14th october, 2005

14th october, 2005

Alphabet
Inspirations
in Coloured
Bobbin Lace

Sandi Woods

BATSFORD

Dedication

To The U.M.

Acknowledgements

Once again I wish to thank my long-suffering husband Phil Woods, my daughters Melissa and Bethany, family, friends and the many lacemakers at home and abroad for the help, interest and encouragement that they gave while I was designing and working the patterns for this book.

I especially appreciate the input from all those unfortunate enough to have been involved in the pattern-testing process, notably Bobbi Donnelly (USA), Sue Karn and the Swanley Lacemakers (UK). Also much appreciated is the assistance received from Ben Smith, most definitely not a lacemaker, but my personal IT helpdesk.

Grateful thanks again to Patricia Read and Lucy Kincaid for researching the Milanese braids and kindly giving permission for their use, and particularly Patricia Read for allowing me to tap into her wealth of knowledge over the years.

Lastly, recognition is due to my editor, Nicola Birtwisle and her team, who had the unenviable task of squeezing a quart into the pint pot that is this book.

All pieces designed and worked by Sandi Woods
Photography by Sandi Woods

All pieces illustrated worked with Pipers Silks
www.pipers-silks.com

First published 2004

ISBN 0 7134 8905 7

A CIP record for this book is available from the British Library.

Printed in Malaysia

for the publishers
B T Batsford
The Chrysalis Building
Bramley Road
London W10 6SP

An imprint of Chrysalis Books Group

CONTENTS

INTRODUCTION

The traditional parlour game 'Chinese Whispers' provides an analogy with the development of the patterns in this book. In Chinese Whispers, the participants sit in a circle, and a phrase chosen by and known only to the instigator is whispered around the circle until it arrives back at the beginning, whereupon the 'new' version is unveiled for all to hear. In this book, the opening phrase is replaced with a shape which is then developed until the original form appears to be lost. During its development the shape travels along a variety of paths, mutating and changing direction with each new idea. *The Silverfish Collection*, for example, starts with the letter *S* and several patterns later finishes with a cross.

An alphabet was chosen to form the basic shapes, since each letter is, by design, closely linked to the others but yet still retains a separate identity, an identity to which everybody can relate.

Each of the letters and their developed shapes may be used alone or in conjunction with others to form elaborate composite designs as in *Chinese Seedlings* or the *Blossoms*. The versatility of the individual letter patterns is immense: merely by rotating the letter *G*, for example, and then changing the colour set and linking this to another *G*, ocean waves are suggested. The use of a negative shape can be explored in any of the patterns.

Colours and tonal values are used in a painterly way to describe shape and form. 'The Leafy Glades Alphabet' has been designed to suggest leafy shapes in a woodland setting with the sunlight streaming from the upper left direction, thereby providing shadowed areas at the lower right. Although each letter has its own designated colour set, *L for Leaves* best illustrates this concept.

Hellebore (Extra) contains full instructions on how to jigsaw pieces of a shape together, allowing the flow of the colours, pattern texture and shadows to continue describing the form, but without the unsightly bulk of several layers placed one on top of another.

Within the book there are many patterns developed from selected letters to show how it is possible to create a personal motif without necessarily using the original letter itself. An example of this concept is *Blackthorn Sprig*. Originating from *I for Ice*, it could either be worked as a sprig, perhaps to commemorate a fiftieth anniversary, or be appropriate for someone with the initial *I*. Unfortunately there is not enough space for an additional design derived from every letter to be included in this book.

Everything natural or abstract can be broken down into basic shapes. Once this concept is appreciated, the idea of drawing and designing becomes as simple and uncomplicated as writing one's signature.

Threads

The threads have been given numbers – no 1, for example – to allow the same instructions to be used to work a range of colour schemes, using seven (or eight) different colours, the range only being limited by the number of thread colours required to work the piece.

All of the colour schemes are numbered in a tonal sequence ranging from the lightest (no 1) through to the darkest (no 8). Piper's Silks 80/3 spun silk (330 denier) and *90/3 gloss silk (270 denier) were used to work all of

the lace illustrated. The two threads are interchangeable within these patterns. (*denotes gloss silk).

Note: Should any other threads be substituted, the scale of the pricking may have to be changed and the finished piece will not look exactly the same.

Other threads, such as Gütermann S303 100/3 spun silk, may be used.

To work the patterns

- Tw 2 leaders before making edge st.
- No (colour) change edge st is used throughout, unless otherwise stated.
- Passive pairs are to be worked in Cls, unless indicated otherwise.
- Top sewings are used throughout, unless otherwise stated.
- Colours/threads are listed singly in thread order listings, unless otherwise indicated.
- The leader pair is always listed at the bottom of the thread order listing, regardless of its actual position.

- When counting in from the relevant edge for the required thread positions, the leaders and edge pairs should be ignored. Thread or pair positions relate to passive pairs only (see working diagrams 1 & 2).
- The positions of the blind (twice worked) pins are not given in the text instructions as this could be confusing when describing a technique; consult the pin reference plan for their position.
- When T O & T B prs, tie reef knot 3 times (L over R, R over L, L over R).
- Ideally, the Midland bobbins should be of approximately

the same size and weight, with smallish spangles to facilitate sewings.

- Each pair of bobbins should have one bobbin fully wound, and one bobbin wound with approximately 75cm of thread. Thus, when needing to use that particular bobbin again, the estimated amount can be drawn off from the full bobbin and wound onto the empty bobbin, thus reducing thread wastage. However, it is usually advisable to have the edge prs and leader pair fully wound.

- The use of a magic thread will facilitate sewings when joining sections or working the rolled edges.

- The leaders and relevant passive prs must be tw 1 before commencing ½ st or Cls & tw sections.

- Take care when working ½ st sections to maintain the same (i.e. correct) leading thread throughout, and to ensure the correct number of twists are used.

- Support pins, after X T of X T X T X , may be used when working T S, or when working the smooth edge of Tenstick sections. Note: Remove support pins as soon as possible.

- Note: Tenstick smooth edge is indicated by a line on pin reference plans.

- If a locking st (X T X T X) is used when leaving one section of work to continue with another, remember to undo the locking st when returning to that section, before continuing.

- When following L–R instructions written for a previous section where the working direction is reversed (i.e. R–L instead of L–R), simply change the working direction of the notes (i.e. lt becomes rt and rt becomes lt). The exception is at the start pin #, when the relevant diagram is given.

- The instructions and diagrams for working the Milanese braids in this book relate solely to the patterns they describe and in many cases they are worked in a form of variation pertaining to those patterns. Full text and diagrams for working the braids in the traditional manner are to be found in the Milanese books listed in Further Reading, page 143.

Additional tips and suggestions

- Use temporary pins, possibly of a different colour, pushed down into the pillow, to serve as a reminder to work blind (twice worked) pins and marked pin holes (for example, A#, B, C and so on) before commencing work.

- Place an enlarged photocopy of the pin reference plan alongside the relevant working instructions.

- Pay careful attention to the instructions: for example, at the pin or after the pin, edge of braid or side of braid.

- Read ahead of the immediate notes for each row; sometimes there are several techniques to employ at and between pins, and occasionally there are additional notes at the end of a set of instructions.

- Do not worry if, when splitting or joining a braid, or any other section, the work seems unstable; by gradually and carefully tensioning all the threads, the work will eventually fall into place.

- The linear design (order of work diagram) shows the design lines more clearly than the pricking or pin reference plan. When, experimenting with other colour schemes, therefore, the linear design may be photocopied, and a colour study made, before work commences.

Abbreviations

#	start pin
½ st	Half-st
Cls	Cloth st
alt	alternate
cont	continue
diag	diagram
foll	following
L	Left
L edge pr	left edge pr
no	number
nos	numbers
Nr	Next row
patt	pattern
poss	possible
pr/prs	pair/pairs
p pr/prs	passive pair/pairs
R	Right
R edge pr	right edge pair
rep/s	repeat/s
rem	remain/ remaining
s p pr/prs	single passive pair/pairs
s ps	single passives
st	stitch
td	technical diagram
tech	technique
temp	temporary
tog	together
thro	through
T O & T B	Tie Off and Throw Back
T P	Temporary Pin
T S	Turning St (X T X T X)
tw	twist
var	variation
X T	cross twist (½ st)
X T X	cross twist cross (Cls)
X T X T	cross twist cross twist (Cls & tw)
X T X T X	cross twist cross twist cross (Tenstick smooth edge st, locking st or T.S.)

SECTION ONE
The Leafy Glades Alphabet

Each letter in the Leafy Glades Alphabet has two different methods of working: a basic stitch version (shown on the left of the picture) and a version using Milanese braid techniques (shown on the right). Both versions are worked using the same colour study and use seven different tonal colours. Thus it is possible to choose any of the seven colour sets to work any version of any of the letters.

It would be possible to work these patterns in simpler ways, but the methods used were chosen to enhance the flow of the design and offer the most effective uses of colour and texture.

The Leafy Glades Alphabet demands a range of skills, depending upon the requirements of the individual letter shape. Thus, the *A* is not the easiest nor is the *Z* the most difficult.

Note: Before commencing any of the patterns it is essential to read 'To Work the Patterns", page 4.

A for APPLE

Colours
(no 1)	*White
(no 2)	*Honey
(no 3)	*Champagne
(no 4)	Sycamore
(no 5)	Eau de Nil
(no 6)	Pale Lettuce
(no 7)	Apple Green

VERSION 1
Section 1
Start at pin A#:
Using a two-colour point start (tech 1, td 1), (Note L–R working direction), hang 1 pr (no 7) and 1 pr (no 6) to be edge prs (diag a.1).

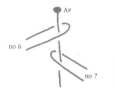

Diagram a1:
Start, Section 1,
Versions 1 and 2

Add magic thread (tech 2, td 2a).
L edge pr is now (no 7).

R edge pr is now (no 6).
On T P, hang 1 pr (no 7) to be leaders. (3 prs)
On T P, hang 2 prs (no 7) and 1 pr (no 6) to be p prs, side by side, in L–R order as foll:
4 x (no 7)
2 x (no 6)
Cls leaders L–R thro 3 p prs and edge st at pin B (tech 3, td 3).
(6 prs)
Nr: add 1 pr (no 6) to be s ps 2 & 3 from R.
Nr: add 1 pr (no 7) to centre.
(8 prs)
Cont in Cls.

After pin C:
add 1 pr (no 5) to be 5th p pr from L.
Nr: add 1 pr (no 4) to be s ps 4 & 5 from R.
Nr: add 1 pr (no 6) to be 2nd p pr from L, and add 1 pr (no 3) to be 3rd p pr from R.
Nr: add 1 p pr (no 2) to be s ps 6 & 7 from R.
(13 prs)

After pin D:
change leaders (no 7) to (no 5), (tech 4, td 4), cont row, adding 1 pr (no 5) to be s ps 4 & 5 from L, and 1 pr (no 1) to be 4th pr from R.
(15 prs)

After pin E:
start patt - Cls thro 3 p prs, tw 1 leaders, work Cls & tw with 4th p pr (no 1), Cls rem p prs.
Cont in patt, working Cls & tw with 4th p pr from R.

After pin F:
split braid (tech 5, td 5) thus: work locking st (tech 6, td 6) and leave.
At pin G:
between 8th and 9th p prs from R, hang 1 pr (no 6) and to the L of it, 1 pr (no 7) on pin G, to be centre edge prs, Cls & tw 2 both prs.

Return to pin F:
undo locking st, cont in patt, working Cls & tw with 4th p pr from R, as before, work edge st with R centre edge pr (no 7)
Secure all bobbins (6 prs) at L side of braid, leave to cont with R side of braid. (11 prs)

Right side of braid, Section 1
Cont in patt, working Cls & tw with 4th p pr (no 1) from R.

After pin H:
cont in Cls.

After pin I:
T O & T B 1 p pr (no 1) from centre.

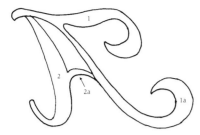

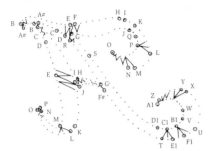

A1: Order of work

A3: Pin reference plan, Version 1

A2: Pricking

Nr: T O & T B 1 p pr (no 2) from centre.
Nr: T O & T B 1 p pr (no 3) from centre.
(8 prs)

After pin J:
change leaders (no 5) to (no 7), (tech 4, td 4), cont row, T O & T B 1 p pr (no 4).
(7 prs)
At pin K:
change leaders (no 7) with R edge pr (no 6), (tech 7, td 7).

After pin K:
add 1 pr (no 7) to be 1st p pr from R, and T O & T B 1 p pr (no 4).
Nr: T O & T B s ps 4 & 5 (no 6) from L, and add 1 pr (no 7) to be s ps 2 & 3 from R.
Nr: add 1 pr (no 7) to be 2nd p pr from R, and T O & T B 2nd p pr (no 6) from L.
(7 prs)

Nr: add 1 p pr (no 6) to be 2nd p pr from L.
Nr: add 1 p pr (no 6) to be s ps 8 & 9 from R.
Nr: add 1 p pr (no 5) to be 3rd p pr from L.
Nr: add 1 p pr (no 4) to be s ps 10 & 11 from R.
(11 prs)
Nr: add 1 p pr (no 3) to be 4th p pr from L.
Nr: add 1 p pr (no 2) to be s ps 12 & 13 from R.
Nr: add 1 p pr (no 1) to be 5th p pr from L.
(14 prs)

After pin L:
start patt: Cls thro 6 p prs, tw 1 leaders,

work Cls & tw with 7th p pr (no 1) from R, Cls rem p prs.
Cont in patt, working Cls & tw with 7th p pr from R.

After pin M:
cont in Cls.

After pin N:
T O & T B 7th p pr (no 1) from R.
Nr: T O & T B s ps 8 & 9 (no 2) from L.
Nr: T O & T B 5th and 7th p prs (no 4/no 5) from R.
Nr: T O & T B 3rd p pr (no 3) from L.
Nr: T O & T B s ps 6 & 7 and 10 & 11 (no 6/no 7) from R.
Nr: T O & T B s ps 2 & 3 (no 6) from L.
(6 prs)
Nr: T O & T B centre p pr (no 7), then Cls leaders thro rem 2 p prs, T O & T B leaders, T O & T B rem 2 p prs, and secure to back of work with previously T B prs.

Finish at pin O:
(tech 8,td 8) Cls & tw both edge prs (no 7), place pin O, Cls prs & T O.
These 2 prs to be used for rolled edge.

Notes for rolled edge
Roll from pin O to pin J (tech 9, td 9):
rolling thread – 1 x (no 7)
rolled threads – 3 x (no 7)
Use edge prs from pin O for roll.
TB 1 thread at pin P and pin Q. Finish at pin J (tech 10, td 10).

Return to left side of braid, Section 1a
(6 prs)
At pin R:
add 1 pr (no 4) to be new leaders, (tech

5, td 5 and tech 36, td 36).
(7 prs)
Nr: add 1 pr (no 2) to be 3rd p pr from R.
Work 1 row.
Nr: T O & T B s ps 2 & 3 (no 6/no 7) from R, and add 1 pr (no 1) to be 4th pr from L.
Work 1 row.
Nr: add 1 pr (no 1) to be 3rd p pr from R.
Work 1 row.
(9 prs)

After pin S:
start patt: Cls thro 2 p prs, tw 1 leaders, work Cls & tw with 3rd p pr, Cls rem p prs.
Cont in patt, working Cls & tw with 3rd p pr from R.

After pin T:
change leaders (no 4) to (no 6), (tech 4, td 4).
Cont in Cls.

Nr: add 1 pr (no 6) to be 6th p pr from R.
Nr: add 1 pr (no 7) to be s ps 2 & 3 from L.
Nr: add 1 pr (no 6) to be s ps 2 & 3 from R, and T O & T B 6th p pr (no 1) from L.
Nr: add 1 pr (no 7) to be 2nd p pr from L.
(12 prs)
Nr: add 1 pr (no 6) to be 2nd p pr from R, and T O & T B s ps 12 & 13 (no 1) from L.
Nr: add 1 pr (no 7) to be 2nd p pr from L.
Nr: T O & T B 4th p pr (no 2) from R, and add 1 pr (no 7) to be 2nd p pr from L.
Nr: add 1 pr (no 6) to be 2nd p pr from L, and T O & T B s ps 6 & 7 (no 5) from R.
(13 prs)

Nr: T O & T B 2nd p pr (no 6) from R, and add 1 pr (no 6) to be s ps 4 & 5 from L.
Nr: add 1 pr (no 5) to be 3rd p pr from L.
Nr: T O & T B 2nd p pr (no 6) from R, and add 1 pr (no 5) to be s ps 6 & 7 from L.
(14 prs)
At pin U:
change leaders (no 6) with L edge pr (no 7), (tech 7, td 7).

After pin U:
add 1 pr (no 4) to be 4th p pr from L.
(15 prs)
At pin V:
change leaders (no 7) with R edge pr (no 6), (tech 7, td 7).

After pin V:
T O & T B 4th p pr (no 6) from R, and add 1 pr (no 3) to be s ps 8 & 9 from L.
Nr: add 1 pr (no 2) to be 5th p pr from L.
Nr: T O & T B s ps 2 & 3 (no 6/no 7) from R, and add 1 pr (no 1) to be s ps 10 & 11 from L.
Nr: add 1 pr (no 1) to be 6th p pr from L.
(17 prs)

After pin W:
T O & T B 2nd p pr from R, start patt, Cls thro 5 prs, tw 1 leaders and 6th p pr from L, work Cls & tw with 6th p pr, Cls rem p prs.
(16 prs)
Nr: T O & T B 2nd p pr (no 7) from R, and Cls & tw as before.
Nr: T O & T B 2nd p pr from R, and cont Cls & tw as before.
(14 prs)

After pin X:
cont in Cls.

After pin Y:
T O & T B 5th and 7th p prs (no 1/no 2) from L.
Nr: T O & T B 5th p pr (no 1) from R.
Nr: T O & T B s ps 8 & 9 (no 3) from L.
Nr: T O & T B 4th p pr (no 4) from R.
(9 prs)
Nr: T O & T B s ps 6 & 7 (no 5) from L.
Nr: T O & T B 3rd p pr (no 5) from R.
Nr: T O & T B s ps 4 & 5 (no 6) from L.
Nr: T O & T B 2nd p pr (no 6) from R.
Work 1 row.
Nr: T O & T B s ps 2 & 3 (no 7) from R.
(4 prs)

After pin Z:
Cls thro rem pr (no 7), T O & T B leaders (no 6), T O p pr (no 7) and set aside for rolled edge.
Finish at pin A1:
(tech 15, td 15), T O & T B L edge pr (no 6).
T O R edge pr (no 7), enclosing set

aside p pr (no 7), these 2 prs to be used for rolled edge.

Notes for rolled edge
Roll from pin A1 to pin D1 (tech 9, td 9):
rolling thread – 1 x (no 7)
rolled threads – 3 x (no 7)
Use R edge pr and enclosed set aside p pr from pin A1 for roll.
T B 1 thread at pin B1 and pin C1.
Finish at pin D1.

Roll from pin A# to pin F1 (tech 9, td 9, tech 16, td 16):
rolling thread – 1 x (no 7)
rolled threads – 3 x (no 7)
Using the magic thread at pin A#, add 2 prs (no 7).
T B 1 thread at pin T and pin E1. Finish at pin F1.

Section 2
Start at pin A#:
using a narrow angle start (tech 17, td 17), (Note R–L working direction), with a top sewing (tech 12, td 12) into the R bar, hang I pr (no 6) to be R edge pr, and into its loop, 1 pr (no 4) to be leaders.
Tw 2 both prs.

Hang 1 pr (no 6) into the L bar, using a top sewing, to be 1st p pr from R.
(3 prs)
At pin B:
in the same manner as before, hang 1 pr (no 7) into R bar to be 1st p pr from L, and 1 pr (no 7) into L bar to be L edge pr.
Tw 2 L edge pr.
(5 prs)
On T P, to hang between 1st p pr from L and 1st p pr from R, add 1 pr (no 6).
Cls leaders (no 4) thro 3 p prs, tw 2 leaders, place pin C, and edge st.
L–R order is:
L edge pr	2 x (no 7)
	2 x (no 7)
	4 x (no 6)
R edge pr	2 x (no 6)
leaders	2 x (no 4)
(6 prs)	

After pin C:
add 1 pr (no 5) to centre.
Nr: add 1 pr (no 4) to centre.
Nr: add 1 pr (no 3) to centre.
Nr: add 1 pr (no 2) to centre.
Nr: add 1 pr (no 1) to centre.
Nr: add 1 pr (no 1) to centre.
(12 prs)

After pin D:
start patt: Cls thro 4 p prs, tw 1 leaders and 5th p pr (no 1) from left, work Cls & tw with 5th p pr, Cls rem p prs.
Cont in patt working Cls & tw with 5th p pr from L.

After pin E:
make locking st with leaders and 1st p pr (tech 6, td 6), secure bobbins and leave to work Section 2a.

Section 2a
Start at pin F#:
using a narrow angle start (tech 17, td 17), (Note R–L working direction) with a top sewing into R bar, hang 1 pr (no 7) to be R edge pr, and into its loop, 1 pr (no 6) to be leaders.
Tw 2 both prs.

Hang 1 pr (no 7) into L bar, using a top sewing, to be 1st p pr from R.
(3 prs)
At pin G:
In the same manner as before, hang 1 pr (no 6) into R bar to be 1st p pr from L, and 1 pr (no 6) into L bar to be L edge pr.
Tw 2 L edge pr.
(5 prs)
On T P, to hang between 1st p pr from L and 1st p pr from R, add 1 pr (no 6).
Cls thro 3 p prs, tw 2 leaders, and make top sewing into R bar at pin G.
(6 prs)

After pin H:
Cls leaders (no 6) thro 2 p prs, T O & T B leaders, leave to return to Section 2.

Return to Section 2
Undo locking st after pin E (diag a.2), and cont row in patt, Cls & tw 5th p pr from L, Cls across p prs only from Section 2, do not tw 2 leaders, leave.
At pin I:
Cls & tw 2 R edge pr (no 6) from Section 2 and L edge pr (no 6) from Section 2a, placing pin I between them.

Cls leaders (no 4) from Section 2 thro both edge prs and 3 p prs from Section 2a, tw 2 leaders and edge st at pin J.
(17 prs)

After pin J:
cont in patt, T O & T B 2nd and 4th p prs (no 6) from R.
Nr: T O & T B 11th p pr (no 6) from L.
Nr: T O & T B 2nd p pr (no 6) from R.
Nr: T O & T B 9th p pr (no 6) from L.
Cont in patt.
(12 prs)

After pin K:
add 1 pr (no 7) to be s ps 2 & 3 from R.
Cont in patt.

After pin L:
Cont in Cls.
Nr: T O & T B 4th and 6th p prs (no 2/no 1) from L.
Nr: T O & T B 4th and 6th p prs (no 4/no 3) from R.

(9 prs)
After completing blind pin M:
change leaders (no 4) to (no 6), (tech 4, td 4) cont row, T O & T B 1 p pr (no 1).
(8 prs)
Work 2 rows.
Nr: T O & T B 1 p pr (no 5).
Work 2 rows.
Nr: T O & T B 1 p pr (no 6).
(6 prs)

After pin N:
T O & T B 1 pr (no 7) from centre.
(5 prs)
After pin O:
(tech 8, td 8), Cls thro 2 rem p prs.
T O & T B leaders and 2 p prs.
Secure to back of work.
Finish at pin P:

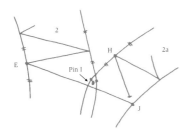

Diagram a2: Joining Sections 2 and 2a, Version 1

(tech 8, td 8), Cls & tw edge prs, place pin P, Cls and T O.
These 2 prs to be used for rolled edge.

Notes for rolled edge
Roll from pin P to pin F#:
rolling thread –1 x (no 7)

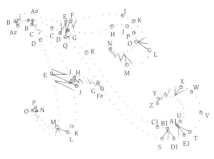

A4: Pin reference plan, Version 2

rolled threads – 3 x (no 7)
Use edge prs from pin P for roll.
Finish at Pin F#.

VERSION 2
Section 1
Start at pin A#:
follow instructions for Version 1, from pin A# to pin E.
After pin E:
Cont in Cls to pin F.

After pin F:
follow instructions for Version 1, from

pins F and G to split braid, working Cls across all p prs, and working edge st at R pinhole below Pin G.
When bobbins for L side have been secured, leave to cont with R side of braid, Section 1.
(11 prs)
Right side of braid, Section 1
Start patt (td a.3): Cls L–R thro 4 p prs, work T S with 5th p pr (no 1) and cont in Archway (var) patt, (diag a.3), using 2 prs from each side to form the 'arches'.
Note: Leaders are only tw 2 to form arches. There are 2 p prs at L and 1 p pr at R.
Work 2 patt reps, working 1 row between each rep.

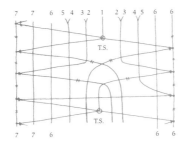

Diagram a3: Patt. 'Archway'(var)

After pin H:
work T S with 4th p pr from L, and cont in Cls, working towards next R pin.
Note Leaders are (no 1/no 2), they and other patt prs will not have returned to their original colour positions.

After pin I:
follow instructions for Version 1, from pin I to pin L.
Note T O & T B lightest prs first near centre, and after pin J, change leaders (no 1/no 2) to (no 7), (tech 4, td 4).
(14 prs)

After pin L:
start patt: Cls R–L thro 6 p prs, work T S with 7th p pr (no 1).
Nr: work 1 section of patt 'Archway' (var), using 2 p prs from each side to form 'arches'.
Use 5th p pr from R as leaders to work to R, then Cls 1 row.
Nr: Cls thro 4 p prs, work T S with 5th p pr from L, work to R.

After pin M:
Note Do not work blind pin.
T O & T B 7th p pr from R.
Nr: T O & T B s ps 8 & 9 from L.
Nr: T O & T B 5th and 7th p prs from R.
Nr: T O & T B 3rd p pr from L.
(9 prs)
Nr: T O & T B s ps 6 & 7 and 10 & 11 from R.
Nr: T O & T B s ps 2 & 3 from L.
(6 prs)

Nr: T O & T B centre pr, then Cls leaders thro rem 2 p prs,
T O & T B leaders, T O & T B rem 2 p prs, and secure to back of work with previously T B prs.

Finish at pin N:
follow instructions for Version 1, pin O.

Notes for rolled edge
As Version 1.

Return to left side of braid, Section 1a
(6 prs)
At pin Q:
follow instructions for Version 1, at pin R.
(7 prs)
Nr: add 1 pr (no 2) to centre.
Work 1 row.
(8 prs)
Nr: *add 1 pr (no 1) to centre.
Work 1 row*.
Nr: rep * to *.
(10 prs)

After pin R:
start patt: Cls to centre,
work T S with centre pr (no 1) and cont in Archway (var) patt, using 2 p prs from each side to form 'arches'.
Work 6 patt reps.

After pin S:
Cls 2 rows.
Nr: *change leaders* to (no 6), (tech 4, td 4) and cont in Cls.
Nr: add 1 pr (no 7) to be s ps 14 & 15 from R.
Nr: add 1 pr (no 6) to be s ps 6 & 7 from L.
Nr: add 1 pr (no 6) to be s ps 4 & 5 from R, and T O & T B s ps 8 & 9 from L.
(12 prs)
Nr: add 1 pr (no 7) to be 2nd p pr from L.
Nr: T O & T B s ps 10 & 11 from R, and add 1 pr (no 7) to be s ps 4 & 5 from L.
Nr: add 1 pr (no 6) to be 2nd p pr from R.
Nr: add 1 pr (no 7) to be s ps 2 & 3 from R, and T O & T B s ps 14 & 15 from L.
(14 prs)
At pin T:
change leaders (no 6) with L edge pr (no 7) (tech 7, td 7).

After pin T:
add 1 pr (no 6) to be s ps 4 & 5 from L.
(15 prs)
At pin U:
change leaders (no 7) with R edge pr (no 6) (tech 7, td 7).

After pin U:
T O & T B s ps 8 & 9 from R edge, and add 1 pr (no 5) to be 3rd p pr from L.

Nr: add 1 pr (no 4) to be s ps 6 & 7 from L, and T O & T B 4th p pr (no 6) from R.
Nr: T O & T B s ps 6 & 7 (no 6) from R, and add 1 pr (no 3) to be 4th p pr from L.
Nr: add 1 pr (no 2) to be s ps 8 & 9 from L.
Nr: T O & T B 3rd p prs (no 6) from R, and add 1 pr (no 1) to be 5th p pr from L.
(16 prs)

After pin V:
start patt: Cls L–R thro 4 p prs, work T S with 5th p pr (no 1) and cont Archway (var) patt, using 2 prs from each side to form 'arches', also, T O & T B s ps 4 & 5 (no 7) from R.
(15 prs)
Nr: T O & T B 2nd p pr (no 7) from R.
Nr: T O & T B 2nd p pr (no 7) from R.
(13 prs)
After crossing 4 patt prs in Archway patt, take 2nd p pr (no 6) from L and work to L, to pin W.

After pin W:
cont in Cls.

After pin X:
T O & T B s ps 8 & 9 (no 3) from L.
Note Do not work blind pin.
Nr: T O & T B 6th p pr (no 2) from R.
(11 prs)
Cont T O & T B 1 p pr per row, lightest colours first.
(5 prs)

Nr: T O & T B s ps 2 & 3 (no 7) from R.
(4 prs)

After pin Y:
follow instructions for Version 1, from pin Z to finish at pin Z, Version 2.

Notes for rolled edges
As Version 1.

Section 2
Start at pin A#:
follow instructions for Version 1, from pin A# to pin E.

After pin D:
start patt: Cls L–R thro 4 p prs, work T S with 5th p pr, and cont in Archway patt, using 2 prs from each side to form 'arches'.
Note When working patt, after crossing of prs, ensure that 2nd p pr is worked to edge st, before Cls row is worked to R, regardless of which pinhole appears to be the next to be worked.
This only applies to 1st 2 patt reps of this section.

After pin E:
work Section 2a.

Section 2a
Start at pin F#:
follow instructions for Version 1.
At pin I:
(td a.2), Cls & tw 2 R edge pr (no 6)

from Section 2 and L edge pr (no 6) from Section 2a, placing pin I between them.

Cls and work T S with centre patt.pr. Work L section of 'arch', leaving 2 prs tw 2 to form L side of 'arch'.

Work R side of 'arch', then also Cls thro both edge prs and 3 p prs from section 2a, tw 2 leaders, and edge st at pin J.
(17 prs)

After pin J:
cont in patt, T O & T B 2nd and 4th p prs (no 6) from R.
Nr: T O & T B 3rd p pr (no 6) from R.
Nr: T O & T B 2nd p pr (no 6) from R.
(13 prs)
Nr: Cross patt prs, and take 2nd pr from L to L edge st.
Work across all prs in patt, T O & T B 2nd pr from R.
(12 prs)
Cont in patt, till 4 patt reps completed. Cont in Cls.

After pin K:
follow instructions for Version 1, cont in Cls, T O & T B where poss, lightest prs first.

Cont to finish at pin P.

Notes for rolled edge
As Version 1.

B for BAUHINIA

Colours
(no 1)	*Rose
(no 2)	*Strawberry
(no 3)	*Hibiscus
(no 4)	Pale Magenta
(no 5)	Mid Purple
(no 6)	*Dark Kingfisher
(no 7)	*Dark Tartan

VERSION 1
Section 1
Start at pin A#:
Using a two colour point start (tech 1, td 1), (Note L–R working direction), hang 1 pr (no 5) and 1 pr (no 4) to be edge prs (diag b.1).
Add magic thread (tech 2, td 2a).

L edge pr is now (no 5).
R edge pr is now (no 4).
On T P, hang 1 pr (no 6) to be leaders.
(3 prs)
On T P, hang 2 prs (no 7) open, to be p prs.

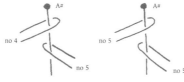

Diagram b1:
Start, Section 1

Diagram b2:
Start, Section 2a

Cls leaders L–R thro 2 p prs, and edge st at pin B (tech 3, td 3).
(5 prs)
Nr: add 2 prs (no 6) to centre.
Nr: add 2 prs (no 5) to centre.
(9 prs)
Nr: *add 1 pr (no 4) to centre*.
Nr: rep * to *.
(11 prs)
After pin C:
T O & T B 1st p pr (no 7) from R, and add 1 pr (no 3) to be 5th p pr from L.
Nr: T O & T B 1st p pr (no 7) from L, and add 1 pr (no 2) to be 5th p pr from R.
Nr: T O & T B 1st p pr (no 6) from R, and add 1 pr (no 2) to be s ps 8 & 9 from L.
Nr: T O & T B 1st p pr (no 6) from L, and add 1 pr (no 1) to be 5th p pr from R.

Nr: T O & T B 1st p pr (no 5) from R, and add 1 pr (no 1) to be s ps 8 & 9 from L.
(11 prs)

After completing blind pin D:
change leaders (no 6) to (no 1), (tech 4, td 4), cont row, adding 1 pr (no 1) to be 5th p pr from R.
(12 prs)
Nr: add 1 pr (no 1) to be s ps 10 & 11 from R.
Nr: add 2 prs (no 2) open, to be 6th & 7th p prs from L.
Nr: add 1 pr (no 1) to be 7th p pr from R.

L–R order is:
L edge pr	2 x (no 5)
	2 x (no 5)
	2 x (no 4)
	2 x (no 2)
	4 x (no 1)
	2 x (no 2)
	2 x (no 1)
	2 x (no 2)
	4 x (no 1)
	2 x (no 2)
	2 x (no 3)

B1: Order of work

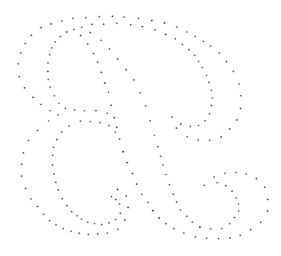

B3: Pin reference
plan, Version 1

B2 : Pricking

	2 x (no 4)
R edge pr	2 x (no 4)
leaders	2 x (no 1)
(16 prs)	

After pin E:
start patt – *Cls thro 3 p prs, tw 1
leaders and 4th & 5th p prs (no 1) from
L, work ½ st with 4th & 5th p prs, Cls
thro 3 prs, tw 1 leaders and 4th & 5th
p prs (no 1) from R, work ½ st with 4th
& 5th p prs, Cls rem 3 prs*.

Cont rep * to *.

After pin F:
cont in Cls, T O & T B 7th p pr (no 1)
from R.
Nr: T O & T B s ps 8 & 9 (no 1) and
s ps 16 & 17 (no 1) from L.
Nr: T O & T B 4th and 7th p prs (no 1)
from R.
Nr: T O & T B s ps 6 & 7 (no 2) and
s ps 10 & 11 (no 2) from L.
(9 prs)
After pin G:
add 1 pr (no 5) to be 1st p pr from R,
and T O & T B s ps 6 & 7 (no 2) from L.
(9 prs)
After pin H:
change leaders (no 1) to (no 4), (tech 4,
td 4) cont row, T O & T B 1 pr (no 2),
and add 1 pr (no 5) to be s ps 2 & 3
from R.
Nr: T O & T B 1 pr (no 3), and add 1 pr
(no 5) to be s ps 2 & 3 from L.
(9 prs)
At pin I:
change leaders (no 4) with L edge pr
(no 5), (tech 7, td 7).

After pin I:
add 1 pr (no 5) to be 2nd p pr from L,
and T O & T B 1 pr (no 4) from centre.
At pin J:
change leaders (no 5) with R edge pr
(no 4), (tech 7, td 7).
After pin J:

T O & T B 1 pr (no 4) from centre, and
add 1 pr (no 4) to be 1st p pr from L.
Nr: add 1 pr (no 3) to be 1st p pr from L.
(10 prs)
Nr: T O & T B 3rd p pr (no 5) from R,
and add 1 pr (no 2) to 2nd pr from L.
Nr: add 1 pr (no 2) to be s ps 4 & 5
from L, and T O & T B s ps 4 & 5 (no 5)
from R.
Nr: T O & T B s ps 4 & 5 (no 5) from R,
and add 1 pr (no 1) to be 3rd pr from L.
(10 prs)
After working 1st part of blind pin K:
change leaders (no 4) to (no 1), (tech 4,
td 4) cont row, adding 1 pr (no 1) to be
s ps 6 & 7 from L.
(11 prs)
Nr: T O & T B 2nd p pr (no 5) from R,
and add 2 prs (no 1) to be s ps 6 & 7
and 10 & 11 from L.
Nr: add 1 pr (no 2) to be 5th p pr from L.
Nr: add 1 pr (no 2) to be s ps 12 & 13
from R.
Nr: add 1 pr (no 1) to be 6th p pr from L.

Cont in Cls.
L–R order is:

L edge pr	2 x (no 4)
	2 x (no 3)
	2 x (no 2)
	4 x (no 1)
	2 x (no 2)
	2 x (no 1)
	2 x (no 2)
	4 x (no 1)
	2 x (no 2)
	2 x (no 4)
	2 x (no 5)
R edge pr	2 x (no 5)
leaders	2 x (no 1)
(15 prs)	

After completing blind pin L:
start patt – *Cls thro 2 prs, tw 1 leaders
and 3rd and 4th p prs (no 1) from L,
work ½ st with 2 p prs, Cls thro 3 prs,
tw 1 leaders and 4th and 5th p prs (no
1) from R, work ½ st with 2 p prs,

Cls rem 3 prs.
Nr: Cls thro 3 p prs, tw 1 leaders and
4th and 5th p prs (no 1) from R, work ½
st with 2 p prs, Cls 3 prs, tw 1 leaders
and 3rd and 4th p prs (no 1) from L,
work ½ st with 2 p prs, Cls rem 2 prs*.

Cont rep * to *.
After pin M:
cont in Cls, work 1 row.

After pin N:
add 1 pr (no 5) to be s ps 2 & 3 from R,
and T O & T B s ps 6 & 7 (no 1) and 16
& 17 (no 1) from L.
(14 prs)
Nr: add 1 pr (no 4) to be 1st p pr from
L, and T O & T B 5th, 7th and 9th p prs
(no 1) from R.
(12 prs)
After pin O:
change leaders (no 1) to (no 4), (tech 4,
td 4) cont row, T O & T B s ps 6 & 7 (no
2) and 10 & 11 (no 2) from L.
(10 prs)
Nr: add 1 pr (no 5) to be 1st p pr from
L, and T O & T B 4th p pr (no 2) and
s ps 10 & 11 (no 2/no 3) from R.
Nr: add 1 pr (no 5) to be 2nd p pr from
R, and T O & T B 3rd p pr (no 2/no 3)
from L.
Nr: T O & T B s ps 4 & 5 (no 4) from L.
(8 prs)
After pin P:
Cls leaders thro all p prs, tw 2 leaders,
and leave, securing bobbins in order.

Note: Section 2 must be worked before
prs from Section 1 may be joined with
top sewings.

Notes for rolled edges
Roll from pin A# to pin T (tech 9, td 9):
rolling thread – 1 x (no 5)
rolled threads – 3 x (no 5)
Using magic thread (tech 16, td 16), add
2 prs at pin A#.

T B 1 thread from roll at pin E and pin S (tech 14, td 14).
Finish at pin T (tech 10, td 10).

Roll from pin J to pin O:
rolling thread – 1 x (no 5)
rolled threads – 3 x (no 5)
Add 1 pr at pin J, using a top sewing (tech 12, td 12), to be rolling thread and 1 rolled thread. Add 1 thread at pin U and pin V, roll as far as pin O.

Note: Rolled edge will be finished and joined to Section 2 with top sewings after prs from Section 1 have joined Section 2.

Section 2
Start at pin A#:
follow instructions for Section 1 from pin A# to pin F.
Note R–L working direction. There is no blind pin at pin D.
After pin F:
Cont in Cls, work 1 row.
Nr: T O & T B 7th p pr (no 1) from R.
Nr: T O & T B s ps 8 & 9 (no 1) and 16 &17 (no 1) from L.
Work 1 row.
Nr: T O & T B 4th and 7th p prs (no 1) from L.
(11 prs)
Nr:*T O & T B 1 p pr (no 2).
Work 1 row*.
Rep *to * 3 more times.
(7 prs)
After pin G:
change leaders (no 1) to (no 4), (tech 4, td 4) cont row.
Work 1 row.
(7 prs)
After pin H:
add 1 pr (no 5) to be s ps 2 & 3 from R, and T O & T B 1 pr (no 3).
Work 1 row.
Nr: T O & T B 2nd p pr (no 4) from L, and add 1 pr (no 5) to be 2nd p pr from R.
Nr: add 1 pr (no 4) to be 2nd p pr from R.
Work 1 row.
Nr: T O & T B 1st p pr (no 4) from L.
(7 prs)
After pin I:
change leaders (no 4) to (no 5) thus: Cls thro 1 p pr (tech 20, td 20), exchange leaders (no 4) with 2nd p pr (no 5), cont row.
Nr: add 1 pr (no 3) to be 3rd p pr from R.
(8 prs)
At pin J:
change leaders (no 5) with L edge pr (no 4), (tech 7, td 7).
After pin J:
add 1 pr (no 3) to be s ps 6 & 7 from L.
Nr: add 1 pr (no 3) to be 4th p pr from R.
Nr: add 1 pr (no 3) to be s ps 8 & 9 from L.
Nr: add 1 pr (no 2) to be 5th p pr from R.

Nr: add 1 pr (no 2) to be s ps 10 & 11 from L.
(13 prs)
After pin K:
change leaders (no 4) to (no 3), (tech 4, td 4) cont row, adding 1 pr (no 3) to be 6th p pr from R.
L–R should be:
L edge pr	2 x (no 5)
	2 x (no 5)
	2 x (no 4)
	4 x (no 3)
	2 x (no 2)
	2 x (no 3)
	2 x (no 2)
	4 x (no 3)
	2 x (no 4)
	2 x (no 5)
R edge pr	2 x (no 5)
leaders	2 x (no 3)
(14 prs)
After pin L:
work locking st with leaders and 1st p pr.
Secure bobbins in order, and leave to complete Section 1.

Return to Section 1
Join Section 1 to Section 2 at pins Q and R, using top sewings.

Finish at pin R:
T O & T B rem prs in a bunch (tech 25, td 25).

Complete rolled edge, finishing at pin R.

Return to Section 2
After pin L:
start patt - *Cls thro 2 prs, tw 1 leaders and 3rd and 4th p prs from L, work ½ st with 2 prs, Cls thro 3 prs, tw 1 leaders and 3rd and 4th p prs from R, work ½ st with 2 prs, Cls rem prs*.

Cont rep * to *.
(14 prs)
After pin M:
cont row in Cls.
Nr: T O & T B 2 p prs (no 2).
Nr: T O & T B 4th and 6th p prs (no 3) from L.
(10 prs)
After completing blind pin N:
work locking st with leaders and 1st p pr from R.
Secure bobbins in order, and leave to work Section 2a.

Section 2a
Start at pin A#:
using a one-colour start (tech 1, td 1 and tech 21, td 21), (Note L–R working direction), hang on 2 prs (no 5) to be edge prs (diag b.2).
Add magic thread (tech 2, td 2).
On T P, hang 1 pr (no 6) to be leaders, (3 prs)

On T P, hang 3 p prs, side by side, in L–R order as foll:
2 x (no 7)
2 x (no 6)
2 x (no 7)
Cls leaders thro 3 p prs and edge st at pin B (tech 3, td 3).
(6 prs)
Nr: add 1 pr (no 6) to centre.
(7 prs)
After pin C:
add 1 pr (no 5) to centre.
Work 1 row.
Nr: rep * to *.
(9 prs)
Nr:*add 1 pr (no 4) to centre*.
Nr: rep * to *.
(11 prs)
Nr: T O & T B 1st p pr (no 7) from R, and add 1 pr (no 3) to be 5th p pr from L.
Nr: T O & T B 1st p pr (no 7) from L, and add 1 pr (no 3) to be s ps 8 & 9 from R.
Nr: T O & T B 1st p pr (no 6) from R, and add 1 pr (no 3) to be 5th p pr from L.
Nr: T O & T B 1st p pr (no 6) from L, and add 1 pr (no 3) to be s ps 8 & 9 from R.
(11 prs)
Nr: add 1 pr (no 2) to centre.
(12 prs)
After pin D:
change leaders (no 6) to (no 3), (tech 4, td 4) cont row, adding 1 pr (no 2) to centre.
Nr: add 1 pr (no 3) to centre.
(14 prs)
After completing blind pin E:
start patt: *Cls thro 2 prs, tw 1 leaders 3rd and 4th p prs (no 3) from L, work ½ st with 2 prs, Cls leaders 3 prs, tw 1 leaders and 3rd and 4th p prs (no 3) from R, work ½ st with 2 prs, Cls rem 2 prs*.
Cont in patt, rep * to *.
After pin F:
cont in Cls.
After pin G:
T O & T B 5th and 7th p prs (no 2) from R.
(12 prs)
After completing blind pin H:
add 1 pr (no 6) to be 1st p pr from L, and T O & T B 4th and 6th p prs (no 3) from R, Cls thro rem prs to R and leave.
Note Do not tw 2 leaders or work edge st.

Return to Section 2
Add 1 pr (no 6) to be 1st p pr from R, and T O & T B 3rd and 5th p prs (no 3) from L, Cls leaders from Section 2 thro rem p prs and leave.
Note Do not tw 2 leaders or work edge st.
Join sections
Cls & tw 2 R edge pr from Section 2a and L edge pr from Section 2, (tech 22, td 22), place pin O.
Cls L leaders thro L edge pr, Cls R

leaders thro R edge pr, work T S with
leaders from both sections, replacing pin
O as a support pin (tech 19,td 19), and
T O & T B 4th pr (no 3) from R, work to
pin P.
(19 prs)
After pin P:
T O & T B s ps:

6 & 7	(no 4)
13 & 14	(no 3)
21 & 22	(no 3)
25 & 26	(no 3) from R.

(15 prs)
After pin Q:
add 1 pr (no 6) to be s ps 2 & 3 from
L, Cls thro 2 prs, change leaders (no 3)
to (no 6), (tech 4, td 4) cont row,
T O & T B s ps:

5 & 6	(no 4)
8 & 9	(no 5)
12 & 13	(no 5)
17 & 18	(no 3) from R.

(12 prs)
Nr: T O & T B s ps 5 & 6 (no 5) and
s ps 10 & 11 (no 4) from R.
(10 prs)
After pin R:
add 1 pr (no 7) to be 1st p pr from L,
and T O & T B s ps 4 & 5 (no 5) and
s ps 7 & 8 (no 4) from R.
Nr: add 1 pr (no 7) to be 1st p pr from
R, and T O & T B s ps 8 & 9 (no 5) from L.
(9 prs)
After pin S:
T O & T B s ps 10 & 11 (no 6/no 7) from L.
(8 prs)
Join to Section 1 at pins T, U and V
using top sewings, T O & T B p prs
primarily from R edge.

Finish at pin V:
retain only L edge pr (no 5) for rolled
edge, T O & T B rem prs in a bunch
(tech 25, td 25) and secure to back of
work with previously T B prs.

Notes for rolled edges
Section 2: roll from pin V to pin W:
rolling thread – 1 x (no 5)
rolled threads – 3 x (no 5)
Add 1 pr (no 5) at pin V.
T B 1 thread from roll at pin R and pin Q.
Finish at pin W.
Section 2: roll from pin A# to pin Y:
rolling thread – 1 x (no 5)
rolled threads – 3 x (no 5)
Add 2 prs (no 5) at pin A#.
T B 1 thread from roll at pin X and pin H.
Finish at pin Y.

Section 2a: from pin A# to pin E:
rolling thread – 1 x (no 5)
rolled threads – 3 x (no 5)
Add 2 prs (no 5) at pin A#.
T B 1 thread from roll at pin Z and pin A1.
Finish at pin E.

VERSION 2
Section 1
Start at pin A#:
Follow instructions for Version 1, from
pin A# to pin E.
(16 prs)
After pin E:
start patt – Cls leaders to centre (diag
b.3), work T S with centre pr (no 1), tw
2 both prs, Cls to L.
Cls both leaders to centre, Tw 2 both
prs, work T S, Cls to R.
Cont in Cls.

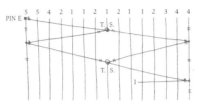

Diagram b3: After pin E, Version 2, Section 1

After pin F:
follow instructions for Version 1, from
pin F to completion of blind pin L.
(15 prs)
After completing blind pin at pin L:
start patt – Cls thro 5 prs, work T S with
6th pr from L, cont in Star patt (diag b,4).
Work 3 patt reps.
Note There is an extra p pr at R side of
braid.
After 3 patt reps,
work T S with leaders in centre patt,
work to R, pin M.

After pin M:
cont in Cls .
After pin N:
follow instructions for Version 1, to
finish at pin R.

Notes for rolled edge
As Version 1.

Section 2
Start at pin A#:
follow instructions for Version 1, from
pin A# to pin E.
(16 prs)
After pin E:
start patt: work T S with 7th p pr and
leaders, cont in patt 'Star' (diag b.4).
Work 1 patt rep.
Note There are extra p prs at each side
of braid.

After completion of final patt rep:
work T S with leaders in patt centre,
work to L, pin F.
After pin F:
cont in Cls, follow instructions for
Version 1, from pin F to pin L.

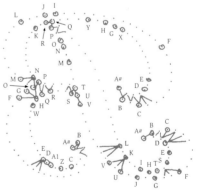

☐ = Leave leaders, return to edge with last pair passed through as new leaders.

Diagram b4: Patt. 'Star'

Return to Section 1
Complete 1 as Version 1.

Return to Section 2
Start Star patt, and work 2 patt reps.

After completion of final rep, work T S
with leaders in patt centre, work to R.
Cont in Cls to pin M.
After pin M:
follow instructions for Version 1 to
locking st after pin N.
Secure bobbins in order, and leave to
work Section 2a.

Section 2a
Start at pin A#:
follow instructions for Version 1 from
pin A# to pin E.
After pin E:

B4: Pin reference plan, Version 2

work 3 more rows.
Start patt; work T.S. with leaders and
centre pr, cont in patt 'Star'.
Work 2 patt reps,
work T.S. with leaders in patt centre,
work to lt.
Cont in Cls.
After pin F:
follow instructions for Version 1,
to finish at pin V.

Notes for rolled edge:
As Version 1.

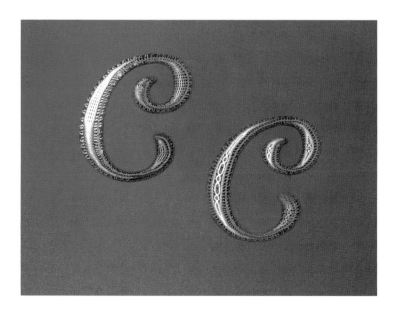

C for COERULEUM

Colours	
(no 1)	*White
(no 2)	Alice Blue
(no 3)	Ocean
(no 4)	Saxe
(no 5)	Royal Blue
(no 6)	*Helio
(no 7)	Navy

VERSION 1
Section 1
Start at pin A#:
Using a one colour point start (tech 23, td 23), (Note R–L working direction), hang 2 prs (no 7) to be edge prs (diag c.1).
Add magic thread (tech 2, td 2b).

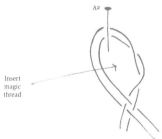

Diagram c1: Start, one colour point start

On T P, hang 1 pr (no 7) to be leaders.
(3 prs)
On T P, hang 1 pr (no 7) and 2 prs (no 5) to be p prs, open, in L–R order as foll:
1 x (no 7)
4 x (no 5)
1 x (no 7)
Cls leaders R–L thro 3 p prs and edge st (tech 3, td 3).
(6 prs)
Cont in Cls, tw 1 leaders to separate the existing 3 p prs (which will form a Cls 'border' alongside the rest of the braid).
Note Cont in this way throughout.
Add p prs to R side of braid, 1 pr per row, in order as foll:
1 pr x (no 6)
1 pr x (no 5)
1 pr x (no 4)
1 pr x (no 3)
1 pr x (no 3)
Work 2 rows.
(11 prs)
After completing blind pin B:
start patt – tw 1 3rd p pr from R, Cls 2 p prs, tw 1 leaders, Cls & tw 3rd p pr, Cls 2 p prs, tw 1 leaders, Cls 'border' prs.
(11 prs)
Nr: tw 1 2nd and 4th p pr from R, Cls 'border' prs, tw 1 leaders, Cls 1 p pr, tw 1 leaders, Cls & tw 3 p prs, Cls rem p prs.
Nr: tw 1 1st & 5th p prs from R, *Cls & tw 5

p prs from R side of braid, tw 1 leaders,
Cls 'border' prs*.
Cont rep * to *.

After pin C:
Cls 'border' prs, tw 1 leaders, Cls 1 p pr,
tw 1 leaders, Cls & tw 3 p prs, Cls 1 p pr.
Nr: Cls 2 p prs, tw 1 leaders, Cls & tw 1
p pr, Cls 2 p prs, tw 1 leaders, Cls '
border' prs.
Nr: Cls 'border' prs, tw 1 leaders, Cls 5
p prs.
Cont in Cls, while still cont tw 1 leaders
to separate 'border' prs.

After pin D:
add 1 pr (no 7) to be 1st p pr from L,
and T O & T B 3rd p pr from R.
(11 prs)
Nr: T O & T B s ps 4 & 5 from R.
Nr: add 1 pr (no 7) to s ps 2 & 3
from L, and T O & T B 2nd p pr from R.
Work 1 row.
(10 prs)
Nr: T O & T B s ps 2 & 3 from R.
Work 2 rows.
Nr: T O & T B 1st p pr from R.
Nr: add 1 pr (no 6) to be 2nd p pr from L.
Work 1 row.
Nr: add I pr (no 6) to be s ps 4 & 5 from L.
(10 prs)
After pin E:
change leaders (no 7) to (no 6), (tech 4,
td 4), cont row.
Nr: add 1 pr (no 5) to be 3rd p pr from L.
Work 3 rows.
Nr: add 1 pr (no 4) to be s ps 6 & 7
from L.
Work 3 rows.
Nr: add 1 pr (no 3) to be 4th p pr from L.
(13 prs)
After pin F:
change leaders (no 6) to (no 5),
(tech 4, td 4), cont row.
Work 2 rows.
Nr: add 1 pr (no 2) to be s ps 8 & 9
from L.
Work 2 rows.
(14 prs)
After pin G:
change leaders (no 5) to (no 3), (tech 4,

td 4), cont row.
Nr: add 1 pr (no 2) to be 5th p pr from L.
Work 3 rows.
Nr: add 1 pr (no 1) to be s ps 10 & 11
from L.
(16 prs)
After pin H:
change leaders (no 3) to (no 2), (tech 4,
td 4), cont row.
Nr: add 1 pr (no 1) to be 6th p pr from L.
Work 1 row.
Nr: add 1 pr (no 1) to be s ps 12 & 13
from L.
(18 prs)
After pin I:
change leaders (no 2) to (no 1), (tech 4,
td 4), cont row.
Nr: T O & T B 2 p.rs (no 6), and add 1
pr (no 1) to centre of (no 1) colour
block.
Nr: start patt: *work Cls & tw with 3
p prs (no 1)*.
Nr: T O & T B 2nd and 10th p prs from L.
Cont in patt, * to *.
(15 prs)
After pin J:
Cls & tw with central p pr (no 1) only.
Nr: Cls all p prs, tw 1 leaders, to main-
tain 'border' throughout.
Nr: T O & T B 5th p pr (no 1) from L.
Work 1 row.
Nr: T O & T B s ps 8 & 9 (no 1) from L.
Work 1 row.
Nr: T O & T B 4th p pr (no 1) from L.
Work 1 row.
Nr: T O & T B s ps 6 & 7 (no 1) from L.
(11 prs)
After pin K:
change leaders (no 1) to (no 2), (tech 4,
td 4) cont row.
Nr: T O & T B 3rd p pr (no 2) from L.
Work 1 row.
Nr: T O & T B s ps 4 & 5 (no 2) from L.
Work 1 row.
Nr: T O & T B 2nd p pr (no 3) from L.
(8 prs)
After pin L:
change leaders (no 2) to (no 3),
(tech 4, td 4) cont row.
Work 1 row.
Nr: add 1 pr (no 6) to be 1st p pr from R.

Nr: T O & T B 1 p pr (no 7) from L, tw
1 leaders either side of 'border' prs, add
1 pr (no 6) to be s ps 2 & 3 from R.
(9 prs)
After pin M:
change leaders (no 3) to (no 5), (tech 4,
td 4) cont row.
Work 2 rows.
Nr: add 1 pr (no 5) to be 2nd p pr from R.
(10 prs)
After pin N:
change leaders (no 5) to (no 6), (tech 4,
td 4) cont row.
Work 2 rows.
Nr: add 1 pr (no 4) to be s ps 4 & 5
from R.
Work 1 row.
Nr: T O & T B 1st p pr (no 7) from L,
and add 1 pr (no 3) to be 3rd p pr from R.
Work 3 rows.
Nr: add 1 pr (no 2) to be s ps 6 & 7
from R.
(12 prs)
After pin O:
start patt: Cls & tw 3rd and 4th p prs
from R.
Nr: Cls & tw 6 p prs from R.
Cont in patt.

After pin P:
Cls & tw 3rd and 4th p prs from R only.
Nr: Cls all p prs, maintain 'border', tw 1
leaders.
Work 1 row.
Nr: T O & T B s ps 6 & 7 (no 2) from R.
Work 2 rows.
Nr: T O & T B 3rd p pr (no 3) from R.
Work 1 row.
(10 prs)
Nr: add 1 pr (no 7) to L, tw 1 leaders to
maintain 'border', and T O & T B s ps 4
& 5 from R.
Work 1 row.
Nr: T O & T B 2nd p pr (no 5) from R.
Nr: T O & T B s ps 2 & 3 (no 6) from R.

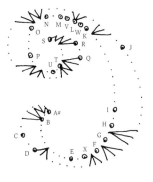

C1: Order of work

C3: Pin reference plan, Version 1

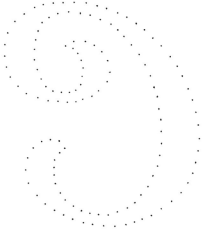

C2: Pricking

Work 4 rows.
(8 prs)
Nr: T O & T B 1st p pr (no 6) from R.
Nr: add 1 pr (no 6) to be s ps 2 & 3 from L.
Work 1 row.
Nr: add 1 pr (no 5) to be 2nd p pr from L.
Work 1 row.
Nr: add 1 pr (no 4) to s ps 4 & 5 from L.
Work 1 row.
(10 prs)
Nr: add 1 pr (no 3) to be 3rd p pr from R.
Work 1 row.
Nr: add 1 pr (no 2) to be s ps 6 & 7 from R.
Nr: add 1 pr (no 1) to be 4th p pr from L.
(13 prs)
After pin Q:
T O & T B 2nd p pr (no 4/no 5) from L, start patt: Cls 1 p pr, tw 1 leaders, Cls & tw next 4 p prs, and work 'border' prs.
Work 1 row.
Nr: T O & T B s ps 2 & 3 (no 6/no 3) from L, Cls 1 p pr, tw 1 leaders, Cls & tw next 3 prs, and work 'border' prs.
Work 1 row.

After pin R:
T O & T B 2nd p pr (no 1) from L.
Nr: Cls all prs, tw 1 leaders, to maintain 'border'.
Nr: T O & T B s ps 2 & 3 (no 2).
Nr: T O & T B 2nd p pr (no 5) from R.
(8 prs)
Nr: T O & T B s ps 2 & 3 (no 3/no 4) from L.
Nr: T O & T B s ps 2 & 3 from R and s ps 2 & 3 from L.
(5 prs)
To finish at pin S:
Cls thro 1st p pr, T O & T B leaders, Cls tog rem 2 p prs, T O & T B, Cls & tw edge prs, place pin S, Cls, T O both prs, T B 1 thread and secure to back of work with previously T B prs.
The rem 3 threads from the edge prs will be used for the rolled edge.

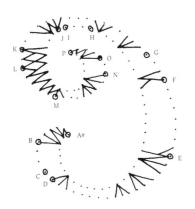

C4: Pin reference plan, Version 2

Notes for rolled edge
Roll from pin S to pin D (tech 9, td 9):
rolling thread – 1 x (no 7)
rolled threads – 2 x (no 7)
Use the 3 threads from the pin S, T B 1 thread from roll at pin T (tech 14, td 14), T B 1 thread from roll at pin U, cont with rolling thread only to pin V, add 1 thread (no 7) to roll at pin V (tech 13, td 13), add 1 thread (no 7) to roll at pin W, T B 1 thread from roll at pin X, T B 1 thread from roll at pin E.
Cont with rolling thread only to pin A#, add 2 threads (no 7) to roll at pin A#, T B 1 thread from roll at pin C.
Finish roll at pin D (tech 10, td 10).

VERSION 2
Section 1
Start at pin A#:
follow instructions for Version 1 till (6 prs).
Note Leaders remain (no 7) throughout. The 'border' is worked in the same manner as Version 1 throughout.
Use the T S when starting and finishing the braid to 'gain' on the outside edge pin (diag c2), this will lessen the need for some of the blind pins, but if used the subsequent instructions may need to be adjusted.
Nr: add 5 prs, 1 pr per row in order:
1 pr x (no 6)
1 pr x (no 5)
1 pr x (no 4)
1 pr x (no 3)
1 pr x (no 7)
to give order shown at pin B (diag c.2).
(11 prs)
After pin B:
start Ovals (var) patt, work T S with 6th p pr (no 7) from L (diag c.2).

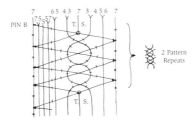

Diagram c2: Patt. 'Ovals' (var) after pin B

After pin C:
complete patt, work T S, cont working to L (diag c.2).

After pin D:
add 1 p pr to L, and T O & T B 3rd p pr from R.
(11 prs).
Cont T O & T B 5 p prs from R, lightest prs first, and adding prs to L, darkest prs first, to give order shown at pin E

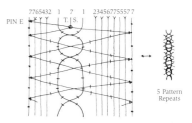

Diagram c3: Patt. 'Ovals' (var) after pin E

(diag c.3).
(15 prs)
After pin E:
start patt – Ovals (var), T S with 5th p pr (no 7) from L (diag c.3).

After pin F:
complete patt, and work T S, cont working to R.
Cont in Cls.

After pin G:
T O & T B 1 p pr (no 7) from patt centre, thereafter T O & T B 1 p pr from patt centre, lightest first, after each L pin.
(8 prs)
After pin H:
add 1 pr (no 7) to be 1st p pr from R.
Note Tw 1 leaders either side of 'border' prs.
Nr: T O & T B 1 p pr (no 6) from L, and add 1 pr (no 6) to be s ps 2 & 3 from R.
(9 prs)
After pin I:
add 1 pr (no 5) to be 2nd p pr from R.
(10 prs)
After completing blind pin J:
add 1 pr (no 4) to be s ps 4 & 5 from R.
Nr: T O & T B 1st p pr (no 7) from L.
Nr: add 1 pr (no 3) to be 3rd p pr from R.
Work 1 row.
Nr: add 1 pr (no 2) to be s ps 6 & 7 from R.
Nr: add 1 pr (no 2) to be 4th p pr from R.
Nr: add 1 pr (no 2) to be s ps 8 & 9 from R.
Nr: add 1 pr (no 7) to be 5th p pr from R, to give order shown at pin K (diag c.4).
(15 prs)
After pin K:
start patt – work T S with 8th p pr from L (diag c.4).
(15 prs)
After pin L:
complete patt, work T S, cont working to L.
Work 2 rows.

Nr: T O & T B 8th p pr (no 7) from L, thereafter T O & T B 1 patt pr per row, lightest first, till (9 prs).

After pin M:
add 1 pr (no 7) to L.
Nr: T O & T B 2nd p pr (no 5).

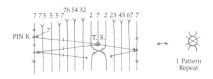

7 7 5 5 5 7 ⁷⁶ ⁵⁴ ³² 2 7 2 23 45 67 7

PIN K ... T.S. ... ↔ ... 1 Pattern Repeat

Diagram c4: Patt. 'Ovals' (var) after pin K

(9 prs)
Cont adding and T O & T B prs to give order shown at pin N (diag c.5).
After pin N:

---

start patt – Ovals (var), T S with 5th pr (no 7) from L (diag c.5).

After pin O:
complete patt, work T S, cont working to L.
Work 1 row.
Nr: T O & T B as many p prs as poss on the row, and cont in this way till 2 p prs (no 7) remain at pin P.
To finish at pin P, follow instructions for Version 1, from pin S.

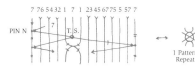

7 76 54 32 1 7 1 23 45 67 75 5 57 7

PIN N ... T.S. ... ↔ ... 1 Pattern Repeat

Diagram c5: Patt. 'Ovals' (var) after pin N

Notes for rolled edge
As Version 1.

D for DELPHINIUM

Colours

(no 1)	*White
(no 2)	*Sky
(no 3)	*Flax
(no 4)	*Delft
(no 5)	*French Navy
(no 6)	*Mid Navy
(no 7)	Navy

VERSION 1
Section 1
Start at pin A#:
using a two-colour point start (tech 1, td 1), (Note R–L working direction), hang 1 pr (no 5) and 1 pr (no 7) to be edge prs (diag d.1).
Add magic thread (tech 2, td 2a).
L edge pr is now (no 5).
R edge pr is now (no 7).

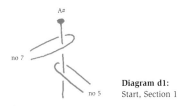

A#

no 7

no 5

Diagram d1:
Start, Section 1

On T P, hang 1 pr (no 6) to be leaders.
(3 prs)
On T P, hang 1 pr (no 5) and 1 pr (no 7), side by side in L–R order:
2 x (no 5)
2 x (no 7)
Cls leaders R–L thro 2 p prs and edge st at pin B (tech 3, td 3).
(5 prs)
Nr: add 1 pr (no 6) to centre.
Nr: add 1 pr (no 5) to be s ps 6 & 7 from R.
Nr: add 1 pr (no 5) to be 2nd p pr from L.
Nr: add 1 pr (no 5) to be s ps 8 & 9 from R.
Work 2 rows.
(9 prs)

Nr: add 1 pr (no 4) to be 2nd p pr from L.
Work 2 rows.
Nr: add 1 pr (no 4) to be s ps 12 & 13 from R.
Work 2 rows.
(11 prs)
Nr: add 1 pr (no 3) to be 3rd p pr from L.
Nr: add 1 pr (no 3) to be s ps 14 & 15 from R.
Nr: add 1 pr (no 2) to be 4th p pr from L.
Nr: add 1 pr (no 2) to be s ps 16 & 17 from R.
(15 prs)
Nr: add 1 pr (no 1) to be 5th p pr from L, start patt: tw 1 leaders, Cls & tw added pr (no 1), Cls rem p prs.
Cont in patt, work 1 row.
Nr: add 1 pr (no 1) to be 5th p pr from L, tw 1 leaders, Cls & tw 2 p prs (no 1), Cls rem p prs.
Cont in Cls & tw 2 p prs (no 1).
After pin C:
T O & T B 4th p pr (no 5) from R.
(16 prs)
After pin D:
Cls & tw 5th p pr (no 1) from R only.
Nr: cont in Cls.
After pin E and also after each 6 foll L edge pins:
T O & T B 2nd p pr from L,
1 pr x (no 4),
1 pr x (no 3),
1 pr x (no 2),
s ps 8 & 9 from lt (no 2/no3), s ps 10 & 11 – (no 4/no 5), 5th p pr – (no 4/no 5), 3rd p pr – (no 1).
Cont in Cls.
(9 prs)
After pin F:
add 1 pr (no 6) to be s ps 4 & 5 from R.
Nr: T O & T B s ps 4 & 5 from L.
Nr: add 1 pr (no 7) to be s ps 2 & 3 from R.
Cont in Cls.
(10 prs)
After pin G:
T O & T B 2nd p pr (no 1/no 3) from L.
Cont in Cls.
(9 prs)
After pin H:
*add 1 pr (no 5) to be 3rd p pr from L.

Work 1 row*.
Rep * to * 3 more times.
(13 prs)
After pin I:
add 1 pr (no 4) to be 4th p pr from L, start patt: tw 1 leaders, Cls & tw added pr (no 4).
Work 1 row.
Nr: T O & T B 2nd p pr (no 7) from R, and add 1 pr (no 4) to be 5th p pr from L, tw 1 leaders, Cls & tw 2 p prs (no 4).
Work 1 row.
Nr: T O & T B 3rd p pr (no 6) from R, and add 1 pr (no 4) to be 6th p pr from L, tw 1 leaders, Cls & tw 3 p prs (no 4).
Cont Cls & tw 3 p prs (no 4)
(14 prs)
After pin J:
T O & T B 6th p pr (no 4) from L, cont Cls & tw 2 p prs (no 4).
Work 1 row.
Nr: T O & T B 5th p pr (no 4) from L, cont Cls & tw 1 p pr (no 4).
(12 prs)
Nr: add 1 pr (no 6) to be 2nd p pr from R.
Nr: T O & T B 4th p pr (no 4) from L, and cont in Cls.
Nr: add 1 pr (no 7) to be 2nd p pr from R.
(13 prs)
After pin K:
*T O & T B 2nd p pr (no 5) from L.
Work 1 row*.
Rep * to * 4 more times.
(8 prs)
At pin L:
change leaders (no 6) with L edge pr (no 5), (tech 7, td 7), cont row, T O & T B 1st p pr from L.
(7 prs)
At pin M:
change leaders (no 5) with R edge pr (no 7), (tech 7, td 7). L–R order is

L edge pr	2 x (no 6)
	4 x (no 6)
	4 x (no 7)
R edge pr	2 x (no 5)
leaders	2 x (no 7)

(7 prs)
After pin N:
add 1 pr (no 6) to be 2nd p pr from R.
Nr: T O & T B 1st p pr (no 6) from L,

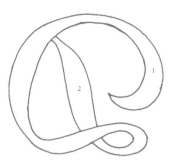

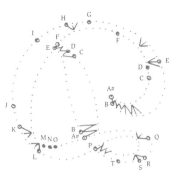

D1: Order of work

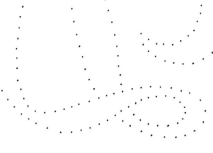

D3: Pin reference plan, Versions 1 and 2

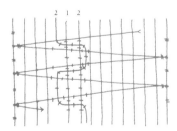

D2: Pricking

and add 1 pr (no 5) to be 2nd p pr from R.
(8 prs)
After pin O:
add 1 pr (no 4) to be 2nd p pr from R,
and start patt: tw 1 leaders, Cls & tw
with added p pr (no 4),
Nr: add 1 pr (no 3) to be 2nd p pr from
R, and Cls & tw 2 p prs: (no 4) and (no 3).
Nr: add 1 pr (no 2) to be 2nd p pr from
R, and Cls & tw 3 p prs: (no 2), (no 3)
and (no 4).
Nr: T O & T B 1st p pr (no 6) from L,
and add 1 pr (no 1) to be 2nd p pr from
R, and Cls & tw 4 p prs: (no 4), (no 3),
(no 2) and (no 1).
(11 prs)
After pin P:
Cls & tw 3 p prs only: (no 3), (no 2)
and (no 1).
Nr: Cls & tw 2 p prs only: (no 1) and
(no 2).
Nr: Cls & tw I p pr only: (no 1).
Cont in Cls.
(11 prs)
After pin Q:
start patt: tw 1 leaders, Cls & tw 2nd
p pr (no 1) from R.
Cont in patt, Cls & tw 2nd p pr (no 1).
At pin R:
change leaders (no 7) with R edge pr
(no 5), (tech 7, td 7).
Cont in Cls.
After pin S:
T O & T B 1 p pr (no 1).
Nr: T O & T B 1 p pr (no 2).
Nr: T O & T B 1 p pr (no 3).
Nr: T O & T B 1 p pr (no 4), and add 1
pr (no 6) to be 2nd p pr from R.
(8 prs)
After pin T:
start patt: tw 1 leaders, Cls & tw 1 p pr
(no 5).
Cont in patt, Cls & tw 1 p pr.

Finish at previously worked pin P:
using top sewings (tech 12, td12), join
to previously worked section of braid,
T O leaders (no 5), R edge pr (no 7),
and 1st p pr (no 5) and set aside for
rolled edge.
T O & T B all rem threads and, secure to

back of work with previously
T B prs.

Notes for rolled edges
Roll from pin P to pin S (tech
9, td 9):
rolling thread – 1 x (no 7)
rolled threads – 1 x (no 7), 1 x (no 5)
Use 3 threads from 3 prs set aside at pin
P for roll.
T B 1 thread (no 5) from roll at pin T
(tech 14, td 14).
Finish at pin S (tech 10, td 10).

Roll from pin P to pin K:
rolling thread – 1 x (no 7)
rolled threads – 1 x (no 7), 1 x (no 5)
Use 3 threads from 3 prs set aside at pin
P for roll.
T B 1 thread (no 5) at pin L.
Finish at pin K.

Roll from pin A# to pin D:
rolling thread – 1 x (no 7)
rolled threads – 1 x (no 7), 1 x (no 5)
Using magic thread at pin A# (tech 16,
td 16), add 1 pr (no 7) and 1 thread (no
5), (tech 24, td 24).
T B 1 thread (no 5) at pin C.
Finish at pin D.

Section 2
Start at pin A#:
using top sewings, hang on 10 prs, to
give L–R order as foll:
Note Leaders (no 5) at pin A#.

R edge pr	2 x (no 7)
	2 x (no 7)
	2 x (no 6)
	6 x (no 5)
	2 x (no 6)
	2 x (no 7)
L edge pr	2 x (no 6)
leaders	2 x (no 5)

(10 prs)
Tw 2 R and L edge prs.
Cls & tw 3 centre p prs, Cls rem p prs.
After pin B:
add 2 prs (no 5) to be 3rd and 7th p prs
from R, these 2 p prs also to be worked
Cls & tw.

(12 prs)
After pin C:
T O & T B 3rd and 7th p prs (no 5) from R.
(10 prs)
After pin D:
T O & T B 3rd and 5th p prs (no 5) from L.
(8 prs)
To finish at pin E and pin F:
join to Section 1, set aside R edge pr (no
7) and 1 thread (no 5) for roll, T O &
T B rem prs in a bunch (tech 25, td 25).

Notes for rolled edge
Roll from pin E to pin A#:
rolling thread – 1 x (no 7)
rolled threads – 1 x (no 7), 1 x (no 5)
Use R edge pr and 1 thread set aside at
pin E for roll.

VERSION 2
Section 1
Start at pin A#:
follow instructions for Version 1, from
pin A# until (16 prs).
Cont in Cls.
Work 1 row.
Nr: Cls 3 p prs, tw 1 leaders,
start patt: Dewdrops (diag d.2) with 4th
p pr (no 2), 5th p pr (no 1) and 6th p pr
(no 2) from L only, Cls rem prs.
Cont in patt.
(16 prs)
Cont in this way, following instructions

Diagram d2: 'Dewdrops' (var)

19

for Version 1.
Cont in patt, working 5 patt reps.
After pin D:
patt. prs will have returned to original colour positions.
Cont in Cls.
After pin E:
follow instructions for Version 1 until (9 prs).
Note: Omit instruction to T O & T B 1 p pr (no 1).
Pay careful attention to the thread colours to be T O & T B as in some cases their numerical position will not be identical to those in Version 1.
After pin F:
follow instructions for Version 1 to pin I.
(13 prs)
After pin I:
add 1 pr (no 4) to be 4th p pr from L.
Work 1 row.
Nr: Cls 3 p prs, tw 1 leaders,
start Dewdrops patt with 3rd p pr (no 4), 4th p pr (no 5) and 5th p pr (no 5) from L only, Cls rem p prs.
Cont in patt, work 9 patt reps.

After pin J:
patt prs will have returned to original colour positions.
Cont in Cls.
Work 2 rows.
Nr: T O & T B 1 p pr (no 4).
(13 prs)
After pin K:
follow instructions for Version 1 to pin O.
After pin O:
follow instructions for Version 1 till (11 prs).
Work 1 row.
Nr: Cls 5 p prs, tw 1 leaders,
start Dewdrops patt with 6th, 7th and 8th p prs from L only, Cls rem p prs.

Cont in patt, work 5 patt reps.
Cont in Cls.
Note Do not work blind pin. There is no pin P to be worked in Version 2.
Follow instructions for Version 1, to finish at pin P.
Note Omit 1 of the blind pins; this will compensate for the earlier unworked blind pin.

Notes for rolled edge
As Version 1.

Section 2
Start at pin A#:
follow instructions for Version 1 till (10 prs).
Work 1 row.
Nr: Cls 2 p prs, tw 1 leaders,
start Dewdrops patt with 3rd, 4th and 5th p prs (no 5) from L, Cls 2 p prs.
Cont in patt.
After pin B:
add 2 prs (no 6) to be 2nd and 8th p prs from R.
(12 prs)
After pin C:
cont in Cls, T O & T B 2nd and 8th p prs (no 6) from L.
(10 prs)
Follow instructions for Version 1, to finish at pin E.

Notes for rolled edge
As Version 1.

E for EGLANTINE

Colours
(no 1)	Flesh
(no 2)	Pastel Pink
(no 3)	*Pale Salmon
(no 4)	*Mint
(no 5)	Pastel Green
(no 6)	Malachite
(no 7)	*Bottle Green

VERSION 1
Section 1
Start at pin A#:
using a two colour point start (tech 1, td 1), (Note L-R working direction), hang 1 pr (no 6) and 1 pr (no 7) to be edge prs (diag e.1).
Add magic thread (tech 2, td 2a).
L edge pr is now (no 6).
R edge pr is now (no 7).

On T P, hang 1 pr (no 5) to be leaders.
(3 prs)
On T P, hang 1 pr (no 6) and 1 pr (no 7), side by side in L-R order:
2 x (no 6)
2 x (no 7)
Cls leaders L-R thro 2 p prs and edge st (tech 3, td 3).
(5 prs)
Nr: add 1 pr (no 7) to centre.
Nr: add 1 pr (no 6) to be 2nd p pr from L.
Nr: add 1 pr (no 5) to be 4th p pr from R.
Nr: add 1 pr (no 5) to be s ps 4 & 5

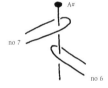

no 7   A#
no 6

Diagram e1:
Start, Section 1

from L.
Cont in Cls.
(9 prs)
After completing blind pin B:
add 1 pr (no 4) to be 3rd p pr from L.
Nr: *add 1 pr (no 4)*.
Nr: rep * to *.
Work 1 row.
L-R order is as foll:
L edge pr	2 x (no 6)
	2 x (no 6)
	2 x (no 5)
	6 x (no 4)
	2 x (no 5)
	2 x (no 6)
	4 x (no 7)
R edge pr	2 x (no 7)
leaders	2 x (no 5)
(12 prs)
After pin C:
start patt – Cls thro 3 p prs, tw 1 leaders, Cls & tw 4th p pr (no 4), Cls rem p prs.

Nr: Cls 4 p prs, tw 1 leaders, Cls & tw 3 p prs (no 4), Cls rem p prs.

Cont in patt, Cls & tw 3 p prs (no 4).
After pin D:

Cls 5 p prs, tw 1 leaders, Cls & tw 6th p pr, Cls rem p prs.
Work 1 row.
Cont in Cls.
Nr: *T O & T B 1 p pr (no 4)*, cont, rep * to * for next 2 rows.
Nr: *T O & T B 1 p.pr (no 5)*.
Nr: rep * to *.
(7 prs)

After pin E:
change leaders (no 5) with 1st p pr from L (no 6), (tech 26, td 26), T O & T B old leaders.
(6 prs)
At pin F:
change leaders (no 6) with R edge pr (no 7), (tech 7, td 7), cont row, adding 1 pr (no 6) to R.
(7 prs)
At pin G:
change leaders (no 7) with L edge pr (no 6), (tech 7, td 7), now
L edge pr	2 x (no 7)
R edge pr	2 x (no 6)
leaders	2 x (no 6),
cont row, adding 1 pr (no 6) to be 1st p pr from R.

Nr: add 1 pr (no 5) to be 2nd p pr from R.
Nr: T O & T B 1st p pr (no 6) from L, and add 1 pr (no 5) to be s ps 4 & 5 from R.
Work 2 rows.
(9 prs)
Nr: add 1 pr (no 4) to be 3rd p pr from R.
Work 3 rows.

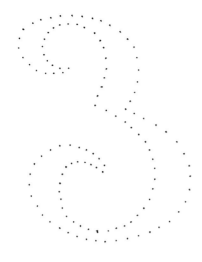

E2: Pricking

E1: Order of work

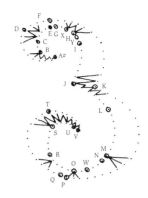

E3: Pin reference plan, Versions 1 and 2

Nr: add 1 pr (no 1) to be s ps 6 & 7 from R.
(11 prs)
After completing blind pin H:
change leaders (no 6) with 1st p pr from L (no 7), (tech 26, td 26), and cont row adding 1 pr (no 1) to be 4th p pr from R.
(11 prs)
Nr: add 1 pr (no 2) to be s ps 8 & 9 from R.
Nr: add 1 pr (no 2) to be 5th p pr from L.
Nr: T O & T B s ps 2 & 3 from R, and add 1 pr (no 3) to be s ps 12 &13 from L, to give L-R order:

L edge pr	2 x (no 7)
	2 x (no 7)
	2 x (no 6)
	2 x (no 5)
	1 x (no 4)
	2 x (no 1)
	2 x (no 2)
	2 x (no 3)
	2 x (no 2)
	2 x (no 1)
	1 x (no 4)
	1 x (no 5)
	1 x (no 6)
R edge pr	2 x (no 6)
leaders	2 x (no 7)
(13 prs)	

After pin I:
start patt – *Cls 5 p prs,
tw 1 leaders, Cls & tw 2 p prs, Cls rem p prs.
Nr: Cls 3 p prs, tw 1 leaders, Cls & tw 2 p prs, Cls rem p prs*.
Cont in patt, rep * to *.

After pin J:
Cls thro 5 p prs only, tw 1 leaders (tech 27, td 27), return to L edge, pin and edge st.
Note Adjust tension carefully.
Cls to pin K.

After pin K:
cont in Cls.

After pin L:
cont in patt – rep * to *.

After pin M:
cont in Cls.

After pin N:
T O & T B 1 p pr (no 3).
Nr: *T O & T B 1 p pr (no 2)*.
Nr: rep * to *.
Nr: *T O & T B 1 p pr (no 1)*.
Nr rep * to *.
Nr: T O & T B 1 p pr (no 4).
Cont in Cls.
(7 prs)
After working 1st part of blind pin O:
T O & T B 2nd p pr (no 5) from R.

After completing blind pin O:
add 1 pr (no 7) to be s ps 2 & 3 from L.
(7 prs)
After pin P:
T O & T B s ps 2 & 3 (no 5/no 6) from R, and add 1 pr (no 6) to L edge.
Nr: add 1 pr (no 6) to s ps 2 & 3 from L.
(8 prs)
At pin Q:
change leaders (no 7) with R edge pr (no 6), (tech 7, td 7).

After pin Q:
T O & T B 1st p pr (no 6) from R, and add 1 pr (no 5) to be 2nd p pr from L.
Nr: add 1 pr (no 5) to be s ps 4 & 5 from L.
Nr: add 1 pr (no 4) to be 5th p pr from R.
Nr: add 1 pr (no 4) to be s ps 6 & 7 from L.
Nr: add 1 pr (no 4) to be 6th p pr from R.
(12 prs)
After pin R:
start patt – Cls 3 p prs, tw 1 leaders, Cls & tw 4th p pr (no 4), Cls rem p prs.
Nr: Cls 4 p prs, tw 1 leaders, Cls & tw 3 p prs (no 4), Cls rem p prs.
Cont in patt, Cls & tw 3 p prs (no 4).

After completing blind pin S:
Cls 3 p prs, tw 1 leaders, Cls & tw 4th p pr, Cls rem p prs.
Nr: rep * to *.
Nr: Cont in Cls.

After pin T:
T O & T B 1 p pr (no 4).
Nr: cont rep * to * for next 2 rows.
(9 prs)
Nr: *T O & T B 1 p pr (no 5)*.
Work 1 row.
Nr: rep * to *.
Work 1 row.
Nr: T O & T B 1 p pr (no 6).
(6 prs)
After pin U:
T O & T B 1 p pr (no 6).
Nr: Cls leaders thro 2 rem p prs (no 7), T O & T B leaders, T O & T B both p prs, and secure to back of work with previously T B prs.

Finish at pin V:
Cls & tw both edge prs (no 7), pin, Cls & T O, these 2 prs to be used for rolled edge.

Notes for rolled edges
Roll from pin V to pin to pin W (tech 9, td 9):
rolling thread – 1 x (no 7)
rolled threads – 3 x (no 7)
Use edge prs from pin V for rolled edge.
T B 1 thread from roll at pin R and pin P (tech 14, td 14).
Finish at pin W (tech 10, td 10).

Roll from pin A# to pin Y:
rolling thread – 1 x (no 7)
rolled threads – 1 x (no 7), 2 x (no 6)
Using magic thread at pin A# (tech 16, td 16), add 1 pr (no 7) and 1 pr (no 6).
T B 1 thread from roll at pin C and pin X.
Finish at pin Y.

VERSION 2
Section 1
Start at pin A#:
follow instructions for Version 1 to pin I.

21

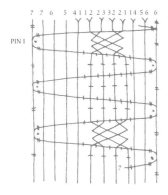

7 7 6 5 4 1 1 2 2 3 3 2 2 1 1 4 5 6 6

PIN I

Diagram e2: Patt. 'Grenades' (var) after pin I

(13 prs)
After pin I:
start Grenades patt (diag e.2), using 5th,
6th, 7th and 8th p prs, work 3 patt reps,
ensuring last rep is completed, to return
threads to original colour order.

Cont follow instructions for Version 1,
to pin L.
After pin L:
start Grenades patt (diag e.2), as before,
work 4 patt reps (the patt prs will not
have returned to their original colour
positions).

After pin N:
T O & T B 5 p prs, 1 pr per row, from
centre of patt, lightest prs first.
(8 prs)
Nr: T O & T B 1 p pr (no 4).
Cont in Cls.

After pin O:
follow instructions for Version 1,
to finish at pin V.

Notes for rolled edge
As Version 1.

F for FAIRY MOSS

Colours
(no 1)	Flesh
(no 2)	*Pale Salmon
(no 3)	*Pale Peach
(no 4)	Pastel Pink
(no 5)	Apple Green
(no 6)	Lime
(no 7)	*Mid Olive

VERSION 1
Section 1
Start at pin A#:
using a two colour point start (tech 1, td
1), (Note L–R working direction), hang
1 pr (no 7) and 1 pr (no 6) to be edge
prs (diag f.1).
Add magic thread (tech 2, td 2a).

L edge pr is now (no 7).

A#

no 6

no 7

Diagram f1:
Start, Section 1

R edge pr is now (no 6).

On T P, hang 1 pr (no 7) to be leaders.
(3 prs)
On T P, hang 2 p prs (no 7) open.
Cls leaders L–R thro 2 p prs and edge st
at pin B (tech 3, td 3).
(5 prs)
Nr: add 2 prs (no 6) to centre.
Nr: *add 1 pr (no 5) to centre*.
Nr: rep * to *.
Nr: *add 1 pr (no 4) to centre braid*.
Nr: rep * to *.
(11 prs)
After pin C:
change leaders (no 7) to (no 4), (tech 4,

td 4), and cont row, adding 1 pr (no 3)
to centre.
(12 prs)
After pin D:
T O & T B 1st p pr (no 7) from R, and
add 1 pr (no 3) to be s ps. 10 & 11 from L.
Nr: add 1 pr (no 2) to be 6th pr from L.
Nr: T O & T B 1st p pr (no 6) from R,
and add 1 pr (no 2) to be s ps. 12 & 13
from L.
(13 prs)
After completing blind pin E:
start patt – Cls thro 5 p prs, tw 1
leaders, tw 1 each of 2 p prs (no 2),
work ½ st with leaders and 2 p prs (no
2), Cls rem p prs.

Nr: T O & T B 1st p pr (no 5) from R,
and cont row working ½ st with
leaders and 2 p prs (no 2).
(12 prs)
Cont working ½ st with leaders and
2 p prs.

After pin F:
when prs have returned to original
colour order, cont in Cls.

After pin G:
T O & T B 1st p pr (no 7) from L.
Work 1 row.
Nr: T O & T B 1st p pr (no 6) from L.
Work 1 row.
(10 prs)
At pin H:
change leaders (no 4) with L edge pr
(no 7), (tech 7, td 7).

After pin H:
change leaders (no 7) to (no 1), (tech 4,
td 4)

After pin I:
T O & T B 1st p pr (no 5) from L.
Nr: add 1 pr (no 1) to centre, L–R order
is as foll:
L edge pr	2 x (no 4)
	2 x (no 4)
	2 x (no 3)
	2 x (no 2)
	2 x (no 1)
	2 x (no 2)
	2 x (no 3)
	2 x (no 4)
R edge pr	2 x (no 6)
leaders	2 x (no 1)
(10 prs)	

After pin J:
start patt – Cls thro 2 prs, tw 1 leaders,
and work ½ st with 3 central prs (no 2),
(no 1) and (no 2), Cls rem p prs.
Cont working ½ st with 3 central prs.

After working 1st part of blind pin K:
when colours have returned to original
colour positions, cont in Cls.

After pin L:
T O & T B 1 pr (no 1) from centre.
Nr: add 1 pr (no 5) to be 1st p pr from
R, and T O & T B s ps. 4 & 5 and 8 & 9
(no 2/no 3) from L.
Work 1 row.
(8 prs)
Nr: add 1 pr (no 6) to be 1st p pr from
R, and T O & T B 1 pr (no 2).
Work 1 row.
Nr: add 1 pr (no 7) to be 1st p pr from
R, and T O & T B 1 pr (no 3).
Work 1 row.
(8 prs)
At pin M:
when working 1st part of blind pin, add
1 pr (no 7) to be s ps. 2 & 3 from R,
then Cls leaders (no 1) thro 1st p pr,
and change leaders (no 1) to (no 7),
(tech 4, td 4), and cont row, T O & T B
2nd p pr (no 4) from L.
Work 1 row.

When completing blind pin at pin M:
change leaders (no 7) with R edge pr
(no 6), (tech 7, td 7) then add 1 pr (no
7) to be s ps. 2 & 3 from R, Cls thro 1st
pr from R and change leaders (no 6) to
(no 7), (tech 4, td 4), and T O & T B 1st

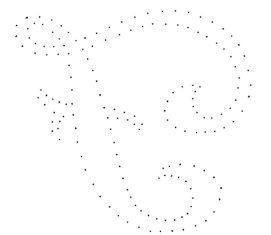

F2: Pricking

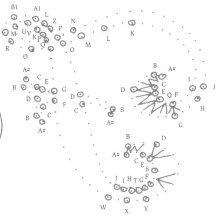

F1: Order of work

F3: Pin reference plan, Versions 1 and 2

p pr (no 4) from L.
(8 prs)
At pin N:
change leaders (no 7) with L edge pr
(no 4), (tech 7, td 7).

After pin N:
change leaders (no 4) to (no 7), (tech 4,
td 4), cont row.
Work 1 row.
Nr: T O & T B 1st p pr (no 5) from L.
Nr: add 1 pr (no 7) to be s ps. 4 & 5
from R.
Nr: T O & T B 1st p pr (no 6) from L.
(7 prs)
After pin O:
work locking st (tech 6, td 6) with
leaders and 1st p pr from L,
leave section to work rolled edge from
pin U to pin Y.

Notes for rolled edge
Roll from pin U to pin Y (tech 9, td 9):
rolling thread – 1 x (no 6)
rolled threads – 3 x (no 6)
Hang on 1 pr (no 6) at pin U,
add 1 thread to roll at pin V and pin K
(tech 13, td 13).
T B 1 thread from roll at pin W and pin
X (tech 14, td 14).
Finish roll at pin Y (tech 10, td 10).

Return to Section 1

Undo locking st, and cont in Cls to
finish at pin P and pin Q, joining to
previously worked braid with top
sewings.
Set aside leaders and L edge pr (no 7),
to be used for rolled edge, pin Q to pin N.
T O & T B rem prs in a bunch (tech 25,
td 25).

Notes for rolled edges
Roll from pin Q to pin N:
rolling thread – 1 x (no 7)

rolled threads – 3 x (no 7)
Use leaders and L edge pr from pin Q
for roll.
T B 1 thread at pin O and pin R.
Finish at pin N.

Roll from pin A# to pin T:
rolling thread – 1 x (no 7)
rolled threads – 3 x (no 7)
Hang 2 prs (no 7) at pin A#.
T B 1 thread from roll at pin S and pin F.
Finish at pin T.

Roll from pin J to pin B1:
rolling thread – 1 x (no 4)
rolled threads – 3 x (no 4)
Hang on 1 pr (no 4) at pin J.
Add 1 thread (no 4) at next 2 following
pins.
T B 1 thread from roll at pin Z and pin A1.
Finish at pin B1.

Section 2
Start at pin A# :
Follow instructions for Section 1, from
pin A# to pin G (diag f.2).
Note Reverse L–R instructions.

After pin G:

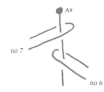

Diagram f2:
Start, Section 2

T O & T B 1st p pr (no 7) from R, and
complete blind pin F.
Work 2 rows.

Nr: T O & T B 1st p pr (no 6) from R.
Work 1 row.
Nr: T O & T B 1st p pr (no 5) from R.
(9 prs)

At pin H:
change leaders (no 4) with L edge pr
(no 6), (tech 7, td 7).

After pin H:
change leaders (no 6) to (no 1), (tech 4,
td 4).

After pin I:
add 1 pr (no 1) to centre.
(10 prs)
After pin J:
T O & T B s ps. 4 & 5 and s ps 10 & 11
(no 2/no 3) from L, Cls thro 1 pr, tw 1
leaders, and work ½ st with 3 central
p prs, Cls rem pr.
Cont in patt, working ½ st with 3 central
prs.
(8 prs)
After pin K:
either when prs have returned to
original colour positions (Version 2),or
to achieve this (Version 1), untwist s
ps.3 & 4 and 7 & 8 (no 2/no 3), and add
1 pr (no 5) to be 1st p pr from R.
Cont in Cls, working ½ st with p pr
(no 1) only.
(9 prs)
Work 1 row.
Nr: add 1 pr (no 6) to be 1st p pr from R.
Work 1 row.
Nr: add 1 pr (no 7) to be 1st p. pr from R.
Work 1 row.
(11 prs)
After pin L:
add 1 pr (no 7) to be s ps. 2 & 3, Cls
thro 1 pr, change leaders (no1) to (no
4), (tech 4, td 4) cont row, T O & T B 1
p pr (no 1).
Cont in Cls.
(11 prs)
Nr: T O & T B 1 p pr (no 2).
Nr: add 1 pr (no 7) to R, and T O & T B
1 p pr (no 3).
Nr: T O & T B 1 p pr (no 4).
(9 prs)

After pin M:
add 1 pr (no 7) to be s ps. 2 & 3,
change leaders (no 4) to (no 7), (tech 4, td 4) cont row, and T O & T B 1 pr (no 4).
(9 prs)
At pin N:
change leaders (no 7) with L edge pr (no 4) (tech 7, td 7).

After pin N:
change leaders (no 4) to (no 7), (tech 4, td 4).
Work 1 row.
Nr: T O & T B 1 pr (no 5) from L.
(8 prs)
Finish at pin O and pin P, using top sewings to join to Section 1 at pin O and pin P.
Use R edge pr and 1st p pr from R edge for rolled edge.
T O & T B rem prs in a bunch.

Notes for rolled edge
Roll from pin O to pin A#:
rolling thread – 1 x (no 7)
rolled threads – 3 x (no 7)
T B 1 thread from roll at pin Q and pin C.
Finish at pin A#.

Section 3
Start at pin A#:
Using a one colour flat start (tech 21, td 21), (Note R–L working direction), hang 2 prs (no 7) to be edge prs, Cls tog, tw 2 L edge pr.

On T P, hang 1 pr (no 7) to be leaders.
(3 prs)
On T P, hang 2 prs (no 7) open.
Cls leaders R–L thro 2 p prs, tw 2 leaders and edge st at pin B.
(5 prs)
Nr: add 1 pr (no 6) to centre, cont in Cls to pin C.

After pin C:
leave to work Section 3a.
(6 prs)

Section 3a
Start at pin A#:
Follow instructions for Section 3, from pin A# to pin C.
Note Reverse R–L working direction.

After pin C:
join sections (tech 22, td 22) thus:

At pin D:
Cls & tw tog, L edge pr from Section 3 and R edge pr from Section 3a, place pin D, Cls both leaders thro respective p prs, work T S in centre, removing pin D and replacing it as a support pin for T S.
Cls tog 3rd and 4th p prs from L,
Cls tog 3rd and 4th p prs from R.
Work T.S and cont working to R.

(12 prs)
After pin E:
work 1 row.
Nr: T O & T B 4th & 6th p prs (no 7) from L.
Nr: T O & T B s ps 4 & 5 and 10 & 11 (no 6/no 7) from R.
(8 prs)
To finish at pin F and pin G:
join to Section 1.

Section 4
Start at pin A#:
follow instructions for Section 3 from pin A# to pin B.
(5 prs)
Nr: add 1 pr (no 7) to centre, cont in Cls.

To finish at pin C and pin D:
join to Section 1.

VERSION 2
Section 1
Start at pin A# :
follow instructions for Version 1, from pin A# (diag f.1) to pin E.
(13 prs)

After completing blind pin E:
add 1 pr (no 4) to be 7th pr from L.
Nr: T O & T B 1st p pr (no 5) from R.
(13 prs)
Nr: Cls thro 6 prs, work T S with 4th pr from R.
Note T S is not positioned centrally.
Start Ovals patt; work 1 patt rep (diag f.3).

Finish patt by working leader from each side, to work T S between 3rd and 4th prs from R. Cont, working leaders to R, cont in Cls.

After pin F:
T O & T B 7th pr (no 4) from L, and cont, following instructions for Version 1 from pin F to pin J.
(10 prs)
After pin J:
Cls thro 3 prs, work T S with centre pr (no 1).
Start Ovals patt, working 8 patt reps (diag f.4).

Finish patt by working leader from each side, to work T S in centre.

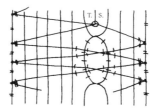

Diagram f3: Patt. 'Ovals' (var)

Cont, working leaders to R, and cont in Cls.

After pin K:
follow instructions for Version 1, to finish at pin P and pin Q.

Notes for rolled edges
As Version 1.

Section 2
Start at pin A# :
follow instructions for Version 1, from pin A# (diag f.2) to pin E.
Note Reverse L–R instructions.

After completing blind pin E:
add 1 pr (no 4) to be 7th pr from R.
(14 prs)
Nr: T O & T B 1st p pr (no 5) from L,

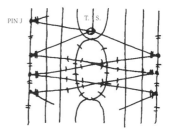

Diagram f4: Patt. 'Ovals' (var) after pin J

Cls thro 3 prs, and work T S with 4th pr (no 4) from L (diag f.5).
Note T S is not positioned centrally.
Start patt: work 1 Maltese Spot, using 3rd and 4th prs (no 2) from L.

Finish patt by working leader from each side, work T S between 3rd and 4th prs (no 2) from L.
Cont working leaders to L, cont in Cls.
(13 prs)
Note In Version 2, Section 2, there is no blind pin at the next inner edge pin.

After working 1st part of blind pin F:
T O & T B 4th pr (no 4) from L.
(12 prs)
After pin G:
follow instructions for Version 1, to pin J.

Note In Version 2, Section 2, there is no pin I.

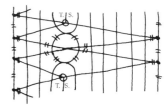

Diagram f5: Patt. 'Maltese Spot'

After pin J:
T O & T B s ps. 4 & 5 and 8 & 9 (no 2/no 3) from L, Cls thro 1 pr, tw 2 leaders (diag f.6), start Ribbon patt with 2 central prs (no 2/no 3), tw 2 leaders, Cls rem pr.
(7 prs)
Work 2 patt reps of Ribbon.

Change 1 patt p pr, 3rd p pr (no 2/no 3) to (no 1) thus:
(diag f.7), *after edge st, leave leaders at L, on T P, hang new patt p pr (no 1), to hang between 2nd and 3rd prs from L. Cls tog new pr (no 1) with 3rd pr (no 2/no 3), T O & T B 3rd pr (no 2/no 3), cont with new pr (no 1) as patt p pr, and cont in patt, Cls 2nd and 3rd patt prs tog.*
(7 prs)
After next patt rep:
change 1 patt p pr, 3rd p pr (no 2/no 3) to (no 1) as before, (see * to *).

Work 5 patt reps:
change 1 patt p pr, 2nd p pr (no 1) to (no 2), (see * to *).

After next patt rep:
change 1 patt p pr, 2nd p pr (no 1) to (no 2), (see * to *).

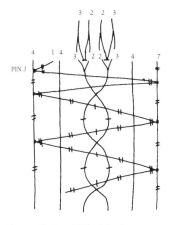

Diagram f6: Patt. 'Ribbon' (var)

After next patt rep:
change 1 patt p pr, 2nd p pr (no 2) to (no 3), (see * to *).
(7 prs)
After pin K:
add 1 pr (no 5) to be 1st p pr from R, cont in patt.
(8 prs)
Nr: cont in Cls.
Nr: add 1 pr (no 6) to be 1st p pr from R. Work 1 row.
Nr: add 1 pr (no 7) to be 1st p. pr from R.
(10 prs)

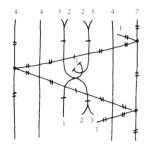

Diagram f7: Patt. 'Ribbon', changing a passive pr

After pin L:
add 1 pr (no 7) to be s ps. 2 & 3 from R, Cls thro 1 pr,
change leaders (no 1) to (no 4), (tech 4, td 4).
(11 prs)
Nr: cont, following instructions for Version 1, to finish at pin O and pin P.

Notes for rolled edge
As Version 1.

Sections 3, 3a and 4
Follow instructions for Version 1.

G for GOLDEN PHEASANT

Colours

(no 1)	*Honey
(no 2)	*Brass
(no 3)	*Marigold
(no 4)	Dark Mauve
(no 5)	Mid Purple
(no 6)	*Helio
(no 7)	Extra Dark Brown

VERSION 1
Section 1
Start at pin A#:
using a one colour point start (tech 23, td 23), (Note L–R working direction), hang 2 prs (no 6) to be edge prs (diag g.1). Add magic thread (tech 2, td 2b).

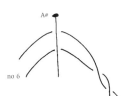

Diagram g1: Start, Section 1

On T P, hang 1 pr (no 7) to be leaders.
(3 prs)
On T P, hang 2 p prs (no 7) open. Cls leaders L–R thro 2 p prs and edge st at pin B (tech 3, td 3).
(5 prs)

After pin B:
add 2 prs (no 6) to centre.
Nr: *add 1 pr (no 5) to centre*.
Nr: rep * to *.
Nr: *add 1 pr (no 4) to centre*.
Work 1 row.
Nr: rep * to *.
(11 prs)

After pin C:
change leaders (no 7) to (no 4), (tech 4, td 4), cont row, adding 1 pr (no 3) to centre.
(12 prs)
At pin D:
change leaders (no 4) with R edge pr (no 6) (tech 7, td 7).

After pin D:
add 1 pr (no 3) to centre.
(13 prs)
After pin E:
change leaders (no 6) to (no 3), (tech 4, td 4) cont row, adding 1 pr (no 2) to centre.

Nr: add 1 pr (no 2) to centre.
(15 prs)
After pin F:
start patt – Cls 6 p prs, tw 1 leaders, Cls rem p prs.
Nr: T O & T B 1st p pr (no 7) from R, Cls 5 p prs, tw 2 leaders, Cls rem p prs.
Nr: Cls 6 p prs, tw 3 leaders, Cls rem p prs.
Nr: T O & T B 1st p pr (no 6) from R, Cls 4 p prs, tw 3 leaders, Cls rem p prs.
Cont Cls, tw 3 leaders as before.
After pin G:
tw 2 leaders as before.
Nr: tw 1 leaders as before.
(13 prs)
After pin H:
cont in Cls.

After working 1st part of blind pin I:
T O & T B 1 p pr (no 2)*.
Nr: rep * to *.
(11 prs)
After completing blind pin I:
change leaders (no 3) to (no 5), (tech 4, td 4), cont row, T O & T B 1 p pr (no 3)
(10 prs)
Nr: T O & T B 1 p pr (no 3).
Nr: T O & T B 1st p pr (no 7) from L.
Nr: T O & T B 3rd p pr (no 4) from R. Work 1 row.
Nr: add 1 pr (no 4) to be 1st p pr from

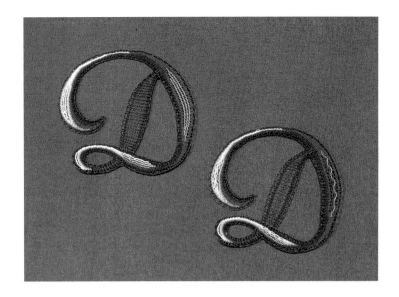

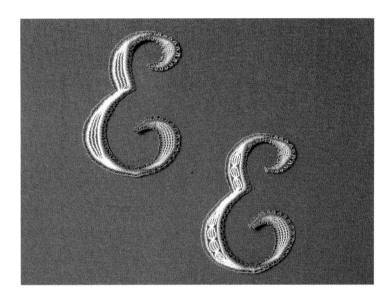

R, and T O & T B 3rd p pr (no 4) from L.
Work 1 row.
(7 prs)
Nr: add 1 pr (no 4) to be s ps 2 & 3
from R, and T O & T B 3rd p pr (no 5)
from L.
Work 1 row.
Nr: add 1 pr (no 4) to be 2nd p pr from
R.
Work 3 rows.
(8 prs)
After pin J:
add 1 pr (no 3) to be 3rd p pr from R.
Nr: add 1 pr (no 3) to be s ps 8 & 9
from L.
Nr: add 1 pr (no 2) to be 4th p pr from R.
(11 prs)

After pin K:
change leaders (no 5) to (no 2), (tech 4,
td 4), cont row, adding 1 pr (no 2) to be
s ps 10 & 11 from L.
Nr: add 1 pr (no 1) to be 5th p pr from R.
Nr: add 1 pr (no 1) to be s ps 12 & 13
from L.
Work 1 row.
(14 prs)
After pin L:
start patt – Cls 6 p prs, tw 1 leaders, Cls
rem p prs.
Nr: tw 2 leaders as before.
Nr: tw 3 leaders as before.
Cont in Cls, tw 3 leaders as before.

After pin M:
tw 2 leaders as before.
Nr: tw 1 leaders as before.

After pin N:
cont in Cls.
Nr: T O & T B 1 p pr (no 1).
(13 prs)
After working 1st part of blind pin O:
change leaders (no 2) to (no 6), (tech 4,
td 4) cont row,
T O & T B 1 p pr (no 1).
(12 prs)
Nr: *T O & T B 1 p pr (no 2)*.
Nr: rep * to *.
Nr: *T O & T B 1 p pr (no 3)*.
Nr: rep * to *.
Nr: T O & T B s ps 4 & 5 (no 4) from R.
Work 1 row.
Nr: T O & T B 2nd p pr (no 4) from R.
Cont in Cls.
(6 prs)
After pin P:
work locking st (tech 6, td 6) with
leaders and 1st p pr from L, secure
bobbins and leave to work Section 1a.

Section 1a
Start at pin A#:
using a two colour point start (tech 1,
td 1), (Note L–R working direction),
hang 1 pr (no 6) and 1 pr (no 4) to be
edge prs (diag g.2).

Add magic thread (tech 2, td 2).
On T P, hang 1 pr (no 7) to be leaders.
(3 prs)
On T P, hang 2 prs (no 7) open.
Cls leaders L–R thro 2 p prs and edge st at pin B.
(5 prs)
Nr: add 2 prs (no 6) to centre.
Nr: add 2 prs (no 5) to centre.
Nr: add 2 prs (no 4) to centre.
(11 prs)
After pin C:
change leaders (no 7) to (no 4), (tech 4, td 4), cont row, adding 2 prs (no 3) to centre.

Nr: T O & T B 1st p pr (no 7) from R, and add 2 prs (no 2) to be 6th and 7th p prs from L.
(14 prs)
After pin D:
change leaders (no 4) to (no 3), (tech 4, td 4), cont row, and start patt – tw 1 leaders between 5th and 6th p prs (no 2) from R.
Nr: T O & T B 1st p pr (no 6) from R, tw 2 leaders between 6th and 7th p prs from L.
Nr: tw 3 leaders between 6th and 7th p prs from L.
Cont in patt, Cls tw 3 leaders as before.
(13 prs)
After pin E:
tw 2 leaders as before.
Nr: tw 1 leaders as before.

After working 1st part of blind pin F:
change leaders (no 3) to (no 5), (tech 4, td 4), cont row, T O & T B 1 p pr (no 2).
Cont in Cls.
(12 prs)
At pin G:
change leaders (no 5) with R edge pr (no 4) (tech 7, td 7).

Diagram g2:
Start, Section 1a

After pin G:
add 1 pr (no 6) to be 1st p pr from R, and T O & T B 1 p pr (no 2).
(12 prs)
Nr: *T O & T B 1 pr (no 3)*.
Nr: rep * to *.
(10 prs)
After working 1st part of pin H:
change leaders (no 4) to (no 6), (tech 4, td 4) cont row, T O & T B 1 p pr (no 4).

At pin I:
change leaders (no 6) with R edge pr (no 5) (tech 7, td 7), cont row, T O & T B 1 p pr (no 4).

After completing blind pin H:
add 1 pr (no 6) to be 1st p pr from L, and T O & T B 1 p pr (no 5).
(8 prs)
Nr: T O & T B 1 p pr (no 5), and add 1 pr (no 5) to be 1st p pr from L.
Nr: add 1 pr (no 4) to be 1st p pr from L, and T O & T B s ps 2 & 3 (no 6) from R.
Nr: T O & T B 1st p pr (no 6) from R, and add 1 pr (no 4) to be s ps 2 & 3 from L.
(8 prs)
At pin J:
change leaders (no 5) with L edge pr (no 6) (tech 7, td 7), cont row, adding 1 pr (no 3) to be 3rd p pr from L.
Nr: add 1 pr (no 3) to be s ps 8 & 9 from R.
Nr: add 1 pr (no 2) to be 4th p pr from L.
Nr: add 1 pr (no 2) to be s ps 10 & 11 from R.
(12 prs)
After completing blind pin K:
change leaders (no 6) to (no 2), (tech 4, td 4) cont row, adding 1 pr (no 1) to be

6th p pr from R.
Nr: add 1 pr (no 1) to be s ps 12 & 13 from R.
(14 prs)
After pin L:
start patt – Cls 5 p prs, tw 1 leaders, Cls rem p prs.
Nr: Cls 6 p prs, tw 2 leaders, Cls rem p prs.
Nr: Cls 5 p prs, tw 3 leaders, Cls rem p prs.
Cont in patt, tw 3 leaders as before.

After pin M:
tw 2 leaders as before.
Nr: tw 1 leaders as before.

After pin N:
cont in Cls.

After pin O:
change leaders (no 2) to (no 6), (tech 4, td 4) cont row, joining sections at pin Q, thus (tech 22, td 22) Cls & tw 2 both edge prs, place pin Q between them.
Cls leaders from respective edges, work T S with both leaders, replacing pin Q to support T S and cont working to R.
(20 prs)
After pin R:
T O & T B s ps 12 & 13 (no 1) from R.
Nr: T O & T B 3rd p pr (no 4), 7th p pr (no 4), and 11th p pr (no 1) from L.
Nr: T O & T B s ps 8 & 9 (no 3/no 2), s ps 12 & 13 (no 2/no 3), and s ps 16 & 17 (no 4) from R.
(13 prs)
Nr: T O & T B 1 p pr (no 2).
Nr: T O & T B 1 p pr (no 3).
(11 prs)
After pin S:
add 1 pr (no 7) to L, and T O & T B 4th p pr (no 4) and s ps 12 & 13 (no 5) from R.
Nr: T O & T B 3rd p pr (no 5) from R.
Nr: T O & T B 3rd p pr (no 5) from L.
Work 1 row.
Nr: T O & T B 3rd p pr (no 6) from L.
Nr: T O & T B s ps 4 & 5 (no 6) from R.
(6 prs)

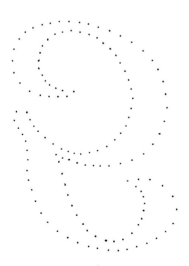

G2: Pricking

G1: Order of work

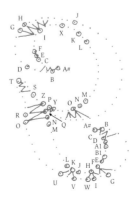

G3: Pin reference plan, Version 1

Nr: T O & T B 2nd p pr (no 6) from L,
Cls tog 2 p prs (no 7), (tech 29, td 29),
Cls leaders (no 6) thro 2 p prs (no 7),
T O & T B all 3 prs, and secure to back
of work with previously T B prs.

Finish at pin T:
Cls & tw both edge prs (no 6), place pin
T, Cls & T O both edge prs; these 2 prs
will be used for rolled edge.

Notes for rolled edges
Roll from pin T to pin W (tech 9, td 9):
rolling thread – 1 x (no 6)
rolled threads – 3 x (no 6)
Use edge prs from pin T for roll.
After 2 pins have been worked, remove
pin T to allow a smoother line to develop.
T B 1 thread at pin U and pin V (tech
14, td 14).
Finish at pin W (tech 10, td 10).

Roll from pin A#, Section 1 to pin Z:
rolling thread – 1 x (no 6)
rolled threads – 3 x (no 6)
Using magic thread (tech 16, td 16), add
2 prs at pin A#.
T B 1 thread at pin X and pin Y.
Finish at pin Z.

Roll from pin A#, Section 1a to pin H:
rolling thread – 1 x (no 6)
rolled threads – 3 x (no 6)
Using magic thread, add 2 prs at pin A#.
T B 1 thread at pin A1 and pin B1.
Finish at pin H.

VERSION 2
Section 1
Start at pin A#:
follow instructions for Version 1 from
pin A# to pin E.
(13 prs)
At pin E:
change leaders (no 6) to (no 4), (tech 4,
td 4) cont row, adding 1 pr (no 2) to
centre.

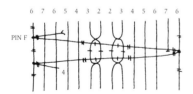

PIN F
6 7 6 5 4 3 2 2 3 4 5 6 7 6
4

Diagram g3: Patt. 'Ribbon' (var) after pin F,
Section 1

Nr: add 1 pr (no 2) to centre.
(15 prs)
After pin F:
start Ribbon patt (diag g.3): Cls 4 p prs,
tw 2 leaders, work Ribbon patt with all
(no 2) and (no 3) p prs, tw 2 leaders,

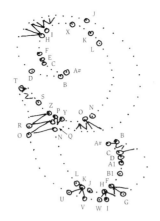

G4: Pin reference plan, Version 2

Cls rem p prs.
Nr: T O & T B 1st p pr (no 7) from R,
cont in patt.
Work 1 row.
Nr: T O & T B 1st p pr (no 6) from R.
(13 prs)
Cont in patt.
Note There is no pin G in Version 2.

After completing blind pin H:
cont in Cls, follow instructions for
Version 1 to pin L:
changing leaders (no 4) to (no 5) after
completing blind pin I, and
changing leaders (no 5) to (no 4) at pin K.

After pin L:
start Ribbon patt – Cls 4 p prs, tw 2
leaders, work Ribbon patt with all (no
1) and (no 2) p prs, tw 2 leaders, Cls
rem p prs.
(14 prs)
Cont in patt.
Note There is no pin M in version 2.

After pin N:
Cls patt prs to complete patt, and return
prs to original colour positions.
Note Do not tw leaders or p prs.
Cont in Cls.
Nr: T O & T B 1 p pr (no 1).
(13 prs)
After working 1st part of blind pin O,
follow instructions for Version 1 to pin P.

Section 1a
Start at pin A#:
follow instructions for Version 1 from
pin A# to pin D.
(14 prs)
After pin D:
cont with leaders (no 4), start Ribbon
patt (diag g.3) – Cls 4p prs, tw 2
leaders, work Ribbon patt with all (no
2) and (no 3) p prs, tw 2 leaders, Cls
rem p prs.
Nr: T O & T B 1 p pr (no 6) from from
R, cont in patt.

(13 prs)
Note There is no pin E in Version 2.

After working 1st part of blind pin F:
change leaders (no 4) to (no 5), (tech 4,
td 4), Cls patt prs to complete patt, and
return prs to original colour positions,
(Note Do not tw leaders or p prs), cont
row, T O & T B 1 p pr (no 2).
Cont in Cls.

At pin G:
change leaders (no 5) with R edge pr
(no 4), (tech 7, td 7).

After pin G:
add 1 pr (no 6) to R, and T O & T B 1
p pr (no 2).
(12 prs)
Cont, follow instructions for Version 1 to
pin L:
changing leaders (no 6) to (no 4) after
completing blind pin K.

After pin L:
start Ribbon patt – Cls 3 p prs, tw 2
leaders, work patt with all (no 1) and
(no 2) p prs, tw 2 leaders, Cls rem p prs.
Cont in patt.
Note There is no pin M in Version 2.

After pin N:
Cls patt prs to complete patt, and return
prs to original colour positions.
Note Do not tw leaders or p prs.
Cont in Cls.

After pin O:
follow instructions for Version 1 to
finish, changing leaders (no 4) to (no
6).

Notes for rolled edge
As Version 1.

H for HELLEBORE

Colours

(no 1)	*Honey
(no 2)	Sycamore
(no 3)	Eau de Nil
(no 4)	*Mint
(no 5)	Light Slate
(no 6)	*Mauve
(no 7)	*Crocus

VERSION 1

Section 1

Start at pin A#:
using a two-colour point start (tech 1, td 1), (Note L–R working direction), hang 1 pr (no 7) and 1 pr (no 5) to be edge prs (diag h.1).
Add magic thread (tech 2, td 2a).
L edge pr is now (no 7).
R edge pr is now (no 5).

Diagram h1:
Start, Section 1

On T P, hang 1 pr (no 7) to be leaders.
(3 prs)
On T P, hang 2 prs (no 7) open to be p prs.
Cls leaders L–R thro 2 p prs and edge st at pin B (tech 3, td 3).
(5 prs)
Nr: *add 1 pr (no 6) to centre*.
Nr: rep * to *.
Nr: * add 1 pr (no 5) to centre*.
Nr: rep * to *.
Nr: add 1 pr (no 4) to centre.
(10 prs)
After pin C:
change leaders (no 7) to (no 5), (tech 4, td 4) cont row, adding 1 pr (no 4) to centre.
Nr: add 1 pr (no 3) to centre.
(12 prs)
After pin D:
change leaders (no 5) to (no 3), (tech 4, td 4) cont row, adding 1 pr (no 3) to centre.
Nr: add 2 prs (no 3) to centre.
(15 prs)
After pin E:
add 1 pr (no 2) to be 6th p pr from L, add 2 prs (no 4) open to be 8th and 9th p prs from L, (Note These 2 p prs (no 4) will become centre edge prs, when braid has split.), and add 1 pr (no 2) to be 11th p pr from L.

(19 prs)
After pin F
split braid, (cont with R braid) thus –
(tech 5, td 5) Cls 7 tw centre edge prs (no 4), 8th and 9th p prs from R, placing pin G as a support pin (tech 19, td 19b).
Secure 9 prs in order, from L side of braid, (to work Section 1a) and leave to work Section 1.

Cont with 10 prs from R side of braid to work Section 1.
After pin F:
T O & T B 1st p pr from R, and add 1 pr (no 2) to be s ps 4 & 5 from L, edge st at pin H.
(10 prs)
After pin H:
start patt – *Cls 1 p pr (no 6), tw 1 leaders, Cls & tw 2nd and 3rd p prs, Cls rem p prs*.

Nr: T O & T B 1st p pr from R, and cont in patt **Cls 3 p prs, tw 1 leaders, Cls & tw 2 p prs, Cls rem pr**.

Cont in patt, rep 2 rows: * to * and ** to **.

After pin I:
cont in Cls.
Nr: work 1 row.
Nr: T O & T B s ps 4 & 5 (no 2) from L.
Work 1 row.
Nr: T O & T B 2nd p pr (no 2) from L.
(7 prs)
After pin J:
add 1 pr (no 4) to be 1st p pr from R.

At pin K:
change leaders (no 3) with R edge pr (no 5), (tech 7, td 7) cont row, adding 1 pr (no 3) to be 1st p pr from R.

At pin L:
change leaders (no 5) with L edge pr (no 4), (tech 7, td 7) cont row, T O & T B s ps 2 & 3 (no 3) from L.
(8 prs)
Nr: add 1 pr (no 3) to be s ps 2 & 3 from R.
Nr: T O & T B 1st p pr (no 3) from L, and add 1 pr (no 2) to be 2nd p pr from R.
Nr: add 1 pr (no 2) to be s ps 4 & 5 from R.
Nr: T O & T B 1st p pr (no 4) from L, and add 1 pr (no 1) to be 3rd p pr from R.
Nr: add 1 pr (no 1) to be s ps 6 & 7 from R.
(11 prs)
After completing blind pin M:
start patt: *Cls 4 p prs, tw 1 leaders, Cls & tw 5th and 6th p prs (no 1), Cls rem p prs.
Nr: Cls 2 p prs, tw 1 leaders, Cls & tw 2

p prs, Cls rem p prs*.
Cont in patt, rep * to *.

At pin N:
change leaders (no 4) with R edge pr (no 3), (tech 7, td 7) cont row, adding 1 pr (no 4) to be 1st p pr from R.
Cont in patt.
(12 prs)
After pin O:
change leaders (no 3) to (no 5), (tech 4, td 4), cont in Cls.
After pin P:
change leaders (no 5) with R edge pr (no 4), (tech 7, td 7) cont row, adding 1 pr (no 5) to be 1st p pr from R.
(13 prs)
Nr: T O & T B s ps 10 & 11 (no 1) from L.
Nr: T O & T B 5th p pr (no 1) from R.
Nr: T O & T B s ps 6 & 7 (no 3/no 2), and s ps 10 & 11 (no 2/no 3) from L.
Nr: Cls tog 3rd and 4th p prs (no 2/no 3) from R, and T O & T B both p prs.
Nr: Cls tog 2nd and 3rd p prs (no 4) from L, and T O & T B both p prs.

To finish at pin Q:
Cls leaders thro rem 2 p prs, T O & T B both p prs. Cls & tw edge prs (no 5), place pin Q, Cls & tw (tech 8, td 8).
These 2 prs to be used for rolled edge.

Notes for rolled edge
Roll from pin Q to pin I (tech 9, td 9):
rolling thread – 1 x (no 5)
rolled threads – 3 x (no 5)
Use edge prs from pin Q for roll.
T B 1 thread at pin M and pin L (tech 14, td 14).
Finish at pin I (tech 10, td 10).

Return to Section 1a

Start at pin E:
On a T P, (Note L–R working direction), add new leaders (no 2), (tech 5, td 5) and cont row, adding 1 pr (no 2) to be s ps 4 & 5 from R, Cls leaders across all p prs, pin and edge st.
(11 prs)
Nr: add 1 pr (no 1) to be 3rd p pr from R.
Nr: add 1 pr (no 1) to be s ps 14 & 15 from L.
(13 prs)
After pin R:
start patt: Cls 6 p prs, tw 1 leaders, Cls & tw 7th and 8th p prs, Cls rem p prs.
Nr: Cls 2 p prs, tw 1 leaders, Cls & tw 2 p prs, Cls rem p prs.
Nr: *Cls 5 p prs, tw 1 leaders, Cls & tw 6th, 7th, 8th and 9th p prs, Cls rem p pr.
Nr: Cls 1 p pr, tw 1 leaders, Cls & tw 4 p prs, Cls rem p prs*.
Cont in patt rep * to *.

After pin S:
Cls 6 p prs, tw 1 leaders, Cls & tw 2

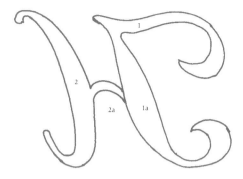

H1: Order of work

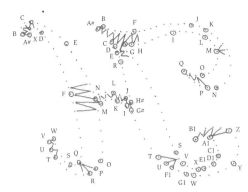

H3: Pin reference plan, Version 1

p prs, Cls rem p prs.
After pin T:
cont in Cls.

After pin U:
cont in Cls.
(13 prs)
Nr: T O & T B s ps 6 & 7 (no 1) from R.
Nr: T O & T B 7th p pr (no 1) from L.

After pin V:
change leaders (no 2) to (no 4), (tech 4,
td 4) cont row, T O & T B s ps 12 & 13
(no 2) from L.
(10 prs)
Nr: T O & T B 6th p pr (no 2) from L.
Nr: T O & T B s ps 2 & 3 (no 3) from R.
Work 1 row.
Nr: T O & T B 1st p pr (no 3) from R.
(7 prs)

At pin W:
change leaders (no 4) with L edge pr
(no 7), (tech 7, td 7).

After pin W:
add 1 pr (no 6) to be 1st p pr from L.

At pin X:
change leaders (no 7) with R edge pr
(no 4), (tech 7, td 7) cont row, T O &
T B 1st p pr (no 4) from R, and adding
1 pr (no 5) to be 1st p pr from L.
(8 prs)
After pin X:
add 1 pr (no 4) to be 1st p pr from L.
Nr: T O & T B 1st p pr (no 5) from R,
and add 1 pr (no 3) to be 1st p pr from L.
Nr: add 1 pr (no 3) to be s ps 2 & 3
from L.
Nr: T O & T B 1st p pr (no 6) from R,
and add 1 pr (no 2) to be 2nd p pr from L.
(10 prs)
Nr: add 1 pr (no 2) to be s ps 4 & 5
from L.
Nr: T O & T B 1st p pr (no 7) from R,
and add 1 pr (no 1) to be 3rd p pr from L.
Nr: add 1 pr (no 1) to be s ps 6 & 7
from L.
Work 1 row.
After pin Y:

start patt – Cls 2 p prs, tw 1 leaders, Cls
& tw 3rd and 4th p prs (no 1), Cls rem
p prs.

Cont in patt, Cls & tw 2 p prs.

After pin Z:
cont in Cls.

After completing blind pin A1:
T O & T B s ps 8 & 9 (no 3/no 2) and
s ps 12 &13 (no 1) from R.
(10 prs)
Nr: T O & T B s ps 5 & 6 (no 1) and
s ps 8 & 9 (no 3/no 4) from L.
Nr: T O & T B 4th p pr (no 2) from R.
Nr: T O & T B s ps 2 & 3 (no 3/no 2)
from L.
Work 1 row.
(6 prs)
Nr: T O & T B 1st p pr (no 3/no 4) from
L, cont row, Cls 2 rem p prs.

Nr: T O & T B leaders (no 4) and 1 p pr
(no 5).
T O rem p pr (no 6) and set aside, this
pr to be used for rolled edge.

Finish at pin B1:
Cls & tw edge prs, place pin B1, Cls tog.

T O & T B L edge pr (no 4) and secure
to back of work with previously T B prs

T O R edge pr (no 7), placing set aside
p pr (no 6) between threads before T O,
these 2 prs to be used for rolled edge.

Notes for rolled edges
Roll from pin B1 to pin E1:
rolling thread – 1 x (no 7)
rolled threads – 1 x (no 7), 2 x (no 6)
Use 2 prs from pin B1 for roll.
T B 1 thread (no 6) at pin C1 and pin D1.
Finish at pin E1.

Roll from pin A# to pin G1:
rolling thread – 1 x (no 7)
rolled threads – 3 x (no 7)
Using magic thread (tech 16, td 16) at
pin A#, add 2 prs (no 7). T B 1 thread at
pin T and pin F1.
Finish at pin G1.

Section 2
Start at pin A#:
using a two colour point start (tech 1, td
1), (Note L–R working direction), hang
1 pr (no 7) and 1 pr (no 4) to be edge
prs (diag h.2).
Add magic thread.

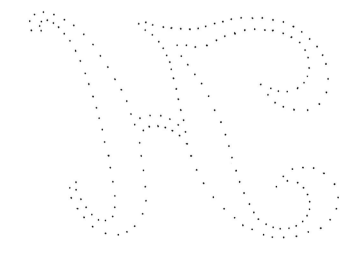

H2: Pricking

L edge pr is now (no 7).
R edge pr is now (no 4).

On T P, hang 1 pr (no 7) to be leaders.
(3 prs)
On T P, hang 2 prs (no 7) open, to be
p prs.
Cls leaders L–R thro 2 p prs, pin and
edge st at pin B.
(5 prs)
Nr: *add 1 pr (no 6) to centre*.
Nr: rep * to *.
Cont in Cls.
(7 prs)
After pin C:
T O & T B 1st p pr (no 7) from R, and
add 1 pr (no 5) to be 3rd p pr from L.
Work 1 row.

Nr: T O & T B 1st p pr (no 6) from R.
Nr: add 1 pr (no 5) to be s ps 6 & 7
from L.
Nr: add 1 pr (no 4) to be 2nd p pr from R.
(8 prs)
After pin D:
change leaders (no 7) to (no 4), (tech 4,
td 4) cont row, adding 1 pr (no 4) to be
s ps 4 & 5 from R.
(9 prs)
Nr: add 1 pr (no 3) to be 3rd p pr from R.
Nr: add 1 pr (no 3) to be s ps 10 & 11
from L.
Nr: T O & T B 1st p pr (no 5) from R,
and add 1 pr (no 2) to be 6th p pr from L.
Nr: add 1 pr (no 2) to be s ps 12 & 13
from L.
(12 prs)
After pin E:
start patt – Cls 2 p prs, tw 1 leaders, Cls
& tw 3rd and 4th p prs (no 2), Cls rem
p prs.
Nr: Cls 5 p prs, tw 1 leaders, Cls & tw 2
p prs, Cls rem p prs.
Nr: *Cls 1 p pr, tw 1 leaders, Cls & tw
2nd, 3rd, 4th and 5th p prs (no 2 and
no 3), Cls rem prs.
Nr: Cls 4 p prs, tw 1 leaders, Cls & tw 4
p prs, Cls rem p prs*.
Cont in patt, rep * to *.
(12 prs)
After pin F:
secure all bobbins in order, and leave to
work Section 2a.

Section 2a
Start at pin G#:
with a top sewing into R bar, hang 1 pr
(no 5) to be R edge pr, tw 2.

At pin H#:
using a narrow angle start (tech 17, td
17), (Note L–R working direction), with
a top sewing into L bar, hang 1 pr (no
5) to be L edge pr, and into its loop, 1
pr (no 6) to be leaders.
Tw 2 both prs.
(3 prs)

Diagram h2:
Start, Section 2

Using pin G# and H#:
in position between leaders (no 6) and
R edge pr (no 5), add 4 p prs in L–R:
4 x (no 5)
4 x (no 6)
Cls leaders thro 4 p prs, edge st at pin I.
Cont in Cls.
(7 prs)
After pin J:
add 1 pr (no 4) to be 1st p pr from L.
Nr: T O & T B 1st p pr (no 6) from R.
Nr: add 1 pr (no 4) to be 1st p pr from L.
(8 prs)
After pin K:
T O & T B 1st p pr (no 6) from R, and
Cls thro 1 p pr (no 5), then change
leaders (no 6) to (no 4), (tech 4, td 4),
cont row.
(7 prs)
At pin L:
change leaders (no 4) with L edge pr
(no 5), (tech 7, td 7).

After pin L:
add 1 pr (no 4) to be 1st p pr from L.
Nr: T O & T B 1st p pr (no 5) from R.
Cont in Cls.
(7 prs)
After working 1st part of blind pin M:
join sections – Cls & tw edge prs (no 4),
place pin N, Cls Section 2a leaders (no
5) thro 4 p prs, and thro both edge prs
(no 4), T O & T B leaders (no 5).
T O & T B 3rd p pr from R (no 4).
Note Care must be taken to ensure
tension of Section 2a p prs remains
undisturbed.

Return to Section 2

Cont in patt:
when leaders next work to R edge, to
complete blind pin M, include p prs
from Section 2a, use R edge pr from
Section 2a to edge st at pin M.

Nr: T O & T B 3rd and 5th p prs (no 4)
from R.
Nr: T O & T B 3rd p pr (no 4) from R.
Nr: T O & T B 2nd p pr (no 4) from R.
Note There are now 2 p prs at R side of
braid.
Cont in patt.
(13 prs)

After pin O:
Cls & tw 2 p prs (no 2) only, Cls rem
p prs.
Work 1 row.

After pin P:
cont in Cls.

After working 1st part of blind pin Q:
change leaders (no 4) to (no 6), (tech 4,
td 4).
(13 prs)
At pin R:
change leaders (no 6) with R edge pr
(no 5), (tech 7, td 7).

After pin R:
T O & T B s ps 8 & 9 (no 2) from R.
Nr: T O & T B 6th p pr (no 2) from L.
Nr: T O & T B s ps 6 & 7 (no 3) from R.
Nr: T O & T B 5th p pr (no 3) from L.
Nr: T O & T B s ps 4 & 5 (no 4) from R.
(8 prs)
After pin S:
change leaders (no 5) to (no 7), (tech 4,
td 4), cont row.
Nr: T O & T B 2nd p pr (no 4) from R.
Work 1 row.
Nr: T O & T B 2nd p pr (no 5) from R.
Nr: add 1 pr (no 7) to be s ps 2 & 3
from L.
(7 prs)

At pin T:
change leaders (no 7) with R edge pr
(no 6), (tech 7, td 7).
After pin T:
T O & T B 1st p pr (no 5) from R.

After pin U:
T O & T B 2nd p pr (no 7) from R.
(5 prs)

After pin V:
Cls leaders thro rem 2 p prs, T O & T B
leaders and 2 p prs, and secure to back
of work with previously T B prs

Finish at pin W:
Cls & tw both edge prs (no 7), place pin
W, Cls prs tog & T O.
These prs to be used for rolled edge.

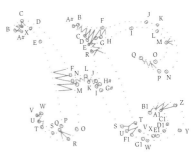

H4: Pin reference plan, Version 2

Notes for rolled edge
Roll from pin W to pin A#:
rolling thread – 1 x (no 7)
rolled threads – 3 x (no 7)
Use prs from pin W for roll.

T B 1 thread at pin D and pin X.
Finish at pin A#.

VERSION 2
Section 1
Start at pin A#:
follow instructions for Version 1, from pin A# to pin H.

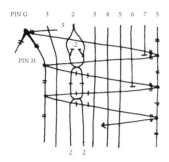

Diagram h3: After pin H, Section 1

After pin H:
start Ribbon (var) patt, with 2nd and 3rd p prs (no 2) from L (diag h.3)
Nr: T O & T B 1st p pr (no 6) from R.
Cont in patt.
(9 prs)

After pin I:
follow instructions for Version 1 to pin M.

After completing blind pin M:
start Ribbon (var) patt, with 5th and 6th p prs (no 1) from L (diag h.4).

At pin N:
change leaders (no 4) with R edge pr (no 3), (tech 7, td 7).
After pin N:
add 1 pr (no 4) to be 1st p pr from R.
Cont in patt.
(12 prs)

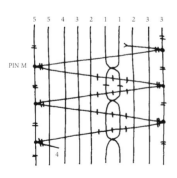

Diagram h4: Patt. 'Ribbon' (var) after pin M

After pin O:
change leaders (no 3) to (no 5), (tech 4, td 4) cont row, Cls tog 4th & 5th patt prs to complete patt. Cont in Cls.

After pin P:
follow instructions for Version 1 to finish at pin Q.

Notes for rolled edge
As Version 1.

Return to Section 1a
Start at pin E:
follow instructions for Version 1 till (13 prs).
Nr: add 1 pr (no 2) to be 4th p pr from R.
(14 prs)

After pin R:
Cls thro 7 p prs, and work T S with 8th p pr from L, and start Orchid 2 patt (diag h.5), using 2nd and 3rd p prs from R, and 6th and 7th p prs from L.
(14 prs)

After pin S and pin T:
work T S, and cont in Cls, working to pin U.
Note There is no blind pin in Version 2.

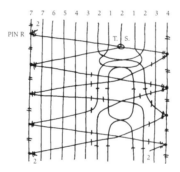

Diagram h5: Patt. 'Orchid 2' (var) after Pin R

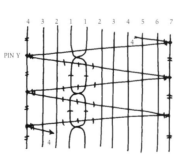

Diagram h6: 'Ribbon' (var) after pin Y, Section 1a

After pin U:
T O & T B 8th p pr (no 2) from L.
(13 prs)
Cont, following instructions Version 1 after pin U (13 prs), to pin Y.

After pin Y:
start Ribbon (var) patt, using 3rd and 4th p prs (no 2) from L (diag h.6).

After pin Z:
follow instructions for Version 1 to finish at pin B1.

Notes for rolled edges
As Version 1.

Section 2
Start at pin A#:
follow instructions for Version 1 from pin A# till (12 prs).
Nr: add 1 pr (no 4) to be 4th p pr from R.
(13 prs)

After pin E:
Cls thro 6 p prs, work T S with 7th p pr (no 4) from L, start Orchid 2 patt (diag h.7). Cont in patt.
After pin F:
when both sides of patt are completed

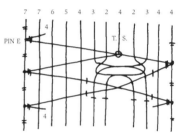

Diagram h7: Patt. 'Orchid 2' (var) after Pin E, Section 2

to match, secure all bobbins in order, and leave to work Section 2a.

Section 2a
Start at pin G#:
follow instructions for Version 1, from pin G# to pin O and pin P, cont in patt.

After pin O and pin P:
work T S in centre of patt with leaders (no 4), cont working to R.
Cont in Cls.
Work 1 row.

After working 1st part of blind pin Q:
change leaders (no 4) to (no 6), (tech 4, td 4), cont row, T O & T B 5th p pr (no 4) from R.
(13 prs)

At pin R:
cont follow instructions for Version 1, to finish at pin W.

Notes for rolled edge
As Version 1.

I for ICE

Colours:

(no 1)	*White
(no 2)	Sycamore
(no 3)	*Ice
(no 4)	*Mint
(no 5)	*Sky
(no 6)	*Helio
(no 7)	*Mid Navy

VERSION 1
Section 1

Start at pin A#:
using a two-colour point start (tech 1, td 1), (Note R–L working direction), hang 1 pr (no 6) and 1 pr (no 7) to be edge prs (diag i.1).
Add magic thread (tech 2, td 2a).

Diagram i1: Start, Section 1

L edge pr is now (no 6).
R edge pr is now (no 7).

On temp in, hang 1 pr (no 6) to be leaders.
(3 prs)
On T P: hang 2 p prs in order L–R, 1 pr (no 6) and 1 pr (no 7). Cls leaders R–L thro 2 p prs and edge st at pin B (tech 3, td 3).
(5 prs)
Nr: add 1 pr (no 7) to be s ps 4 & 5, from L.
Nr: add 1 pr (no 6) to be s ps 6 & 7 from R.
(7 prs)
After pin C:
cont in Cls, and add 2 prs (no 6), 1 pr per row, to centre of braid, then add 2 prs (no 4), 1 pr per row, to centre of braid.
(11 prs)
Nr: T O & T B 2nd p pr (no 7) from R.
(10 prs)
Add 2 prs (no 2), (Note Continue colour sequence), 1 pr per row, to near centre.
Nr: T O & T B 2nd p pr (no 6) from L, and add 1 pr (no 1) to centre.
Nr: add 1 pr (no 1) to centre.
(13 prs)
After completing blind pin D:
change leaders (no 6) to (no 1) (tech 4, td 4), cont row, adding 1 pr (no 1) to centre of braid, L–R order should be as foll:
L edge pr 2 x (no 6)
4 x (no 6)

2 x (no 4)
2 x (no 2)
6 x (no 1)
2 x (no 2)
2 x (no 4)
2 x (no 6)
2 x (no 7)
R edge pr 2 x (no 7)
leaders 2 x (no 1)
(14 prs)
After pin E:
start patt: Cls 4 p prs, tw 1 leaders, ½ st 3 p prs (no 1), Cls rem p prs.
Nr: Cls 3 p prs, tw 1 leaders, ½ st 5 p prs (no 1) and (no 2).
Cls rem p prs.

Cont ½ st 5 p prs.

After pin F:
when ½ st prs have returned to their original colour positions, cont in Cls, T O & T B 6 p prs from centre, 1 pr per row, lightest prs first, until 8 prs rem.
(8 prs)
After pin G:
change leaders (no 1) to (no 7), (tech 4, td 4), cont row, T O & T B rem p pr (no 4).
Nr: T O & T B 1 p pr (no 6) from centre.
(6 prs)
At pin H:
edge st (diag i.2), then set aside R edge pr to be collected later.

Cont in Cls, at each of the central pins (tech 30, td 30), tw 2 leaders, pin, and set aside 1st p pr on R, after working, to be collected later.

Work blind pins, as indicated on pin reference plan, around the point.

At pin I:
change leaders (no 7) with L edge pr (no 6), (tech 7, td 7).

Cont, collecting prs thus:
work to R, include pr hanging from pin, tw 2 leaders, replacing pin underneath leaders.
When pin H is reached again:

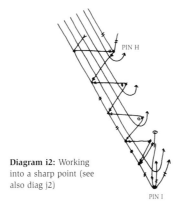

Diagram i2: Working into a sharp point (see also diag j2)

PIN H

PIN I

tw 2 leaders, make a side sewing into pin H, previously worked, tw 2 leaders and cont Cls.

After pin J:
add 1 pr (no 6) to be 2nd p pr from L.

At pin K:
change leaders (no 6) with R edge pr (no 7), (tech 7, td 7).
After pin K:
add 1 pr (no 6), to be s ps 6 & 7 from R.
(8 prs)

After pin L:
add 1 pr (no 5), to be 4th p pr from L.
Nr: add 1 pr (no 5), to be s ps 6 & 7 from R.
Nr: add 1 pr (no 3), to be 5th p pr from L
Nr: add 1 pr (no 3), to be s ps 8 & 9 from R.
(12 prs)
Nr: add 1 pr (no 1) to be 6th p pr from L.
Nr: add 1 pr (no 1) to be s ps 10 & 11 from R.
Nr: add 1 pr (no 1), to be 7th p pr from L.
(15 prs)
After pin M:
change leaders, (no 7) to (no 1), (tech 4, td 4), cont row, L–R order should be as foll:
L edge pr 2 x (no 7)
6 x (no 6)
2 x (no 5)
2 x (no 3)
6 x (no 1)
2 x (no 3)
2 x (no 5)
2 x (no 6)
2 x (no 7)
R edge pr 2 x (no 6)
leaders 2 x (no 1)
(15 prs)
After pin N:
start patt – Cls 5 p prs, tw 1 leaders, ½ st 3 p prs (no 1), Cls rem p prs.
Next row: Cls 3 p prs, tw 1 leaders, ½ st 5 p prs (no 1) and (no 3), Cls rem p prs.
Cont ½ st 5 p prs.

After pin O:
add 1 pr (no 5), to be s ps 8 & 9 from L.
Nr: add 1 pr (no 5) to be s ps 6 & 7 from R.
Nr: add 1 pr (no 7) to be 1st p pr from L.
Nr: add 1 pr (no 7) to be 1st p pr from R.
(19 prs)
After pin P:
change leaders (no 1) to (no 7), (tech 4, td 4), cont in Cls.
Nr: T O & T B 8th and 10th p prs (no 1) from L.
Nr: T O & T B 6th and 8th p prs (no 3) from R.
Nr: T O & T B 5th, 7th and 9th p prs, 2 p prs (no 5) and 1 p pr (no 1) from L.

I1: Order of work

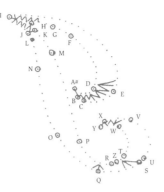

I3: Pin reference plan, Versions 1 and 2

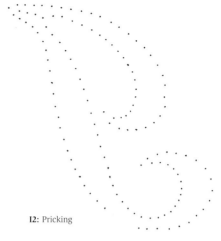

I2: Pricking

(12 prs)
Nr: T O & T B s ps 8 & 9 (no 5) from R.
Nr: T O & T B 5th p pr(no 5) from L.
Nr: *T O & T B 1 p pr (no 6)*.
Rep * to * 3 more times.
Work 1 row.
L–R order should be as foll:
L edge pr   2 x (no 7)
             6 x (no 7)
R edge pr   2 x (no 6)
leaders   2 x (no 7)
(6 prs)
After pin Q:
add 1 pr (no 6) to be 1st p pr from L.
Work 1 row.
Nr: add 1 pr (no 6) to be s ps 2 & 3
from L.
Work 1 row.
Nr: add 1 pr (no 6) to be 2nd p pr from L.
(9 prs)
At pin R:
change leaders (no 7) with R edge pr
(no 6), (tech 7, td 7).

After pin R:
T O & T B 2nd p pr from R (no 7), and
add 1 pr (no 4) to be 3rd p pr from L.
(9 prs)
Nr: add 1 pr (no 4) to be s ps 6 & 7 from L.
Nr: add 1 pr (no 2) to be 5th p pr from R.
Nr: add 1 pr (no 2) to be s ps 8 & 9 from L.
Work 1 row.
Nr: add 1 pr (no 1) to be 5th p pr from L.
Nr: add 1 pr (no 1) to be s ps 12 & 13
from R.
(14 prs)
At pin S:
change leaders (no 6) with L edge pr
(no 7), (tech 7, td 7).

After pin S:
add 1 pr (no 1) to be 6th p pr from L.
(15 prs)
After pin T:
change leaders (no 7) to (no 1), (tech 4,
td 4).

After pin U:
start patt: Cls 4 p prs, tw 1 leaders, ½ st

3 p prs (no 1), Cls rem p prs.
Nr: Cls 4 p prs, tw 1 leaders, ½ st 5
p prs (no 1) and (no 2), Cls rem p prs.
Cont ½ st 5 p prs.

After pin V:
when patt prs have returned to their
original colour positions, cont in Cls.

After pin W:
change leaders (no 1) to (no 7), (tech 4,
td 4), cont row, T O & T B 6th and 8th
p prs (no 1) from R.
(13 prs)
Nr: T O & T B 4th and 6th p prs (no 2)
from L.
Nr: T O & T B 5th p pr (no 1) from R.
Nr: T O & T B s ps 6 & 7 (no 4) from L,
and 3rd p pr (no 6) from R.
(8 prs)
Nr: T O & T B 3rd p pr (no 4) from R.
Nr: T O & T B 2nd p pr (no 6) from L.
Nr: T O & T B 2nd p pr (no 7) from R.
(5 prs)
After pin X:
Cls leaders thro 2 rem p prs, T O & T B
leaders and 2 rem p prs.
Cls & tw edge prs, place pin Y, and Cls
& T O both edge prs.
T B 1 thread (no 6), and secure to back
of work with previously T B prs.
Use rem 3 threads for rolled edge.

Notes for rolled edges
Roll from pin Y to pin Z (tech 9, td 9):
rolling thread – 1 x (no 7)
rolled threads – 1 x (no 7), 1 x (no 6)

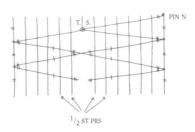

Diagram i3: Patt. 'Mittens' after pin N, Version 2

Use 3 threads from rem 2 edge prs for roll.
T B 1 thread (no 6) from roll at pin T
(tech 14, td 14).
Finish at pin Z (tech 10, td 10).

Roll from pin A# to pin H:
rolling thread – 1 x (no 7)
rolled threads – 1 x (no 7), 1 x (no 6)
Using magic thread at pin A#, add 3
threads (tech 16, td 16).
Finish at pin H.

VERSION 2
Section 1
Start at pin A#:
follow instructions for Version 1 until
pin E.
(14 prs)
After pin E:
work T S (tech 19, td 19) with leaders
(no 1), and central p pr (no 1), and start
Mittens patt (diag i.3).
Note Diag i3 illustrates Mittens after pin
N, the difference being the number of
p prs. The 4 central patt prs are worked
using the same method.
After pin F:
Cls both leaders from each side thro 3
p prs, tw 1 leaders, ½ st leaders thro
2 p prs, work T S, then cont in Cls,
working to R side of braid.
Note When completing patt section
using Mittens, the p prs will not have
returned to their original colour positions.
Cont in Cls,
T O & T B 1 p pr per row from centre.

At pin G:
change leaders, (no 1) to (no 7), (tech
4, td 4).
Cont in Cls,
T O & T B 1 p pr per row from centre,
until 6 prs rem.

Follow instructions for Version 1 from pin H
to pin N.
(15 prs)
After pin N:
work T S with leaders (no 1) and central pr
(no 1), then start Mittens patt (diag i.3).
Note There are 15 prs in this section of patt,
therefore it will be necessary to Cls thro 4
p prs on L and 3 p prs on R, when working
patt.

After pin O:
add 2 prs (no 5), to be s ps 8 & 9 from L
and s ps 6 & 7 from R.
(17 prs)
After the next pins at each edge have been
placed, add 1 pr (no 7) to be 1st p prs at
each side.
(19 prs)
After the next pins at each edge have been
placed, work to centre, work T S with leader
prs, cont in Cls, working to R.

After pin P:
follow instructions for Version 1, until pin U.
Note In Version 2, the thread colours to be
T O & T B will not be identical to those of
Version 1.
(15 prs)
After pin U:
work T S with leaders (no 1) and central pr
(no 1),
start Mittens patt (diag i.3).
Note There are 15 prs in this section of patt,
therefore it will be necessary to Cls thro 3
p prs on the L and 4 p prs on the R, when
working patt.

After pin V:
Cls to centre, work T S with leader prs, and
cont in Cls, working to R.
Note In Version 2, the thread colours to be
T O & T B will not be identical to those of
Version 1.

After pin W:
change leaders, (no 1) to (no 7),(tech 4, td
4), cont row, T O & T B 6th and 8th p prs
from R.
(13 prs)
Nr: follow instructions for Version 1 to
finish.

Notes for rolled edges
As Version 1.

J for JAY

Colours

(no 1)	*White
(no 2)	Pastel Pink
(no 3)	*Sky
(no 4)	*Delft
(no 5)	Dark Mulberry
(no 6)	*French Navy
(no 7)	*Mid Navy

VERSION 1

Section 1

Start at pin A#:

using a two colour point start (tech 1, td 1), (Note R–L working direction), hang 1 pr (no 6) 1 pr (no 7) to be edge prs (diag j.1).
Add magic thread (tech 2, td 2a).
L edge pr is now (no 6).
R edge pr is now (no 7).

PIN A#

no 7

no 6

Diagram j1:
Start, Section 1

On T P, hang 1 pr (no 6) to be leaders.
(3 prs)
On T P, hang 2 prs in order L–R, 1 pr (no 6) and 1 pr (no 7).
Cls leaders R–L thro 2 p prs and edge st at pin B (tech 3, td 3).
(5 prs)
Nr: add 1 pr (no 7) to be s ps 4 & 5 from L.
Nr: add 1 pr (no 6) to be s ps 6 & 7 from R.
(7 prs)
Cont in Cls, adding 4 prs (no 6) 1 pr per row, to centre.
Work 1 row.
(11 prs)
Cont in Cls, adding 1 pr (no 4) to centre, on next and following alternate row.
(13 prs)
Nr: T O & T B 2nd p pr from R (no 7), and add 1 pr (no 4) to be 6th p pr from L.
Nr: T O & T B 2nd p pr from L (no 6), and add 1 pr (no 4) to be s ps 10 & 11 from R.
Nr: T O & T B 2nd p pr from R (no 6), and add 1 pr (no 3) to be 6th p pr from L.
Nr: T O & T B 2nd p pr from L (no 6), and add 1 pr (no 3) to be s ps 10 & 11 from R.
(13 prs)
Work 1 row.
Nr: T O & T B 2nd p pr from L (no 6),

and add 1 pr (no 1) to be 6th p pr from R.
Nr: add 1 pr (no 1) to be s ps 12 & 13 from R.
Nr: add 1 pr (no 1) to be 6th p pr from L.
(15 prs)
After pin C:
change leaders (no 6) to (no 1), (tech 4, td 4), cont row,
start patt – tw 1 leaders, and work ½ st with 7th p pr (no 1) from R.
Nr: work ½ st with 5th, 6th and 7th p prs (no 1) from L.
Cont ½ st 3 p prs.

After pin D:
T O & T B s ps 4 & 5 (no 4) from L.
Nr: T O & T B s ps 6 & 7 (no 4) from R.
L–R order should be as foll:

L edge pr	2 x (no 6)
	2 x (no 6)
	2 x (no 4)
	2 x (no 3)
	6 x (no 1)
	2 x (no 3)
	2 x (no 4)
	2 x (no 6)
	2 x (no 7)
R edge pr	2 x (no 7)
leaders	2 x (no 1)

(13 prs)
After pin E:
work ½ st with 6th p pr from R, Cls rem prs.
Work 3 rows.

After pin F:
cont in Cls.

After pin G:
change leaders (no 1) to (no 7), (tech 4, td 4) cont row, T O & T B 1 central p pr (no 1).
(12 prs)
Nr: *T O & T B 1 pr (no 1)*.
Nr: rep * to *.
Nr: *T O & T B 1 pr (no 3)*.
Nr: rep * to *.
Nr: *T O & T B 1 pr (no 4)*.
Nr: rep * to *.
(6 prs)
At pin H:
edge st (diag j.2), and then set aside R edge pr to be collected later.
Cont in Cls, at each of the central pins (tech 30, td 30), tw 2 leaders, pin, and set aside 1st p pr on R, after working, to be collected later.

Work blind pins, as indicated on pin reference plan, around the point.

At pin I:
change leaders (no 7) with L edge pr (no 6), (tech 7, td 7).

Cont, collecting prs thus: work to R, include pr hanging from pin, tw 2

leaders, replacing pin underneath leaders.
When pin H is reached again:
tw 2 leaders, make a side sewing into pin H, previously worked, tw 2 leaders and cont Cls.

After pin J:
add 1 pr (no 6) to be 2nd p pr from L.
(7 prs)

At pin K:
change leaders (no 6) with R edge pr (no 7), (tech 7, td 7).
After pin K:
add 1 pr (no 6) to be s ps 6 & 7 from R.

After pin L:
add 1 pr (no 5) to be 4th p pr from L.
Nr: add 1 pr (no 5) to be s ps 6 & 7 from R.
(10 prs)
After pin M:
add 1 pr (no 2) to be 5th p pr from L.
Nr: add 1 pr (no 2) to be s ps 8 & 9 from R.
Nr: T O & T B 2nd p pr from L, and add 1 pr (no 2) to be 5th p pr from R.
(12 prs)
Nr: add 1 pr (no 2) to be s ps 10 & 11 from R.
Nr: add 1 pr (no 2) to be 6th p pr from L.
Nr: T O & T B s ps 2 & 3 (no 7/no 6) from R, and add 1 pr (no 2) to be s ps 12 & 13 from left.
Work 1 row.
(14 prs)
After pin N:
change leaders (no 7) to (no 2), (tech 4, td 4).
Cont row, starting patt: tw 1 leaders and central 2 p prs (no 2), work ½ st with these 2 p prs only.

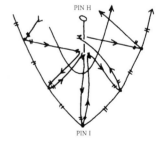

PIN H

PIN I

Diagram j2: Working into a sharp point, (see also diag i2)

Nr: tw 1 leaders and 2nd and 5th central p prs (no 2), work ½ st with 4 central p prs (no 2).
L–R order should be as foll:

L edge pr	2 x (no 7)
	4 x (no 6)
	2 x (no 5)
	12 x (no 2)
	2 x (no 5)
	1 x (no 6)
	1 x (no 7)

R edge pr   2 x (no 6)
leaders   2 x (no 2)
(14 prs)
After pin O:
add 1 pr (no 5) to be s ps 6 & 7 from L.
Nr: add 1 pr (no 5) to be s ps 4 & 5
from R.
(16 prs)
Nr: add 1 pr (no 7) to be 1st p pr from
L, and work ½ st with 2 central p prs
(no 2) only.
Nr: add 1 pr (no 7) to be 1st p pr from R.
Cont in Cls.
(18 prs)
After pin P:
change leaders (no 2) to (no 7), (tech 4,
td 4), cont row, T O & T B 7th and 10th
p prs (no 2) from L.
(16 prs)
Nr: T O & T B 2 prs (no 2) s ps 10 & 11,
and 14 & 15 from R.
Nr: T O & T B s ps 12 & 13 from L.
Nr: T O & T B 5th p pr from R.
Nr: *T O & T B 1 central p pr (no 5)*.
Repeat * to * 3 more times.

At the same time, after pin Q:
add 1 pr (no 7) to be 1st p pr from L ,
and *T O & T B s ps 4 & 5 (no 6) from R*.
Work 1 row.
Rep * to *.
(7 prs)
Work 1 row.
Nr: T O & T B 3rd p pr from L (no 6/no 7).
Work 1 row.
L–R order should be as foll:
L edge pr   2 x (no 7)
                 6 x (no 7)
R edge pr   2 x (no 6)
leaders   2 x (no 7)
(6 prs)

J2: Pricking

After pin R:
add 1 pr (no 6) to be 1st p pr from L.
Work 1 row.
Nr: add 1 pr (no 6) to be s ps 2 & 3
from L.
Work 1 row.
Nr: add 1 pr (no 4) to be 2nd p pr from L.
(9 prs)
At pin S:
change leaders (no 7) with R edge pr
(no 6), (tech 7, td 7).
Work 1 row.
Nr: add 1 pr (no 4) to be s ps 4 & 5
from L.
Work 1 row.
Nr: add 1 pr (no 3) to be 3rd p pr from L.
Work 1 row.
(11 prs)
Nr: add 1 pr (no 3) to be s ps 6 & 7
from L.
Work 1 row.
Nr: add 1 pr (no 1) to be 4th p pr from L.
Work 1 row.
Nr: add 1 pr (no 1) to be s ps 8 & 9
from L, and
T O & T B 2nd p pr (no 7) from R.
Nr: add 1 pr (no 1) to be 7th p pr from R.
(14 prs)
At pin T:
change leaders (no 6) with L edge pr
(no 7), (tech 7, td 7).

After pin U:
change leaders (no 7) to (no 1), (tech 4,
td 4), cont row, starting patt: tw 1
leaders and 3 p prs (no 1), work ½ st
with 3 p prs (no 1).

After pin V:
work ½ st with 1 centre pr (no 1).
Work 1 row.
Nr: cont in Cls.

After pin W:
change leaders (no 1) to (no 7), (tech 4,
td 4), cont row, T O & T B 6th and 8th
p prs (no 1) from R.
(12 prs)

Nr: T O & T B 1 p pr (no 1).
Nr: T O & T B s ps 8 & 9, and 12 & 13
(no 3/no 4).
Nr: T O & T B 1 pr (no 3).
Nr: T O & T B 1 p pr (no 4).
Nr: T O & T B 2nd p pr (no 6) from L.
(6 prs)
After pin X:
T O & T B 1 p pr (no 6).
Work 1 row.
(5 prs)
After pin Y:
Cls leaders thro rem 2 p prs (no 7), T O
& T B leaders and 2 p prs.
Cls & tw both edge prs, place pin Z, Cls
& T O both edge prs.
T B 1 thread (no 6) and secure to back
of work with previously T B prs.
Use 3 rem threads for rolled edge.

Notes for rolled edges
Roll from pin Z to pin A1 (tech 9, td 9):
rolling thread – 1 x (no 7)
rolled threads – 1 x (no 7), 1 x (no 6)
Use 3 threads from rem 2 edge prs for roll.
T B 1 thread (no 6) from roll at pin S
(tech 14, td 14).
Finish at pin A1 (tech 10, td 10).

Roll from pin A# to pin H:
rolling thread – 1 x (no 7)
rolled threads – 1 x (no 7), 1 x (no 6)
Using magic thread at pin A# , add 3
threads (tech 16, td 16).
Finish at pin H.

VERSION 2
Section 1
Start at pin A#:
Follow instructions for Version 1 until
pin C.
Note Only add 2 prs (no 1) to centre of
braid, and do not change leaders.
At pin C:

L–R order should be as foll:
L edge pr   2 x (no 6)

J1: Order of work

J3: Pin reference plan, Version 1

2 x (no 6)
4 x (no 4)
2 x (no 3)
4 x (no 1)
2 x (no 3)
4 x (no 4)
2 x (no 6)
2 x (no 7)

R edge pr   2 x (no 7)
leaders   2 x (no 6)
(14 prs)

After pin C:
start Kisses patt with 2nd to 9th p prs
inclusive, from L edge (diag j.3).
Note There is an extra p pr on R side of
braid.

After pin D:
when patt prs have returned to their
original colour positions, cont in Cls.
As braid narrows, T O & T B prs from
centre, lightest prs first, until 6 p prs
remain.
(6 prs)

After pin E:
change leaders (no 6) to (no 7), (tech 4,
td 4).
After pin F:
and at pins G, H, I, J and K, follow
instructions for Version 1 from pin H to
pin M.
After pin K:
add 4 p prs (no 2) and 2 p prs (no 1),
also T O & T B 1 p pr (no 6) from L,
and 1 p pr (no 6/no 7) from R.

At pin L:
L–R order should be as foll:
L edge pr   2 x (no 7)
                   4 x (no 6)
                   2 x (no 5)
                   4 x (no 2)
                   4 x (no 1)
                   4 x (no 2)
                   2 x (no 5)
                   1 x (no 6)
                   1 x (no 7)

R edge pr   2 x (no 6)
leaders   2 x (no 7)
(14 prs)

After pin L:
change leaders (no 7) to (no 5), (tech 4,
td 4).

Nr: start Kisses patt with 8 p prs (diag
j.3), (no 5), (no 2), & (no 1).

After pin M:
cont in Cls, and add 2 prs (no 5) to be
s ps 4 & 5 from R, and s ps 6 & 7 from L.
Nr: add 1 pr (no 7) to be 1st p pr from L.
Nr: add 1 pr (no 7) to be 1st p pr from R.
(18 prs)

After pin N:
change leaders (no 5) to (no 7), (tech 4,
td 4), then start T O & T B 10 p prs, (no
1), (no 2), & (no 5), from centre as
braid narrows.
(8 prs)

After pin O:
follow instructions for Version 1.
Note Pins Q, P, R Version 1, will be pins
O, P, Q, Version 2).
(9 prs)
At pin Q:
change leaders (no 7) with R edge pr
(no 6), (tech 7, td 7).

Work 1 row.
Nr: add 7 p prs on next and following
alternate rows, to give L–R order as foll:
L edge pr   2 x (no 7)
                   2 x (no 6)
                   4 x (no 4)
                   2 x (no 3)
                   4 x (no 1)
                   2 x (no 3)
                   4 x (no 4)
                   2 x (no 6)
                   6 x (no 7)
R edge pr   2 x (no 7)
leaders   2 x (no 6)
(16 prs)
At pin R:
change leaders (no 6) with L edge pr
(no 7), (tech 7, td 7), cont row, T O &
T B 1st p pr (no 7) from R, and start
Kisses patt with 2nd to 9th prs inclusive,
from L (diag j.3).

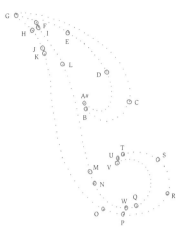

J4: Pin reference plan, Version 2

(15 prs)
After pin S:
when prs have returned to their original
colour positions, cont in Cls.
Nr: T O & T B 9 p prs from centre, 1 pr
per row, lightest prs first.
(6 prs)

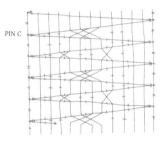

Diagram j3: Patt. 'Kisses' after pin C, Version 2

After pin T:
follow instructions for Version 1.
Note Pins X, Y, Z Version 1, will be pins
T, U, V Version 2.

To finish,
follow instructions for Version 1.

Notes for rolled edges
As Version 1.

Diagram K1: Order of work

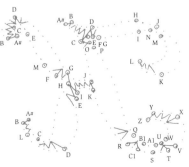

Diagram K3: Pin reference plan,
versions 1 and 2

K for KINGFISHER

Colours

(no 1)	Alice Blue
(no 2)	Ocean
(no 3)	Saxe
(no 4)	*Royal
(no 5)	*Honeybird
(no 6)	Kingfisher
(no 7)	*Dark Kingfisher

VERSION 1

Section 1

Start at pin A#:
using a two colour point start (tech 1, td 1), (Note L-R working direction), hang 1 pr (no 7) and 1 pr (no 6) to be edge prs (diag k.1).
Add magic thread (tech 2, td 2a).
L edge pr is now (no 7).
R edge pr is now (no 6).

On T P, hang 1 pr (no 4) to be leaders.
(3 prs)
On T P, hang 2 prs (no 7) and 2 prs (no 6) to be p prs, to give order:
2 x (no 7)
4 x (no 6)
2 x (no 7)
Cls leaders L-R thro 4 p prs and edge st at pin B (tech 3, td 3).
(7 prs)
After pin B:
add 2 prs (no 4), 1 pr per row, to centre.
Nr: add 2 prs (no 5), 1 pr per row, to centre.
Nr: add 2 prs (no 4), 1 pr per row, to centre.
Nr: add 2 prs (no 6) open, to centre.

At pin C:
L-R order should be:

L edge pr	2 x (no 7)
	2 x (no 7)
	2 x (no 6)
	2 x (no 4)
	2 x (no 5)
	2 x (no 4)
	4 x (no 6)
	2 x (no 4)
	2 x (no 5)
	2 x (no 4)
	2 x (no 6)
	2 x (no 7)
R edge pr	2 x (no 7)
leaders	2 x (no 4)
(15 prs)	

After pin D:
split braid (tech 5, td 5) thus – working locking st (tech 6, td 6) and leave.

At pin E:
between p prs 6 & 7 from R, hang 1 pr (no 4) and to the L of it, 1 pr (no 7) to

be centre edge prs, Cls prs tog and tw 2 both prs.

Undo locking st after pin D:
cont across all p prs, adding 1 pr (no 3) to be s ps 8 & 9 from R.

Secure all bobbins (8 prs) at L side of braid, leave to cont with R side of braid, Section 1
(10 prs)

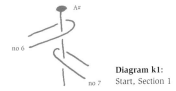

Diagram k1:
Start, Section 1

Return to Section 1

After pin F:
add 1 pr (no 2) to be 4th p pr from L.
(11 prs)
Nr: T O & T B s ps 2 & 3 (no 7/no 6) from R, and add 1 pr (no 1) to be s ps 8 & 9 from L.

After pin G:
start patt – *Cls 3 prs, tw 1 leaders, Cls 2 p prs, tw 1 leaders, Cls rem prs.*
Cont in patt, rep * to *.

After pin H:
cont in Cls.

After pin I:
T O & T B 3rd and 6th p prs (no 3/no 5) from L.
Nr: T O & T B s ps 6 & 7 (no 1) from R.
Nr: T O & T B 3rd p pr (no 2) from L.
Nr: T O & T B 1 p pr (no 4) from centre.
(6 prs)

At pin J:
change leaders (no 4) with R edge pr (no 6), (tech 7, td 7).
After pin J:
add 1 pr (no 4) to be 1st p pr from R, and T O & T B 1 p pr (no 4) from centre.
Nr: add 1 pr (no 5) to be 1st p pr from R.
Nr: add 1 pr (no 4) to be 1st p pr from R.
Nr: add 1 pr (no 3) to be 1st p pr from R.
Nr: add 1 pr (no 2) to be 1st p pr from R.
Nr: *add 1 pr (no 1) to be s ps 1 & 3 from R.*
Nr: rep * to *.

Cont in Cls, L-R order is:

L edge pr	2 x (no 7)
	3 x (no 6)
	1 x (no 7)
	2 x (no 4)
	2 x (no 5)
	2 x (no 4)

	2 x (no 3)
	1 x (no 2)
	1 x (no 1)
	1 x (no 2)
	3 x (no 1)
R edge pr	2 x (no 4)
leaders	2 x (no 6)
(12 prs)	

At pin K:
change leaders (no 6) with R edge pr (no 4), (tech 7, td 7).
After pin K:
T O & T B s ps 2 & 3 (no 1) from R.
Work 1 row.
Nr: T O & T B 2nd p pr (no 1/no 2) from R.
Nr: T O & T B s ps 10 & 11 (no 4/no 3) from L.
Nr: T O & T B 1st p pr (no 1/no 2) from R.
Nr: T O & T B s ps 6 & 7 (no 4/no 5) from L.
Nr: T O & T B 1st p pr (no 3/no 4) from R.
(6 prs)

To finish at pin L:
Cls thro 3 rem p prs, T O & T B leaders and 3 rem p prs, tie in a bunch, and secure to back of work with previously T B prs (tech 8, td 8).
Cls & tw edge prs, place pin L, Cls & T O both prs.
These prs to be used for rolled edge.

Notes for rolled edge
Roll from pin L to pin I (tech 9, td 9):
rolling thread – 1 x (no 7)
rolled thread – 1 x (no 7), 2 x (no 6)
Use edge prs from pin L for roll.
T B 1 thread (no 6) at pin M and pin N (tech 14, td 14).
Finish at pin I (tech 10, td 10).

Return to Section 1a

At pin C:
add 1 pr (no 6) to be leaders at L side of L section (tech 5, td 5), adding 1 pr (no 5) to be s ps 8 & 9 from L, edge st at pin O, and cont.
Nr: add 1 pr (no 3) to be 4th p pr from R.
Nr: add 1 pr (no 2) to be s ps 10 & 11 from L.
(12 prs)
After pin P:
start patt – *Cls 3 p prs, tw 1 leaders, Cls 2 p prs, tw 1 leaders, Cls rem p prs.
Nr: Cls 4 p prs, tw 1 leaders, Cls 2 p prs, tw 1 leaders, Cls rem p prs*.
Cont in patt rep * to *.

After pin Q:
cont in Cls.

After pin R:
T O & T B s ps 6 & 7 (no 4/no 5), and s ps 14 & 15 (no 5/no 4) from L.
(10 prs)
Nr: T O & T B s ps 6 & 7 (no 2) from R.
Work 1 row.

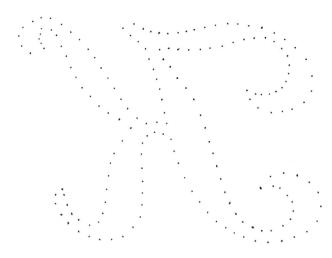

Diagram K2:
Pricking

Nr: T O & T B 3rd p pr (no 3) from R.
Nr: T O & T B s ps 6 & 7 (no 5) from L.
Nr: T O & T B 2nd p pr (no 4) from R.
(6 prs)
After pin S:
add 1 pr (no 6) to be 1st p pr from L.
Work 1 row.
Nr: add 1 pr (no 5) to be 1st p pr from L.
Work 1 row.
(8 prs)
At pin T:
change leaders (no 6) with L edge pr
(no7), (tech 7, td 7).

After pin T:
add 1 pr (no 4) to be 1st p pr from L.
(9 prs)
When completing blind pin U:
change leaders (no 7) with R edge pr
(no 4), (tech 7, td 7).

At pin V:
change leaders (no 4) with L edge pr
(no 6), (tech 7, td 7).
After pin V:
add 1 pr (no 3) to be 1st p pr from L.
(10 prs)

After pin W:
T O & T B 2nd p pr (no 6) from R, and
add 1 pr (no 7) to be 1st p pr from R,
and add 1 pr (no 2) to be 1st p pr from L.
(11 prs)
Nr: add 1 pr (no 1) to be s ps 1 & 3 from L.
Nr: T O & T B 2nd p pr (no 6) from R,
and add 1 pr (no 7) to be 1st p pr from R.
Nr: add 1 pr (no 1) to be s ps 1 & 3 from L.
(13 prs)
After pin X:
T O & T B s ps 8 & 9 (no 3/no 4) and
s ps 12 & 13 (no 5/no 6) from L.
Work 1 row.
Nr: T O & T B 2nd p pr (no 2/no 1) from L.
Nr: T O & T B 5th p pr (no 4/no 3) from R.
Nr: T O & T B 2nd p pr (no 1/no 2) from L.
Nr: T O & T B 5th p pr (no 1) from L.
(7 prs)
At pin Y:
change leaders (no 6) with L edge pr

(no 4), (tech 7, td 7).
After pin Y:
T O & T B 1st p pr (no 5/no 6) from L,
then Cls thro rem 3 p prs, T O & T B 3
rem p prs and leaders, tie in a bunch
and secure to back of work with
previously T B prs (tech 8, td 8).

Finish at pin Z:
Cls & tw edge prs, place pin Z, Cls & T O.
These prs to be used for rolled edge.

Notes for rolled edges
Roll from Pin Z to pin B1:
rolling thread – 1 x (no 7)
rolled threads – 1 x (no 7), 2 x (no 6)
Use edge prs from pin Z fro roll.
T B 1 thread (no 6) and pin W and pin A1.
Finish at pin B1.

Roll from pin A# to pin S:
rolling thread – 1 x (no 7)
rolled threads – 3 x (no 7)
Add 2 prs (no 7) at pin A#(tech 16, td 16a).
T B 1 thread from roll at Pin R and pin C1.
Finish at pin S.

Section 2
Start at pin A#:
using a two colour point start (tech 1, td
1), (Note L–R working direction), hang
1 pr (no 7) and 1 pr (no 6) to be edge
prs (diag k.1).
Add magic thread.
L edge pr is now (no 7).
R edge pr is now (no 6).

On T P, hang 1 pr (no 4) to be leaders.
(3 prs)
On T Ps, hang 6 prs in order as foll
(diag k.2):
2 x (no 7)
2 x (no 6)
1 x (no 5)
2 x (no 4)
1 x (no 5)
2 x (no 6)
2 x (no 7)
Cls leaders thro 6 p prs and edge st at pin B.

(9 prs)
Nr: add 1 pr (no 3) to centre.
Nr: add 1 pr (no 2) to centre.
(11 prs)
After pin C:
T O & T B 1 p pr (no 2) from centre.
Nr: T O & T B 1 p pr (no 3) from centre.
Nr: T O & T B 1 p pr (no 4) from centre.
Nr: T O & T B 1 p pr (no 5) from centre.
Nr: T O & T B 1 p pr (no 6) from centre.
(6 prs)
After pin D:
add 1 pr (no 6) to be 1st p pr from R,
and T O & T B 2nd p pr (no 6) from L.
Work 1 row.
Nr: add 1 pr (no 6) to be s ps 2 & 3
from R, and T O & T B 2nd p pr (no 7)
from L.
(6 prs)
Nr: add 1 pr (no 4) to be 3rd p pr from L.
Nr: add 1 pr (no 4) to be s ps 4 & 5 from R.
Nr: add 1 pr (no 3) to be 4th p pr from L.
Nr: add 1 pr (no 2) to be s ps 6 & 7 from R.

After pin E:
L–R order is as foll:
L edge pr	2 x (no 7)
	2 x (no 7)
	2 x (no 6)
	2 x (no 4)
	1 x (no 3)
	2 x (no 2)
	1 x (no 3)
	2 x (no 4)
	2 x (no 6)
R edge pr	2 x (no 7)
leaders	2 x (no 4)

(10 prs)
Start patt: *Cls 3 p prs, tw 1 leaders, Cls
2 p prs, tw 1 leaders, Cls rem p prs.
Nr: Cls 2 p prs, tw 1 leaders, Cls 2
p prs, tw 1 leaders, Cls rem prs*.
Cont in patt, rep * to *.
After pin F:
cont in Cls.
Work 1 row.
Nr: T O & T B 1 p pr (no 2).
Nr: T O & T B 1 p pr (no 3).
(8 prs)
After pin G:
Cls across all p prs, do not tw leaders,
do not work edge st.
Secure all prs in order and leave to work
Section 2a.

Section 2a
Start at pin A#:
using a one colour point start (tech 23,
td 23), (Note R–L working direction),
hang 2 prs (no 7) open, to be edge prs
(diag k.3).
Add magic thread.
On T P, hang 1 pr (no 4) to be leaders.
(3 prs)
On T P, hang 2 prs (no 7) and 1 pr (no
6) open, to be p prs, to give order:
2 x (no 7)

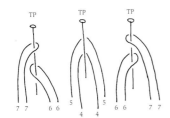

Diagram k2: Adding passive pairs, Section 2

2 x (no 6)
2 x (no 7)
Cls leaders R–L thro 3 p prs and edge st
at pin B.
(6 prs)
Nr: add 1 pr (no 6) to centre.

After pin C:
add 1 pr (no 4) to centre.
Work 2 rows.
(8 prs)
Nr: add 1 pr (no 4) to centre.
Nr: add 1 pr (no 6) to be s ps 4 & 5 from R.
Nr: add 1 pr (no 6) to be s ps 4 & 5 from L.
Work 1 row.
Nr: add 1 pr (no 4) to centre.
Nr: add 1 pr (no 2) to centre.

After pin D:
L–R order is:

L edge pr	2 x (no 7)
	2 x (no 7)
	4 x (no 6)
	3 x (no 4)
	2 x (no 2)
	3 x (no 4)
	4 x (no 6)
	2 x (no 7)
R edge pr	2 x (no 7)
leaders	2 x (no 4)

(13 prs)
Start patt: Cls 4 p prs, tw 1 leaders, Cls
2 p prs, tw 1 leaders, Cls rem prs.
Cont in patt.
After pin E:
Cls across all p prs, do not tw leaders,
do not work edge st.
Join Sections 2 and 2a
Work Cls & tw 2 with both edge prs
(tech 22, td 22), place pin H, Cls leaders
thro respective edge prs.
Work T.S, removing and replacing pin H
as a support pin, and work to L, pin I,
T O & T B s ps 10 & 11 (no 2) from L.
(20 prs)
After pin I:
T O & T B, 3rd p pr (no 6), 5th p pr (no

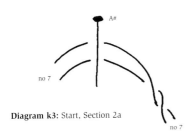

Diagram k3: Start, Section 2a

4), 7th p pr (no 6), and s ps 30 & 31 (no
4) from L.
(16 prs)
Nr: T O & T B 2nd p pr (no 4), 9th p pr
(no 6), and s ps 20 & 21 (no 4) from R.
(13 prs)
Nr: T O & T B , 3rd p pr (no 4), 5th p pr
(no 7), and 7th p pr (no 7) from L.
(10 prs)
Nr: T O & T B 3rd p pr (no 7), and 5th
p.r (no 7) from R.
(8 prs)
Cont in Cls to finish at pin J:
join to Section 1, and T O.
At pin K:
set aside L edge pr (no 7) and 1st p pr
(no 7) from L, to be used for rolled
edge, T O & T B rem prs in a bunch and
secure to back of work with previously
T B prs.

Notes for rolled edges
Roll from pin K to pin A#, Section 2a:
rolling thread – 1 x (no 7)
rolled threads – 3 x (no 7)
Use set aside threads from pin K for
rolled edge.
T B 1 thread from roll at pin L and pin B.
Finish at pin A#, Section 2a.

Roll from pin A# to pin H, Section 2:
rolling thread   1 x (no 7)
rolled threads   3 x (no 7)
Add 2 prs (no 7) at pin A#, Section 2,
(tech 16, td 16).
T B 1 thread at pin M and pin F.
Finish at pin H.

VERSION 2
Section 1
Start at pin A#:
follow instructions for Version 1, from
pin A# to pin G.

After pin G:
start Ribbon (var) patt – *Cls 3 p prs,
tw 1 leaders, work Ribbon (var) with 2
p prs (diag k.4), tw 1 leaders, Cls rem p prs*.
Cont in patt rep * to *.

After pin H:
follow instructions for Version 1, from
pin H to finish at pin L.

Notes for rolled edge
As Version 1.

Return to Section 1a
Follow instructions for Version 1, from
pin C to pin P.
After pin P:
work 1 row.
Nr: start Ribbon (var) patt – *Cls 4
p prs, tw 1 leaders, work Ribbon (var)
patt with 2 p prs (diag k. 4), tw 1
leaders, Cls rem p prs.

Nr: Cls 3 p prs, tw 1 leaders, work
Ribbon (var) with 2 p prs, tw 1 leaders,
Cls rem p prs*.
Cont in patt, rep * to *.
After pin Q:
cont in Cls, and follow instructions for
Version 1,
to finish at pin Z.

Notes for rolled edges
As Version 1.

Section 2
Start at pin A#:
follow instructions for Version 1, from
pin A# to pin E.

After pin E:
start Ribbon (var) patt – *Cls 3 p prs,
tw 1 leaders, work Ribbon (var) patt
with 2 p prs (diag k.4), tw 1 leaders, Cls
rem p prs.

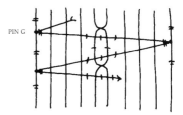

Diagram k4: Patt. 'Ribbon' (var) after pin G,
Section 1

Nr: Cls 2 p prs, tw 1 leaders, work
Ribbon (var) patt with 2 p prs, tw 1
leaders, Cls rem p prs*.
Cont in patt, rep * to *.

After pin F:
cont in Cls, following instructions for
Version 1, from pin F to pin G, including
instructions for pin G.
Secure all bobbins in order, and leave to
work Section 2a.

Section 2a
Start at pin A#:
follow instructions for Version 1, from
pin A# to pin D.

After pin D:
start Ribbon (var) patt – *Cls 4 p prs,
tw 1 leaders, work Ribbon (var) patt
with 2 p prs (diag k.4), tw 1 leaders, Cls
rem p prs*.
Cont in patt, rep * to *.

After pin E:
Cls across all p prs, do not tw leaders,
do not work edge st.
Join Sections 2 and 2a
Follow instructions for Version 1 to finish.

Notes for rolled edges
As Version 1.

L for LEAVES

Colours

(no 1)	Sycamore
(no 2)	Pale Lettuce
(no 3)	Apple Green
(no 4)	*Jade
(no 5)	Pastel Green
(no 6)	Malachite
(no 7)	*Tartan

VERSION 1

Section 1

Start at pin A#:
using a one colour point start (tech 23, td 23), (Note R–L working direction), hang 2 prs (no 7) open, to be edge prs (diag l.1).
Add magic thread (tech 2, td 2b).

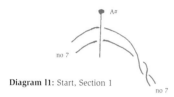

Diagram l1: Start, Section 1

On T P, hang 1 pr (no 7) to be leaders.
(3 prs)
On T P, add 2 prs (no 7) open, to be p prs. Cls leaders R–L thro 2 p prs and edge st (tech 3, td 3).
(5 prs)
Nr: add 1 pr (no 6) to be 1st p pr from L.
Nr: add 1 pr (no 6) to be s ps 2 & 3 from L.
Nr: add 1 pr (no 5) to be 1st p pr from L.
Nr: add 1 pr (no 5) to be s ps 2 & 3 from L.
Work 1 row.
(9 prs)
Nr: add 1 pr (no 4) to be 2nd p pr from L.
Nr: add 1 pr (no 4) to be s ps 4 & 5 from L.
Nr: add 1 pr (no 4) to be 3rd p pr from L.
Nr: add 1 pr (no 4) to be s ps 6 & 7 from L.
Work 1 row.

At pin B:
L–R order should be:

L edge pr	2 x (no 7)
	2 x (no 5)
	8 x (no 4)
	2 x (no 5)
	4 x (no 6)
	4 x (no 7)
R edge pr	2 x (no 7)
leaders	2 x (no 7)

(13 prs)
After pin B:
add 1 pr (no 3) to be 4th p pr from L.
Nr: T O & T B 2nd p. pr (no 7) from R, and add 1 pr (no 3) to be s ps 8 & 9 from L.
Nr: add 1 pr (no 2) to be 5th p. pr from L.
Nr: add 1 pr (no 2) s ps 10 & 11 from L.

Nr: add 1 pr (no 2) 6th p. pr from L.
(17 prs)
At pin C:
change leaders (no 7) to (no 3), (tech 4, td 4), cont row.
Nr:* start patt: working ½ st, with 5th, 6th, and 7th p prs (no 2) from L, Cls with rem prs*.
Nr: T O & T B 2nd p pr from R (no 6) and, cont rep * to *.
(16 prs)
After pin D:
when leaders have returned to their original colour (no 3), cont in Cls.

After pin E:
add 1 pr (no 7) to be 1st p pr from R, and T O & T B 1 p pr (no 2).
Nr: T O & T B 1 p pr (no 2), and add 1 pr (no 7) to be 2nd p pr from R.
Nr: T O & T B 1 p pr (no 2).
Nr: T O & T B s ps 6 & 7 (no 4/no 3) and s ps 10 & 11 (no 3/no 4) from L.
(13 prs)

At pin F:
change leaders (no 3) with R edge pr (no 7), (tech 7, td 7).
After pin F:
add 1 pr (no 5) to R, and T O & T B 1 p pr (no 3) and 2nd p pr (no 4) from L.
(12 prs)
Nr: T O & T B 3rd p pr (no 4) from L.
Nr: add 1 pr (no 3) to be 1st p pr from R.
Nr: T O & T B 1 p pr (no 5) from L.
Nr: add 1 pr (no 3) to be 1st p pr from R, and T O & T B 1st p pr from L.
Nr: T O & T B 1st p pr from L, and add 1 pr (no 3) to be 1st p pr from R.
(11 prs)
Nr: change leaders (no 7) to (no 3), (tech 20, td 20), T O & T B leaders (no 7), using 1st p pr (no 3) as new leaders, cont row, adding 1 pr (no 2) to become 1st p pr at R edge, Cls leaders thro this 1st p pr, and T O & T B 1st p pr from L.
(10 prs)
Nr: T O & T B 1 p pr (no 7) from left.
Nr: add 1 pr (no 2) to be 1st p pr from R.
Nr: add 1 pr (no1) to be 1st p pr from R.
Work 1 row.
Nr: add 1 pr (no 1) to be 1st p pr from R.
Work 3 rows.
Nr: add 1 pr (no 7) to be 1st p pr from L.
(13 prs)
After pin G:
start patt: working ½ st with 2 p prs (no 3) from centre of braid.

After completing blind pin H:
T O & T B 1 p pr (no 1) from R.
Nr: T O & T B 1 p pr (no 1) from R, and cont in Cls.

Nr: T O & T B 1 p pr (no 2) from R.
Nr: T O & T B 1 p pr (no 2) from R, and add 1 pr (no 6) to be s ps 2 & 4 from L.

Nr: T O & T B 1 p pr (no 3) from R edge.
Nr: T O & T B 1 p pr (no 3) from R edge.
(8 prs)

At pin I:
change leaders (no 3) with L edge pr (no 7), (tech 7, td 7).
After pin I:
add 1 pr (no 6) to be s ps 6 & 8 from L.

At pin J:
change leaders (no 7) with R edge pr (no 3), (tech 7, td 7).

After pin J:
T O & T B 1 pr (no 5) from R edge, and change leaders (no 3) to (no 7), (tech 4, td 4), cont in Cls.
L–R order should be:

L edge pr	2 x (no 3)
	1 x (no 7)
	1 x (no 6)
	1 x (no 7)
	1 x (no 6)
	1 x (no 7)
	1 x (no 6)
	1 x (no 7)
	1 x (no 6)
	2 x (no 7)
R edge pr	2 x (no 7)
leaders	2 x (no 7)

(8 prs)
After pin K:
add 1 pr (no 7) to be 1st p pr from L.
Nr: add 1 pr (no 7) to be 1st p pr from L, and T O & T B 2nd p pr (no 7/no 6) from R.
Nr: *add 2 prs (no 7), to be 1st p pr from each edge, and T O & T B 1p pr (no 7/no 6) from R.*
Rep * to * twice more.
(12 prs)
Finish at pin L:
L–R order should be:

L edge pr	2 x (no 3)
	18 x (no 7)
R edge pr	2 x (no 7)
leaders	2 x (no 7)

(12 prs)
Join to previously worked section, (tech 12, td 12).
T O all prs, set aside leaders, R edge pr and 1st p pr from R, these 3 prs to be used for rolled edges.
T B rem prs in a bunch.

Notes for rolled edges
Roll from pin L to pin J (tech 9, td 9):
rolling thread – 1 x (no 7)
rolled threads – 2 x (no 7)
Use 3 of the threads (no 7) at pin L for roll.
T B 1 thread at each of the 2 pins before pin J (tech 14, td 14).
Finish at pin J (tech 10, td 10).
Roll from pin L to pin A#:
rolling thread – 1 x (no 7)
rolled threads – 2 x (no 7)

Use rem 3 threads (no 7) at pin L for roll.
T B 1 thread at each of the 2 pins before pin A#.
Finish at pin A#.

Section 2
Start at pin # :
using top sewings (tech 12, td 12),
(Note R–L working direction), hang on 12 prs in the same order as at pin L, the finish of Section 1.
Tw 2 both edge prs.
Work 2 rows, and cont in Cls.

After pin M:
add 1 pr (no 6) to be s ps 6 & 8 from R.
Nr: add 1 pr (no 6) to be s ps 5 & 7 from R.
Nr: add 1 pr (no 6) to be s ps 8 & 9 from R, and T O & T B 1st p pr (no 7) from L.
Nr: add 1 pr (no 6) to be 5th p pr from R.
Nr: add 1 pr (no 6) to be s ps 10 & 11 from R.
(16 prs)
Nr: T O & T B 1st p pr (no 7) from L, and add 1 pr (no 5) to be 6th p pr from R.
Nr: add 1 pr (no 6) to be s ps 12 & 13 from R.
Nr: add 1 pr (no 5) to be 7th p pr from R.
Nr: add 1 pr (no 5) to be s ps 14 & 15 from R.
(19 prs)
Nr: T O & T B 1st p pr (no 7) from L, and add 1 pr (no 3) to be 8th p pr from R.
Nr: add 1 pr (no 3) to be s ps 16 & 17 from R.
Nr: add 1 pr (no 2) to be 9th p pr from R.
Nr: add 1 pr (no 2) to be s ps 18 & 19 from R, and T O & T B 1st p pr (no 7) from L.
(21 prs)
Nr : T O & T B 1 p pr (no 6) from L, and add 1 pr (no 1) to be 10th p pr from R.
Nr: T O & T B 1 p pr (no 6) from R, and add 1 pr (no 1) to be s ps 18 & 19 from R.
Next row: T O & T B 1st pr (no 7) from L, and add 1 pr (no 1) to be 10th p pr from R.
Next 3 rows: T O & T B 2nd p pr from L.

(18 prs)
Cont in Cls for 5 rows.
Nr: *T O & T B 1 p pr (no 1) from near centre.
Work 1 row*.
Rep * to* twice more.
(15 prs)
Nr: *T O & T B 1 p pr (no 2) from near centre.
Work 1 row.*
Rep * to * once more.
(13 prs)
Next 2 rows: T O & T B 1 p pr (no 3), 1 pr per row.
(11 prs)
Next 2 rows: T O & T B 1 p pr (no 5), 1 pr per row.
Work 1 row.
(9 prs)
Nr: T O & T B 1 p pr (no 6/no 5).
Cont in Cls, L–R order should be:

L edge pr	2 x (no 3)
	2 x (no 7)
	2 x (no 6)
	1 x (no 7)
	1 x (no 6)
	4 x (no 7)
R edge pr	2 x (no 7)
leaders	2 x (no 7)

(8 prs)
After pin N:
T O & T B 2nd p pr (no 6) from L.
Nr: add 1 pr (no 7) to be 1st p pr from R.

At pin O:
change leaders (no 7) with L edge pr (no 3), (tech 7, td 7).

After pin O:
change leaders (no 3) to (no 6), (tech 31, td 31), T O & T B leaders (no 3).
(8 prs)
After completing blind pin P:
add 1 pr (no 6) to be s ps 6 & 8 from L.
(9 prs)
After pin Q:
add 1 pr (no 6) to be 3rd p pr from L.
Nr: add 1 pr (no 6) to be s ps 6 & 7 from L.

Nr: add 1 pr (no 5) to be 4th p pr from L.
Nr: add 1 pr (no 4) to be s ps 8 & 9 from L.
(13 prs)
After completing blind pin R:
start patt: working ½ st with 3rd, 4th, 5th and 6th p prs from L.

After pin S:
when both leaders have returned to original colours, and 4th p pr is (no 4), T O & T B 4th p pr (no 4) and cont in Cls.
(12 prs)
Nr: T O & T B 1 p pr (no 5).
Nr: T O & T B 2 p prs (no 6).
Nr: *T O & T B 1 p pr (no 7/no 6)*.
Rep * to * twice more.
Work 1 row.
(6 prs)
Nr: after working R edge st, change leaders (no 6) to (no 7), (tech 31, td 31), T O & T B leaders (no 6).
Note All prs are now (no 7).
(6 prs)
Work as far as pin T:
secure all bobbins in order, and leave to work rolled edge.

Notes for rolled edge
Roll from pin# to pin P:
rolling thread – 1 x (no 7)
rolled threads – 2 x (no 7)
Add 3 threads (no 7) at pin # (tech 16, td 16).
T B 1 thread 2 pins before pin P.
Finish at pin P.

Return to pin T
To finish at pin U:
join to previously worked section (tech 12, td 12), using top sewings.
T O all prs.
Set aside L edge pr and 1 thread from 1st p pr from L,to use for rolled edge.
T B rem prs in a bunch.

Notes for rolled edge
Roll from pin U to pin V:
rolling thread – 1 x (no 7)

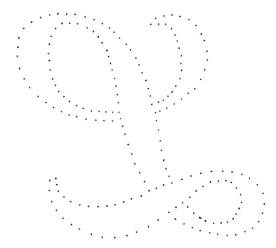

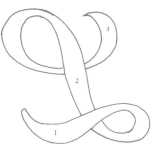

L1: Order of work

L2: Pricking

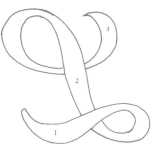

L3: Pin reference plan, Version 1

43

rolled threads – 2 x (no 7)
Use L edge pr and 1 thread from 1st
p pr from L for roll.
T B 1 thread 2 pins before pin V.
Finish at pin V.

Section 3
Start at pin #:
using top sewings (tech 12, td 12),
(Note R–L working direction), hang on 6
prs (no 7).
Cls 2 rows.
Nr: add 1 pr (no 6) to centre.
Work 1 row.
Nr: add 1 pr (no 7) to centre.
Work 1 row.
Nr: add 1 pr (no 6) to centre.
Work 1 row.
(9 prs)
Nr: add 1 pr (no 4) to centre.
Work 1 row.
Nr: add 1 pr (no 4) to centre.
Work 1 row.
Nr: add 1 pr (no 3) to centre.
Nr: add 1 pr (no 2) to centre.
(13 prs)

After pin W:
change leaders (no 7) to (no 3), (tech
31, td 31), T O & T B old leaders (no 7).
Nr: start patt: working ½ st with 2
central p prs (no 2/no 3).

After completing 1st part of blind pin X:
change leaders (no 3) to (no 7), (tech
31, td 31), T O old leaders (no 3), cont
row, T O & T B 2 central p prs (no 2/no
3), and cont in Cls.
(11 prs)
Nr: T O & T B 2 p prs (no 6/no 7) and 1
p pr (no 4).
Nr: T O & T B 1 p pr (no 4).
Nr: T O & T B 1 p pr (no 6).
Nr: T O & T B 1 p pr (no 7).
(5 prs)
To finish at pin Y:
(tech 8, td 8), Cls leaders thro rem p prs
and T O.
Cls & tw edge prs, place pin Y,
Cls & T O.
Set aside 3 threads from edge prs to use
for rolled edge.
T B rem prs and secure to back of work
with previously T B prs.

Notes for rolled edge
Roll from pin Y to pin Z:
rolling thread – 1 x (no 7)
rolled threads – 2 x (no 7)
Use 3 threads from edge prs at pin Y.
T B 1 thread from roll 2 pins before pin Z.
Finish at pin Z.

VERSION 2
Section 1
Start at pin A# :

using a one colour point start (tech 23,
td 23), (Note R–L working direction),
hang 2 prs (no 7) open, to be edge prs
(diag l.1).
Add magic thread.

On T P, hang 1 pr (no 7) to be leaders.
(3 prs)

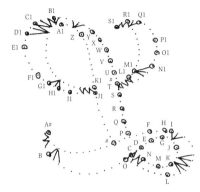

Diagram L4: Pin reference plan, Version 2

On T P, add 2 prs (no 7) to be p prs.
Cls leaders R–L thro 2 p prs and edge st
(tech 3, td 3).
(5 prs)
Nr: add 1 pr (no 6) to be 1st p pr from L.
Nr: add 1 pr (no 5) to be 1st p pr from L.
Nr: add 1 pr (no 4) to be 1st p pr from L.
Nr: add 1 pr (no 3) to be 1st p pr from L.
Nr: add 1 pr (no 2) to be 1st p pr from L.
Work 1 row.

At pin B:
L–R order should be
L edge pr   2 x (no 7)
                   2 x (no 2)
                   2 x (no 3)
                   2 x (no 4)
                   2 x (no 5)
                   2 x (no 6)
                   2 x (no 7)
                   2 x (no 7)
R edge pr   2 x (no 7)
leaders   2 x (no 7)
(10 prs)
After pin B:
start Lattice 1 patt, also working Cls &
Tw with 1st p pr from R throughout patt
(diag l.2).
Note Blind pins are not shown in diags.

After pin C:
after Cls patt prs tog, T O & T B 1 pr (no 2).
Cont, keeping patt correct.
(9 prs)
After pin D:
after Cls patt prs tog, T O & T B 1 pr
(no 3).
Cont, keeping patt correct.
(8 prs)
After pin E:
after Cls patt prs tog, T O & T B 1 pr
(no 5).

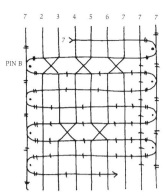

Diagram l2: Patt. 'Lattice' (var) after pin B,
Section 1

Cont, keeping patt correct.
(7 prs)
After pin F:
cont in Cls, L–R order should be
L edge pr   2 x (no 7)
                   2 x (no 4)
                   2 x (no 6)
                   4 x (no 7)
R edge pr   2 x (no 7)
leaders   2 x (no 7)
(7 prs)

After pin G:
T O & T B 1 p pr (no 4) from L.
(6 prs)
After pin H:
add 1 pr (no 6) to be 1st p pr from R.
Nr: T O & T B 1 pr (no 6) from L.

After pin I:
add 1 pr (no 3) to be 1st p pr from R.
Work 1 row.
Nr: add 1 pr (no 2) to be 1st p pr from R.
Work 1 row.
Nr: add 1 pr (no 1) to be 1st p pr from R.
Nr: add 1 pr (no 2) to be s ps 4 & 5
from R.
Nr: add 1 pr (no 1) to be 2nd p pr from R.
(11 prs)
After pin J:
start Lattice 1 patt, using 4 p prs from R,
only (diag l.3).
T O & T B the innermost pr (no 1), after
Cls with patt pr (no 2).
Cont in patt.
T O & T B the rem pr (no 1), after Cls
with patt pr (no 2).
Cont in patt.
(9 prs)
After pin K:
Cls rem 2 patt prs (no 2) tog.
Cont in Cls.

At pin L:
*T O & T B 1st p pr from R.
Work 1 row*.
Rep * to * 3 more times.

Note At the same time:
At pin M:

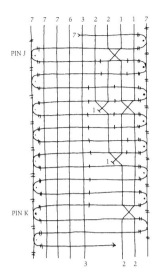

Diagram 13: Patt. 'Lattice 1'(var) after pin J, Section 1

*add 1 pr (no 7) to be 1st p pr from L.
Work 1 row*.
Rep * to * twice more.
All prs should now be (no 7).
(8 prs)

After pin N,
start Lattice 1 patt – (Cls tog, 2 sets of 2 prs), also working, Cls & Tw with 1st p pr from L throughout patt.

Finish at pin O:
join to previously worked braid, (tech 12, td 12).
T O all prs, set aside leaders, R edge pr and 1st p pr from R, these 3 prs to be used for rolled edges.
T B rem prs in a bunch.

Notes for rolled edges
As Version 1.

Section 2
Start at pin #:
using top sewings (tech 12, td 12),
(Note R–L working direction), hang on 10 prs (no 7).
Tw 2 both L and R edge prs.
Cls R–L thro 6 prs, Tw 1 leaders, Cls & Tw 1st p pr from L, and edge st at pin P.

After pin P:
start patt: 'Lattice 1' (Cls tog, 3 sets of 2 prs), also working, Cls & Tw with 1st p pr from L throughout patt.

After pin Q:
change 2nd and 5th patt prs from R (no 7) to (no 6), (tech 28, td 28).
Note After changing prs, remember to Cls patt prs to complete patt.

After pin R:
change 1st patt pr from R (no 7) to (no

5), and change 6th patt pr from R (no 7) to (no 6), (tech 28, td 28).

After pin S:
change 3rd patt pr from R (no 6) to (no 3), and change 5th patt pr from R (no 6) to (no 5), (tech 28, td 28).

After pin T:
change 1st patt pr from R (no 7) to (no 2), change 4th patt pr from R (no 5) to (no 2), and change 6th patt pr from R (no 7) to (no 3), (tech 28, td 28)

After pin U:
change 2nd patt pr from R (no 2) to (no 1), and change 5th patt pr from R (no 3) to (no 2), (tech 28, td 28).

After pin V:
change 1st patt pr from R (no 3) to (no 1), and change 6th patt pr from R (no 6) to (no 2), (tech 28, td 28).

After pin W:
change 5th patt pr from R (no 2) to (no 1), (tech 28, td 28)

After pin X:
T O & T B 6th patt pr from R (no 5) after Cls with 5th patt pr from R (no 1).
(9 prs)
After pin Y:
T O & T B 2nd patt pr from R (no 2) after Cls with 3rd patt pr from R (no 1).
Cont in Cls.
(8 prs)
After pin Z:
add 1 pr (no 6) to be 1st p pr from R.
(9 prs)
Nr: T O & T B 1 pr (no 1).
Nr: add 1 pr (no 7) to be 1st p pr from R.
Nr: T O & T B 1 pr (no 1).
Work 1 row.
(8 prs)
Nr: T O & T B 1 pr (no 1).
Work 1 row.
Nr: T O & T B 1 pr (no 2) and add 1 pr (no 7) to be 1st p pr from R.

After pin A1:
L–R order is
L edge pr	2 x (no 7)
	2 x (no 7)
	2 x (no 6)
	4 x (no 7)
R edge pr	2 x (no 7)
leaders	2 x (no 7)
(7 prs)
Cont in Cls, adding 1 pr (no 7) to be 2nd p pr from R.
Work 1 row.
Nr: add 1 pr (no 7) to be s ps 4 & 5 from R.
(9 prs)
After pin B1:
T O & T B 1 pr (no 6).

Nr: add 1 pr (no 6) to be 4th p pr from R.
Work 1 row.
Nr: add 1 pr (no 6) to be s ps 8 & 9 from R.
(10 prs)
After pin C1:
start Lattice 1 patt, using 6 p prs from L (Cls tog, 3 sets of 2 prs), also working, Cls & tw 1st p pr from R throughout patt.

After pin D1:
change 2nd and 5th patt prs from L (no 7) to (no 5), (tech 28, td 28).

After pin E1:
change 1st and 6th patt prs from L (no 7) to (no 4), (tech 28, td 28).

After pin F1:
change 2nd and 5th patt prs from L (no 5) to (no 6), (tech 28, td 28).

After pin G1:
change 3rd and 4th patt prs from L (no 4) to (no 7), (tech 28, td 28).

After pin H1:
Cls tog patt prs to complete patt, cont in Cls, and T O & T B 2 p prs (no 6).
Nr: *T O & T B 1 p pr (no 6)*.
Nr: rep * to *.
Note All prs are now (no 7).
(6 prs)
Work as far as pin I1:
secure all bobbins in order, and leave to work rolled edge.

Notes for rolled edge
Roll from pin # to pin A1:
rolling thread – 1 x (no 7)
rolled threads – 2 x (no 7)
Add 3 threads (no 7) at pin # (tech 16, td 16).
T B 1 thread 2 pins before pin A1.
Finish at pin A1.

Return to pin I1
After pin I1:
cont in Tenstick, (tech 32, td 32b), working smooth edge at R side, Cls R edge pr with 1st p pr from R, pinned edge is at L side.

Finish at pin J1 and pin K1:
join to previously worked section using top sewings, set aside L edge pr and 1 thread from 1st p pr from L, to use for rolled edge.
T O rem prs in a bunch.

Notes for rolled edge
Roll from pin J1 to pin F1:
rolling thread – 1 x (no 7)
rolled threads – 2 x (no 7)
Use L edge pr and 1 thread from 1st p pr from L for roll.
T B 1 thread at pin G1.
Finish at pin F1.

Section 3

Start at pin #:
using top sewings (tech 12, td 12),
(Note R–L working direction), hang on
7 prs (no 7), and cont in Tenstick,
working smooth edge at R side, pinned
edge is at L side.
(7 prs)

At pin L1:
change to a pinned edge (tech 33, td
33), cont in Cls, adding 1 pr (no 6) to
be 3rd p pr from R.
Work 1 row.
Nr: add 1 pr (no 6) to be s ps 6 & 7 from R.
(9 prs)

After completing blind pin M1:
T O & T B s ps 2 & 3 (no 7) from R.
(8 prs)

After pin N1:
start Lattice 1 patt (Cls tog, 2 sets of 2
prs), change 1st and 4th patt prs (no 7)
to (no 5) from R, working Cls & tw with
1st p pr from L throughout patt.

After pin O1:
change 2nd and 3rd patt prs (no 5) to
(no 3) from R.

After pin P1:
change 1st and 4th patt prs (no 6) to
(no 2) from R.

After pin Q1:
Cls patt prs tog to complete patt, and
T O & T B 2 patt prs (no 2), cont in Cls.
(6 prs)

After pin R1:
T O & T B centre pr (no 3).
Work 1 row.
(5 prs)

To finish at pin S1:
(tech 8, td 8), Cls leaders thro rem p prs
and T O.
Cls & tw edge prs, place pin S1, Cls & T O.
Set aside 3 threads from edge prs to use
for rolled edge.
T B rem prs and secure to back of work
with previously T B prs.

Notes for rolled edge
As Version 1.

M for MELISSA OFFICINALIS

Colours
(no 1)	*White
(no 2)	*Honey
(no 3)	Sycamore
(no 4)	Eau de Nil
(no 5)	*Mauve
(no 6)	*Mahogany
(no 7)	Extra Dark Brown

VERSION 1
Section 1

Start at pin A#:
using a two colour point start (tech 1, td 1), (Note L–R working direction), hang 1 pr (no 7) and 1 pr (no 5) to be edge prs (diag m.1).
Add magic thread (tech 2, td 2a).
L edge pr is now (no 7).
R edge pr is now (no 5).

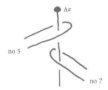

Diagram m1:
Start, Section 1

On T P, hang 1 pr (no 5) to be leaders.
(3 prs)
On T P, hang 1 pr (no 7) and 2 prs (no 6) to be p prs, in L–R order as foll:
2 x (no 7)
4 x (no 6)
Cls leaders L–R thro 3 p prs and edge st at pin B (tech 3, td 3).
(6 prs)
Nr: add 1 pr (no 5) to be 1st p pr from R.
Nr: add 1 pr (no 5) to be s ps 8 & 9 from L.
Nr: add 1 pr (no 5) to be 2nd p pr from R.
Nr add 1 pr (no 5) to be s ps 10 & 11 from L.
(10 prs)
After pin C:
add 1 pr (no 5) to be 3rd p pr from R.
Nr: T O & T B 1st p pr (no 7) from L, and add 1 pr (no 5) to be s ps 6 & 7 from R.
Nr: add 1 pr (no 4) to be 4th p pr from R.
Nr: T O & T B 1st p.r (no 6) from L, and add 1 pr (no 4) to be s ps 8 & 9 from R.
(12 prs)
Nr: add 1 pr (no 3) to be 5th p pr from R, and add 1 pr (no 5) to be s ps 6 & 7 from L.
Nr: T O & T B 1st p pr (no 6) from L, and add 1 pr (no 3) to be s ps 10 & 11 from R.
Nr: add 1 pr (no 2) to be 6th p pr from R, and add 1 pr (no 5) to be 3rd p pr

from L.
Nr: add 1 pr (no 2) to be s ps 16 & 17 from L.
(17 prs)
After pin D:
split braid (tech 5, td 5) thus – work locking st (tech 6, td 6) and leave.
At pin E:
between 10th and 11th p prs from R, hang 2 prs (no 5) open on pin F, to be centre edge prs, Cls to pin F (diag m.2), replacing pin E under leaders for support (not shown in diag m.2). Cls & tw 2 centre edge prs (no 5).
Note Insert magic thread.
(19 prs)

At pin F:
change leaders (no 5) with L edge pr (no 7), (tech 7, td 7).
After pin F:
change leaders (no 7) to (no 5), (tech 4, td 4), cont row, adding 1 pr (no 5) to be 3rd p pr from R, Section 1a.
At pin G:
edge st with L centre edge pr (no 5).
After pin G:
add 1 pr (no 5) to be s ps 6 & 7 from R.
After pin H:
work locking st (tech 6, td 6), secure all bobbins at L side of braid and leave to cont with Section 1.

Return to Section 1
At pin D:

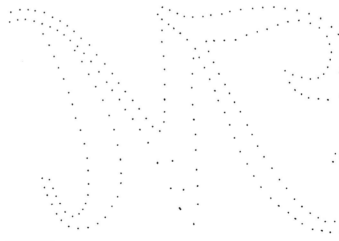

M2: Pricking

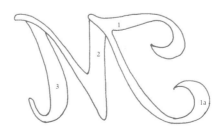

M1: Order of work

add 1 pr (no 2) to be new leaders (diag m.2), (tech 5, td 5), cont row, adding 1 pr (no 1) to be 5th p pr from L.
(14 prs)
At pin I:
edge st with R centre edge pr (no 5).
After pin I:
start patt: Cls 4 p prs, tw 1 leaders, work ½ st with 5th p pr (no 1), Cls rem p prs.
After pin J:
T O & T B 1st p pr (no 5) from R, cont Cls 4 p prs, tw 1 leaders, work ½ st with 5th, 6th and 7th p prs from R, Cls rem p prs.
Nr: cont in patt, working ½ st with 3 p prs.
Nr: T O & T B 1st p pr (no 5) from R, cont in patt.
L–R order should be as foll:

L edge pr	2 x (no 5)
	2 x (no 5)
	2 x (no 4)
	2 x (no 3)
	2 x (no 2)
	2 x (no 1)
	2 x (no 2)
	2 x (no 3)
	2 x (no 4)
	2 x (no 5)
R edge pr	2 x (no 5)
leaders	2 x (no 2)

(12 prs)
After pin K:
Note Patt prs will not have returned to

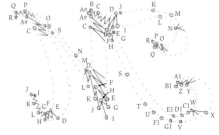

M3: Pin reference plan, Version 1

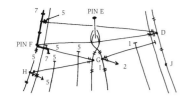

Diagram m2: Splitting a braid, changing leaders and left edge pair, also adding passive pairs

original colour positions.
T O & T B 1 p pr (no 1) from centre,
cont in Cls.
Nr: T O & T B 1 pr (no 2) from centre.
Nr: add 1 pr (no 5) to be s ps 2 & 3
from R, and T O & T B s ps 4 & 5 and
s ps 7 & 8 (no 3/no 4) from L.
(9 prs)
After pin L:
change leaders (no 2) to (no 5), (tech 4,
td 4), cont row, T O & T B 4th p pr (no
3) from R.
Nr: add 1 pr (no 5) to be 2nd p pr from
R, and T O & T B s ps 4 & 5 (no 3/no 4)
from L.
Nr: T O & T B 2nd p pr (no 4) from L.
(7 prs)
After pin M:
add 1 pr (no 4) to be 2nd p pr from R.
Nr: add 1 pr (no 4) to be s ps 8 & 9
from L.
Nr: T O & T B 1st p pr (no 5) from L,
and add 1 pr (no 3) to be s ps 6 & 7
from R.
Nr: add 1 pr (no 2) to be 4th p pr from R.
(11 prs)
After completing blind pin N:
change leaders (no 5) to (no 3), (tech 4,
td 4),
L–R order should now be:

L edge pr	2 x (no 5)
	4 x (no 5)
	2 x (no 4)
	2 x (no 3)
	2 x (no 2)
	2 x (no 3)
	2 x (no 4)
	2 x (no 5)
R edge pr	2 x (no 5)
leaders	2 x (no 3)

(11 prs)
Cont row, starting patt – Cls 3 p prs, tw
1 leaders, work ½ st with 4th p pr
(no 2) from R, Cls rem p prs.
Nr: Cls 2 p prs, tw 1 leaders, work ½ st
with 3rd, 4th and 5th p prs from R, Cls
rem p prs.
Cont in patt, working ½ st with 3 p prs.

After working 1st part of blind pin O:
cont in Cls.
Note Patt prs will not have returned to
their original colour positions.
After completing blind pin O:
change leaders (no 3) to (no 5), (tech 4,
td 4), cont row, T O & T B 3rd and 5th

p prs (no 2/no 3) from R.
Nr: T O & T B 3rd p pr (no 2/no 3) from R.
(8 prs)
After working 1st part of blind pin P:
add 1 pr (no 6) to be 1st p pr from L,
and T O & T B s ps 4 & 5 (no 4) from R.
Nr: add 1 pr (no 6) to be 1st p pr from
R, and T O & T B 4th p pr (no 4) from L.
Nr: T O & T B 2nd and 4th p prs (no 5)
from L.
(6 prs)
After pin Q:
T O & T B 1 pr (no 5) from centre, Cls
tog 2 rem p prs (no 6), (tech 29, td 29),
Cls leaders thro rem p prs,
T O & T B leaders and 2 p prs, and
secure to back of work with previously
T B prs.

Finish at pin R:
Cls & tw edge prs (no 5), place pin R,
Cls & T O edge prs, these 2 prs will be
used for rolled edge.

Notes for rolled edge
Roll from pin R to pin E (tech 9, td 9):
rolling thread – 1 x (no 5)
rolled threads – 3 x (no 5)
Use edge prs from pin R for roll.
T B 1 thread at pin N and pin L (tech
14, td 14).
Finish at pin E, using magic thread (tech
16, td 16a).

Return to Section 1a
After pin H:
undo locking st, cont in Cls, adding 1 pr
(no 4) to centre.
Work 1 row.
(10 prs)
Nr: T O & T B 2nd p pr (no 5) from L,
and add 1 pr (no 4) to be s ps 8 & 9 from R.
Work 1 row.
Nr: T O & T B s ps 2 & 3 (no 5) from L,
and add 1 pr (no 4) to be 5th p pr from R.
Work 1 row.
Nr: add 1 pr (no 3) to be s ps 6 & 7 from L.
(11 prs)
Nr: T O & T B 2nd p pr (no 5) from R.
Nr: add 1 pr (no 3) to be 4th p pr from L.
Nr: T O & T B s ps 2 & 3 (no 5) from L.
Nr: add 1 pr (no 3) to be s ps 8 & 9 from L.
After pin S:
change leaders (no 5) to (no 4), (tech 4,
td 4),
L–R order should be

L edge pr	2 x (no 5)
	2 x (no 5)
	3 x (no 4)
	6 x (no 3)
	3 x (no 4)
	2 x (no 5)
R edge pr	2 x (no 5)
leaders	2 x (no 4)

(11 prs)
Cont row, starting patt – Cls thro 2

p prs, tw 1 leaders,
work ½ st with 4th and 5th p prs (no 3)
from R, Cls rem p prs.
Cont in patt, working ½ st with 2 p prs.
After pin T:
threads will have returned to original
colour positions, change leaders (no 4)
to (no 5), (tech 4, td 4), cont in Cls
After pin U:
add 1 pr (no 5) to be s ps 2 & 3 from L,
and T O & T B s ps 8 & 9 (no 3) from R.
Nr: T O & T B 4th p pr (no 3) from R.
Nr: add 1 pr (no 5) to be 2nd p pr from
L, and T O & T B s ps 6 & 7 (no 3) from R.
Nr: T O & T B 3rd p pr (no 4) from R.
Work 2 rows.
Nr: add 1 pr (no 5) to be s ps 4 & 5
from L, and T O & T B s ps 4 & 5 (no 4)
from R.
Work 2 rows.
Nr: T O & T B 2nd p pr (no 4) from R.
(8 prs)
After pin V:
add 1 pr (no 4) to be 2nd p pr from L.
Nr: T O & T B 2nd p pr (no 5) from R,
and add 1 pr (no 4) to be s ps 4 & 5 from L.
Nr: add 1 pr (no 3) to be 3rd p pr from L.
Nr: T O & T B 2nd p pr (no 5) from R,
and add 1 pr (no 3) to be s ps 6 & 7 from L.
Nr: add 1 pr (no 2) to be 4th p pr from L.
Work 1 row.
Nr: add 1 pr (no 2) to be s ps 8 & 9 from L.
Work 1 row.
Nr: add 1 pr (no 1) to be 5th p pr from L.
(13 prs)
After completing blind pin W:
change leaders (no 5) to (no 2), (tech 4,
td 4).
L–R order should be:

L edge pr	2 x (no 5)
	2 x (no 5)
	2 x (no 4)
	2 x (no 3)
	2 x (no 2)
	2 x (no 1)
	2 x (no 2)
	2 x (no 3)
	2 x (no 4)
	4 x (no 5)
R edge pr	2 x (no 5)
leaders	2 x (no 2)

(13 prs)
After pin X:
start patt: Cls 4 p prs, tw 1 leaders,
work ½ st with 5th p pr (no 1), Cls rem
prs.
Nr: Cls 4 p prs, tw 1 leaders, work ½ st
with 5th, 6th and 7th p prs, Cls rem p prs.
Cont in patt, working ½ st with 3 p prs.

After working 1st part of blind pin Y:
cont in Cls.
Note Patt prs will not have returned to
their original colour positions.
After completing blind pin Y:
change leaders (no 2) to (no 5), (tech 4,
td 4), cont row, T O & T B 5th p pr (no

1) and 7th p pr (no 3) from L.
Nr: T O & T B 3rd p pr (no 3) and 5th
p pr (no 2) from L.
(9 prs)
After working 1st part of blind pin Z:
add 1 pr (no 6) to be 1st p pr from R,
and T O & T B 3rd p pr (no 2) from L.
Nr: add 1 pr (no 6) to be 1st p pr from
L, and T O & T B s ps 8 & 9 (no 4) from R.
After completing blind pin Z:
T O & T B s ps 4 & 5 from R, and 3rd
p pr (no 4) from L.
(7 prs)
After pin A1:
Cls tog 2nd and 3rd p prs (no 5) from L,
T O & T B 2 p prs.
Cls leaders thro 2 rem p prs (no 6), T O
& T B leaders and 2 p prs and secure to
back of work with previously T B prs.
Finish at pin B1:
Cls & tw edge prs, place pin B1, Cls &
T O edge prs, these 2 prs to be used for
rolled edge.

Notes for rolled edges
Roll from pin B1 to pin E1:
rolling thread – 1 x (no 5)
rolled threads – 3 x (no 5)
Use edge prs from pin B1 for roll.
T B 1 thread at pin C1 and pin D1.
Finish at pin E1.
Roll from pin A# to pin V:
rolling thread – 1 x (no 7)
rolled threads – 1 x (no 7), 2 x (no 6)
Using magic thread at pin A#, hang on 1
pr (no 7), and into its loop, 1 pr (no 6).
T B 1 thread (no 6) from roll at pin F1
and pin G1.
Finish at pin V.

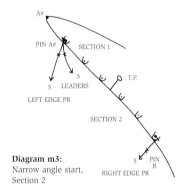

Diagram m3:
Narrow angle start,
Section 2

Section 2
Start at pin A#:
using a narrow angle start (tech 17, td
17), (Note L-R working direction), hang
1 pr (no 5) to be leaders, and into its
loop, 1 pr (no 5) to be L edge pr (diag
m.3), tw 2 both prs.
Hang 1 pr (no 5) to be R edge pr at pin
B, tw 2.
(3 prs)
Hang 11 prs more into Section 1,
using top sewings and/or T Ps, to give

L-R order as foll:
L edge pr   2 x (no 5)
                   4 x (no 5)
                   4 x (no 4)
                   6 x (no 3)
                   4 x (no 4)
                   4 x (no 5)
R edge pr   2 x (no 5)
leaders   2 x (no 5)
(14 prs)
Cls across all p prs, joining to Section 1
with a top sewing, into the L bar at pin B.
Cont in Cls.

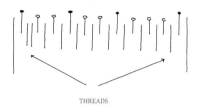

THREADS

Diagram m4: Working into a deep point and creating decorative holes

After pin C:
change leaders (no 5) to (no 4), (tech 4,
td 4), cont row, starting patt, Cls 2
p prs, tw 1 leaders, work ½ st with 4th,
5th, 6th, 7th and 8th p prs from R, Cls
rem p prs.
Cont in patt, working ½ st with 5 p prs.
(14 prs)
After working 1st part of blind pin D:
it will be necessary to work into a deep
point (diag m.4), see also (tech 30, td
30), cont in patt to pin E.
After pin E:
work 7 patt prs, give leaders an extra
tw, place pin F and work in patt to pin G.
After pin G:
work 4 patt prs, give leaders an extra
tw, place pin H and work in patt to pin I.
After pin I:
Cont in Cls.
Note Patt prs will not have returned to
their original colour positions.
Cls 1 p pr, tie ½ knot, (to keep 1st p pr
in position against pin), Cls 3 p prs, tw
2 leaders, remove pin H and replace
under leaders, Cls to pin J.
Note Using support pins will aid correct
tension of p prs, (diag m.4).

After pin J:
Cls 7 p prs to pin F.
At pin F:
tw 2 leaders, remove pin F and replace
under leaders, Cls to pin K.

After pin K:
Cls thro all p prs to pin D.
At pin D:
complete blind pin, and cont in Cls.
After pin L:
adjust tension of p prs to give required
effect of 'decorative holes' between Pin

D and Pin I.
(14 prs)
After pin M:
T O & T B 4th and 8th p prs (no 3/no 4)
from L.
Nr: T O & T B 4th and 6th p prs (no 3/
no 4) from R.
Nr: T O & T B 4th p pr (no 4) from L.
Work 1 row.
Nr: T O & T B s ps 6 & 7 (no 4) from L.
Work 1 row.
(8 prs)
After pin N:
change leaders (no 3/no 4) to (no 5),
(tech 4, td 4), cont row, T O & T B 3rd
p pr (no 4) from R.
(7 prs)
After pin O:
add 1 pr (no 6) to be 1st p pr from R,
and T O & T B 2nd p pr (no 5) from L.
Nr: T O & T B 2nd p pr (no 5) from L.
Work 2 rows.
Nr: add 1 pr (no 7) to be 1st p pr from
R, and T O & T B 2nd p pr (no 5) from L.
(6 prs)
After pin P:
T O & T B 1st p pr (no 5) from L, and
add 1 pr (no 6) to be s ps 4 & 5 from R.

After pin Q:
T O & T B 2nd p pr (no 6) from L, Cls
leaders thro 2 rem p prs, and T O rem 2
p prs and leaders (no 5), T B leaders,
set aside rem 2 p prs.
These 2 p prs will be used for rolled edge.
(4 prs)
Finish at pin R:
Cls & tw both edge prs (no 5), place pin
R, Cls & T O.
T B L edge pr, and secure all T B
threads, to back of work with previously
T B prs.
Place rem R edge pr (no 5) and p pr (no
6), between p pr (no 7), tie a knot to
include them.
These 3 prs will be used for rolled edge.

Notes for rolled edges
Roll from pin R to pin B:
rolling thread – 1 x (no 7)
rolled threads – 1 x (no 7), 2 x (no 6),
2 x (no 5)
Use 3 prs from pin R for rolled edge,
placing lightest threads closest to pinned
edge.
T B 1 thread (no 6) from roll at pin O
and pin S.
At pin I:
work 3 sewings to ease roll around corner.
After 1st sewing, tie tog and T B rolling
thread (no 7) and 1 rolled thread (no 7),
cont, with rolling thread (no 5) taken
from roll, and 1 rolled thread (no 5).
Finish at pin B.

Roll from pin A# to pin D:
rolling thread – 1 x (no 5)

rolled threads – 3 x (no 5)
Hang 1 pr (no 5) into pin A#, and I pr (no 5) into its loop.
Finish at pin D.

Section 3
Start at pin A#:
follow instructions for Section 2, from pin A# to pin C.
Cont in patt, as Section 2.
(14 prs)
After pin D:
cont in Cls.
Note Patt prs will not have returned to their original colour positions.

After pin E:
T O & T B 5th, 7th and 9th p prs (no 3/no 4) from L.
Nr: T O & T B s ps 6 & 7 and 10 & 11 (no 3/no 4) from R.
(9 prs)
After pin F:
change leaders (no 4) to (no 5), (tech 4, td 4), cont row, T O & T B s ps 6 & 7 (no 4) from R.
Nr: T O & T B 3rd p pr (no 4) from R.
(7 prs)
After working 1st part of blind pin G:
T O & T B s ps 4 & 5 (no 5) from L.
(6 prs)
After pin H:
add 1 pr (no 6) to be 1st p pr from R, and T O & T B 2nd p pr (no 5) from L. Work 3 rows.
Nr: add 1 pr (no 7) to be 1st p pr from R, and T O & T B 2nd p pr (no 5) from L. Work 3 rows.
Nr: add 1 pr (no 7) to be 1st p pr from R, and T O & T B 1st p pr (no 5) from L.
(6 prs)
After pin I:
Cls leaders (no 5) thro 3 p prs, T O & T B leaders, T O 3 p prs and set aside, these 3 prs will be used for rolled edge.

Finish at pin J:
Cls & tw edge prs (no 5), place pin J, Cls & T O. T B L edge pr, and secure all T B threads, to back of work with previously T B prs.

Notes for rolled edges
Roll from pin J to pin D:
rolling thread – 1 x (no 7)

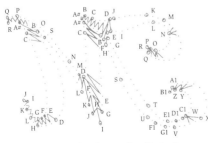

Diagram M4: Pin reference plan, Version 2

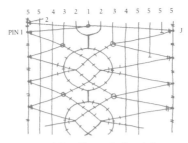

Diagram m5: Patt. 'Crossnet' after pin I

rolled threads – 1 x (no 7), 2 x (no 5)
Use R edge pr (no 5) and 1st p pr (no 7) from R for rolled edge.
Make 1st sewing for roll into pin J.
T B 1 thread (no 5) from roll at pin K and pin L.
Finish at pin D.
Roll from pin I to pin A#:
rolling thread – 1 x (no 7)
rolled threads – 1 x (no 7), 2 x (no 6)
Use 2 p prs (no 6) and (no 7) from pin I for rolled edge.
Finish at pin A#.

VERSION 2
Section 1
Start at pin A#:
follow instructions for Version 1, from pin A# to pin I.
(14 prs)
After pin I:
start Crossnet patt – Cls L–R thro 4 p prs, work T S with leaders (no 2) and 5th p pr (no 1), (diag m.5) cont in patt.
After pin J:
T O & T B 1st p pr (no 5) from R.

After next pin at R edge:
T O & T B 1st p pr (no 5) from R.
(12 prs)
After completing 2 patt reps, work T S with leaders, cont in Cls, working to R edge.
Note Patt prs will not have returned to their original colour positions.
After pin K:
follow instructions for Version 1, T O & T B p prs from centre, lightest prs first where poss, to pin N.
After pin N:
change leaders (no 5) to (no 3), (tech 4, td 4), cont row, start Crossnet patt, working T S with 4th p pr (no 2) from R.
After completing 3 patt reps, work T S with leaders, cont in Cls, working to R edge.
Note As patt prs will not have returned to their original colour positions, it will not be possible to finish with an exact reverse of patt 'Crossnet' start, make adjustments to fit remaining pinholes.
(11 prs)
After completing blind pin O:
follow instructions for Version 1 to finish.

Notes for rolled edge
As Version 1.

Return to Section 1a
Follow instructions for Version 1, from pin H (9 prs) until (10 prs), including 2 p prs (no 3) only, L–R order is now:

L edge pr	2 x (no 5)
	2 x (no 5)
	3 x (no 4)
	4 x (no 3)
	3 x (no 4)
	2 x (no 5)
R edge pr	2 x (no 5)
leaders	2 x (no 5)

(10 prs)
Cont in Cls to pin S.

After pin S:
change leaders (no 5) to (no 4), (tech 4, td 4), cont row, start Crossnet patt, work T S with centre p pr (no 3), cont in patt.
After completing 2 patt reps: work T S in centre with leaders, using a support pin (tech 19, td 19b), cont in Cls, working to R edge at pin T.
After pin T:
change leaders to (no 5), (tech 4, td 4).
Note Patt prs will not have returned to their original colour positions.
After pin U:
follow instructions for Version 1, from pin U.
Note On the row following pin U, add 1 pr (no 5) to be s ps 2 & 3 from L, (11 prs). There will be no need to T O & T B 1 p pr (no 3) to achieve correct no. of p prs.
After pin X:
start Crossnet patt, Cls thro 4 p prs, work T S with 5th p pr (no 1), cont in patt.
After completing 2 patt reps, work T S in centre with leaders, cont in Cls, working to R edge.
Note Patt prs will not have returned to their original colour positions.
After completing blind pin Y:
follow instructions for Version 1 to finish.

Notes for rolled edges
As Version 1.

Section 2
Start at pin A#:
follow instructions for Version 1, from pin A# to pin C.
(14 prs)
After pin C:
change leaders (no 5) to (no 4), (tech 4, td 4), cont row, start Crossnet patt, working T S with centre p pr (no 3), cont in patt.
After completing 3 patt reps:
Note: There is no pin E instruction, in Version 2.

Cont with L side of braid
After working 1st part of blind pin D:

Cls leaders thro 3 p prs, tw 1 leaders, Cls 1 p pr, tw 1 leaders, Cls 1 p pr, tw 1 leaders, place pin F between centre patt.prs, leave to work R side of braid.

Cont with R side of braid
Cls & tw centre patt pr thro 2 p prs, Cls thro 3 p prs, tw 2 leaders, edge st at pin G, place pin H between 3rd and 4th p prs from R, Cls leaders thro 3 p prs, tw 1 leaders, Cls & tw 2 p prs.
Work T S with leaders,
using pin F as a support pin (tech 19, td 19b), tw 1 R leaders, Cls 1 p pr, tw 1 leaders, Cls 1 p pr, tw 1 leaders, Cls 3 p prs to pin I.

After pin I:
cont in Cls, Cls 1 p pr, tie ½ knot, (to keep 1st p pr in position against pin), Cls 3 p prs, tw 2 leaders, remove pin H and replace under leaders, Cls to pin J.

Note Using support pins will aid correct tension of p prs, (diag m.4).
After pin J:
follow instructions for Version 1 to finish.

Notes for rolled edges
As Version 1.

Section 3
Start at pin A#:

follow instructions for Version 2, Section 2, from pin A# to after pin C.
Start Crossnet patt – work T S with centre p pr, cont in patt.
After completing 5 patt reps, work T S with leaders, cont in Cls, working to R edge, pin D.
Note Patt prs will not have returned to their original colour positions.
Cont in Cls to pin E:
follow instructions for Version 1 to finish.

Notes for rolled edges
As Version 1.

N for NUTMEG

Colours
(no 1)	*White
(no 2)	Pastel Pink
(no 3)	*Soft Beige
(no 4)	*Deep Beige
(no 5)	Dark Mulberry
(no 6)	Dark Claret
(no 7)	Extra Dark Brown

VERSION 1
Section 1
Start at pin A#:
using a two colour point start (tech 1, td 1), (Note L–R working direction), hang 1 pr (no 7) and 1 pr (no 5) to be edge prs (diag n.1).
Add magic thread (tech 2, td 2a).

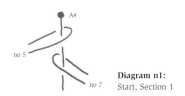

Diagram n1:
Start, Section 1

L edge pr is now (no 7).
R edge pr is now (no 5).

On T P, hang 1 pr (no 5) to be leaders.
(3 prs)
On T P, hang 1 pr (no 7) and 2 prs (no 6) to be p prs, in L–R order as foll:
2 x (no 7)
4 x (no 6)
Cls leaders L–R thro 3 p prs and edge st at pin B (tech 3, td 3).
(6 prs)
Nr: add 1 pr (no 5) to be 1st p pr from R.
Nr: add 1 pr (no 5) to be s ps 8 & 9 from L.
Nr: add 2 prs (no 5) open, to be 2nd

and 3rd p prs from R.
Nr: add 2 prs (no 5) open, to be 6th and 7th p prs from L.
(12 prs)
After pin C:
add 1 pr (no 4) to be 4th p pr from R.
Nr: T O & T B 1st p pr (no 7) from L, and add 1 pr (no 4) to be s ps 8 & 9 from R.
Nr: add 1 pr (no 3) to be 5th p pr from R, and add 1 pr (no 5) to be s ps 8 & 9 from L.
(15 prs)
Nr: T O & T B 1st p pr (no 6) from L, and add 1 pr (no 3) to be s ps 10 & 11 from R.
Nr: add 1 pr (no 2) to be 6th p pr from R, and add 1 pr (no 5) to be 4th p pr from L.
Nr: T O & T B 1st p pr (no 6) from L, and add 1 pr (no 2) to be s ps 12 & 13 from R.
(17 prs)
After pin D:
split braid (tech 5, td 5) thus – work locking st (tech 6, td 6) and leave.
At pin E:
between 10th and 11th p prs from R, hang 2 prs (no 5) open on pin E, to be centre edge prs, Cls to pin F (see 'M', diag m.2), replacing pin E under leaders for support (not shown in 'M',diagram.2). Cls & tw 2 centre edge prs (no 5).
Note Insert magic thread.
(19 prs)
At pin F:
change leaders (no 5) with L edge pr (no 7), (tech 7, td 7).
After pin F:
change leaders (no 7) to (no 5), (tech 4, td 4), cont row, adding 1 pr (no 5) to be 3rd p pr from R, Section 1a.
At pin G:
edge st with L centre edge pr (no 5).
After pin G:
add 1 pr (no 5) to be s ps 6 & 7 from R.

After pin H:
work locking st (tech 6, td 6), secure all bobbins at L side of braid and leave to cont with Section 1.

Return to Section 1
At pin D:
add 1 pr (no 2) to be new leaders (see 'M', diag m.2), (tech 5, td 5), cont row, adding 1 pr (no 1) to be 5th p pr from L.
(14 prs)
At pin I:
edge st with R centre edge pr (no 5).

After pin I:
start patt: Cls 4 p prs, tw 1 leaders, work Cls & tw with 5th p pr (no 1), Cls rem p prs.
After pin J:
T O & T B 1st p pr (no 5) from R, cont in patt.
Nr: cont in patt.
Nr: T O & T B 1st p pr (no 5) from R, cont in patt.
L–R order should be as foll:
L edge pr	2 x (no 5)
	2 x (no 5)
	2 x (no 4)
	2 x (no 3)
	2 x (no 2)
	2 x (no 1)
	2 x (no 2)
	2 x (no 3)
	2 x (no 4)
	2 x (no 5)
R edge pr	2 x (no 5)
leaders	2 x (no 2)
(12 prs)
After pin K:
T O & T B 1 p pr (no 1) from centre, cont in Cls.
Nr: T O & T B 1 pr (no 2) from centre.
Nr: add 1 pr (no 5) to be s ps 2 & 3 from R, and T O & T B s ps 4 & 5 (no 3/no 4) and s ps 7 & 8 (no 2) from L.
(9 prs)

After pin L:

change leaders (no 2) to (no 5), (tech 4, td 4), cont row, T O & T B 4th p pr (no 3) from R.

Nr: add 1 pr (no 5) to be 2nd p pr from R, and T O & T B s ps 4 & 5 (no 3/no 4) from L.

Nr: T O & T B 2nd p pr (no 4) from L.

(7 prs)

After pin M:

add 1 pr (no 4) to be 2nd p pr from R.

Nr: add 1 pr (no 4) to be s ps 8 & 9 from L.

Nr: add 1 pr (no 3) to be 3rd p pr from R.

Nr: T O & T B 1st p pr (no 5) from L, and add 1 pr (no 3) to be s ps 6 & 7 from R.

Nr: add 1 pr (no 2) to be 4th p pr from R.

After completing blind pin N:

change leaders (no 5) to (no 3), (tech 4, td 4),

L–R order should now be:

L edge pr	2 x (no 5)
	4 x (no 5)
	2 x (no 4)
	2 x (no 3)
	2 x (no 2)
	2 x (no 3)
	2 x (no 4)
	2 x (no 5)
R edge pr	2 x (no 5)
leaders	2 x (no 3)

(11 prs)

Cont row, start patt – Cls 3 p prs, tw 1 leaders, work Cls & tw with 4th p pr (no 2) from R, Cls rem p prs.

Cont in patt, Cls & tw 1 p pr.

After working 1st part of blind pin O:
cont in Cls.

After completing blind pin O:

change leaders (no 3) to (no 5), (tech 4, td 4), cont row, T O & T B 3rd and 5th p prs (no 3) from R.

Nr: T O & T B 3rd p pr (no 2) from R.

(8 prs)

After working 1st part of blind pin P:

add 1 pr (no 6) to be 1st p pr from L, and T O & T B s ps 4 & 5 (no 4) from R.

Nr: add 1 pr (no 6) to be 1st p pr from R, and T O & T B 4th p pr (no 4) from L.

Nr: T O & T B 2nd and 4th p prs (no 5) from L.

(6 prs)

After pin Q:

T O & T B 1 pr (no 5) from centre, Cls tog 2 rem p prs (no 6), (tech 29, td 29), Cls leaders thro rem p prs, T O & T B leaders and 2 p prs, and secure to back of work with previously T B prs.

Finish at pin R:

Cls & tw edge prs (no 5), place pin R, Cls & T O edge prs, these 2 prs will be used for rolled edge.

Notes for rolled edge

Roll from pin R to pin E (tech 9, td 9):

rolling thread – 1 x (no 5)

rolled threads – 3 x (no 5)

Use edge prs from pin R for roll.

T B 1 thread at pin N and pin L (tech 14, td 14).

Finish at pin E, using magic thread (tech 16, td 16a).

Return to Section 1a

After pin H:

undo locking st, cont in Cls, adding 1 pr (no 4) to centre.

Work 1 row.

(10 prs)

Nr: T O & T B 2nd p pr (no 5) from L, and add 1 pr (no 4) to be s ps 8 & 9 from R.

Work 1 row.

Nr: T O & T B s ps 2 & 3 (no 5) from L, and add 1 pr (no 4) to be 5th p pr from R.

Work 1 row.

Nr: add 1 pr (no 3) to be s ps 6 & 7 from L.

Nr: T O & T B 2nd p pr (no 5) from R.

Nr: add 1 pr (no 3) to be 4th p pr from L.

Nr: T O & T B s ps 2 & 3 (no 5) from R.

Nr: add 1 pr (no 3) to be s ps 8 & 9 from L.

(11 prs)

After pin S:

change leaders (no 5) to (no 4), (tech 4, td 4), cont in Cls.

After pin T:

change leaders (no 4) to (no 5), (tech 4, td 4), cont in Cls.

After pin U:

add 1 pr (no 5) to be s ps 2 & 3 from L, and T O & T B s ps 8 & 9 (no 3) from R.

Nr: T O & T B 4th p pr (no 3) from R.

Nr: add 1 pr (no 5) to be 2nd p pr from L, and T O & T B s ps 6 & 7 (no 3) from R.

Nr: T O & T B 3rd p pr (no 4) from R.

Work 2 rows.

Nr: add 1 pr (no 5) to be s ps 4 & 5 from L, and T O & T B s ps 4 & 5 (no 4) from R.

Work 2 rows.

Nr: T O & T B 2nd p pr (no 4) from R.

(8 prs)

After pin V:

add 1 pr (no 4) to be 2nd p pr from L.

Nr: T O & T B 2nd p pr (no 5) from R, and add 1 pr (no 4) to be s ps 4 & 5 from L.

Nr: add 1 pr (no 3) to be 3rd p pr from L.

Nr: T O & T B 2nd p pr (no 5) from R, and add 1 pr (no 3) to be s ps 6 & 7 from L.

Nr: add 1 pr (no 2) to be 4th p pr from L.

Nr: add 1 pr (no 2) to be s ps 8 & 9 from R.

Nr: add 1 pr (no 1) to be 5th p pr from L.

After completing blind pin W:

change leaders (no 5) to (no 2), (tech 4, td 4).

L–R order should be as foll:

L edge pr	2 x (no 5)
	2 x (no 5)
	2 x (no 4)
	2 x (no 3)
	2 x (no 2)
	2 x (no 1)
	2 x (no 2)
	2 x (no 3)
	2 x (no 4)
	4 x (no 5)
R edge pr	2 x (no 5)
leaders	2 x (no 2)

(13 prs)

After pin X:

start patt: Cls 4 p prs,

tw 1 leaders,

work Cls & tw with 5th p pr (no 1), Cls rem prs.

Cont in patt, working Cls & tw with 1 p pr.

After working 1st part of blind pin Y:
cont in Cls.

After completing blind pin Y:

change leaders (no 2) to (no 5), (tech 4, td 4), cont row, T O & T B 5th p pr (no 1) and 7th p pr (no 3) from L.

Nr: T O & T B 3rd p pr (no 3) and 5th p pr (no 2) from L.

(9 prs)

After working 1st part of blind pin Z:

add 1 pr (no 6) to be 1st p pr from R, and T O & T B 3rd p pr (no 2) from L.

Nr: add 1 pr (no 6) to be 1st p pr from L, and T O & T B s ps 8 & 9 (no 4) from R.

After completing blind pin Z:

T O & T B s ps 4 & 5 from R, and 3rd p pr (no 4) from L.

(7 prs)

After pin A1:

Cls tog 2nd and 3rd p prs (no 5) from L, T O & T B 2 p prs.

Cls leaders thro 2 rem p prs (no 6), T O & T B leaders and 2 p prs and secure to back of work with previously T B prs.

Finish at pin B1:

Cls & tw edge prs, place pin B1, Cls & T O edge prs, these 2 prs to be used for rolled edge.

Notes for rolled edges

Roll from pin B1 to pin E1:

rolling thread – 1 x (no 5)

rolled threads – 3 x (no 5)

Use edge prs from pin B1 for roll.

T B 1 thread at pin C1 and pin D1.

Finish at pin E1 (tech 10, td 10).

Roll from pin A# to pin V:

rolling thread – 1 x (no 7)

rolled threads – 1 x (no 7), 2 x (no 6)

Using magic thread at pin A#, hang on 1 pr (no 7),

and into its loop, 1 pr (no 6).

T B 1 thread (no 6) from roll at pin F1 and pin G1.

Finish at pin V.

Section 2

Start at pin A#:

using a narrow angle start (tech 17, td 17), (Note L–R working direction), hang 1 pr (no 5) to be leaders, and into its loop, 1 pr (no 5) to be L edge pr (see 'M', diag m.3), tw 2 both prs.

Hang 1 pr (no 5) to be R edge pr at pin B, tw 2.

(3 prs)

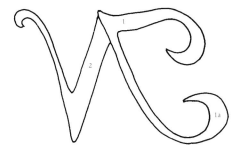

N1: Order of work

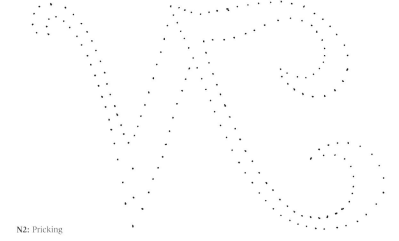

N2: Pricking

Hang 11 prs more into Section 1, using top sewings and/or T Ps, to give L–R order as foll:

L edge pr 2 x (no 5)
4 x (no 5)
4 x (no 4)
6 x (no 3)
4 x (no 4)
4 x (no 5)
R edge pr 2 x (no 5)
leaders 2 x (no 5)
(14 prs)

Cls across all p prs, joining to Section 1 with a top sewing, into the L bar at pin B. Cont in Cls.
After pin C:
change leaders (no 5) to (no 4), (tech 4, td 4), cont row, start patt – Cls 2 p.rs, tw 1 leaders, work Cls & tw with 3rd and 4th p prs (no 4) from L, tw 1 leaders, again, Cls 3 p prs (no 3), tw 2 leaders, work Cls & tw with 3rd and 4th p prs (no 4), Cls rem p prs.
Cont in patt, as before.

After working 1st part of blind pin D:
it will be necessary to work into a deep point (see 'M', diag m.4), see also (tech 30, td 30), cont in patt to pin E.
After pin E:
work 7 patt prs, give leaders an extra tw, place pin F and work in patt to pin G.
After pin G:
work 4 patt prs, give leaders an extra tw, place pin H and work in patt to pin I.
After pin I:
cont in Cls – Cls 1 p pr, tie ½ knot, (to keep 1st p pr in position against pin) Cls 3 p prs, tw 2 leaders, remove pin H and replace under leaders, Cls to pin J.
Note Using support pins will aid correct tension of p prs, (see 'M', diag m.4)
After pin J:
Cls 7 p prs to pin F.
At pin F:
tw 2 leaders, remove pin F and replace under leaders, Cls to pin K.

After pin K:
Cls thro all p prs to pin D.
At pin D:
complete blind pin, cont in Cls.
After pin L:
adjust tension of p prs to give required effect of 'decorative holes' between Pin D and Pin I.
(14 prs)
After pin M:
T O & T B s ps 16 & 7 and s ps 16 & 17 (no 4) from L.
Nr: T O & T B 4th and 6th p prs (no 3) from R.
Nr: T O & T B 4th p pr (no 3) from L.
Work 1 row.
Nr: T O & T B s ps 6 & 7 (no 4) from L.
Work 1 row.
(8 prs)
After pin N:
change leaders (no 4) to (no 5), (tech 4, td 4), cont row, T O & T B 3rd p pr (no 4) from R.
(7 prs)
After pin O:
add 1 pr (no 6) to be 1st p pr from R.
Work 1 row.
Nr: add 1 pr (no 6) to s ps 2 & 3 from R.
Work 1 row.
Nr: add 1 pr (no 7) to be 1st p pr from R, and T O & T B s ps 4 & 5 (no 5) from L.
Work 1 row.
Nr: add 1 pr (no 7) to be s ps 2 & 3 from R, and T O & T B 2nd p pr (no 5) from L.
Work 1 row.
Nr: T O & T B 5th p pr (no 5) from R.
(8 prs)
After pin P:
start patt – tw 1, 1st p pr (no 5) from L, work Cls & tw with 1 p pr, Cls rem prs.
Cont in patt, Cls & tw 1 p pr.

After working 1st part of blind pin Q:
T O & T B 3rd p pr (no 6) from R, cont in Cls.
Nr: T O & T B 1st p pr (no 5) from L.

(6 prs)
After completing blind pin Q:
T O & T B 2nd p pr (no 7) from R.
Nr: Cls leaders (no 5) thro rem 2 p prs (no 6 and no 7) and T O. T O & T B leaders.
(4 prs)
Finish at pin R:
Cls & tw edge prs (no 5), place pin R, Cls & T O. T B L edge pr, and secure to back of work with previously T B prs. Place rem R edge pr (no 5) and T O p pr (no 6) between T O p pr (no 7) and tie knot with p pr (no 7).
These 3 prs to be used for rolled edge.

Notes for rolled edges
Roll from pin R to pin B:
rolling thread – 1 x (no 7)
rolled threads – 1 x (no 7), 2 x (no 6), 2 x (no 5)
Use 3 prs from pin R for rolled edge, placing lightest threads closest to pinned edge.
T B 1 thread (no 6) at pin S and pin O.
At pin I:
work 3 sewings to ease around the corner – after 1st sewing, tie tog and T B rolling thread (no 7) and rolled thread (no 7), cont, with rolling thread (no 5) taken from roll, and 1 rolled thread (no 5).
Finish at pin B.
Roll from pin A# to pin D:
rolling thread – 1 x (no 5)
rolled threads – 3 x (no 5)
Hang 1 pr (no 5) into pin A#, and 1 pr (no 5) into its loop.
Finish at pin D.

VERSION 2
Section 1
Start at pin A#:
follow instructions for Version 1, from pin A# to pin I.
(14 prs)
After pin I:

start Ovals' (var) patt – Cls & tw
throughout with patt prs (no 2), (diag
n.2) cont in patt.
After pin J:
T O & T B 1st p pr (no 5) from R.
After next R pin: T O & T B 1st p pr (no
5) from R.
(12 prs)
After 5 patt reps:
work T S with leaders, cont in Cls,
working to R edge.
After pin K:
follow instructions for Version 1 to after
pin N.
Note When patt sections are complete,
leaders and centre patt pr will have
changed positions, therefore ignore
colour positions in notes for Version 1.
(11 prs)
After pin N:
change leaders (no 5) to (no 3), (tech 4,
td 4), cont row – start Ovals (var) patt,
work T S with 4th p pr (no 2) from R,
cont in patt.
After 5 patt reps: work T S with leaders,
cont in Cls, working to R edge.
After completing blind pin O:
follow instructions for Version 1 to finish.

Notes for rolled edge
As Version 1.

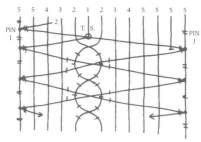

Diagram n2: Patt. 'Ovals' (var)

Return to Section 1a
After pin H:
follow instructions for Version 1 to pin X.
(13 prs)
After pin X:
start Ovals (var) patt – work T S with
5th p pr (no 1) from L, cont in patt.
After 5 patt reps:
work T S with leaders, cont in Cls,
working to L edge.
Note There is no blind pin Y in Version 2.
After pin Y:
change leaders (no 2) to (no 5), (tech 4,
td 4), cont row, T O & T B 5th p pr (no
1) and 7th p pr (no 3) from L. (11 prs)
Cont follow instructions for Version 1 to
finish.

Notes for rolled edges

As Version 1.

Section 2

Start at pin A#:
follow instructions for Version 1, from
pin A# to pin C.
(14 prs)
After pin C:
change leaders (no 5) to (no 4), (tech 4,
td 4), cont row – start Pinwheel (var)
patt, work T S with centre pr.
Cont in patt, Cls crossing of centre patt
prs, there is no T S at centre of
Pinwheel (diag n.3).
Work 3 patt reps (diag n.3):
patt to centre, work T S, cont working
Cls & tw 1 with patt prs, Cls 2 p prs to R
edge.
Nr: Cls & tw 1, 7 patt prs, Cls 2 p prs at
both edges, as in patt.
After working 1st part of blind pin D:
cont Cls & tw patt prs, and Cls 2 p prs
while following instructions for Version
1 to finish.

Notes for rolled edges
As Version 1.

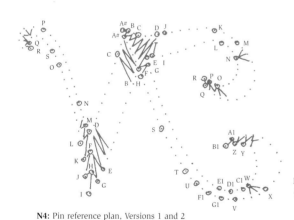

N4: Pin reference plan, Versions 1 and 2

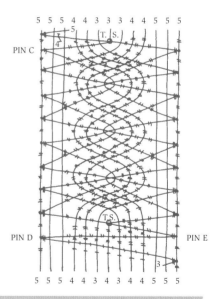

Diagram n3 (right): 'Pinwheel'
(Var) After Pin C

O for ORCHID

Colours
(no 1)   *White
(no 2)   Flesh
(no 3)   Sycamore
(no 4)   *Stone
(no 5)   Pale Lettuce
(no 6)   *Dove
(no 7)   Dark Mulberry

VERSION 1
Section 1

Start at pin A#:
using a one colour point start (tech 23,
td 23), (Note R–L working direction),
hang 2 prs (no 7) open, to be edge prs
(diag o.1).
Add magic thread (tech 2, td 2b).

On T P, hang 1 pr (no 7) to be leaders.
(3 prs)
On T P, add 2 prs (no 7) open, to be p prs.
Cls leaders R–L thro 2 p prs and edge st
(tech 3, td 3).
(5 prs)

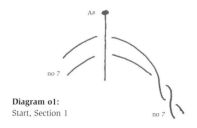

Diagram o1:
Start, Section 1

Nr: add 2 prs (no 6) to be s ps 2, 4, 5
and 7 from L.
Nr: add 2 prs (no 7) to be s ps 2, 3, 10
and 11 from R.
Nr: add 2 prs (no 4) to centre.

Nr: add 2 prs (no 2) to be s ps 8, 10, 11 and 13 from R.
Nr: add 2 prs (no 2) to be s ps 6 & 7 from L.
(15 prs)
After pin B:
start patt: tw 1 leaders between s ps 6 & 7.
Nr: *tw 2 leaders between s ps 6 & 7.
Nr: tw 1 leaders between s ps 4 & 5, 6 & 7 and 8 & 9.
Nr: tw 2 leaders between s ps 4 & 5 and 8 & 9.
Nr: tw 1 leaders between s ps 4 & 5, 6 & 7 and 8 & 9*.
Rep * to * once more.

At pin C:
change L edge pr (tech 34, td 34), add new edge pr (no 5), place pin C, T O & T B old edge pr (no 7), cont rep 1st 3 rows * to *.
After pin D:
add 1 pr (no 5) to be 1st p pr from L.
Note Cont patt in same position as before.
(16 prs)
Nr: tw 1 leaders between s ps 4 & 5 and 8 & 9.
Nr: cont in Cls, *T O & T B 1 pr (no 2) from centre*.
Nr: rep * to *.
Nr: add 1 pr (no 5) to be s ps 2 & 3 from L, and T O & T B 1 pr (no 7) from L and 1 pr (no 2) from centre.
Nr: T O & T B 2 prs (no 2/no 4) from near centre.
(11 prs)
At pin E:
change leaders (no 7) with L edge pr (no 5), (tech 7, td 7).
After pin E:
T O & T B 1 pr (no 4) from centre.
Nr: T O & T B 1 pr (no 6/no 7) from R.
Nr: add 1 pr (no 6) to be 1st p pr from L, and T O & T B 1 pr (no 6/no 7) from R.
Nr: T O & T B 1 pr (no 6/no 7) from R, and add 1 pr (no 4) to be 3rd p pr from L.
Nr: add 1 pr (no 3) to be s ps 6 & 7 from L, and T O & T B 1 pr (no 6/no 7) from R.
Nr: add 1 pr (no 3) to be 4th p pr from L.
Nr: add 1 pr (no 3) to be s ps 8 & 9 from L.
(11 prs)
At pin F:
change leaders (no 5) with R edge pr (no 7), (tech 7, td 7).
After pin F:
T O & T B 1st p pr from R (no 7).
Nr: add 1 pr (no 2) to be 5th p pr from L.
Nr: add 1 pr (no 2) to be s ps 8 & 9 from R.
Work 1 row.
(12 prs)
Cont adding 1 pr (no 1) on next and foll 3 alternate rows,
to give L–R order as foll:
L edge pr   2 x (no 7)
              2 x (no 6)
              2 x (no 5)
              1 x (no 4)
              3 x (no 3)
              2 x (no 2)
              8 x (no 1)
              2 x (no 2)

3 x (no 3)
1 x (no 4)
2 x (no 5)
R edge pr   2 x (no 5)
leaders   2 x (no 7)
(16 prs)
After pin G:
start patt – *tw 1 leaders in centre of 4
p prs (no 1)*.
Nr: rep * to *.
Nr: *tw 2 leaders in centre of 4 p prs
(no 1)*.
Nr: rep * to *.
After pin H:
cont, tw 1 leaders as before.
After pin I:
cont in Cls.
After pin J:
T O & T B 6 p prs, 1 p pr per row,
lightest prs first, from centre.
(10 prs)
*Work 1 row.
Nr: T O & T B 1 p pr (no 3)*.
Rep * to * twice more.
(7 prs)
At pin K:
change leaders (no 7) with R edge pr
(no 5), (tech 7, td 7).
After working 1st part of blind pin L:
T O & T B 1 pr (no 4).
L–R order should be:
L edge pr   2 x (no 7)
                2 x (no 6)
                4 x (no 5)
R edge pr   2 x (no 7)
leaders   2 x (no 5)
(6 prs)
After completing blind pin L:
add 1 pr (no 7), to be 1st p pr from R.
Rep * to * twice more, adding p prs to
centre of (no 7) colour block.
(9 prs)
After pin M:
T O & T B 1 pr (no 5) and rep * to *.
Nr: rep * to *.
After pin N:
T O & T B 1 p pr (no 5) and rep * to *.
Nr: rep * to *.
(11 prs)
At pin O:
change leaders (no 5) with L edge pr

(no 7), (tech 7, td 7).
After pin O:
add 1 pr (no 6) to centre.
L–R order should be:
L edge pr   2 x (no 5)
                         2 x (no 6)
                         6 x (no 7)
                         2 x (no 6)
                         8 x (no 7)
R edge pr   2 x (no 7)
leaders   2 x (no 7)
(12 prs)
Cont, adding 1 pr per row, to centre, in
order:
1 pr   (no 7)
1 pr   (no 6)
1 pr   (no 6)
(15 prs)
Cont, on next and foll alternate rows:
T O & T B 2nd p pr from each side, and
adding 1 pr per row to centre, in order:
1 pr   (no 4)
1 pr   (no 6)
2 prs   (no 4)
6 prs   (no 2)
(15 prs)
After T O & T B 12 p prs:
add 8 prs (no 1), 1 pr per row.
L–R order is as foll:
L edge pr   2 x (no 5)
                         2 x (no 6)
                         2 x (no 4)
                         6 x (no 2)
                        16 x (no 1)
                         6 x (no 2)
                         2 x (no 4)
                         2 x (no 7)
R edge pr   2 x (no 7)
leaders   2 x (no 7)
(21 prs)
After pin P:
add 1 pr (no 5) to be s ps 1 & 3 from L.
Nr: *T O & T B 1 p pr (no 1)*.
Nr: add 1 pr (no 3) to be s ps 5 & 7 from L.
Nr: rep * to *.
Nr: add 1 pr (no 3) to be s ps 9 & 11 from L.
Nr: rep * to *.
Nr: add 1 pr (no 5) to be s ps 1 & 3
from L, and rep * to *.
Cont, T O & T B 1 p pr (no 1) per
row, then 1 p pr (no 2) per row.

(13 prs)
After pin Q:
add 1 pr (no 3) to be s ps 4 & 6 from R,
and T O & T B 1 p pr (no 2).
Nr: *T O & T B 6th p pr from L (no 3/no 2).
Work 1 row*.
Rep * to * once.
(11 prs)
Nr: *T O & T B 1 p pr (no 3/no 4) from lt*.
Rep * to * 3 more times.
(7 prs)
Nr: T O & T B s ps 2 & 3 (no 7/no 6)
from R.
Nr: T O & T B 1st p pr (no 5/no 7) from R.
Work 1 row.
Nr: T O & T B 1st p pr (no 6/no 5) from R.
(4 prs)
Finish at pin R:
Cls leaders (no 7) thro rem p pr (no 5),
T O both prs, T B p pr (no 5).
Cls & tw edge prs, place pin R, Cls &
T O both prs, enclosing leaders in knot
of R edge pr.
T B L edge pr (no 5).
Set aside R edge pr (no 7) and leaders
(no 7) for rolled edge.
T B rem threads and secure to back of
work with previously T B prs.

Notes for rolled edges
Roll from pin R to pin K (tech 9, td 9):
rolling thread – 1 x (no 7)
rolled threads – 3 x (no 7)
Use R edge pr and leaders from pin R
for roll.
T B 1 thread at pin S and pin T (tech
14, td 14).
Finish at pin K (tech 10, td 10).

Roll from pin A# to pin V:
rolling thread – 1 x (no 7)
rolled threads – 2 x (no 7)
Using magic thread at pin A# (tech 16,
td 16a), add 1 pr (no 7), and 1 single
thread (no 7) for roll, (tech 24, td 24).
T B 1 thread at pin U.
Finish at pin V.

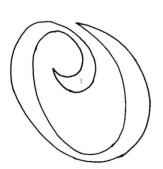

O1: Order of work

O3: Pin reference plan, Version 1

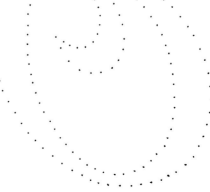

O2: Pricking

VERSION 2
Section 1

Start at pin A#:
Follow instructions for Version 1, from pin A# till (5 prs).

Cont, adding 9 prs, 2 prs per row, to centre in order:
2 prs   (no 6)
2 prs   (no 4)
4 prs   (no 2)
Nr: add 1 pr (no 7).
(14 prs)
After pin B:
start Bubbles (var) patt –work T S with 6th p pr (no 7) from L (diag o.2).

At pin C:
follow instructions for Version 1, to change edge prs.

After pin D:
add 1 pr (no 5) to be 1st p pr from L, and T O & T B centre p pr (no 7).
Work 2 rows.
Nr: T O & T B 1 p pr (no 2) from centre.
Nr: add 1 pr (no 5) to be s ps 2 & 3 from L, and T O & T B 1 p pr (no 2) from centre.
Nr: T O & T B s ps 6 & 7 and 10 & 11 (no 2/no 4).
(11 prs)
At pin E:
change leaders (no 7) with L edge pr

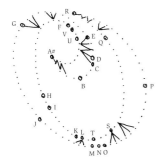

O4: Pin reference plan, Version 2

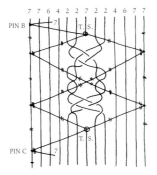

Diagram o2: Patt. 'Bubbles' (var)

(no 5), (tech 7, td 7).
After pin E:
T O & T B 1 centre p pr (no 2).
Nr: T O & T B 3rd p pr (no 4) from R.
Nr: add 1 pr (no 6) to be 1st p pr from L, and T O & T B s ps 4 & 5 (no 6) from R.
Nr: T O & T B 2nd p pr (no 6) from R, and add 1 pr (no 4) to be 3rd p pr from L.
Nr: add 1 pr (no 3) to be s ps 6 & 7 from L, and T O & T B s ps 2 & 3 (no 7) from R.
Nr: add 1 pr (no 3) to be 4th p pr from L.
Nr: add 1 pr (no 3) to be s ps 8 & 9 from L.
(11 prs)

At pin F:
change leaders (no 5) with R edge pr (no 7), (tech 7, td 7).
After pin F:
T O & T B 1st p pr (no 7) from R.
Nr: add 1 pr (no 2) to be 5th p pr from L.
Nr: add 1 pr (no 2) to be s ps 8 & 9 from R.
Work 1 row.
Cont, adding 3 prs (no 1), on next and foll alternate rows.
(15 prs)

After pin G:
(diag o.3), start patt: Cls & tw 7th p pr (no 1) from L.
Work 1 row.
Nr: patt 'Ribbon' with 5th & 6th and 8th

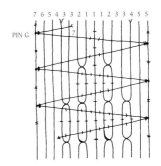

Diagram o3: Patt. 'Ribbon' (var)

& 9th p prs from L.
Work 1 row.
Nr: patt 'Ribbon' with 3rd, 4th, 5th, 6th and 8th, 9th, 10th, 11th p prs from L.
Cont in Ribbon patt and Cls & tw 7th p pr from L.
After pin H:
cont in patt with 5th & 6th and 8th & 9th p prs and Cls & tw p pr only, Cls rem p prs.
Note Patt prs will have returned to their original colour positions.

After pin I:
cont Cls & tw 7th p pr from L only, Cls rem p prs.
Note Patt prs will have returned to their original colour positions.
Work 1 row.
Nr: cont in Cls.
(15 prs)
After pin J:
work 1 row, then follow instructions for Version 1, from pin J, T O & T B 5 p prs from near centre till (10 prs).
Cont following instructions for Version 1, after (10 prs), to finish.

Notes for rolled edges
As Version 1.

P for PRIMULA

Colours

(no 1)	*White
(no 2)	Dark Ivory
(no 3)	*Honey
(no 4)	*Champagne
(no 5)	*Mint
(no 6)	Pale Sage
(no 7)	Dark Sage

VERSION 1
Section 1

Start at pin A#:
using a two colour point start (tech 1, td 1), (Note R–L working direction), hang 1 pr (no 7) and 1 pr (no 6) to be edge prs (diag p.1).
Add magic thread (tech 2, td 2a).
L edge pr is now (no 7).
R edge pr is now (no 6).

On T P, hang 1 pr (no 6) to be leaders.
(3 prs)
On T P, hang 3 prs in L-R order:
4 x (no 7)

Diagram p1:
Start, Section 1

2 x (no 6)
Cls leaders R-L thro 3 p prs and edge st (tech 3, td 3) at pin B.
(6 prs)
After pin B:
add 1 pr (no 6) to be s ps 6 & 7 from L.
Nr: add 1 pr (no 5) to be 2nd p pr from R.

57

Nr: add 1 pr (no 5) to be s ps 8 & 9 from L.
Nr: add 1 pr (no 4) to be 3rd p pr from R.
Nr: add 1 pr (no 5) to be s ps 10 & 11 from L.
Work 2 rows.
L–R order should be:

L edge pr	2 x (no 7)
	4 x (no 7)
	2 x (no 6)
	2 x (no 5)
	1 x (no 4)
	2 x (no 5)
	1 x (no 4)
	2 x (no 5)
	2 x (no 6)
R edge pr	2 x (no 6)
leaders	2 x (no 6)

(11 prs)
After pin C:
change leaders (no 6) to (no 4), (tech 4, td 4).

After pin D:
start patt: *Cls 5 p prs, tw 1 leaders, Cls rem p prs.
Nr: Cls 3 p prs, tw 1 leaders, Cls rem p prs*.
Cont in patt, rep * to *, tw 2 leaders.

After pin E:
rep * to *, tw 1 leaders.
After pin F:
cont in Cls.
At pin G:
change leaders (no 4) with R edge pr (no 6), (tech 7, td 7).

After pin G:
change leaders (no 6) to (no 4), (tech 4, td 4).

After pin H:
add 1 pr (no 4) to be 1st p pr from R, and T O & T B 5th p pr (no 4/no 5) from L.
Work 1 row.
(11 prs)
Nr: add 1 pr (no 4) to be 1st p pr from R, and T O & T B 5th p pr (no 5/no 4)

from L.
Work 1 row.
Nr: add 1 pr (no 3) to be s ps 2 & 3 from R, and T O & T B s ps 8 & 9 (no 5) from L.
Nr: T O & T B 4th p pr (no 5) from L.
(10 prs)
Nr: add 1 pr (no 3) to be 2nd p pr from R, and T O & T B s ps 6 & 7 (no 6) from L.
Nr: T O & T B 3rd p pr (no 6) from L.
Nr: add 1 pr (no 2) to be s ps 4 & 5 from R, and T O & T B s ps 2 & 3 (no 7) from L.
(9 prs)
Nr: start patt – *Cls 4 p prs, tw 1 leaders, Cls rem p prs.
Nr: Cls 2 p prs, tw 1 leaders, Cls rem p prs*.
Cont in patt, rep * to *.

After pin I:
cont in Cls.
Nr: T O & T B s ps 8 & 9 (no 2) from L.
Nr: add 1 pr (no 7) to be s ps 10 & 11 from R.
Nr: T O & T B 5th p pr (no 3) from L.
Nr: add 1 pr (no 7) to be 5th p pr from R.
(9 prs)
Nr: T O & T B s ps 10 & 11 (no 3) from L.
Nr: add 1 pr (no 7) to be s ps 8 & 9 from R.
Nr: T O & T B s ps 10 & 11 (no 4) from L.
Nr: T O & T B 1st pr (no 4) from R.
(7 prs)
After completing blind pin J:
change leaders (no 4) to (no 7), (tech 4, td 4).

At pin K:
change leaders (no 7) with R edge pr (no 4), (tech 7, td 7).

After pin K:
change leaders (no 4) to (no 6), (tech 4, td 4).

After pin L:
change leaders (no 6) to (no 7), (tech 4, td 4).

Finish at pin M:
join to previously worked section.
T O all prs.
Set aside leaders, R edge pr and 1st p pr (no 7) from R, for rolled edge.
T B rem prs in a bunch.

Notes for rolled edges
Roll from pin M to pin K (tech 9, td 9):
rolling thread – 1 x (no 7)
rolled threads – 2 x (no 7)
Use 3 threads from pin M for roll.
T B 1 thread from roll, 2 pins before pin K (tech 14, td 14).
Finish at pin K (tech 10, td 10).

Roll from pin M to pin A#:
rolling thread – 1 x (no 7)
rolled threads – 2 x (no 7)
Use 3 threads from pin M for roll.
T B 1 thread from roll, 2 pins before pin A#.
Finish at pin A#.

Section 2
Start at pin #:
using top sewings (tech 12 , td 12),
(Note R–L working direction), and T Ps, hang on 12 prs.
Order is as foll:

L edge pr	2 x (no 7)
	18 x (no 7)
R edge pr	2 x (no 7)
leaders	2 x (no 7)

(12 prs)
Tw 2 both edge prs, Cls leaders R–L thro p prs, tw 2 leaders and edge st at pin N, (tech 3, td 3).

After pin N:
add 2 prs per row to centre.
L–R order:

L edge pr	2 x (no 7)
	9 x (no 7)
	1 x (no 6)
	1 x (no 5)
	4 x (no 4)
	1 x (no 5)
	1 x (no 6)

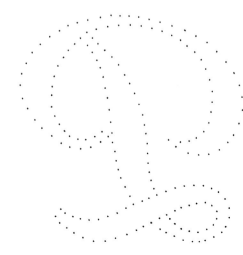

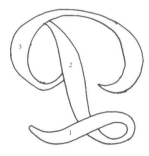

P1: Order of work

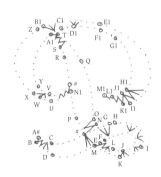

P3: Pin reference plan, Versions 1 & 2

P2: Pricking

9 x (no 7)
R edge pr   2 x (no 7)
leaders   2 x (no 7)
(16 prs)

After pin O:
change leaders (no 7) to (no 4), (tech 4, td 4), cont row, T O & T B 3rd p prs (no 7) from each side, and add 2 prs (no 3) to centre.
Nr: add 1 pr (no 4) to centre, and start patt: Cls 7 p prs, tw 1 leaders, Cls rem p prs.
(17 prs)
Nr: add 2 prs (no 2) to be 7th p prs from each side, tw 2 leaders in centre.
(19 prs)
Nr: T O & T B s ps 4 & 5 (no 7) from each side, tw 3 leaders in centre.
Nr: T O & T B 2nd p prs (no 7) from each side, tw 3 leaders in centre.

After pin P:
cont in patt: Cls 6 p prs, tw 3 leaders, Cls rem 6 p prs.
L–R order is as foll:
L edge pr   2 x (no 7)
    3 x (no 7)
    1 x (no 6)
    1 x (no 5)
    2 x (no 4)
    1 x (no 3)
    2 x (no 2)
    1 x (no 3)
    2 x (no 4)
    1 x (no 3)
    2 x (no 2)
    1 x (no 3)
    2 x (no 4)
    1 x (no 5)
    1 x (no 6)
    3 x (no 7)
R edge pr   2 x (no 7)
leaders   2 x (no 4)
(15 prs)
After pin Q:
tw 2 leaders in centre.
Nr: tw 1 leaders in centre.
Nr: cont in Cls.

After pin R:
T O & T B 2 p prs (no 2).
Work 1 row.
Nr: T O & T B 2 p prs (no 3).
Nr: T O & T B 2 p prs (no 4).
(9 prs)

After pin S:
change leaders (no 4) to (no 7), (tech 4, td 4), cont row, T O & T B 1 p pr (no 4).
Work 1 row.
Nr: T O & T B 1 p pr (no 5).
Work 1 row.
Nr: T O & T B 1 p pr (no 6).

After pin T:
Cls L–R thro all p prs, secure all bobbins in order and leave to work Section 3.

Notes for rolled edge
Roll from pin # to pin S:
rolling thread – 1 x (no 7)
rolled threads – 2 x (no 7)
Add 3 threads at pin # (tech 24, td 24).
Roll to pin S, secure all bobbins and leave to work Section 3.

Section 3

Start at pin #:
using a narrow angle start (tech 17, td 17), (Note L–R working direction), with top sewings (tech 12, td 12), and T Ps, hang on 6 prs.
Order as foll:
L edge pr   2 x (no 7)
    6 x (no 7)
R edge pr   2 x (no 7)
leaders   2 x (no 7)
(6 prs)
Tw 2 both edge prs, cont in Cls.

After pin U:
add 1 pr (no 6) to centre.

After pin V:
change leaders (no 7) to (no 5), (tech 4, td 4).

After pin W:
add 1 pr (no 6) to centre.

After pin X:
add 1 pr (no 5) to centre.
Nr: add 1 pr (no 5) to centre.
Work 1 row.
(10 prs)
After pin Y:
change leaders (no 5) to (no 4), (tech 4, td 4), cont row, adding 1 pr (no 4) to centre.
(11 prs)
Nr: start patt: Cls 4 p prs, tw 1 leaders, Cls rem p prs.
Nr: tw 2 leaders in centre.
Nr: tw 3 leaders in centre.
Cont in patt, tw 3 leaders in centre.

After pin Z:
tw 2 leaders in centre.
Nr: tw 1 leaders in centre.

After pin A1:
cont in Cls.

After pin B1:
T O & T B 1 p pr per row from centre, till 3 p prs rem.
L–R order should be:
L edge pr   2 x (no 7)
    6 x (no 7)
R edge pr   2 x (no 7)
leaders   2 x (no 4)
(6 prs)
After pin C1:
add 1 pr (no 6) to be 1st p pr from L.
Nr: add 1 pr (no 5) to be s ps 2 & 3 from L.

(8 prs)
After completing blind pin D1:
add 1 pr (no 4) to be 2nd p pr from L, and T O & T B 2nd p pr (no 7) from R.
Work 1 row.
Nr: add 1 pr (no 4) to be s ps 4 & 5 from L, and T O & T B s ps 2 & 3 (no 7) from R.
Work 1 row.
Nr: add 1 pr (no 3) to be 3rd p pr from L.
Nr: T O & T B 1st p pr (no 7) from R.
Nr: add 1 p pr (no 3) to be s ps 6 & 7 from L.
(9 prs)
At pin E1:
change leaders (no 4) with R edge pr (no 7), (tech 7, td 7).

After pin E1:
T O & T B 1st p pr (no 6/no 5) from R.
(8 prs)
After pin F1:
change leaders (no 7) to (no 4), (tech 4, td 4).
Nr: add 1 pr (no 2) to be 3rd p pr from R.
Work 1 row.
Nr: add 1 pr (no 2) to be s ps 6 & 7 from R.
Nr: add 1 pr (no 1) to be 5th p pr from L.
Nr: add 1 pr (no 1) to be s ps 8 & 9 from R.
(12 prs)
After pin G1:
start patt: Cls 5 p prs, tw 1 leaders, Cls rem p prs.
Nr: tw 2 leaders.
Nr: tw 3 leaders.
Cont in patt, tw 3 leaders.

After completing blind pin H1:
tw 2 leaders.

After pin I1:
tw 1 leaders.

After pin J1:
cont in Cls.

After pin K1:
T O & T B 1 pr (no 1).
(11 prs)
Nr: T O & T B s ps 6 & 7 and 12 & 13 (no 3/no 2) from L.
Nr: T O & T B 2nd and 4th p prs (no 3/no 2) from R.
(7 prs)
After pin L1:
change leaders (no 4) to no 7), (tech 4, td 4), cont row, T O & T B 1 p pr (no 1).
(6 prs)
Nr: T O & T B 1 p pr (no 4) from centre.
Cls 2 rem p prs, and T O & T B.
T O leaders, T B 1 thread and set aside rem thread for rolled edge.

Finish at pin M1:
Cls & tw edge prs, pin Cls & T O both prs.

T B R edge pr (no 4), and secure to
back of work with previously T B prs.
Set aside L edge pr for rolled edge.

Notes for rolled edges
Roll from pin M1 to pin #:
rolling thread – 1 x (no 7)
rolled threads – 2 x (no 7)
Use 1 thread from leaders and L edge pr
from pin M1 for roll.
T B 1 thread from roll at pin H1.
Add 1 thread (no 7) to roll at pin T.
T O 1 thread from roll at pin Y.
Finish at pin #.

Roll from pin N1 to pin W:
rolling thread – 1 x (no 7)
rolled thread – 2 x (no 7)
Add 3 threads at pin N1, using top
sewings.
T B 1 thread from roll at pin U.
Finish at pin W.

Return to complete Section 2
Cont in Cls.
Join Section 2 to Section 3 using top
sewings.
Complete rolled edge at pin A1.
T O & T B all prs in a bunch (tech 25, td
25).

VERSION 2
Section 1
Start at pin A#:
follow instructions for Version 1, from
pin A# to pin B.

After pin B:
add 1 pr per row.
L–R order as foll:

L edge pr	2 x (no 7)
	4 x (no 7)
	2 x (no 6)
	2 x (no 5)
	4 x (no 4)
	2 x (no 5)
	2 x (no 6)
R edge pr	2 x (no 6)
leaders	2 x (no 6)

(11 prs)
Cont following instructions for Version
1, to pin D.

After pin D:
start Grenades patt (diag p.2) – Cls 3
p prs, work patt with 4th, 5th, 6th and

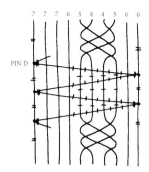

7 7 7 6 5 4 4 5 6 6

PIN D

Diagram p2: Patt. 'Grenades' after pin D

7th p prs from L, Cls rem p pr.
Cont in patt.
Note There is no pin E or pin F in
Version 2.
After 5 patt reps are completed, and patt
prs have returned to their original colour
positions, cont in Cls.

After pin G:
follow instructions for Version 1, to
finish at pin M.
Note Colours will not be exactly as
Version 1, therefore T O & T B prs by
position, not colour.

Notes for rolled edges
As Version 1.

Section 2
Start at pin #:
follow instructions for Version 1, from
pin # until prs have been added after
pin O.
L–R order as foll:

L edge pr	2 x (no 7)
	7 x (no 7)
	1 x (no 6)
	1 x (no 5)
	2 x (no 4)
	4 x (no 3)
	2 x (no 4)
	1 x (no 5)
	1 x (no 6)
	7 x (no 7)
R edge pr	2 x (no 7)
leaders	2 x (no 4)

(16 prs)
Nr: add 2 prs (no 2) to centre, and T O
& T B 2nd p prs (no 7) from each side.
Nr: add 1 pr (no 4) to centre, and T O &
T B s ps 4 & 5 (no 7) from each side.
On the same row, start Grenades patt

(diag p.2):
Cls 4 p prs, patt with 5th, 6th, 7th and
8th p prs from L, Cls rem p prs.

After 5 patt reps are completed, cont in
Cls.
Note There is no pin P or pin Q in
Version 2.

After pin R:
follow instructions for Version 1.
Note Colours will not be exactly as
Version 1, therefore T O & T B prs by
position, not colour.

Notes for rolled edge
As Version 1.

Section 3
Start at pin #:
follow instructions for Version 1, from
pin # to pin Y.

After pin Y:
change leaders (no 5) to (no 4), (tech 4,
td 4), cont row, adding 1 pr (no 4) to
centre, start Grenades patt with 3rd, 4th,
5th and 6th p prs from L.
(11 prs)
Cont in patt, till 5 patt reps are completed.

After pin A1:
cont in Cls, following instructions for
Version 1, to pin G1.

After pin G1:
work 2 rows,
Nr: start Grenades patt with 4th, 5th,
6th and 7th p prs from L.

Cont in patt, till 5 patt reps are completed.
Note There is no pin H1 in Version 2.

After pin I1:
cont in Cls.
Note There is no pin J1 in Version 2.

After pin K1:
follow instructions for Version 1, to
finish at pin M1.

Notes for rolled edges
As Version 1.

Return to Section 2
Follow instructions for Version 1, to
finish at pin A1.

Q for QUINCE

Colours
(no 1)	*Pale Salmon
(no 2)	*Pale Peach
(no 3)	*Rose
(no 4)	*Strawberry
(no 5)	*Hibiscus
(no 6)	*Dark Coral
(no 7)	Dark Cerise

VERSION 1
Section 1
Start at pin A#:
using a one colour point start (tech 23, td 23), (Note R–L working direction), hang 2 prs (no 7) open, to be edge prs (diag q.1).
Add magic thread (tech 2, td 2b).

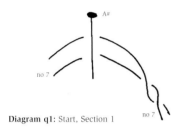

Diagram q1: Start, Section 1

On T P, hang 1 pr (no 7) to be leaders.
(3 prs)
On T P, add 2 prs (no 7) open to be p prs.
Cls leaders R–L thro 2 p prs and edge st (tech 3, td 3).
(5 prs)
Nr: add 1 pr (no 6) to be 1st p pr from L.
Nr: add 1 pr (no 6) to be s ps 2 & 3 from L.
Nr: add 1 pr (no 5) to be 1st p pr from L.
Nr: add 1 pr (no 5) to be s ps 2 & 3 from L.
Work 1 row.
Nr: add 1 pr (no 4) to be 2nd p pr from L.
Nr: add 1 pr (no 4) to be s ps 4 & 5 from L.
After completing blind pin B, L–R order should be:

L edge pr	2 x (no 7)
	2 x (no 5)
	4 x (no 4)
	2 x (no 5)
	4 x (no 6)
	4 x (no 7)
R edge pr	2 x (no 7)
leaders	2 x (no 7)
(11 prs)	

Cont row, adding 1 pr (no 3) to be 3rd p pr from R.

Nr: add 1 pr (no 3) to be s ps 6 & 7 from L, and T O & T B 2nd p pr (no 7) from R.

Nr: add 1 pr (no 1) to be 4th p pr from L.
Nr: add 1 pr (no 1) to be s ps 8 & 9 from L.
Nr: add 1 pr (no 1) to be 5th p pr from L.
(15 prs)
After pin C:
change leaders (no 7) to (no 2), (tech 4, td 4).

After pin D:
start patt: Cls 3 p prs, tw 1 leaders, ½ st 4th, 5th and 6th p prs from L, Cls rem p prs.

Cont in patt, ½ st 3 p prs.

After pin E:
T O & T B 1 p pr (no 6), and cont in patt.

After pin F:
cont in Cls.
Note Patt prs will have returned to their original colour positions.

After pin G:
T O & T B 3 p prs (no 1), 1 pr per row.
(11 prs)
At pin H:
change leaders (no 2) with R edge pr (no 7), (tech 7, td 7).

After pin H:
add 1 pr (no 4) to be 1st p pr from R, and T O & T B s ps 6 & 7 (no 3) from L.
Nr: T O & T B 3rd p pr (no 3) from L.
Nr: add 1 pr (no 3) to be 1st p pr from R, and T O & T B s ps 4 & 5 (no 4) from L.
Nr: T O & T B 2nd p pr (no 4) from L.
(9 prs)
Nr: add 1 pr (no 1) to be 1st p pr from R, and T O & T B 2nd p pr (no 5) from L.
Nr: T O & T B s ps 2 & 3 (no 5/no 6) from L.
Nr: add 1 pr (no 1) to be 1st p pr from R, and T O & T B 1st p pr (no 5/no 6) from L.
(8 prs)
After completing blind pin I:
change leaders (no 7) to (no 1), (tech 4, td 4), cont row, start patt – Cls 3 p prs, tw 1 leaders,
½ st 2 p prs (no 1).
Cont in patt, ½ st 2 p prs.

After pin J:
cont in patt, add 1 pr (no 3) to be 1st p pr from R.
Work 1 row.
Nr: add 1 pr (no 4) to be 1st p pr from R.
Work 1 row.
Nr: add 1 pr (no 5) to be 1st p pr from R.
(11 prs)
After completing blind pin K:
change leaders (no 1) to (no 7), (tech 4, td 4), cont in Cls.
At pin L:
change leaders (no 7) with R edge pr (no 2), (tech 7, td 7).

After pin L:
add 1 pr (no 7) to be 1st p pr from R.
Nr: T O & T B 1 p pr (no 1).

After pin M:
T O & T B 1 p pr (no 1).
(10 prs)
After completing blind pin N:
change leaders (no 2) to (no 7), (tech 4, td 4), cont row, T O & T B 1 p pr (no 3).
Nr: T O & T B 1 p pr (no 3).
Nr: add 1 pr (no 6) to be 2nd p pr from L, and T O & T B 1 p pr (no 4).
Nr: T O & T B 1 p pr (no 4).
Nr: add 1 pr (no 6) to be 2nd p pr from L, and T O & T B 1 p pr (no 5).

L–R order should be:

L edge pr	2 x (no 7)
	2 x (no 7)
	4 x (no 6)
	2 x (no 7)
R edge pr	2 x (no 7)
leaders	2 x (no 7)
(7 prs)	

Cont in Cls to finish at pin O:
join to existing braid using top sewings (tech 12, td 12).
T O all prs.
Set aside R edge pr, leaders and 1st p pr from R (no 7), for rolled edge.
T B rem prs in a bunch (tech 25, td 25).

Notes for rolled edges
Roll from pin O to pin M (tech 9, td 9):
rolling thread – 1 x (no 7)
rolled threads – 2 x (no 7)
Use 3 threads from pin O for roll.
T B 1 thread from roll, 2 pins before pin M (tech 14, td 14).
Finish at pin M (tech 10, td 10).

Roll from pin O to pin A#:
rolling thread – 1 x (no 7)
rolled threads – 2 x (no 7)
Use 3 threads from pin O for roll.
T B 1 thread from roll, 2 pins before pin A#.
Finish at pin A#.

Section 2
Start at pin A#:
using top sewings (tech 12, td 12), (Note L–R working direction), and T Ps, hang on 7 prs.
This gives order:

L edge pr	2 x (no 7)
	2 x (no 7)
	4 x (no 6)
	2 x (no 7)
R edge pr	2 x (no 7)
leaders	2 x (no 7)
(7 prs)	

Tw 2 both edge prs, Cls to pin B.

At pin B:
Note Make a sewing with leaders, do not work edge st at pin B.

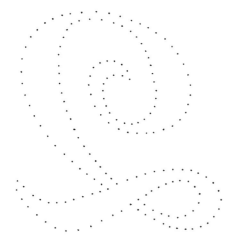

Q1: Order of work

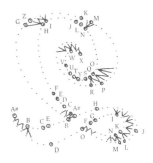

Q3: Pin reference plan, Versions 1 & 2

Q2: Pricking

After pin C:
add 4 p prs, 1 pr per row to centre, in order as foll:

2 prs	(no 4)
1 pr	(no 3)
1 pr	(no 2)
(11 prs)	

After pin D:
T O & T B 1st p pr (no 7) from L, also change leaders (no 7) to (no 6), (tech 4, td 4), cont row, adding 1 pr (no 2) to centre, as before.
Nr: add 1 pr (no 1) to be s ps 10 & 11 from R.
Nr: T O & T B s ps 2 & 3 (no 6/no 5) from L, and add 1 pr (no 1) to be 6th p pr from R.
Nr: T O & T B s ps 4 & 5 (no 6/no 4) from R, and add 1 pr (no 1) to be s ps 8 & 9 from L.
(12 prs)
At pin E:
change leaders (no 6) with L edge pr (no 7), (tech 7, td 7).

After pin E:
change leaders (no 7) to (no 2), (tech 4, td 4).
L–R order should be:

L edge pr	2 x (no 6)
	1 x (no 6)
	1 x (no 4)
	1 x (no 3)
	2 x (no 2)
	6 x (no 1)
	2 x (no 2)
	1 x (no 3)
	1 x (no 4)
	1 x (no 6)
	2 x (no 7)
R edge pr	2 x (no 7)
leaders	2 x (no 2)
(12 prs)	

After pin F:
start patt: Cls 2 p prs, tw 1 leaders, ½ st

3rd, 4th, 5th and 6th p prs from L, Cls rem p prs.
Cont in patt, ½ st 4 p prs.

After pin G:
cont in Cls.
Note Patt prs will have returned to their original colour positions.

After completing blind pin H:
change leaders (no 2) to (no 7), (tech 4, td 4), cont row, T O & T B s ps 10 & 11 from R.
(11 prs)
Nr: T O & T B 5th p pr (no 1) from R.
Nr: T O & T B s ps 6 & 7 (no 1) from L.
Nr: T O & T B 4th p pr (no 2) from R.
(8 prs)
After completing blind pin I:
change leaders (no 7) with L edge pr (no 6), (tech 7, td 7), then change leaders (no 6) to (no 7), (tech 4, td 4), cont row, T O & T B 1 p pr (no 2).
(7 prs)
Nr: add 1 pr (no 5) to be 1st p pr from R, and T O & T B 2nd p pr (no 3) from L.
Work 1 row.
Nr: add 1 pr (no 5) to be s ps 2 & 3 from R, and
T O & T B 1 p pr (no 4).
Work 1 row.
Nr: add 1 pr (no 4) to be 2nd p pr from R.
Nr: T O & T B 1st p pr (no 6) from L, and add 1 pr (no 3) to be s ps 4 & 5 from R.
(8 prs)
After pin J:
change leaders (no 7) to (no 1), (tech 4, td 4), cont row, adding 1 pr (no 3) to be 4th p pr from L.
(9 prs)
At pin K:
change leaders (no 1) with R edge pr (no 7), (tech 7, td 7).

After pin K:
add 1 pr (no 1) to be s ps 6 & 7 from R.
(10 prs)
After pin L:
change leaders (no 7) to (no 1), (tech 4, td 4), cont row, adding 1 pr (no 1) to be 5th p pr from L.

Nr: add 1 pr (no 1) to be s ps 8 & 9 from R.
(12 prs)
After pin M:
T O & T B 1st p pr (no 5) from R.

After completing blind pin N:
start patt – Cls 3 p prs, tw 1 leaders, ½ st 4th, 5th, 6th and 7th p prs from L, Cls rem p prs.

Cont in patt, ½ st 4 p prs.

After pin O:
cont in Cls.
Note Patt prs will have returned to their original colour positions.

After pin P:
T O & T B 1 p pr (no 1).
Nr: T O & T B 1 p pr (no 1).
Nr: T O & T B 1 p pr (no 1).
(8 prs)
After pin Q:
change leaders (no 1) to (no 7), (tech 4, td 4).

At pin R:
change leaders (no 7) with R edge pr (no 1), (tech 7, td 7).
After pin S:
change leaders (no 1) to (no 6), (tech 4, td 4).
After pin T:
add 1 pr (no 7) to be s ps 2 & 3 from L, and T O & T B 2nd p pr (no 3) from R.
Nr: T O & T B 1 pr (no 3), and add 1 pr (no 6) to be 2nd p pr from L.

At pin U:
change leaders (no 6) with L edge pr (no 7), (tech 7, td 7).

After pin U:
change leaders (no 7) to (no 6), (tech 4, td 4), cont row, adding 1 pr (no 5) to be s ps 4 & 5 from L.
(9 prs)
Nr: T O & T B 1st p pr (no 4) from R, and add 1 pr (no 4) to be 3rd p pr from L.
Nr: add 1 pr (no 4) to be s ps 6 & 7 from L, and T O & T B 1 p pr (no 5) from R.

After pin V:
start patt – Cls 2 p prs, tw 1 leaders,
½ st 2 p prs (no 4), Cls rem p prs.

Cont in patt, ½ st 2 p prs.

After working 1st part of blind pin W:
cont in Cls.
Note: Patt prs will have returned to their
original colour positions.
Nr: T O & T B 1 p pr (no 4) from centre.
Nr: T O & T B 1 p pr (no 4) from centre.
Nr: T O & T B 1 p pr (no 5) from centre.
Nr: T O & T B 1 p pr (no 6) from centre.
Work 2 rows.
(5 prs)
To finish at pin X:
Cls leaders thro rem 2 p prs, and T O &
T B prs.
Cls & tw edge prs tog, place pin X, Cls &
T O.
T B 1 thread (no 7) from R edge pr.
Set aside L edge pr (no 6) and 1 thread
from R edge pr (no 7) for rolled edge.
T B rem threads and secure to back of
work with previously T B prs.

Notes for rolled edges
Roll from pin X to pin Y:
rolling thread – 1 x (no 6)
rolled threads – 1 x (no 7), 1 x (no 6)
Use L edge pr and 1 thread from R edge
pr at pin X for roll.
T B 1 thread (no 6) from roll at pin U.
Finish at pin Y.

Roll from pin B to pin Z:
rolling thread – 1 x (no 7)
rolled threads – 2 x (no 7)
Add 3 threads at pin B (tech 24, td 24)
for roll.
T B 1 thread from roll 2 pins before pin Z.
Finish at pin Z.

VERSION 2
Section 1
Start at pin A#:
follow instructions for Version 1, from
pin A# to pin D.
(15 prs)
After pin D:
T O & T B 1 p pr (no 6).
(14 prs)
After pin E:
start Figure-of-Eight 3 (var) patt – Cls 4
p prs, work T S with 5th p pr (no 1),

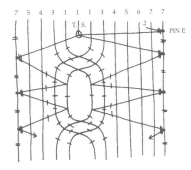

7 5 4 3 1 1 1 3 4 5 6 7 7 T. S. 2 PIN E

Diagram q2: Patt. 'Figure-of-eight' (var)
after pin E

work patt with 2 p prs (no 1) and 2
p prs (no 3), (diag q.2).
Work 3 patt reps.

After pin F:
work T S in centre of patt prs, cont in
Cls working to L.

After pin G:
follow instructions for Version 1 to
finish at pin O.

Notes for rolled edges
As Version 1.

Section 2
Start at pin A#:
follow instructions for Version 1, from
pin A# to pin F.
Note After pin D, add 2 prs (no 1) only.
(11 prs)
After pin F:
Start Figure-of-Eight 3 (var) patt – Cls 3
p prs, work T S with 4th p pr (no 1),
work patt with 1 p pr (no 1), 2 p prs
(no 2) and 1 p pr (no 3).
Note There is no pin G or pin I in
Version 2.

Work 6 patt reps.
Note Patt prs will not have returned to
their original colour positions.

Work T S in centre of patt prs.
Cont in Cls, working to R.

After completing blind pin H:
change leaders (no 1) to (no 7), (tech 4,
td 4), cont row
T O & T B 3rd p pr (no 2/no 1) from R.
Nr: T O & T B 2nd p pr (no 1/no 2)

from L.
Nr: T O & T B 3rd p pr (no 2) from L.
Nr: T O & T B s ps 6 & 7 (no 3) from R.
(7 prs)
After completing blind pin I:
change leaders (no 7) with L edge pr
(no 6), (tech 7, td 7), then change
leaders (no 6) to (no 7), (tech 4, td 4),
cont row, T O & T B 1 p pr (no 2), and
add 1 pr (no 5) to be 1st p pr at R edge.
Work 1 row.
(7 prs)
Nr: T O & T B 1 p pr (no 4), and
add 1 pr (no 5) to be s ps 2 & 3 from R.
Work 1 row.
Nr: add 1 pr (no 4) to be 2nd p pr from R.
Work 1 row.
Nr: T O & T B 1st p pr from L (no 6),
and add 1 pr (no 3) to be s ps 4 & 5
from R.
L–R order should be:

L edge pr	2 x (no 7)
	2 x (no 7)
	2 x (no 5)
	1 x (no 4)
	2 x (no 3)
	1 x (no 4)
	2 x (no 5)
R edge pr	2 x (no 7)
leaders	2 x (no 7)

(8 prs)
After pin J:
follow instructions for Version 1 to pin M.

After pin M:
add 1 pr (no 1) to be 6th p pr from L,
and T O & T B 1st p pr (no 5) from R.

After completing blind pin N:
start Figure-of-Eight 3 (var) patt – Cls 5
p prs, work T S with 6th p pr (no 1),
work patt with 3 p prs (no 1) and 1 p pr
(no 3).
Work 5 patt reps.
Work T S in centre of patt prs.
Cont in Cls, working to R.

After completing blind pin O:
T O & T B 6th p pr (no 1) from L.
(11 prs)

After pin P:
follow instructions for Version 1 to
finish at pin X.

Notes for rolled edges
As Version 1.

R for RHODODENDRON

Colours

(no 1)	Pastel Pink
(no 2)	*Rose
(no 3)	*Strawberry
(no 4)	*Hibiscus
(no 5)	Pale Magenta
(no 6)	Dark Mauve
(no 7)	Mid Purple

VERSION 1

Section 1

Start at pin A#:
using a two colour point start (tech 1, td 1), (Note L–R working direction), hang 1 pr (no 7) and 1 pr (no 6) to be edge prs (diag r.1).
Add magic thread (tech 2, td 2a).
L edge pr is now (no 7).
R edge pr is now (no 6).

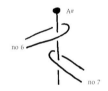

Diagram r1:
Start, Section 1

On T P, hang 1 pr (no 6) to be leaders.
(3 prs)
On T P, hang 2 prs in order L–R:
1 pr (no 7) and 1 pr (no 6).
Cls leaders L–R thro 2 p prs and edge st at pin B (tech 3, td 3)
(5 prs)
Nr: add 1 pr (no 6) to be s ps 2 & 3 from R.
Nr: add 1 pr (no 5) to be 3rd p pr from L.
Nr: add 1 pr (no 4) to be s ps 4 & 5 from R.
Nr: add 1 pr (no 3) to be 4th p pr from L.
Nr: add 1 pr (no 2) to be s ps 6 & 7 from R.
Nr: add 1 pr (no 1) to be 5th p pr from L.
Work 1 row.
L–R order is now:

L edge pr	2 x (no 7)
	2 x (no 7)
	2 x (no 6)
	1 x (no 5)
	1 x (no 4)
	1 x (no 3)
	1 x (no 2)
	2 x (no 1)
	1 x (no 2)
	1 x (no 3)
	1 x (no 4)
	1 x (no 5)
	2 x (no 6)
R edge pr	2 x (no 6)
leaders	2 x (no 6)

(11 prs)
After completing blind pin C:
start patt – Cls thro 4 p prs, tw 1 leaders, work Cls & tw with 5th p pr (no 1) from L, Cls rem p prs.

Nr: Cls thro 2 p prs, tw 1 leaders, work Cls & tw with 3rd, 4th and 5th p prs from L, Cls rem p prs.
Cont in patt, Cls & tw 3 p prs.

After pin D:
rearrange threads (by untwisting), to return to original colour positions, cont in Cls
Nr: T O & T B 1 p pr (no 1) from centre.
Nr: T O & T B 1 p pr (no 2) from centre.
Nr: add 1 pr (no 7) to be s ps 2 & 3 from L, and T O & T B 1 p pr (no 3).
Nr: T O & T B 1 p pr (no 4), and add 1 pr (no 7) to be 2nd p pr from L.
Nr: add 1 pr (no 7) to be s ps 4 & 5 from L, and T O & T B 1 p pr (no 5).
Nr: T O & T B s ps 2 & 3 (no 6) from R, and add 1 pr (no 6) to be 1st p pr from L.
(9 prs)

At pin E:
change leaders (no 6) with L edge pr (no 7), (tech 7, td 7).
After pin E:
add 1 pr (no 6) to be s ps 2 & 3 from L.
(10 prs)

At pin F:
change leaders (no 7) with R edge pr (no 6), (tech 7, td 7).
After pin F:
T O & T B 1 p pr (no 6) from R, and add 1 pr (no 5) to be 2nd p pr from L.
Work 1 row.
Nr: add 1 pr (no 4) to be s ps 12 & 13 from R.
Nr: add 1 pr (no 3) to be 3rd p pr from L.
Nr: T O & T B 3rd p pr (no 7) from R, and add 1 pr (no 2) to be s ps 6 & 7 from L.
(12 prs)
Nr: add 1 pr (no 2) to be 4th p pr from L.
Nr: T O & T B s ps 4 & 5 (no 7) from R, and add 1 pr (no 1) to be s ps 8 & 9 from L.
Nr: add 1 pr (no 1) to be 5th p pr from L.
Nr: T O & T B 2nd p pr (no 7) from R.
(13 prs)

After completing blind pin G:
start patt – Cls thro 3 p prs, tw 1 leaders, work Cls & tw with 4th, 5th and 6th p prs from L, Cls rem p prs.
Cont in patt, Cls & tw 3 p prs.
After pin H:
cont in Cls.

After pin I:
T O & T B 1 p pr per row, lightest prs first, till 6 prs rem.
Secure all bobbins in order and leave

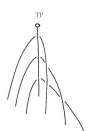

Diagram r2:
Staggered start, Section 2a

leaders, at L side of braid, to work Section 2.
Note Do not work edge st.

Notes for rolled edges

Roll from pin A# to pin E (tech 9, td 9):
rolling thread – 1 x (no 7)
rolled threads – 2 x (no 7)
Add 3 threads at pin A# for roll (tech 24, td 24).
T B 1 thread from roll 2 pins before pin E (tech 14, td 14).
Finish at pin E (tech 10, td 10).

Roll from pin F to pin I:
rolling thread – 1 x (no 7)
rolled threads – 1 x (no 7)
Using top sewing (tech 12, td 12) add 1 pr at pin F, work 2 pins, then add 1 thread (no 7) to roll.
At pin I, secure threads and leave.
Note Roll will be completed after Section 1 is joined to Section 2.

Section 2

Start at pin A#:
follow instructions for Version 1, from pin A# to pin D.
Note: R–L working direction.
(11 prs)
After pin D:
rearrange threads, to return to original colour positions, cont in Cls.

After pin E:
T O & T B 1 p pr (no 1).
(10 prs)
After pin F:
T O & T B 1 p pr (no 2).
Nr: T O & T B 1 p pr (no 3).
Nr: T O & T B 1 p pr (no 4).
Work 1 row.
Nr: T O & T B 1 p pr (no 5).
(6 prs)
After pin G:
add 1 pr (no 7) to be 1st p pr from L.
Work 1 row.
Nr: add 1 pr (no 7) to be s ps 2 & 3 from L.
(8 prs)
After pin H:
add 1 pr (no 5) to be 4th p pr from L.
Work 1 row.
Nr: add 1 pr (no 5) to be s ps 8 & 9 from L.
(10 prs)
After completing blind pin I:
add 1 pr (no 4) to be 4th p pr from R.

Nr: add 1 pr (no 4) to be s ps 10 & 11 from L.
Nr: add 1 pr (no 3) to be 5th p pr from R.
(13 prs)
After pin J:
start patt – Cls thro 5 p prs, tw 1 leaders, work Cls & tw with 6th p pr (no 3) from L, Cls rem prs.
Nr: Cls thro 3 p prs, tw 1 leaders, work Cls & tw with 4th, 5th and 6th p prs, Cls rem p prs.
Cont in patt, Cls & tw 3 p prs.
At pin K:
leave to complete Section 1.

Return to Section 1
Join to Section 2 at pin J and pin K, using top sewings, and complete rolled edge to finish at pin J.

Return to Section 2
After pin K:
cont in Cls.

After pin L:
T O & T B 1 p pr (no 3).
Nr: T O & T B 1 p pr (no 4).
Nr: T O & T B 1 p pr (no 4).
Nr: T O & T B 1 p pr (no 5).
(9 prs)
After pin M:
work locking st (tech 6, td 6), and leave to work Section 2a.

Section 2a
Start at pin A#:
follow instructions for Version 1, from pin A# till 3 prs.
Note: R–L working direction.

On T P, add 3 prs (no 7) staggered (diag r.2), to be p prs (tech 35, td 35).
Cls leaders R–L thro 3 p prs, and edge st

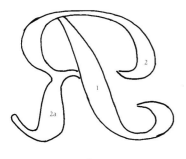

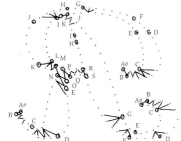

at pin B.
(6 prs)
Nr: add 1 pr (no 6) to be 2nd p pr from L.
(7 prs)
After pin C:
add 1 pr (no 6) to be s ps 6 & 7 from R.
Work 1 row.
Nr: add 1 pr (no 5) to be 4th p pr from R.
Work 1 row.
Nr: add 1 pr (no 5) to be s ps 8 & 9 from R.
Nr: add 1 pr (no 4) to be 4th p pr from L.
Nr: add 1 pr (no 4) to be s ps 10 & 11 from R.
Work 1 row.
Nr: add 1 pr (no 3) to be 5th p pr from L.
(13 prs)
After pin D:
start patt – Cls thro 4 p prs, tw 1 leaders, work Cls & tw with 5th p pr (no 3) from L, Cls rem p prs.
Nr: Cls thro 4 p prs, tw 1 leaders, work Cls & tw with 5th, 6th and 7th p prs, Cls rem p prs.
Cont in patt, Cls & tw 3 p prs.
After pin E:
cont in Cls across all p prs, do not tw leaders, do not work edge st, and leave.

Return to Section 2

Undo locking st after pin M, and Cls across all p prs, do not tw leaders, do not work edge st.

Join Sections 2 and 2a

Work Cls & tw 2 with both edge prs (tech 22, td 22), place pin N, Cls leaders thro respective edge prs, work T S, removing and replacing pin N as a support pin, cont working to L, pin O.
(22 prs)

After pin O:
T O & T B 5 p prs, on one row, as foll:
s ps 6 & 7 (no 5/no 4),

R1: Order of work

s ps 9 & 10 (no 3),
s ps 12 & 13 (no 4/no 5),
s ps 33 & 34 (no 5), and
s ps 36 & 37 (no 6/no 7) from L.
(17 prs)
After pin P:
T O & T B 4 p prs, on one row, as foll:
s ps 4 & 5 (no 6/no 7),
s ps 9 & 10 (no 6),
s ps 13 & 14 (no 6), and
s ps 22 & 23 (no 4) from R.
(13 prs)
After pin Q:
T O & T B s ps 5 & 6 (no 5) and s ps 13 & 14 (no 6) from L.
Nr: T O & T B 1 pr (no 6) near lt*.
Nr: rep * to *.
Nr: T O & T B 1 pr (no 7) from centre.
(8 prs)
At pin R and pin S:
join to Section 1, using top sewings (tech 12, td 12).
T O all prs, set aside L edge pr (no 7), and 1 thread (no 7) for rolled edge.
T B rem prs in a bunch.

Notes for rolled edges
Roll from pin S to pin A#, Section 2a:
rolling thread – 1 x (no 7)
rolled threads – 2 x (no 7)
Use 3 threads from pin S for roll.
T B 1 thread from roll at pin B.
Finish at pin A#.

Roll from pin A# to pin E, Section 2:
rolling thread – 1 x (no 7)
rolled threads – 2 x (no 7)
Hang 3 threads from pin A# (tech 24, td 24).
T B 1 thread from roll at pin C.
Finish at pin E.

VERSION 2
Section 1
Start at pin A#:

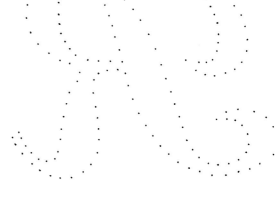

R3: Pin reference
plan, Version 1

R2: Pricking

follow instructions for Version 1, from pin
A# to pin B.
(5 prs)
After pin B:
add 7 p prs to centre, 1 pr per row, in order
as foll:
1 pr (no 6)
1 pr (no 5)
1 pr (no 4)
1 pr (no 3)
1 pr (no 2)
1 pr (no 1)
1 pr (no 6)
(12 prs)
After completing blind pin C:
start Maltese spot (var) patt, (diag r.3) –
work T S with centre p pr (no 6).
After pin D:
complete patt after crossing 4 centre patt prs
(diag r.3), work T S, cont in Cls working to R.

After completing blind pin E:
T O & T B s ps 7 & 8 (no 2/no 1) from L.
Nr: T O & T B s ps 7 & 8 (no 2/no 1) from R.
Nr: T O & T B s ps 5 & 6 (no 4/no 3) from L.
Nr: T O & T B s ps 5 & 6 (no 4/no 3) from R.
Nr: add 1 pr (no 6) to be 1st p pr from L,
and T O & T B s ps 7 & 8 (no 6/no 5) from R.
Nr: T O & T B s ps 3 & 4 (no 6/no 5) from
R, and add 1 pr (no 6) to be s ps 2 & 3 from L.
(8 prs)
At pin F:
change leaders (no 6) with L edge pr (no 7),
(tech 7, td 7).
After pin F:
add 1 pr (no 6) to be 2nd p pr from L.
(9 prs)
At pin G:
change leaders (no 7) with R edge pr (no 6),
(tech 7, td 7).
After pin G:
T O & T B s ps 2 & 3 (no 6) from R, and add
1 pr (no 5) to be s ps 4 & 5 from L.
Nr: add 1 pr (no 4) to be 3rd p pr from L.
and add 1 pr (no 7) to be s ps 4 & 5 from R.
Nr: T O & T B 1 p pr (no 6) from R, and add
1 pr (no 3) to be s ps 6 & 7 from L.
Nr: add 1 pr (no 2) to be 4th p pr from L.
Nr: add 1 pr (no 1) to be s ps 12 & 13 from R.
Nr: add 1 pr (no 6) to be 5th p pr from L.
(14 prs)
After pin N:

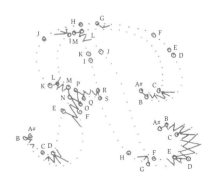

R4: Pin reference plan, Version 2

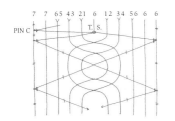

Diagram r1: Patt. 'Maltese Spot'(var) after pin C

start Maltese Spot (var) patt – work T S with 7th p pr (no 6).
Nr: patt 3rd, 4th, 5th and 6th p prs from L edge.
Note Tw 2 leaders in patt.

After pin I and pin J:
complete patt after crossing 4 centre patt prs, to return patt prs to their original colour positions, work T S, cont in Cls working to R.
After pin K:
T O & T B 6th and 8th p prs (no 1/no 2) from R.
(12 prs)
Nr: T O & T B 3rd & 5th p prs (no 3/no 4) from L.
Nr: T O & T B 4th & 6th p prs (no 5/no 6) from R.
Nr: T O & T B 2nd p pr (no 6) from L.
Nr: T O & T B s ps 6 & 7 (no 6) from R.
(6 prs)
Work 2 rows.
Secure all bobbins in order and leave leaders, at L side of braid, to work Section 2.
Note Do not work edge st.

Notes for rolled edges
As Version 1.

Section 2
Start at pin A#:
follow instructions for Version 1, from pin A# to pin D.
Note R–L working direction.
After 1st working blind pin C: work T S to start patt.

(12 prs)
After pin D:
complete patt after crossing 4 centre patt prs, work T S, cont in Cls, working to L.

After pin E:
T O & T B 7th p pr (no 2/no 1) from L.
Work 1 row.
Nr: T O & T B 3rd p pr (no 2/no 1) from L.
(10 prs)

After pin F:
T O & T B 5th p pr (no 4/no 3) from L.
Work 1 row.
Nr: T O & T B 3rd p pr (no 4/no 3) from L.
Nr: T O & T B 2nd p pr (no 6/no 5) from R.
Nr: T O & T B 2nd p pr (no 6/no 5) from L.
(6 prs)

After pin G:
follow instructions for Version 1, from pin G to pin H.
(8 prs)

After pin H:
add 1 pr (no 5) to be 4th p pr from L.
Work 1 row.
Nr: add 1 pr (no 5) to be s ps 8 & 9 from L.
(10 prs)
After completing blind pin I:
add 1 pr (no 4) to be 4th p pr from R.
Nr: add 1 pr (no 3) to be s ps (10 & 11) from L.
Nr: add 1 pr (no 6) to be 5th p pr from R.
(13 prs)

After pin J:
start Maltese Spot (var) patt – work T S with 6th p pr from L.
Nr: patt 4th, 5th, 6th and 7th p prs from L.
Note Tw 1 leaders in patt.
After pin K:
work T S at pin L.
After pin L:
cont in Cls working to L.
Leave to complete Section 1.

Return to Section 1
Join to Section 2 at pin L and pin M:
using top sewings, and complete rolled edge to finish at pin M.

Return to Section 2
Cont, T O & T B 5th and 7th p prs (no 3/no 4) from L.
Nr: T O & T B 3rd p pr (no 5) from R.
Nr: T O & T B 4th p pr (no 5) from L.
(9 prs)
After pin M:
work locking st (tech 6, td 6), and leave to work Section 2a.

Section 2a
Start at pin A#:
follow instructions for Version 1, from pin A# to pin D.
Note R–L working direction.
Only 1 p pr (no 4) is added, followed by 1 p pr (no 3), work 1 row, then add 1 p pr (no 6) to be 5th p pr from L.
(13 prs)
After completing blind pin D:
start patt – work T S with 6th p pr from R.
Nr: patt 4th, 5th, 6th and 7th patt prs from L.
Note Tw 1 leaders in patt.

After pin E:
complete patt after crossing 4 centre patt prs, work T S, cont in Cls working to L.
After pin F:
Cls across all p prs, do not tw leaders, do not work edge st, and leave.

Return to Section 2

Undo locking st after pin M, and follow instructions for Version 1, to finish.
Note Use pin reference plan for Version 1, from pin M to pin S.
Thread colour order will not be the same as Version 1, therefore T O & T B lightest colours first.

Notes for rolled edges
As Version 1.

S for SILVERFISH

Colours
(no 1)	*White
(no 2)	Flesh
(no 3)	*Stone
(no 4)	*Mint
(no 5)	*Dove
(no 6)	Steel Blue
(no 7)	*Pewter Grey

VERSION 1
Section 1
Start at pin A#:
using a two colour point start (tech 1, td 1), (Note L–R working direction), hang 1 pr (no 6) and 1 pr (no 5) to be edge prs (diag s.1).
Add magic thread (tech 2, td 2a).
Lt edge is now (no 6).
R edge is now (no 5).

On T P, hang 1 pr (no 3) to be leaders.
(3 prs)
On T P, hang 2 p prs (no 7) open.

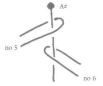

Diagram s1:
Start, Section 1

Cls leaders L–R thro 2 p prs and edge st (tech 3, td 3).
(5 prs)
Nr: *add 1 pr (no 5) to centre*.
Nr: rep * to *.
Nr: *add 1 pr (no 3) to centre*.
Nr: rep * to *.

(9 prs)
Cont, adding 6 prs (no 2), 1 pr per row
to centre.
Work 1 row.
(15 prs)
After pin B:
add 1 pr (no 1) to centre.
Nr: add 2 prs (no 1) to be 7th and 9th
p prs from R.
Nr: add 2 prs (no 1) to be 7th and 11th
p prs from L.
Work 1 row.
(20 prs)
Nr: T O & T B 8th and 10th p prs (no 1)
from L.
Nr: T O & T B 5th p pr (no 2), 8th p pr
(no 1) and 11th p pr (no 2) from R.
Nr: T O & T B s ps 8 & 9 (no 2), 12 & 13
(no 1) and 16 & 17 (no 2) from L.
Nr: T O & T B 5th p pr (no 1) from R.
(11 prs)

After pin C:
add 1 pr (no 6) to be 2nd p pr from L,
and T O & T B s ps 8 & 9 (no 2) from R.
Nr: T O & T B 4th p pr (no 2) from R,
and add 1 pr (no 6) to be s ps 4 & 5
from L.
Nr: T O & T B s ps 10 & 11 (no 3) from L.
Nr: T O & T B 3rd p pr (no 3) from R.
Work 1 row.
(9 prs)
After pin D:
T O & T B s ps 4 & 5 (no 5) from R.
Nr: add 1 pr (no 4) to be 4th p pr from L.
Work 1 row.
Nr: add 1 pr (no 4) to be s ps 8 & 9
from L.
Work 1 row.
Nr: add 1 pr (no 4) to be 5th p pr from L.
Work 3 rows.
(11 prs)
After pin E:
add 1 pr (no 1) to be 4th p pr from L.
Nr: T O & T B s ps 4 & 5 (no 6) from L,
and add 1 pr (no 3) to be 7th p pr from R.
L–R order should be:
L edge pr   2 x (no 6)
                 2 x (no 7)
                 2 x (no 6)

2 x (no 3)
2 x (no 1)
6 x (no 4)
2 x (no 5)
2 x (no 7)
R edge pr   2 x (no 5)
leaders   2 x (no 3)
(12 prs)
After completing blind pin F:
change leaders (no 3) to (no 1), (tech 4,
td 4), cont row, adding 1 pr (no 2) to be
4th p pr from L.
Work 1 row.
(13 prs)
Nr: add 1 pr (no 3) to be s ps 6 & 7
from L.
Work 1 row.
Nr: add 1 pr (no 2) to be s ps 10 & 11
from L.
(15 prs)
After pin G:
T O & T B 1 p pr (no 6).
Nr: add 1 pr (no 1) to centre.
Work 1 row.
Nr: add 1 pr (no 1) to centre.
Work 1 row.
L–R order should be:
L edge pr   2 x (no 6)
                 2 x (no 7)
                 4 x (no 3)
                 4 x (no 2)
                 6 x (no 1)
                 6 x (no 4)
                 2 x (no 5)
                 2 x (no 7)
R edge pr   2 x (no 5)
leaders   2 x (no 1)
(16 prs)
After pin H:
start patt:
work ½ st with 3 central p prs (no 1)
only.
After pin I:
cont in Cls.

After completing blind pin J:
add 1 pr (no 6) to be 2nd p pr from R,
and T O & T B 1 p pr (no 1) from centre.
Nr: T O & T B 1 p pr (no 1).
Nr: add 1 pr (no 7) to be 2nd p pr from

R, and T O & T B 1 p pr (no 1).
Nr:*T O & T B 1 p pr (no 2/no 4)*.
Next 2 rows: rep * to *.
(12 prs)
After pin K:
change leaders (no 1) to (no 6), (tech 4,
td 4), cont row, T O & T B 1 p pr (no
2/no 4).
Nr:*T O & T B 1 p pr (no 3/no 4).
Work 1 row*.
Next 2 rows: rep * to *.
Nr: T O & T B 1 p pr (no 3).
(8 prs)
At pin L:
change leaders (no 6) with R edge pr
(no 5), (tech 7, td 7).
After pin L:
change leaders (no 5) to (no 6), (tech 4,
td 4).

Cont in Cls.
L–R order should be:
L edge pr   2 x (no 6)
                 2 x (no 7)
                 2 x (no 5)
                 2 x (no 6)
                 4 x (no 7)
R edge pr   2 x (no 6)
leaders   2 x (no 6)
(8 prs)
After pin M:
add 1 pr (no 5) to be s ps 4 & 5 from L.
Nr: add 1 pr (no 6) to be s ps 6 & 7
from R.
Nr: add 1 pr (no 5) to be 5th p pr from L.
Nr: add 1 pr (no 6) to be s ps 6 & 7
from R.
(12 prs)
After pin N:
add 1 pr (no 4) to be 2nd p pr from L.
Work 1 row.
Nr: add 1 pr (no 4) to be 4th p pr from L.
Work 1 row.
Nr: add 1 pr (no 4) to be s ps 4 & 5
from L.

S1: Order of work

S3: Pin reference plan, Version 1 & 2

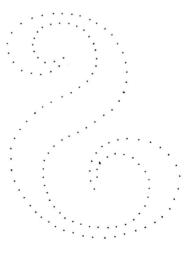

S2: Pricking

Work 1 row.
Nr: add 1 pr (no 1) to be 2nd p pr from L.
Work 1 row.
Nr: add 1 pr (no 1) to be s ps 4 & 5
from L, and T O & T B 2nd p pr (no 7)
from R.
(16 prs)

After pin O:
T O & T B s ps 14 & 15 (no 4/no 5) from L.
Nr: T O & T B 6th p pr (no 4/no 5) from R.
Nr: T O & T B s ps 12 & 13 (no 5/no 6)
from L.
Nr: T O & T B 5th p pr (no 5/no 6) from R.
Nr: T O & T B s ps 10 & 11 (no 4/no 5)
from L.
Nr: T O & T B s ps 8 & 9 (no 4) from R.
Nr: T O & T B s ps 6 & 7 (no 1/no 4)
from L.
Work 2 rows.
Nr: T O & T B 2nd p pr (no 6) from R.
Work 2 rows.
Nr: T O & T B 3rd p pr (no 1/no 5) from L.
(7 prs)
After pin P:
T O & T B s ps 2 & 3 (no 7/no 6) from R.
(6 prs)
After pin Q:
T O & T B 1 p pr (no 1).
Nr: T O & T B central p pr (no 6/no 7).
(4 prs)
After pin R:
Cls thro rem p pr, T O & T B leaders and
rem p pr.
(2 prs)
At pin S:
Cls & tw edge prs, place pin S, add
magic thread (tech 2, td 2a), Cls and
T O prs.
Edge prs will be used for rolled edge.

Notes for rolled edges
Roll from pin S to pin L (tech 9, td 9):
rolling thread – 1 x (no 6)
rolled threads – 3 x (no 6)
Use edge prs from pin S for roll.

T B I thread from roll at pin T and pin U
(tech 14, td 14).
Finish at pin L (tech 10, td 10).

Roll from pin A# to pin V:
rolling thread – 1 x (no 6)
rolled threads – 2 x (no 6)
Add 1 pr and 1 single thread at pin A#
for roll, (tech 24, td 24).
T B 1 thread from roll at pin E.
Finish at pin V.

VERSION 2
Section 1
Start at pin A#:
follow instructions for Version 1, from
pin A# to pin D.
(9 prs)
After pin D:
T O & T B s ps 4 & 5 (no 5) from R.
Nr: add 1 pr (no 4) to be 4th p pr from L.
Work 1 row.
Nr: add 1 pr (no 4) to be s ps 8 & 9 from L.
Work 1 row.
Nr: add 1 pr (no 1) to be 4th p pr from L.
(11 prs)
After pin E:
add 1 pr (no 1) to be s ps 8 & 9 from L.
Nr: add 1 pr (no 3) to be 7th p pr from
R, and T O & T B s ps 4 & 5 (no 6) from L.
(12 prs)
After completing blind pin F:

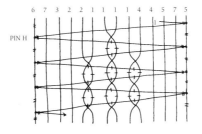

Diagram s2: Patt. 'Ribbon'(var) after pin H

change leaders (no 3) to (no 1), (tech 4,
td 4), cont row, adding 1 pr (no 2) to be
7th p pr from R.
Work 3 rows.
Nr: add 1 pr (no 2) to be s ps 8 & 9 from L.
(14 prs)
After pin G:
T O & T B 1 p pr (no 6).
Nr: add 1 pr (no 1) to centre.
Work 1 row.
Nr: add 1 pr (no 1) to centre.
Work 1 row.
L–R order should be:

L edge pr	2 x (no 6)
	2 x (no 7)
	2 x (no 3)
	4 x (no 2)
	8 x (no 1)
	4 x (no 4)
	2 x (no 5)
	2 x (no 7)
R edge pr	2 x (no 5)
leaders	2 x (no 1)

(15 prs)
After pin H:
start Ribbon (diag s.2) patt gradually,
with 6 central prs, thus –
1st & 2nd rows, work Ribbon with 1 set
of prs,
3rd & 4th rows, work Ribbon with 3 sets
of prs.

After completing 1st blind pin at R edge,
gradually return patt prs to original
colour positions, cont in Cls to pin J,
following instructions for Version 1,
from pin J to finish at pin S.
Note Adjust numbers and colours of prs
T O & T B between pins J and L from
centre of braid accordingly.
Version 2 has only 15 prs whereas
Version 1 has 16 prs.

Notes for rolled edges
As Version 1.

T for TILIA

Colours
(no 1)	*White
(no 2)	Sycamore
(no 3)	Eau de Nil
(no 4)	Pale Lettuce
(no 5)	Apple Green
(no 6)	Lime
(no 7)	*Mid Olive

VERSION 1
Section 1
Start at pin A#:
Using a one colour point start (tech 23,

td 23), (Note L–R working direction),
hang 2 prs (no 7) open, to be edge prs
(diag t.1).
Add magic thread (tech 2, td 2b).

On T P, hang 1 pr (no 7) to be leaders.
(3 prs)
On T P, add 3 prs (no 7) staggered (tech
35, td 35), to be p prs.

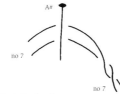

Diagram t1: Start, Section 1

Cls leaders L–R thro 3 p prs and edge st
at pin B (tech 3, td 3).
(6 prs)
Nr: add 1 pr (no 6) to be 2nd p pr from
R, and add 1 pr (no 7) to be 2nd p pr
from L.
Nr: add 1 pr (no 5) to be s ps 8 & 9
from L.
(9 prs)
After pin C:
add 1 pr (no 7) to be s ps 4 & 5 from L.
(10 prs)
After pin D:
add 1 pr (no 6) to be s ps 6 & 7 from R.
Work 1 row.
Nr: add 1 pr (no 5) to be 3rd p pr from R.
Work 1 row.
Nr: add 1 pr (no 4) to be s ps 6 & 7

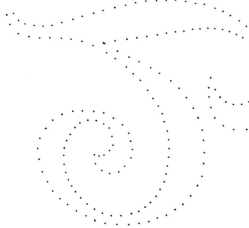

T1: Order of work

T3: Pin reference plan, Version 1

T2: Pricking

from R.
(13 prs)
After pin E:
Cls thro 3 p prs, tw 1 leaders, cont in
Cls, adding 1 pr (no 5) to be 4th p pr
from R.

Nr: add 1 pr (no 4) to be s ps 8 & 9
from R, and tw 1 leaders as before.
Nr: tw 1 leaders as before, and add 1 pr
(no 5) to be 5th p pr from R.
(16 prs)
After pin F:
add 1 pr (no 4) to be s ps 10 & 11 from
R, and tw 2 leaders as before, leave to
split braid.
(17 prs)
At pin G:
between 3rd and 4th p prs from L, hang
2 prs (no 7) open on pin G, tw 2, to be
centre edge prs (diag t.2).

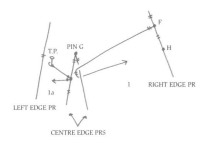

Diagram t2: Splitting braid

R side of braid, Section 1

Note Do not edge st.
Pass leaders, tw 2, over and under R
centre edge pr, hanging from pin G,
work back to R edge.
L–R order should be:

L edge pr	2 x (no 7)
	2 x (no 7)
	3 x (no 6)
	2 x (no 5)
	1 x (no 4)
	1 x (no 5)
	1 x (no 4)
	1 x (no 5)
	2 x (no 4)
	1 x (no 5)
	1 x (no 4)
	1 x (no 5)
	1 x (no 4)
	2 x (no 5)
	1 x (no 6)
	2 x (no 7)
R edge pr	2 x (no 7)
leaders	2 x (no 7)
(14 prs)	

Leave.

L side of braid, Section 1a.
On T P,
hang 1 pr (no 7) to be new leaders (tech
36, td 36), work to R, and edge st with
L centre edge pr, hanging from pin G,
work to L with new leaders, edge st,
work locking st with leaders and 1st
p pr from L.
L–R order should be:

L edge pr	2 x (no 7)
	6 x (no 7)
R edge pr	2 x (no 7)
leaders	2 x (no 7)
(6 prs)	

Leave.

Cont with Section 1.
After pin H:
start patt: Cls thro 5 p prs, tw 1 leaders,
Cls rem p prs.
Nr: tw 2 leaders as before.
Cont in patt, tw 2 leaders, as before.

After pin I:
cont in patt, tw 1 leaders, as before.

After pin J:
cont in Cls.
(14 prs)
After pin K:
T O & T B s ps 12 & 13 (no 4) from L.
After pin L:
T O & T B 5th p pr (no 5) from R.
Nr: T O & T B s ps 10 & 11 (no 4) from L.
Nr: T O & T B 4th p pr (no 5) from R.

Nr: T O & T B s ps 8 & 9 (no 4) from L.
Nr: T O & T B 3rd p pr (no 5) from R,
and add 1 pr (no 7) to be s ps 2 & 3 from L.
Nr: T O & T B s ps 8 & 9 (no 5) from L.
Nr: add 1 pr (no 7) to be s ps 2 & 3 from
R, and T O & T B s ps 6 & 7 (no 6) from L.
Nr: add 1 pr (no 7) to be 2nd p pr from
L, and T O & T B 1 p pr (no 6).
All rem prs are now (no 7).
(8 prs)

After pin M:
add 1 pr (no 6) to be 1st p pr from R.
Nr: T O & T B 2nd p pr (no 7) from L.
Nr: add 1 pr (no 6) to be s ps 2 & 3
from R.
Work 1 row.
Nr: add 1 pr (no 5) to be 2nd p pr from
R, and T O & T B 2nd p pr (no 7) from L.
Work 1 row.
Nr: add 1 pr (no 4) to be s ps 4 & 5 from R.
Work 1 row.
(10 prs)

Nr: add 1 pr (no 3) to be 3rd p pr from
R, and T O & T B 2nd p pr (no 7) from L.
Work 3 rows.
Nr: add 1 pr (no 2) to be s ps 6 & 7 from R.
Work 3 rows.
Nr: add 1 pr (no 1) to be 4th p pr from
R, and T O & T B s ps 2 & 3 (no 7) from L.
Work 3 rows.
Nr: add 1 pr (no 1) to be s ps 8 & 9 from R.
(12 prs)

After completing blind pin N:
start patt: Cls thro 5 p prs, tw 1 leaders,
Cls rem p prs.
Nr: tw 2 leaders, as before.
Cont in patt, tw 2 leaders, as before.

After pin O:
cont in patt, tw 1 leaders, as before.

After pin P:
cont in Cls, T O & T B s ps 8 & 9 (no 1)
from R.
Nr: T O & T B 5th p pr (no 1) from L.
Nr: T O & T B s ps 6 & 7 (no 2) from R.
Nr: T O & T B 4th p pr (no 3) from L..
Nr: T O & T B s ps 4 & 5 (no 4) from R.
Nr: T O & T B 3rd p pr (no 5) from L.
(6 prs)
After pin Q:

T O & T B s ps 2 & 3 (no 6) from R,
then T O & T B leaders and 2 rem p prs.
Finish at pin R:
Cls & tw edge prs, place pin R, Cls & T O.
T B 1 thread and secure to back of work
with previously T B prs.
Use rem 3 threads for rolled edge.

Notes for rolled edge
Roll from pin R to pin S (tech 9, td 9):
rolling thread – 1 x (no 7)
rolled threads – 2 x (no 7)
Use 3 threads from pin R for roll.
T B 1 thread from roll 2 pins before pin
S (tech 14, td 14).
Finish at pin S (tech 10, td 10).

Return to Section 1a

Undo locking st, and cont in Cls to pin T.
(6 prs)
After pin T:
add 1 pr (no 6) to centre.

Cont adding 5 prs, 1 pr per row, in foll
order:
1 pr   (no 5)
2 prs   (no 4)
2 prs   (no 3)
(12 prs)
After pin U:
T O & T B s ps 2 & 3 (no 7) from R, and
add 1 pr (no 2) to centre as before.
Next 2 rows: rep * to *.
(14 prs)
After pin V:
start patt: Cls thro 6 p prs, tw 1 leaders,
Cls rem p prs.
Nr: tw 1 leaders, as before.
Nr: tw 2 leaders, as before.
Cont in patt, tw 2 leaders, as before.

After pin W:
cont in patt, tw 1 leaders, as before.

After pin X:
cont in Cls.
Work 1 row.
Nr: T O & T B s ps 12 & 13 (no 2) from L.
Nr: T O & T B s ps 7 & 8 and 11 & 12
(no 2/no 3) from R.
Nr: T O & T B s ps 7 & 8 and 11 & 12
(no 3/no 4) from L.
Nr: T O & T B 3rd p pr (no 2) from R.
Nr: add 1 pr (no 7) to be 2nd p pr from
L, and T O & T B 1 p pr (no 4).
Work 1 row.
Nr: T O & T B 1 p pr (no 5).
Nr: add 1 pr (no 7) to be 4th p pr from R.
Work 1 row.
Nr: T O & T B 1 p pr (no 6), and add 1
pr (no 7) to be 2nd p pr from L.
(8 prs)
After pin Y:
add 1 pr (no 6) to be 2nd p pr from L.
Work 3 rows.
Nr: add 1 pr (no 6) to be s ps 4 & 5

from L.
Nr: T O & T B 2nd p pr (no 7) from R,
and add 1 pr (no 5) to be 3rd p pr from L.
Work 1 row.
Nr: add 1 pr (no 5) to be s ps 8 & 9
from R.
Work 1 row.

After pin Z:
start patt: Cls thro 4 p prs, tw 1 leaders,
Cls rem p prs.
Nr: tw 1 leaders, as before.
Nr: tw 2 leaders, as before.

Cont in patt, tw 2 leaders, as
before.

After pin A1:
tw 1 leaders, as before.
Nr: tw 1 leaders, as before.

Nr: cont in Cls,
T O & T B 1 p pr from centre,
lightest prs first, till 4 p prs rem.
(7 prs)

After pin B1:
add 1 pr (no 6) to be 1st p pr from
R.
Work 1 row.
Nr: add 1 pr (no 6) to be s ps 2 & 3
from R.
Nr: T O & T B 1 p pr (no 7), and add 1
pr (no 5) to be 2nd p pr from R.
Nr: add 1 pr (no 4) to be s ps 4 & 5
from R.
Nr: T O & T B 1 p pr (no 7), and add 1
pr (no 3) to be 3rd p pr from R.
Nr: add 1 pr (no 3) to be s ps 6 & 7
from R.
(11 prs)

After pin C1:
start patt: Cls thro 3 p prs, tw 1 leaders,
Cls rem p prs.
Nr: tw 1 leaders, as before.
Nr: tw 2 leaders, as before.
Cont in patt, tw 2 leaders, as before.

After pin D1:
tw 1 leaders, as before.
Nr: tw 1 leaders, as before.

After pin E1:
cont in Cls, T O & T B s ps 6 & 7 (no 3)
from R.
Nr: T O & T B s ps 6 & 7 (no 6/no 5)
from L, and 3rd p pr (no 3) from R.
Nr: T O & T B 1 pr (no 4).
Nr: T O & T B s ps 6 & 7 (no 6/no 5)
from L.
(6 prs)
Finish at pin F1:
T O & T B 1 p pr (no 6), Cls thro rem 2
p prs, T O & T B leaders and rem p prs.
Cls & tw edge prs. place pin F1, Cls & T O.
T B 1 thread and secure to back of work

with previously T B prs.
Use rem 3 threads for rolled edge.

Notes for rolled edge
Roll from pin F1 to pin A#:
rolling thread – 1 x (no 7)
rolled threads – 2 x (no 7)
Use 3 threads from pin F1 for roll (tech
9, td 9).
T B 1 thread from roll 2 pins before pin A#.
Finish at pin A# (tech 10, td 10).

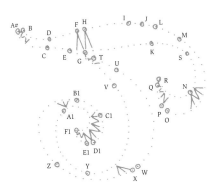

T4: Pin reference plan, Version 2

VERSION 2
Section 1
Start at pin A#:
follow instructions for Version 1, from
pin A# to pin H.
Note After pin F do not add 1 p pr (no
4), 16 prs only in total before splitting
braid. Therefore thread order, after pin
G, will not include central p pr (no 4).
(13 prs)

Cont with Section 1
After pin H:
start patt: Cls thro 4 p prs, Cls & tw 5th
p pr (no 5), Cls rem p prs.
Nr: start Ribbon (var) patt – Cls thro 3
p prs, tw 1 leaders, Cls tog 4th & 5th
p prs and 7th & 8th p prs, Cls & tw 6th
p pr (no 5) from L.
Cont in patt (diag t.3): Ribbon (var).
Note There is no pin I in Version 2.

After pin J:
Cls thro 4 p prs, Cls & tw 5th p pr, Cls
rem p prs.
Cont in Cls.

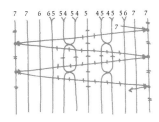

Diagram t3: Patt. 'Ribbon' (var) after pin H

71

After pin K:
work 1 row.
After pin L:
follow instructions for Version 1 to pin N.
Note Do not add 2nd p pr (no 1)
(11 prs)

After completing blind pin N:
start patt: Cls thro 4 p prs, Cls & tw 5th
p pr (no 1) from L, Cls rem p prs.
Nr: cont in patt, Cls & tw 1 p pr (no 1),
as before.
Note There is no pin O in Version 2.

After pin P:
work 1 row.
Nr: follow instructions for Version 1,
from 1 row after pin P, to finish at pin R.

Notes for rolled edge
As Version 1.

Return to Section 1a

Undo locking st, and cont to pin T.
(6 prs)
After pin T:
add 6 prs to centre, 1 pr per row, in foll
order:
1 pr	(no 6)
1 pr	(no 5)
1 pr	(no 4)
2 prs	(no 3)
1 pr	(no 2)
(12 prs)
After pin U:
T O & T B s ps 2 & 3 (no 7) from R, and
add 1 pr (no 2) as before.

Nr: add 1 pr (no 2) as before.
(13 prs)
After pin V:
start patt: Cls thro 5 p prs, tw 1 leaders,
Cls & tw 6th p pr from L, Cls rem p prs.
Nr: cont in patt, Cls & tw 5th p pr, as
before.
Nr: start Ribbon (var) patt – Cls thro 3
p prs, tw 1 leaders, Cls tog 4th & 5th
p prs and 7th & 8th p,prs, Cls & tw 6th
p pr from L.
Cont in Ribbon (var).

After pin W:
patt 1 row, patt prs will have returned to
their original colour positions.
Nr: Cls thro 5 p prs, Cls & tw 6th p pr
from L, Cls rem p prs.

After pin X:
Work 1 row.
Cont in Cls.
(13 prs)
Nr: T O & T B 6th p pr (no 2) from L.
Nr: T O & T B s ps 8 & 9 (no 2) from R.
Nr: T O & T B 4th and 6th p prs (no 3)
from L.
Nr: T O & T B 3rd p pr (no 2) from R.
Nr: add 1 pr (no 7) to be 2nd p pr from
L, and T O & T B 1 p pr (no 4).
Work 1 row.
Nr: T O & T B 1 p pr (no 5).
Nr: add 1 pr (no 7) to be 4th p pr from R.
Work 1 row.
Nr: T O & T B 1 pr (no 6), and add 1 pr
(no 7) to be 2nd p pr from L.
(8 prs)
After pin Y:

follow instructions for Version 1, until
only 1 pr (no 5) has been added.

After pin Z:
start patt: Cls thro 4 p prs, Cls & tw
with 5th p pr from R, Cls rem p prs.

Cont in patt, Cls & tw 1 p pr.

After pin A1:
cont in patt for 2 rows.
Nr: cont in Cls, T O & T B 1 p pr from
braid, lightest prs first, till 4 p prs rem.
(7 prs)
After pin B1:
follow instructions for Version 1, until
only 1 pr (no 3) has been added.
(10 prs)
After pin C1:
start patt: Cls thro 2 p prs, Cls & tw 3rd
p pr from R, Cls rem p prs.
Cont in patt, Cls & tw 1 p pr.

After pin D1:
cont in patt for 2 rows.

After pin E1:
follow instructions for Version 1, to
finish at pin F1.
Note There will only be 1 p pr (no 3) to
be T O & T B.

Notes for rolled edge
As Version 1.

U for UMBRA

Colours
(no 1)	*Marigold
(no 2)	*PO Red
(no 3)	*Dark Peony
(no 4)	Cardinal
(no 5)	Dark Claret
(no 6)	Extra Dark Brown
(no 7)	Navy

VERSION 1
Section 1
Start at pin A#:
using a two colour point start (tech 1,td1):
Note L–R working direction
hang 1 pr (no 7) and 1 pr (no 3) to be
edge prs (diag u.1).
Add magic thread (tech 2, td 2a).
L edge pr is now (no 7).
R edge pr is now (no 3).
On T P, hang 1 pr (no 4) to be leaders.
(3 prs)

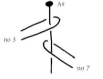

Diagram u1:
Start, Section 1

On T P, hang 2 prs in order L–R:
1 pr (no 7) and 1 pr (no 4).
Cls leaders L–R thro 2 p prs and edge st
at pin B (tech 3, td 3).
(5 prs)
Nr: add 1 pr (no 6) to be 2nd p pr from R.
Nr: add 1 pr (no 7) to be s ps 2 & 3
from L, and add 1 pr (no 5) to be 2nd
p pr from R.
Nr: add 1 pr (no 4) to be s ps 2 & 3
from R, and add 1 pr (no 6) to be s ps 6
& 7 from L.
Nr: add 1 pr (no 5) to be s ps 10 & 11
from L, and add 1 pr (no 3) to be 2nd
p pr from R.
Nr: add 1 pr (no 3) to be s ps 4 & 5
from R.
Nr: add 1 pr (no 2) to be 9th p pr from L.

Nr: add 1 pr (no 2) to be s ps 6 & 7
from R.
Nr: add 1 pr (no 2) to be 10th p pr from L.
(16 prs)
After pin C:
start patt: Cls thro 2 p prs, (Note Tie ½
knot with leaders after 1st p pr to hold
pr in position close to pin), tw 1
leaders,
work ½ st with 3 p prs (no 2), Cls rem
p prs.
Nr: Cls thro 8 p prs, tw 1 leaders, work
½ st with 3 p prs, Cls rem p prs.
Cont in patt, ½ st 3 p prs.
After pin D:
when patt prs have returned to their
original colour positions, cont in patt,
add 1 pr (no 5) to be 6th p pr from L.
Nr: add 1 pr (no 4) to be s ps 14 & 15
from R.
Nr: add 1 pr (no 5) to be s ps 12 & 13
from L.
Nr: add 1 pr (no 4) to be 8th p pr from R.
Nr: add 1 pr (no 5) to be 7th p pr from L.
Nr: add 1 pr (no 6) to be 16th p pr from R.

Nr: add 1 pr (no 7) to be 2nd p pr from L.
(23 prs)
After pin E:
when patt prs have returned to their
original colour positions, T O & T B 4th
p pr (no 2) from R, and in addition,
work ½ st with 8th, 9th and 10th p prs
(no 5) from L.
Nr: cont in patt.
Nr: cont in patt, and T O & T B s ps 6 &
7 (no 2) from R.
Nr: cont in patt.
Nr: cont in patt, and T O & T B 3rd p pr
(no 2) from R.
(20 prs)
Nr: cont in patt.
Nr: T O & T B s ps 4 & 5 (no 3) from R.
Nr: T O & T B 15th p pr (no 3) from L.
Nr: T O & T B 2nd p pr (no 4) from R.
Nr: T O & T B 13th p pr (no 4) from L.
Nr: T O & T B 2nd p pr (no 4) from R.
Nr: cont in patt.
Nr: T O & T B 1st p pr (no 4) from R.
Nr: cont in patt.
Nr: when patt prs have returned to their
original colour positions, cont in Cls.
(14 prs)
When completing blind pin F:
change leaders (no 4) with L edge pr
(no 7), (tech 7, td 7).

At pin G:
change leaders (no 7) with R edge pr
(no 3), (tech 7, td 7).
After pin G:
T O & T B 2nd p pr (no 5) from R.
(13 prs)

After 1st working blind pin H:
change leaders (no 3) cont with 1st p pr
(no 7) from L, (tech 37, td 37).

Nr: T O & T B 2nd p pr (no 5) from R.

Nr: T O & T B 7th p pr (no 5) from L.
Nr: T O & T B 2nd p pr (no 5) from R.
Nr: T O & T B 5th p pr (no 6) from L.
Nr: T O & T B 1st p pr (no 5) from R.
(7 prs)

After pin I:
T O & T B s ps 4 & 5 (no 6/no 7) from L.
(6 prs)

After pin J:
T O & T B 2nd p pr (no 6/no 7) from R,
Cls leaders thro 2 rem p prs, and T O &
T B 3 prs, and secure to back of work
with previously T B prs.
Finish at pin K:
Cls & tw L edge pr (no 4) and R edge pr
(no 7), place pin K, Cls & T O.
These 2 prs to be used for rolled edge.

Notes for rolled edge
Roll from pin K to pin A# (tech 9, td 9):
rolling thread – 1 x (no 7)
rolled threads – 1 x (no 7), 2 x (no 4)
Use edge prs from pin K for roll.
At pin L and pin H, T B 1 thread (no 4)
and add 1 thread (no 7) to roll.
Finish at pin A#.

Section 2
Start at pin A#:
using a two colour point start (tech 1, td
1), (Note L–R working direction), hang
1 pr (no 7) and 1 pr (no 1) to be edge
prs (diag u.2).
Add magic thread (tech 2, td 2a).

On T P, hang 1 pr (no 2) to be leaders.
(3 prs)
On T P, hang 2 prs in order L–R:
1 pr (no 7) and 1 pr (no 1).
Cls leaders thro 2 p prs and edge st at
pin B.

(5 prs)
Nr: add 1 pr (no 1) to be s ps 2 & 3
from R, and add 1 pr (no 3) to be 2nd
p pr from L.
(7 prs)
Nr: add 1 pr (no 6) to be 2nd p pr from
L, and add 1 pr (no 2) to be 4th p pr
from L, and add 1 pr (no 1) to be 2nd
p pr from R.
(10 prs)
Nr: add 1 pr (no 2) to be s ps 8 & 9
from R, and add 1 pr (no 3) to be s ps
12 & 13 from R, and add 1 pr (no 5) to
be 3rd p pr from L.
(13 prs)
Nr: add 1 pr (no 4) to be 4th p pr from
L, and add 1 pr (no 2) to be 8th p pr
from L, and add 1 pr (no 1) to be s ps 4
& 5 from R.
(16 prs)
Nr: add 1 pr (no 1) to be 3rd p pr from
R, and add 1 pr (no 4) to be s ps 8 & 9
from L.
Nr: add 2 prs (no 2) to be 9th and 11th
p prs from L.
(20 prs)

After pin C:
start patt: Cls thro 1st p pr, tw 1 leaders,
work ½ st with 2nd, 3rd and 4th p prs
(no 1), Cls rem p prs.

After pin D:
work locking st (tech 6, td 6) and leave
to split braid (tech 38, td 38).
At pin E:
between 10th and 11th p prs from L,
hang 2 prs (no 4) open on pin E, tw 2,
to be centre edge prs.

Return to pin D
Undo locking st, work across all prs to
pin F, cont in patt, ½ st 3 p prs.

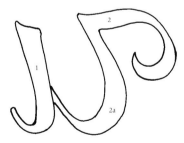

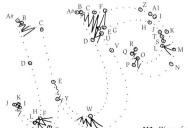

U1: Order of work

U3: Pin reference plan, Version 1

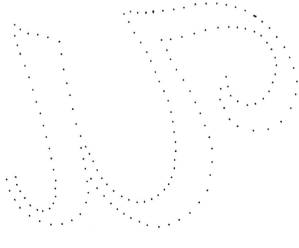

U2: Pricking

At pin E:
Cls & tw 2 centre edge prs, add magic thread (tech 2, td 2b).

Cont with R side of braid, Section 2

Cont in patt, ½ st 3 p prs, as before.
(10 prs)
At pin G:
work edge st with R centre edge pr.

After pin H:
when patt prs have returned to their original colour positions, cont in Cls.
At pin I:
change leaders (no 2) with R edge pr (no 1), (tech 7, td 7).
After pin I:
add 1 pr (no 2) to be 1st p pr from R.
Nr: T O & T B 1st p pr (no 2) from L.
Nr: add 1 pr (no 2) to be s ps 2 & 3 from R.
Nr: T O & T B 1st p pr (no 2) from L.
Work 1 row.
(10 prs)
At pin J:
change leaders (no 1) with L edge pr (no 4), (tech 7, td 7).

At pin K:
change leaders (no 4) with R edge pr (no 2), (tech 7, td 7).
Work 2 rows.
Nr: add 1 pr (no 3) to be 1st p pr from R.
Work 1 row.
Nr: add 1 pr (no 4) to be 1st p pr from R.
(12 prs)
After working 1st part of blind pin L:
T O & T B 3rd p pr (no 1) from L.
(11 prs)

After pin M:
start patt: Cls thro 5 p prs, tw 1 leaders, ½ st 6th and 7th p prs (no 1) from R, Cls rem prs.
Cont in patt, ½ st 2 p prs.
After pin N:
add 1 pr (no 4) to be s ps 2 & 3 from R.
(12 prs)
After working 1st part of blind pin O:
when patt prs have returned to their original colour positions cont in Cls.
After pin P:
T O & T B s ps 12 & 13 (no 1) and s ps 15 & 16 (no 1) from R.
Nr: T O & T B 2nd p pr (no 1) and s ps 6 & 7 (no 2) from L.
Nr: T O & T B 2nd p pr (no 4) from R.
Nr: T O & T B s ps 4 & 5 (no 2/no 3) from L.
(6 prs)
After pin Q:
T O & T B 2nd p pr from R (no 2/no 3), Cls thro rem 2 p prs, T O leaders and rem 2 p prs, T B leaders and 1st p pr (no 4) from R.
Set aside rem p pr (no 1) to be used for rolled edge.

Finish at pin R:
Cls & tw edge prs, place pin R, Cls edge prs

& T O, placing set aside p pr (no 1) between L edge pr (no 1) to enclose when tying knot.
These 2 prs to be used for rolled edge.
T B R edge pr (no 4).
Secure T B threads to back of work with previously T B prs.

Notes for rolled edge
Roll from pin R to pin T:
rolling thread – 1 x (no 1)
rolled threads – 3 x (no 1)
Use L edge pr and 1st p pr from L for roll.
T B 1 thread at pin L and pin S (tech 14, td 14).
Finish at pin T (tech 10, td 10).

Return to L side of braid, Section 2a

At pin D:
add 1 pr (no 3) to be leaders (tech 38, td 38), cont row.
(13 prs)
At pin U:
work edge st with L centre edge pr.
After pin U:
add 1 pr (no 3) to be 5th p pr from R.
Work 1 row.
(14 prs)
Nr: T O & T B 1st p pr from R, and add 1 pr (no 4) to be 5th p pr from L.
Work 1 row.
Nr: T O & T B 1st p pr (no 2) from R.
Work 1 row.
(13 prs)
After pin V:
T O & T B 1st p pr (no 2) from R, and start patt: Cls thro 1st p pr,
tw 1 leaders, ½ st 2nd, 3rd, 4th and 5th p prs, Cls rem p prs.
(12 prs)
Cont in patt, ½ st 4 p prs.

After working 1st part of blind pin W: cont in Cls.
Note Leaders will have returned to original colour position,
2 p prs (no 3) will have changed position with 2 p prs (no 4).

After pin X:
add 1 pr (no 4) to be 1st p pr from R.
Work 1 row.
Nr: T O & T B 2nd p pr (no 3) from R.
Nr: T O & T B s ps 10 & 11 (no 3) from L.
Nr: T O & T B 4th p pr (no 3) from R.
Nr: T O & T B s ps 10 & 11 (no 4) from L.
Nr: T O & T B 2nd p pr (no 4) from R, and add 1 pr (no 5) to be s ps 6 & 7 from L.
(9 prs)
At pin Y:
join to Section 1 using top sewings, T O & T B prs from R side as braid narrows.

Finish at pin E, Section 1:
use 1st p pr (no 4) from R, R edge pr

(no 4), L edge pr (no 7) and 1st p pr from L (no 7) for rolled edges.
Secure rem prs to back of work with previously T B prs.

Notes for rolled edges
Roll from pin Y to pin E:
rolling thread – 1 x (no 4)
rolled threads – 3 x (no 4)
Use R edge pr and 1st p pr from R for roll.
T B 1 thread from roll at pin X.
Finish at pin E (tech 16, td 16a).

Roll from pin E, Section 1, to pin A#, Section 2:
rolling thread – 1 x (no 7)
rolled threads – 3 x (no 7)
Use L edge pr and 1st p pr from L for roll.
T B 1 thread at pin W.
Finish at pin A#, also adding 2 prs (no 1) into loop of rolling thread (no 7) when making last sewing.

Roll from pin A# to pin A1:
rolling thread – 1 x (no 1)
rolled threads – 3 x (no 1)
Use 2 prs added at pin A# (tech 16, td 16a), when finishing previous rolled edge.
T B 1 thread from roll at pin F and pin Z.
Finish at pin A1.

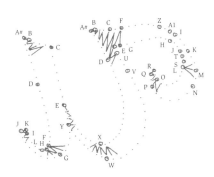

U4: Pin reference plan, Version 2

VERSION 2
Section 1
Start at pin A#:
Follow instructions for Version 1, from pin A# to pin C.
(16 prs)
After pin C:
start Basketweave (var) patt – Cls thro 2 p prs (diag u.3), (Note Tie ½ knot after 1st p pr to keep p pr close to pin), tw 1 leaders, Cls 3rd and 4th p prs tog, work patt with 3p prs from R only, Cls rem p prs.
After pin D:
follow instructions for Version 1 to pin E.
After pin E:
follow instructions for Version 1 to finish at pin K, working Basketweave (var) patt as before, with 8th, 9th and 10th p prs (no 5) from L.

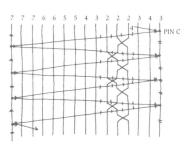

Diagram u3: Patt. 'Basketweave' (var) after pin C

Note Cls 9th and 10th p prs tog to commence patt.
Notes for rolled edge
As Version 1.

Section 2
Start at pin A#:
Follow instructions for Version 1, from pin A# to pin C.

Diagram u2: Start, Section 2

(20 prs)
After pin C:
start Basketweave (var) patt with 2nd, 3rd and 4th p prs (no 1) from R.
Note Cls 2nd and 3rd p prs tog to commence patt.
After pin D:
follow instructions for Version 1 to pin M, cont in patt.

After 1st working blind pin L:
cont in Cls.
(12 prs)
After pin M:
start Basketweave (var) patt with 6th, 7th and 8th p prs (no 1) from R.
Note Cls 6th and 7th p prs tog to commence patt.
Cont in patt.
After pin N:
add 1 pr (no 4) to be s ps 2 & 3 from R.
(13 prs)

After 1st working blind pin O:
T O & T B 3rd p pr (no 1) from L, and cont in Cls
(12 prs)
After pin P:
follow instructions for Version 1 to finish at pin R.

Notes for rolled edge
As Version 1.

Return to L side of braid, Section 2a
(12 prs)
At pin D:

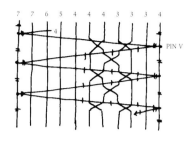

Diagram u4: Patt. 'Basketweave' (var) after pin V

follow instructions for Version 1, from pin D to pin V.
After pin V:
T O & T B 1st p pr (no 2) from R, and start Basketweave (var) patt with 2nd, 3rd, 4th and 5th p prs from R (diag u.4). Note Cls 2nd and 3rd p prs tog and 4th and 5th p prs tog, to commence patt.
Cont in patt.
After pin W: cont in Cls.
After 1st working blind pin X:
T O & T B 7th p pr (no 3) from L.

Nr: T O & T B 1st p pr (no 3) from R.
Nr: T O & T B 5th p pr (no 3) from L.
Nr: T O & T B 1st p pr (no 4) from R, and add 1 pr (no 5) to be s ps 6 & 7 from L.
(9 prs)
At pin Y:
follow instructions for Version 1 to finish at pin E, Section 1.

Notes for rolled edges
As Version 1.

V for VIOLA

Colours
(no 1)	*Champagne
(no 2)	Eau de Nil
(no 3)	Baby Blue
(no 4)	*Flax
(no 5)	*Pansy
(no 6)	Mid Purple
(no 7)	*Helio

VERSION 1
Section 1
Start at pin A#:
using a two colour point start (tech 1, td 1), (Note R–L working direction), hang 1 pr (no 7) and 1 pr (no 1) to be edge prs (diag v.1).
Add magic thread (tech 2, td 2a).

Diagram v1:
Start, Section 1

L edge pr is now (no 7).
R edge pr is now (no 1).

On T P, hang 1 pr (no 4) to be leaders.
(3 prs)
On T P, hang 4 prs in order L–R:
1 pr	(no 7)
1 pr	(no 6)
1 pr	(no 4)
1 pr	(no 1)

Cls leaders R–L thro 4 p prs and edge st at pin B (tech 3, td 3).
(7 prs)
Nr: add 3 prs as foll:
1 pr (no 5) to be 3rd p pr,
1 pr (no 3) to be 5th p pr, and
1 pr (no 2) to be 6th p pr from L.
(10 prs)
Nr: add 3 prs as foll:

1 pr (no 1) to be s ps 2 & 3,
1 pr (no 2) to be s ps 6 & 7, and
1 pr (no 3) to be s ps 10 & 11 from R.
(13 prs)
Nr: add 3 prs as foll:
1 pr (no 5) to be s ps 6 & 7,
1 pr (no 4) to be s ps 10 & 11, and
1 pr (no 3) to be s ps 15 & 16 from L.
(16 prs)
Nr: add 1 pr (no 3) to be s ps 12 & 13, and add 1 pr (no 4) to be s ps 19 & 20 from R.
Nr: add 1 pr (no 5) to be 4th p pr, and add 1 pr (no 4) to be s ps 14 & 15 from L.
Nr: add 1 pr (no 5) to be s ps 28 & 29 from R.
Work 1 row.
(21 prs)

After pin C:
start patt – Cls thro 6 p prs, tw 1 leaders, Cls rem p prs.
Nr: tw 2 leaders, as before.
Cont in patt, tw 2 leaders, as before.

After pin D:
work locking st (tech 6, td 6) and leave to split braid (tech 38, td 38).
At pin E:
between 8th and 9th p prs from L, hang 2 prs (no 4) open on pin E, tw 2, to be centre edge prs.

Return to pin D
Undo locking st, work across all prs, cont in patt, tw 2 leaders.

At pin E:
Cls & tw 2 centre edge prs.
Cont with R side of braid, Section 1

Cont in patt, tw 2 leaders, as before.
(13 prs)
At pin F:
work edge st with R centre edge pr.

After pin G:
cont in patt, tw 1 leaders, as before.
After pin H:
cont in Cls.

After pin I:
T O & T B s ps 8 & 9 (no 3) from L.
Nr: T O & T B 6th p pr (no 3) from R.
Nr: T O & T B 2nd p pr (no 4) from L.
(10 prs)

At pin J:
change leaders (no 4) with R edge pr (no 1), (tech 7, td 7).
After pin J:
T O & T B 5th p pr (no 3) from R.
Nr: T O & T B 1st p pr (no 4) from L.
(8 prs)
After pin K:
add 1 pr (no 2) to be 1st p pr from R.
Nr: T O & T B 1st p pr (no 3) from L.
Nr: add 1 pr (no 3) to be 1st p pr from R.
(9 prs)

At pin L:
change leaders (no 1) with L edge pr (no 4), (tech 7, td 7).
After pin L:
T O & T B 1st p pr (no 2) from L, and add 1 pr (no 2) to be s ps 4 & 5 from R.
Nr: add 1 pr (no 4) to be 1st p pr from R.
Nr: T O & T B 1st p pr (no 2) from L, and add 1 pr (no 3) to be s ps 4 & 5 from R.
Nr: add 1 pr (no 4) to be 1st p pr from R.
Nr: add 1 pr (no 3) to be 6th p pr from L.
Work 1 row.
Nr: add 1 pr (no 3) to be s ps 12 & 13 from L.
(13 prs)

After pin M:
start patt: Cls thro 4 p prs, tw 1 leaders, Cls rem p prs.
Nr: tw 1 leaders, as before.
Nr: tw 2 leaders, as before.
Cont in patt, tw 2 leaders as before.
After pin N:
tw 1 leaders, as before.
Nr: cont in Cls.
After pin O:
T O & T B s ps 8 & 9 (no 3) and s ps 14 & 15 (no 2) from R.
Nr: T O & T B 4th and 6th p prs (no 3) from L.

Nr: T O & T B 3rd p pr (no 3) and 5th
p pr (no 1) from R.
Nr: T O & T B 2nd p pr (no 2) from L.
Nr: T O & T B 2nd p pr (no 4) from R.
(5 prs)
After pin P:
Cls thro 2 p prs, T O leaders and 2
p prs, T B leaders and 1 p pr (no 4).
Set aside 1 p pr (no 1) to be used for
rolled edge.

Finish at pin Q:
Cls & tw edge prs, place pin Q, Cls.
T O & T B R edge pr (no 4), and secure
to back of work with previously T B prs.
T O L edge pr (no 1), enclosing set
aside p pr (no 1) when tying knot.
These 2 prs to be used for rolled edge.

Notes for rolled edge
Roll from pin Q to pin L (tech 9, td 9):
rolling thread – 1 x (no 1)
rolled threads – 3 x (no 1)
Use 2 prs (no 1) from pin Q for roll.
T B 1 thread from roll at pin R and pin
S (tech 14, td 14).
Finish at pin L (tech 10, td 10).

Return to L side of braid, Section 1a
After pin D:
add 1 pr (no 4) to be leaders (tech 38,
td 38), cont in Cls.
(11 prs)

At pin T:
work edge st with L centre edge pr.
After pin T:
add 1 pr (no 4) to be 2nd p pr from R.
Nr: add 1 pr (no 4) to be s ps 16 &17
from L.
Nr: add 1 pr (no 3) to be 3rd p pr from R.
Nr: add 1 pr (no 3) to be s ps 18 & 19
from L.
(15 prs)
After pin U:
add 1 pr (no 2) to be 4th p pr from R,
and T O & T B s ps 8 & 9 (no 5) from L.
Nr: add 1 pr (no 2) to be s ps 18 & 19
from L.
Nr: add 1 pr (no 1) to be 5th p pr from
R, and T O & T B 4th p pr (no 5) from L.
Nr: add 1 pr (no 1) to be s ps 18 & 19

from L.
Nr: T O & T B s ps 22 & 23 (no 5) from R.
(16 prs)

After pin V:
start patt: Cls thro 8 p prs, tw 1 leaders,
Cls rem p prs.
Nr: tw 2 leaders, as before.
After pin W:
add 1 pr (no 5) to be 1st p pr from R.
Work 1 row.
Nr: add 1 pr (no 5) to be s ps 2 & 3
from R.
Work 1 row.
Nr: add 1 pr (no 5) to be 2nd p pr from R.
(19 prs)
After pin X:
tw 1 leaders, as before.

After pin Y:
cont in Cls.
Nr: T O & T B s ps 16 & 17 (no 1) from L.
Nr: T O & T B 8th p pr (no 1) from R.
Nr: T O & T B s ps 14 & 15 (no 2) from L.
Nr: T O & T B 7th p pr (no 2) from R.
Nr: T O & T B s ps 10 & 11 (no 4/no 3)
and s ps 14 & 15 (no3/no 4) from L.
Nr: T O & T B s ps 10 & 11 (no 3) from R.
Nr: T O & T B 5th p pr (no 4) from L.
Nr: T O & T B s ps 8 & 9 (no 4) from R.
(10 prs)
After pin Z:
add 1 pr (no 7) to be s ps 2 & 3 from L,
and T O & T B 4th p pr (no 4) from R.
Nr: T O & T B s ps 4 & 5 (no 5) from R.
Nr: add 1 pr (no 6) to be 1st p pr from L.
(10 prs)
After pin A1:
change leaders (no 4) to (no 6), (tech 4,
td 4), cont row T O & T B 3rd p pr (no
5) from R.
(9 prs)
At pin B1:
change leaders (no 6) with L edge pr
(no 7), (tech 7, td 7).
After pin B1:

add 1 pr (no 6) to be s ps 2 & 3 from L.
Nr: T O & T B 1st p pr (no 5) from R.
Nr: add 1 pr (no 6) to be 2nd p pr from L.
Nr: T O & T B 1st p pr (no 5) from R.
Nr: add 1 pr (no 6) to be s ps 4 & 5
from L.
(10 prs)

At pin C:
change leaders (no 7) with R edge pr
(no 4), (tech 7, td 7).
After pin C⁴:
T O & T B 1st p pr (no 6) from R, then
change leaders (no 4) to (no 7), (tech 4,
td 4).
(9 prs)
After pin D1:
add 1 pr (no 5) to be 5th p pr from R.
Work 1 row.
Nr: add 1 pr (no 5) to be s ps 10 & 11
from R.
Work 1 row.
Nr: add 1 pr (no 4) to be 6th p pr from R,
Work 1 row.
Nr: add 1 pr (no 4) to be s ps 12 & 13
from R.
(13 prs)

After pin E:
start patt: Cls thro 6 p prs, tw 1 leaders,
Clr rem p prs.
Nr: tw 1 leaders, as before.
Nr: tw 2 leaders, as before.
Cont in patt, tw 2 leaders, as before.
After completing blind pin F1:
tw 1 leaders, as before.
Nr: cont in Cls.

After working 1st part of blind pin G1:
T O & T B s ps 4 & 5 (no 6/no 5), s ps 8
& 9 (no 4), and s ps 12 & 13 (no 5/no
6) from L.
Nr: T O & T B 3rd p pr (no 6), and 5th
p pr (no 4) from R.
Nr: T O & T B s ps 4 & 5 (no 5) from R.
(7 prs)

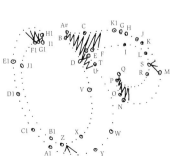

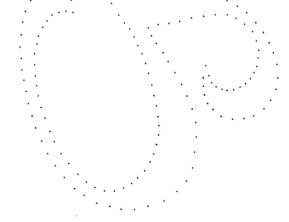

V1: Order of work   **V3:** Pin reference plan, Version 1   **V2:** Pricking

After pin H1:
T O & T B s ps 2 & 3 (no 7), and s ps 6
& 7 (no 6) from R.
Cls thro rem 2 p prs, T O & T B leaders
and 2 rem p prs, and secure to back of
work with previously T B prs.

Finish at pin I1:
Cls & tw edge prs, place pin I, Cls & T O.
These 2 prs to be used for rolled edge.

Notes for rolled edges
Roll from pin I1 to pin A# (tech 9, td 9):
rolling thread – 1 x (no 7)
rolled threads – 1 x (no 7), 2 x (no 6)
Use edge prs from pin I1 for roll.
T B 1 thread (no 6) at pin J1 and pin B1.
Finish at pin A#, also adding 2 prs (no
1) into loop of rolling thread when
making last sewing.

Roll from pin A# to pin J, Section 1:
rolling thread – 1 x (no 1)
rolled threads – 3 x (no 1)
Use 2 prs added at pin A# (tech 16, td
16a),when finishing previous rolled edge.
T B 1 thread at pin K1 and pin H.
Finish at pin J.

VERSION 2
Section 1
Start at pin A#:
follow instructions for Version 1, from
pin A# to pin C.
(21 prs)
After pin C:
start Haloed Fish patt (diag v.2).
After pin D:
work locking st (tech 6, td 6) and leave
to split braid (tech 38, td 38).

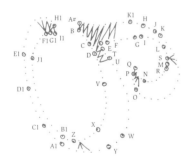

V4: Pin reference plan, Version 2

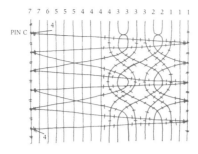

Diagram v2: Patt. 'Haloed Fish' after pin C

At pin E:
between 8th and 9th p prs from L, hang
2 prs (no 4) open on pin E, tw 2, to be
centre edge prs.

Return to pin D
Work across all prs, cont in patt, Haloed
Fish.

At pin E:
Cls & tw 2 centre edge prs.

Cont with R side of braid, Section 1

Cont in patt.
(13 prs)
At pin F:
work edge st with R centre edge pr.
After pin G and pin H:
cont in patt.

After pin I:
when prs have returned to their original
colour positions, cont in Cls.
Nr: T O & T B s ps 10 & 11 (no 3), and
s ps 14 & 15 (no 3) from R.
Nr: T O & T B 2nd p pr (no 4) from L.
(10 prs)
At pin J:
cont follow instructions for Version 1 to
pin M.
(13 prs)

After pin M:
start patt: Haloed Fish (diag v.3).
Cont in patt.
After pin N:
when patt prs have returned to their
original colour positions, cont in Cls.

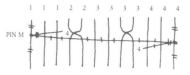

Diagram v3: Patt. 'Haloed fish' after pin M

After pin O:
follow instructions for Version 1 to
finish at pin Q.

Notes for rolled edge
As Version 1.

Return to L side of braid, Section 1a

Follow instructions for Version 1, from
pin D to pin V.
(16 prs)

After pin V:
start Haloed Fish patt (diag v.4).
After pin W:

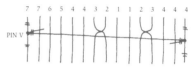

Diagram v4: Patt. 'Haloed fish' after pin V

add 1 pr (no 5) to be 1st p pr from R.
(17 prs)

After pin X:
cont in Cls.
Nr: add 1 pr (no 5) to be s ps 2 & 3
from R.
(18 prs)

After pin Y:
add 1 pr (no 5) to be 2nd p pr from R.
(19 prs)
Cont, follow instructions for Version 1 to
finish.

Notes for rolled edges
As Version 1.

W for WATERFALL

Colours

(no 1)	*White
(no 2)	Eau de Nil
(no 3)	*Ice
(no 4)	Alice Blue
(no 5)	Ocean
(no 6)	*Honeybird
(no 7)	Dark Kingfisher

VERSION 1
Section 1

Start at pin A#:

using a one colour point start (tech 23, td 23), (Note R–L working direction), hang 2 prs (no 7) open, to be edge prs (diag w.1).

Add magic thread (tech 2, td 2b).

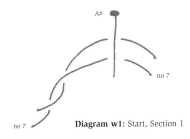

Diagram w1: Start, Section 1

On T P, hang 1 pr (no 6) to be leaders. (3 prs)

On T P, add 2 prs (no 7) open, to be p prs. Cls leaders R–L thro 2 p prs and edge st at pin B (tech 3, td 3). (5 prs)

W1: Order of work

After pin B:

add 2 p prs (no 6) to centre.

Nr: add 2 p prs (no 5) to centre.

Nr: add 2 p prs (no 6) to be s ps 4 & 5 from L, and s ps 4 & 5 from R.

Work 1 row.

Nr: add 1 p pr (no 4) to centre.

Nr: add 1 p pr (no 4) to centre.

Work 2 rows.

(13 prs)

After pin C:

start patt: Cls thro 2 p prs, tw 1 leaders, work ½ st with 6 p prs in centre, Cls rem p prs.

Cont in patt, ½ st 6 p prs.

After pin D:

when patt prs have returned to their original colour positions, cont in Cls.

(13 prs)

After pin E:

T O & T B 4 p prs from centre, 1 pr per row, till 6 p prs rem.

(9 prs)

Nr: *add 1 pr (no 7) to be 1st p pr from L.

Nr: T O & T B 2nd p pr from R*.

Rep * to * 3 more times, till all p prs (no 7).

(9 prs)

At pin F:

change leaders (no 6) with L edge pr (no 7), (tech 7, td 7).

After pin G:

add 1 pr (no 6) to be 1st p pr from L.

Nr: add 1 pr (no 6) to be s ps 14 & 15 from R.

Nr: add 1 pr (no 5) to be 2nd p pr from L.

Nr: T O & T B 2nd p pr (no 7) from R, and 1 pr (no 4) to be s ps 4 & 5 from L.

Nr: add 1 pr (no 3) to be 3rd p pr from L, and T O & T B 2nd p pr (no 7) from R.

Nr: T O & T B 2nd p pr (no 7) from R, and add 1 pr (no 3) to be s ps 6 & 7 from L.

(12 prs)

Nr: add 1 pr (no 2) to be 4th p pr from L.

Nr: T O & T B 2nd p pr (no 7) from R, and add 1 pr (no 2) to be s ps 8 & 9 from L.

Nr: add 1 pr (no 1) to be 5th p pr from L.

Nr: T O & T B 2nd p pr (no 7) from R, and add 1 pr (no 1) to be s ps 10 & 11 from L.

Nr: add 1 pr (no 1) to be 6th p pr from L.

(15 prs)

After pin H:

T O & T B 1st p pr (no 7) from R, Cls thro 1 p pr and change leaders (no 7) to (no 1), (tech 4, td 4), cont row starting patt – Cls thro 1 p pr,

tw 1 leaders, work ½ st with 7 p prs in centre, Cls rem p prs.

Cont in patt, ½ st 7 p prs.

(14 prs)

After pin I:

when patt prs have returned to their original colour positions, cont in Cls.

After pin J:

T O & T B 3 p prs from centre, 1 pr per row, lightest prs first, till 8 p prs rem.

(11 prs)

After pin K:

change leaders (no 1) to (no 7), (tech 4, td 4), cont row.

Nr: cont T O & T B p prs from centre, 1 pr per row, lightest prs first on next and foll alt rows, till 4 p prs rem.

(7 prs)

After pin L:

add 1 pr (no 7) to be 1st p pr from R.

Nr: T O & T B s ps 4 & 5 (no 4) from L, and add 1 pr (no 7) to be s ps 2 & 3 from R.

Nr: add 1 pr (no 6) to be 2nd p pr from R.

Nr: T O & T B 2nd p pr (no 5) from L, and add 1 pr (no 6) to be s ps 4 & 5 from R.

(9 prs)

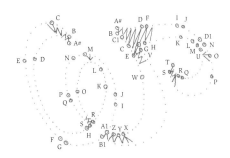

W3: Pin reference plan, Version 1

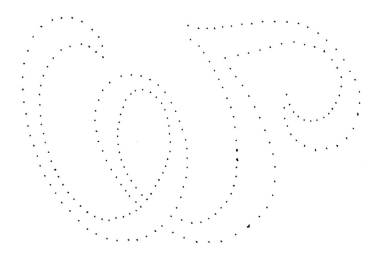

W2: Pricking

Nr: add 1 pr (no 6) to be 3rd p pr from R.
Nr: T O & T B s ps 2 & 3 (no 6) from L,
and add 1 pr (no 6) to be s ps 6 & 7
from R.
Work 1 row.
Nr: T O & T B 1st p pr (no 6) from L,
and add 1 pr (no 5) to be 4th p pr from R.
(10 prs)

At pin M:
change leaders (no 7) with L edge pr
(no 6), (tech 7, td 7).

After pin M:
add 1 pr (no 5) to be s ps 8 & 9 from L.
Nr: add 1 pr (no 4) to be 5th p pr from R.
Nr: add 1 pr (no 4) to be s ps 10 & 11
from L.

After pin N:
start patt: Cls thro 2 p prs, tw 1 leaders,
work ½ st with 6 p prs in centre, Cls
rem p prs.
Cont in patt, ½ st 6 p prs.

After pin O:
when patt prs have returned to their
original colour positions, cont in Cls.

After pin P:
add 1 pr (no 7) to be 1st p pr from L,
and T O & T B 1 p pr from centre.
Nr: add 1 pr (no 7) to be 1st p pr from
R, and T O & T B 1 p pr from centre.
(13 prs)

After pin Q:
change leaders (no 6) to (no 7), tech 4,
td 4), cont row, T O & T B 1 p pr from
centre.
Cont T O & T B 1 p pr from centre, 1 pr
per row, till all p prs (no 7).
(7 prs)
Work several more rows, work locking
st (tech 6, td 6), secure bobbins in order
and leave to work rolled edge.
Note Rolled edge must be worked before
this section may be completed.

Notes for rolled edge
Roll from Pin A# to pin R (tech 9, td 9):
rolling thread – 1 x (no 7)
rolled threads – 3 x (no 7)
Add 2 prs (no 7) to pin A# using magic
thread (tech 16a, td 16a).
T B 1 thread at pin D (tech 14, td 14).
Add 1 thread (no 7) at pin L (tech 13, td
13), cont to pin O.
Note Leave to complete Section 1.
(After completing Section 1, cont roll to
finish at pin R.)

Return to Section 1
Undo locking st, and cont in Cls, to
finish at pin R and pin S, joining to
previously worked section with top
sewings.

Note Complete rolled edge to finish at
pin R.

Section 2
Start at pin A#:
using a two colour point start (tech 1, td
1), (Note R–L working direction), hang
1 pr (no 7) and 1 pr (no 6) to be edge
prs (diag w.2).

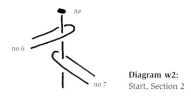

Diagram w2:
Start, Section 2

Add magic thread (tech 2, td 2a).
L edge pr is now (no 7).
R edge pr is now (no 6).

On T P, hang 1 pr (no 3) to be leaders.
(3 prs)
On T P, hang 4 prs in order L–R:
2 prs   (no 7)
1 pr   (no 6)
1 pr   (no 5)
Cls leaders thro 4 p prs and edge st at
pin B.
(7 prs)

After pin B:
add 1 pr (no 5) to be s ps 8 & 11 from L,
and add 1 pr (no 4) to be s ps 9 & 10
from L.
Nr: add 1 pr (no 4) to be s ps 4 & 7
from R, and add 1 pr (no 3) to be s ps 5
& 6 from R.
Nr: add 1 pr (no 6) to be s ps 6 & 7
from L, and add 1 pr (no 3) to be s ps 6
& 7 from R.
Nr: add 1 pr (no 2) to be 4th p pr from
R, and add 1 pr (no 5) to be 4th p pr
from L.
Nr: add 1 pr (no 2) to be s ps 18 & 19
from L.
Nr: add 1 pr (no 1) to be 5th p pr from R.
(17 prs)

After pin C:
start patt – Cls thro 6 p prs, tw 1 leaders,
work ½ st with 7 p prs in centre, Cls
rem p prs.
Cont in patt, ½ st 7 p prs.
After pin D:
add 1 pr (no 6) to be 10th p pr from R.
(18 prs)

After pin E:
add 1 pr (no 4) to be s ps 8 & 9 from L,
and add 1 pr (no 6) to be s ps 20 & 21
from R.
(20 prs)
After pin F:
work locking st (tech 6, td 6) and leave
to split braid (tech 39, td 39).

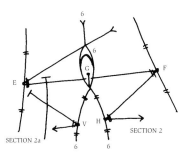

Diagram w3: Splitting braid

At pin G:
Cls & tw 2 tog, 10th and 11th p prs from
R, to be centre edge prs (diag w.3), placing
pin G, and adding magic thread (tech
2b, td 2b).

Return to pin F

Undo locking st, work across 9 p prs,
edge st with R centre edge pr at pin H.

Cont with R side of braid, Section 2

Cont in patt, ½ st 7 p prs.
(12 prs)
After pin I:
when patt prs have returned to their
original colour positions, cont in Cls.

After pin J:
T O & T B 5th p pr (no 1) from R.
(11 prs)
After pin K:
add 1 pr (no 6) to be 1st p pr from L,
Cls thro 1 more p pr, then change
leaders (no 3) to (no 7), (tech 4, td 4),
cont row T O & T B s ps 8 & 9 (no 2)
from R.
(11 prs)
Nr: add 1 pr (no 6) to be 1st p pr from
R, and T O & T B 5th p pr (no 2) from L.
Nr: add 1 pr (no 7) to be 1st p pr from
L, and T O & T B s ps 6 & 7 (no 4/no
3), and s ps 10 & 11 (no 3/no 4) from R.
Nr: T O & T B s ps 6 & 7 from R.
(9 prs)

At pin L:
change leaders (no 7) with L edge pr
(no 6), (tech 7, td 7).
After pin L:
T O & T B 4th p pr from L.
Nr: add 1 pr (no 7) to be 1st p pr from
R, and T O & T B s ps 6 & 7 (no 5) from L.
(8 prs)
After pin M
add 1 pr (no 7) to be 1st p pr from L,
Cls thro 1 more p pr, then change leaders (no 6) to (no 7), (tech 4, td 4).
(9 prs)

At pin N:
change leaders (no 7) with R edge pr

(no 6), (tech 7, td 7).
After pin N:
add 1 pr (no 7) to be 1st p pr from R,
and T O & T B 4th p pr (no 5) from L.
Nr: add 1 pr (no 7) to be 1st p pr from
L, and T O & T B s ps 6 & 7 (no 6) from R.
Nr: add 1 pr (no 7) to be 1st p pr from
R, and T O & T B 4th p pr (no 6) from L.
(9 prs)

After pin O:
add 1 pr (no 6) to be 3rd p pr from R.
Nr: add 1 pr (no 6) to be s ps 10 & 11
from L.
Nr: add 1 pr (no 6) to be 4th p pr from R.
Nr: add 1 pr (no 6) to be s ps 12 & 13
from L.
Nr: add 1 pr (no 4) to be 5th p pr from R.
Nr: add 1 pr (no 5) to be s ps 13 & 14,
and add 1 pr (no 4) to be s ps 16 & 17,
and add 1 pr (no 5) to be s ps 19 & 20
from L.
(17 prs)

After pin P:
start patt: Cls thro 3 p prs, tw 1 leaders,
work ½ st with 6 p prs, Cls rem p prs.
Cont in patt, ½ st 6 p prs.
Nr: T O & T B 2nd p pr from L.
Nr: T O & T B 2nd p pr from R.
Nr: T O & T B 2nd p pr from L.
Work 1 row.
Nr: T O & T B 2nd p pr from L.
Cont in patt, ½ st 6 p prs.
(13 prs)
After pin Q:
cont in Cls.
After pin R:
T O & T B 1 pr per row from centre, till
3 p prs rem.
(6 prs)
After pin S:
T O & T B central p pr, Cls 2 rem p prs,
T O & T B 2 rem p prs.
T O leaders (no 6), and set aside to be
used for rolled edge.

Finish at pin T:
Cls & tw both edge prs, place pin T, Cls
& T O.
T B R edge pr and secure to back of
work with previously T B prs.
Set aside L edge pr (no 7) to be used for
rolled edge.

Notes for rolled edge
Roll from pin T to pin G:
rolling thread – 1 x (no 7)
rolled threads – 1 x (no 7), 2 x (no 6)
Use L edge pr and leaders set aside at
pin T for roll.
T B 1 thread (no 7) at pin U.
Exchange rolling thread (no 7) with 1
thread (no 6) from roll at pin M.
T B 1 thread (no 7) from roll at pin K.
Finish at pin G (tech 16 a, td 16 a).
Return to Section 2a

Start at pin E:
add new leaders (no 2), (tech 31, td 31),
(diag w.3), cont row, adding 1 pr (no 3)
to be 5th p pr from L, Cls across all
p prs and edge st at pin V, using L
centre edge pr (no 6).
(10 prs)
After pin V:
add 1 pr (no 3) to be s ps 6 & 7 from R.
Nr: add 1 pr (no 3) to be 6th p pr from L.
Nr: add 1 pr (no 2) to be s ps 8 & 9
from R.
Nr: add 1 pr (no 2) to be 7th p pr from L.
Nr: add 1 pr (no 2) to be s ps 10 & 11
from R.
Nr: T O & T B 1st p pr (no 7) from L,
and add 1 pr (no 1) to be 6th p pr from R.
(15 prs)

After pin W:
T O & T B 1st p pr (no 7) from L, and
start patt: Cls thro 2 p prs, tw 1 leaders,
work ½ st with 7 p prs, Cls rem p prs.
Cont in patt, ½ st 7 p prs.
After pin X:
add 1 pr (no 7) to be 1st p pr from L.
Nr: add 1 pr (no 7) to be 1st p pr from R.
(16 prs)

After pin Y:
cont in Cls, add 1 pr (no 7) to be 1st
p pr from L, and T O & T B s ps 8 & 9
(no 2/no 3), and s ps 13 & 14 (no 1)
and s ps 18 & 19 (no 2/no 3) from R.
Note Patt prs will not have returned to
their original colour positions.
Nr: add 1 pr (no 7) to be 1st p pr from
R, and T O & T B s ps 8 & 9 (no 4/no
3), and s ps 12 & 13 (no 2), and s ps 16
& 17 (no 3/no 4) from L.
(12 prs)

After pin Z:
change leaders (no 2) to (no 7), (tech 4,
td 4), cont row T O & T B 5th p pr (no
2) from R.
Nr: T O & T B s ps 8 & 9 (no 2) from R,
and join to Section 1 at pin A1, using
top sewings.
After pin A1:
T O & T B 4th p pr (no 5) from L.

Finish at pin B1:
Set aside L edge pr (no 7) and 1st p pr
(no 7) from L for rolled edge.
T B rem prs in a bunch (tech 25, td 25)
and secure to back of work with
previously T B prs.

Notes for rolled edges
Roll from pin A1 to pin A#:
rolling thread – 1 x (no 7)
rolled threads – 3 x (no 7)
Use L edge pr and 1st p pr from L, set
aside at pin A1 for roll.
T B 1 thread at pin C1 and pin B.
Finish at pin A# adding 2 prs (no 6), to

be used for following rolled edge (tech
16a, td 16a).

Roll from pin A# to pin D1
rolling thread – 1 x (no 6)
rolled threads – 3 x (no 6)
Use 2 prs added at pin A# for rolled edge.
T B 1 thread from roll at pin F and pin J.
Finish at pin D1 (tech 10, td 10).

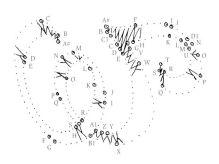

W4: Pin reference plan, Version 2

VERSION 2
Section 1
Start at pin A#:
follow instructions for Version 1, from
pin A# till (13 prs).
Work 1 row.
Nr: add 1 pr (no 6) to centre.
(14 prs)

After pin C:
start Horseshoes patt – Cls to centre
(diag w.4), work T S with centre p pr
(tech 19, td 19), cont in patt.
Work 3 patt reps,
finishing with the crossing of 6 central
patt. prs.

After pin D:
Cls both leaders to centre, (Note Patt prs
will not have returned to their original
colour positions), work a rearranged T S

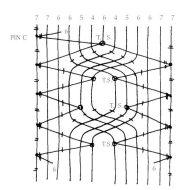

Diagram w4: Patt. 'Horseshoes' after pin C

(by twisting threads, e.g. diag w.5) to
ensure that the continuing leaders will
be (no 6), when working to R.
Cont in Cls.

After pin E:
T O & T B 1 p pr per row, from centre,
till 6 p prs rem.
Work 1 row.
(9 prs)

Nr: *add 1 pr (no 7) to be 1st p pr from L.
Nr: T O & T B 2nd p pr (no 6) from R*.
Rep * to * 3 more times, till all prs (no 7).
(9 prs)
At and after pin F:
follow instructions for Version 1 to pin H.

At pin H:
T O & T B 1st p pr (no 7), Cls thro 1
p pr and change leaders (no 7) to (no
1), (tech 4, td 4), cont row starting
Horseshoes patt – working T S with 6th
p pr from L.

Cont in patt.
Work 3 patt reps, finishing with the
crossing of 6 patt.prs.
Cls leaders to centre, (Note Patt prs will
not have returned to their original
colour positions), work T S, and cont in
Cls, working to L.
(14 prs)

After pin I:
follow instructions for Version 1, from
pin I till (13 prs).
Note This will be a few rows after pin M.
Nr: add 1 pr (no 6) to be 6th p pr from R.
(14 prs)

After pin N:
start Horseshoes patt – Cls thro 5 p prs,
work T S with centre p pr, cont in patt.
Work 1 patt rep, finishing with the
crossing of 6 central p prs.
Cls leaders to centre, (Note Patt prs will
not have returned to their original
colour positions), work a rearranged T S
to ensure that the continuing leaders
will be (no 6), when working to L.
Cont in Cls.

After pin O:
work 3 rows.
Nr: T O & T B 6th p pr (no 5) from L.
(13 prs)

After pin P:
follow instructions for Version 1, to
finish at pin R and pin S.

Notes for rolled edge
Roll as Version 1.

Section 2
Start at pin A#:
follow instructions for Version 1, from
pin A# to pin C.
(17 prs)

After pin C:
start Horseshoes patt – Cls thro 9 p prs,
work a rearranged T S with 10th p pr

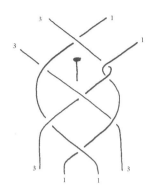

Diagram w5: An example of rearranging threads
when working Turning

(no 1), to ensure leaders will have a
mirror image colour combination
(diag w.5).
Cont in patt, using 2nd, 3rd, 4th, 5th,
6th and 7th p prs from R, Cls rem p prs.

After pin D:
add 1 pr (no 6) to be 6th p pr from L.
(18 prs)

After pin E:
add 1 pr (no 4) to be s ps 8 & 9 from L,
and add 1 pr (no 6) to be s ps 20 & 21
from R.
(20 prs)

After pin F:
when 1 patt rep has been worked, cont
in patt,
follow instructions for Version 1, to split
braid, from pin F till (12 prs).

Cont with R side of braid, Section 2
Cont in patt.
Work 3 patt reps, finishing with the
crossing of 6 patt prs.
Cls leaders to centre, (Note Patt prs will
not have returned to their original
colour positions), work a rearranged T S
to ensure that the continuing leaders
will be (no 3), when working to R.
Cont in Cls.
(12 prs)

After pin I:
follow instructions for Version 1, from
pin I to pin P.
(17 prs)

After pin P:
add 1 pr (no 6) to be 7th p pr from R.
(18 prs)
Nr: T O & T B 2nd p pr from L, start
Horseshoes patt – work T.S with 7th

p pr (no 6) from R, cont in patt, also
T O & T B 2nd p pr from L edge twice
more, and R edge once, after each
subsequent pin.
Cont in patt.
(14 prs)
Work 3 patt reps, finishing with the
crossing of 6 patt.prs, (Note Patt prs will
not have returned to their original
colour positions), work a rearranged T S
to ensure that the continuing leaders
will be (no 6), when working to R, T O
& T B 5th p pr from R.
Cont in Cls.
(13 prs)

After pin Q:
T O & T B 4th and 6th p prs from R.
Nr: T O & T B 4th p pr from L.
Nr: T O & T B 4th p pr from R.
(9 prs)

After completing blind pin R:
T O & T B 2nd and 5th p prs from L.
Nr: T O & T B 1 pr from centre.
(6 prs)

After pin S:
follow instructions for Version 1, to
finish at pin T.

Notes for rolled edge
As Version 1.

Return to Section 2a

Start at pin E:
follow instructions for Version 1, from
pin E to pin W
(15 prs)

After pin W:
start Horseshoes patt – Cls thro 5 p prs,
work a rearranged T S with 6th p pr (no
1), to ensure leaders will have a mirror
image colour combination.
Cont working patt upside-down, to
match patt direction of Section 1, also
T O & T B 1st p pr from L, after working
next L edge pin.
Work 6 patt reps, finishing with the
crossing of 6 patt prs, (Note Patt prs will
not have returned to their original
colour positions), work a rearranged T S
to ensure that the continuing leaders
will be (no 2), when working to R, cont
in Cls.
Note There is no blind pin in Version 2.

After pin X
work 1 row, then follow instructions for
Version 1, to finish at pin B1.

Notes for rolled edges
As Version 1.

X for XENON

Colours

(no 1)	*Honey
(no 2)	*Champagne
(no 3)	Sycamore
(no 4)	*Mint
(no 5)	*Jade
(no 6)	Kingfisher
(no 7)	Dark Tartan

VERSION 1

Section 1

Start at pin A#:

using a straight edge start (tech 40, td 40), (Note R–L working direction), hang 1 pr (no 6) and 1 pr (no 7) to be edge prs (diag x.1).
Add magic thread (tech 2, td 2a).
L edge pr is now (no 6).
R edge pr is now (no 7).

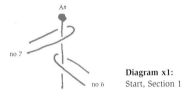

Diagram x1:
Start, Section 1

On T P, hang 1 pr (no 6) to be leaders, (diag x.2).
(3 prs)
On T P, hang 3 prs (no 6), side by side, to be p prs.
Cls leaders R–L thro 3 p prs and edge st at pin B (tech 3, td 3).
(6 prs)
After pin C:
add 1 pr (no 7) to be 1st p pr from R. Work 1 row.
Nr: add 1 pr (no 7) to be s ps 2 & 3 from R, and T O & T B 2nd p pr (no 6) from L.
Nr: add 1 pr (no 7) to be 4th p pr from L.
Nr: add 1 pr (no 6) to be 3rd p pr from R, and T O & T B s ps 2 & 3 (no 6) from L.

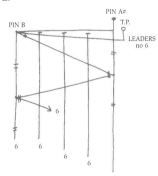

Diagram x2 : Straight edge start, R–L working direction

Work 1 row.
(8 prs)
Nr: add 1 pr (no 6) to be s ps 6 & 7 from R.
Nr: T O & T B 1st p pr (no 6) and, add 1 p pr (no 5) to be 4th p pr from R.
Nr: add 1 pr (no 5) to be s ps 8 & 9 from R.
Nr: add 1 pr (no 4) to be 4th p pr from L.
Nr: add 1 pr (no 4) to be s ps 10 & 11 from R.
Nr: T O & T B 1st p pr (no 7) from L, and add 1 p pr (no 3) to be 6th p pr from R.
(12 prs)
After pin D:
change leaders (no 6) to (no 4), (tech 4, td 4), cont row, adding 1 pr (no 3) to be s ps 8 & 9 from L.
(13 prs)
Nr: T O & T B 1st p pr (no 6) from L, and add 1 pr (no 2) to be 7th p pr from R.
Nr: add 1 pr (no 2) to be s ps 14 & 15 from R.
Nr: add 1 pr (no 1) to be 5th p pr from L.
Nr: add 1 pr (no 1) to be s ps 16 & 17 from R.
(16 prs)

After pin E:
start patt: Cls thro 2 p prs, tw 1 leaders, work ½ st with 6 p prs, Cls rem p prs.
Nr: T O & T B 2nd p pr (no 7) from R, cont in patt.
Cont in patt ½ st 6 p prs, as before.
(15 prs)
After pin F:
when patt prs have returned to their original colour positions, cont in Cls.

After pin G:
add 1 pr (no 7) to be 1st p pr from R, and add 1 pr (no 6) to be 1st p pr from L. Work 2 rows.
(17 prs)
After pin H:
change leaders (no 4) to (no 6), (tech 4, td 4), cont row T O & T B s ps 16 & 17 (no 1) from R.

Nr: T O & T B 8th p pr (no 1) from R.
Nr: T O & T B s ps 10 & 11 (no 2) from L.
Nr: T O & T B 7th p pr (no 2) from R.
Nr: T O & T B s ps 6 & 7 (no 4/no 3) and s ps 10 & 11 (no 3/no 4) from L.
(11 prs)

At pin I:
change leaders (no 6) with R edge pr (no 7), (tech 7, td 7).
After pin I:
T O & T B s ps 10 & 11 (no 3) from R.

(10 prs)
At pin J:
change leaders (no 7) with L edge pr (no 6), (tech 7, td 7).

After pin J:
T O & T B 3rd p pr (no 4) from L.
Nr: T O & T B s ps 8 & 9 (no 5) from R.
Nr: T O & T B 2nd p pr (no 5) from L.
Nr: add 1 pr (no 6) to be 1st p pr from R, and T O & T B s ps 2 & 3 (no 6) from L.

After pin K:
T O & T B 1st p pr (no 6) from L, and add 1 pr (no 6) to be s ps 2 & 3 from R. Work 2 rows.
Nr: add 1 pr (no 5) to be 2nd p pr from R.
Nr: add 1 pr (no 5) to be s ps 8 & 9 from L.
Nr: add 1 pr (no 4) to be 3rd p pr from R.
Nr: add 1 pr (no 4) to be s ps 10 & 11 from L.
(11 prs)
After pin L:
T O & T B 1st p pr (no 6) from R, and add 1 pr (no 3) to be 6th p pr from L.
Nr: add 1 pr (no 3) to be s ps 12 & 13 from L.
Nr: add 1 pr (no 2) to be 4th p pr from R.
Nr: add 1 pr (no 2) to be s ps 14 & 15 from L.
(14 prs)
After pin M:
change leaders (no 6) to (no 4), (tech 4, td 4), cont row.

After pin N:
start patt: Cls thro 4 p prs, tw 1 leaders, work ½ st with 6 p prs, Cls rem p pr.
Cont in patt, ½ st with 6 p prs.

After pin O:
when patt prs have returned to their original colour positions, cont in Cls,

Diagram X1: Order of work

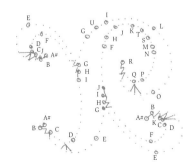

Diagram X3: Pin reference plan, Versions 1 and 2

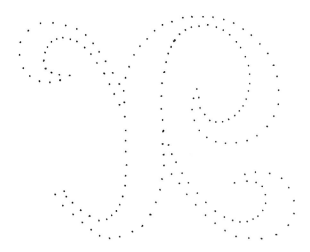

X2: Pricking

adding 1 pr (no 6) to be 1st p pr from R.
(15 prs)
After pin P:
change leaders (no 4) to (no 7), (tech 4,
td 4), cont row T O & T B s ps 10 & 11
(no 2) from R.
Nr: add 1 pr (no 6) to be s ps 2 & 3
from R, and T O & T B 7th p pr (no 2)
from L.
Nr: T O & T B s ps 12 & 13 (no 3) from L.
Nr: add 1 pr (no 7) to be 1st p pr
from R, and T O & T B 6th p pr (no 3)
from L.
Nr: T O & T B s ps 10 & 11 (no 4) from L.
(12 prs)
After completing blind pin Q:
T O & T B 5th p pr (no 4) from L.
Nr: T O & T B s ps 8 & 9 (no 5) from R.
Work 1 row.
Nr: T O & T B 4th p pr (no 5) from R.
Work 1 row.
(9 prs)
Nr: T O & T B 3rd p pr (no 6) from R.
Nr: T O & T B s ps 6 & 7 (no 6) from L.
Nr: T O & T B 2nd p pr (no 6) from R.
Nr: T O & T B 2nd p pr (no 7) from L.
(5 prs)

Finish at pin R:
T O & T B s ps 2 & 3 (no 7) from R, Cls
thro rem p pr (no 7), T O & T B rem p pr.
T O leaders and set aside, they will be
used for rolled edge.
Cls & tw both edge prs, place pin R, T O
both prs, and T B R edge pr,
set aside L edge pr.
L edge pr to be used for rolled edge.

Notes for rolled edges
Roll from pin R to pin K (tech 9, td 9):
rolling thread – 1 x (no 7)
rolled threads – 3 x (no 7)
Use leaders and L edge pr from pin R,
for roll.
T B 1 thread at pin S and pin T (tech
14, td 14).
Finish at pin K (tech 10, td 10).

Roll from pin A# to pin I:
rolling thread – 1 x (no 7)
rolled threads – 3 x (no 7)
Add 2 prs (no 7) to pin A# using magic
thread, (tech 16, td 16a).
T B 1 thread at pin G and pin U.
Finish at pin I.

Section 2

Start at pin A#:
using a two colour point start (tech 1, td
1), (Note L–R working direction), hang
1 pr (no 7) and 1 pr (no 6) to be edge
prs (diag x.3).
Add magic thread (tech 2, td 2a).
L edge pr is now (no 7).
R edge pr is now (no 6).

Diagram x3:
Start, Section 2

On T P, hang 1 pr (no 6) to be leaders.
(3 prs)
On T P, hang 2 prs in order L–R:
1 pr (no 7) and 1 pr (no 6).
Cls leaders thro 2 p prs and edge st at
pin B.
(5 prs)
Nr: *add 1 pr (no 6) to centre*.
Nr: rep * to *.
Nr: add 1 pr (no 5) to be 2nd p pr from R.
Nr: add 1 pr (no 5) to be s ps 8 & 9
from L.
Nr: add 1 pr (no 4) to be 3rd p pr from R.
Nr: add 1 pr (no 4) to be s ps 10 & 11
from L.
Nr: add 1 pr (no 3) to be 4th p pr from R.
(12 prs)
After completing blind pin C:
change leaders (no 6) to (no 3), (tech 4,
td 4), cont row.

After pin D:
start patt: Cls thro 4 p prs, tw 1 leaders,
work ½ st with 3 p prs,
Cls rem p prs.
Cont in patt, ½ st with 3 p prs.
(12 prs)

After pin E:
when patt prs have returned to their
original colour positions, cont in Cls.
(12 prs)

After pin F:
change leaders (no 3) to (no 7), (tech 4,
td 4), cont row T O & T B 4th p pr (no
3) from R.
Nr: T O & T B s ps 6 & 7 (no 4) from R.
Nr: T O & T B 5th p pr (no 4) from L.
Nr: T O & T B s ps 4 & 5 (no 5) from R.
Nr: T O & T B 4th p pr (no 5) from L.
Work 1 row.
(7 prs)
Nr: add 1 pr (no 7) to be s ps 2 & 3
from L.
Nr: T O & T B 2nd p pr (no 6) from R.
Nr: add 1 pr (no 7) to be 2nd p pr from L.
Nr: T O & T B s ps 2 & 3 (no 6) from R.
Work 1 row.
Nr: T O & T B 1st p pr (no 6) from R.
(6 prs)
At pins G & H:
join to Section 1, using top sewings
(tech 12, td 12), sewing leaders into pin H.

Finish at pin I:
T O & T B rem threads, setting aside L
edge pr (no 7), and 1st p pr (no 7) from
L, to be used for rolled edge.

Notes for rolled edge
Roll from pin I to pin A#:
rolling thread – 1 x (no 7)
rolled threads – 3 x (no 7)
Use L edge pr and 1st p pr from L for
roll.
T B 1 thread from roll at pin D and pin J.
Finish at pin A#.

Section 3

Start at pin A#:
follow instructions for Section 2 from
pin A# to pin E.
(12 prs)
After pin E:
cont in Cls.
Note Patt prs will not have returned to
their original colour positions.

After pin F:
follow instructions for Section 2 to pin
G, T O & T B p prs, lightest colours first.
At pin G, pin H and pin I:
join to Section 1, using top sewings, sew
leaders into pin I.

Finish at pin J:
T O & T B rem threads, setting aside L

edge pr (no 7), and 1st p pr (no 7) from
L, to be used for rolled edge.

Notes for rolled edge
Roll from pin A# to pin J:
rolling thread – 1 x (no 7)
rolled threads – 3 x (no 7)
Use L edge pr and 1st p pr from L for
roll.
T B 1 thread at pin D and pin K.
Finish at pin A#.

VERSION 2
Section 1
Start at pin A#:
follow instructions for Version 1, from
pin A# to pin E.
(16 prs)

After pin E:
start Dewdrops patt (diag x.4) – Cls thro
2 p prs, work patt with 3rd, 4th, 5th,
6th, 7th and 8th p prs, Cls rem p prs.
Nr: T O & T B 1st p pr (no 7) from R,
cont in patt with 6 prs, as before.
Cont in patt, with 6 patt prs.
(15 prs)

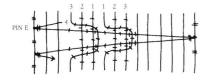

Diagram x4: Patt. 'Dewdrops' after pin E,
Section 1

After pin F:
complete patt to return patt prs to
original colour positions, cont in Cls.
After pin G:

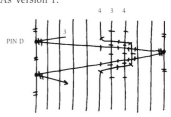

Diagram x5: Patt. 'Dewdrops' after pin N,
Section 1

follow instructions for Version 1 to pin N.
(14 prs)
After pin N:
start Dewdrops patt (diag x.5) – Cls
leaders thro 4 p prs, work patt with 5th,
6th, 7th, 8th, 9th and 10th p prs, Cls
rem p pr.
Cont in patt, with 6 patt prs.
(14 prs)
After pin O:
add 1 pr (no 6) to be 1st p pr from R,
cont in patt.
(15 prs)
After pin P:
complete patt to return patt prs to original colour positions, change leaders (no
4) to (no 7), (tech 4, td 4), cont in Cls,
follow instructions for Version 1, to
finish at pin R.

Notes for rolled edges
As Version 1.

Section 2
Start at pin A#:
follow instructions for Version 1, from
pin A# to pin D.
(12 prs)
After pin D:
start Dewdrops patt (diag x.6) – Cls thro
4 p prs, work patt with 5th, 6th and 7th
p prs, Cls rem p prs.
Cont in patt, with 3 patt prs.
(12 prs)
After pin E:
cont in Cls, follow instructions for
Version 1, to finish at pin I.

Notes for rolled edge
As Version 1.

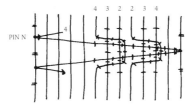

Diagram x6: Patt. 'Dewdrops' after pin D, Section
2

Section 3
Start at pin A#:
follow instructions for Version 2, Section
2, from pin A# to finish at pin J.

Notes for rolled edge
As Version 1.

Y for
THE REASON
BECAUSE...

Colours
(no 1)	*White
(no 2)	*Honey
(no 3)	Dark Ice
(no 4)	Powder Blue
(no 5)	Light Slate
(no 6)	Deep Marine
(no 7)	Steel Blue

VERSION 1
Section 1
Start at pin A#:
using a two colour point start (tech 1, td
1), (Note R–L working direction), hang
1 pr (no 5) and 1 pr (no 7) to be edge
prs (diag y.1).
Add magic thread (tech 2, td 2a).

Diagram y1:
Start, Section 1

L edge pr is now (no 5).
R edge pr is now (no 7).
On T P, hang 1 pr (no 7) to be leaders.
(3 prs)
On T P, hang 2 prs in order L–R:
1 pr (no 5) and 1 pr (no 6).
Cls leaders R–L thro 2 p prs and edge st
at pin B (tech 3, td 3).
(5 prs)
Nr: add 1 pr (no 4) to be s ps 2 & 4
from L, and add 1 pr (no 5) to be s ps 2
& 4 from R.
Nr: add 1 pr (no 6) to be 1st p pr from
R, and add 1 pr (no 4) to be 2nd p pr
from L.
Nr: add 1 pr (no 3) to be s ps 4 & 5
from L.

(10 prs)
After pin C:
change leaders (no 7) to (no 2), (tech 4,
td 4), cont row, adding 1 pr (no 2) to be
3rd p pr from L.
Nr: add 1 pr (no 2) to be s ps 6 & 7
from L.
Work 1 row.
L–R order should be:
L edge pr	2 x (no 5)
	1 x (no 5)
	2 x (no 4)
	1 x (no 3)
	4 x (no 2)
	1 x (no 3)
	1 x (no 4)
	1 x (no 5)
	1 x (no 4)
	1 x (no 5)
	1 x (no 6)
	1 x (no 5)
	3 x (no 6)
R edge pr	2 x (no 7)
leaders	2 x (no 2)
(12 prs)	

After pin D:
start patt – Cls thro 3 p prs, tw 1 leaders, Cls rem p prs.
Nr: tw 2 leaders, as before.
Nr: tw 3 leaders, as before.
Cont in patt, tw 3 leaders.

After pin E:
tw 2 leaders, as before.
Nr: rep * to *.
Nr: *tw 1 leaders, as before*.
Nr: rep * to *.
Cont in Cls.

After pin F:
T O & T B s ps 6 & 7 (no 2) from L.
(11 prs)
After pin G:
change leaders (no 2) to (no 7), (tech 4, td 4), cont row T O & T B 3rd p pr (no 2) from L.
Nr: T O & T B s ps 4 & 5 (no 3) from L.
Nr: T O & T B 5th p pr (no 4) from R.
Nr: T O & T B s ps 4 & 5 (no 4/no 5) from L.
(7 prs)
After pin H:
add 1 pr (no 7) to be 1st p pr from R, and T O & T B s ps 2 & 3 (no 5/no 4) from L.
Work 1 row.
Nr: add 1 pr (no 6) to be 1st p pr from R, and T O & T B 2nd p pr (no 6/no 5) from L.
Work 1 row.
Nr: add 1 pr (no 6) to be 1st p pr from R.
Nr: T O & T B 1st p pr (no 5/no 6) from L.
(7 prs)

At pin I:
change leaders (no 7) with L edge pr (no 5), (tech 7, td 7).
After pin I:
T O & T B 1st p pr (no 6) from L.
(6 prs)

At pin J:
change leaders (no 5) with R edge pr (no 7), (tech 7, td 7).
After pin J:
add 1 pr (no 5) to be 1st p pr from R.
Nr: add 1 pr (no 5) to be s ps 8 & 9 from L.
(8 prs)
After pin K:
change leaders (no 7) to (no 1), (tech 4, td 4), cont row.
Nr: add 1 pr (no 3) to be 5th p pr from L.
Nr: add 1 pr (no 3) to be s ps 4 & 5 from R.
Nr: add 1 pr (no 3) to be 6th p pr from L.
Nr: add 1 pr (no 1) to be s ps 6 & 7 from R.
Nr: add 1 pr (no 1) to be 7th p pr from L.
Work 2 rows.
Nr: add 1 pr (no 1) to be s ps 8 & 9 from R.
L–R order should be:
L edge pr   2 x (no 7)
                   2 x (no 7)
                   4 x (no 6)
                   2 x (no 5)
                   3 x (no 3)
                   6 x (no 1)
                   3 x (no 3)

Y1: Order of work

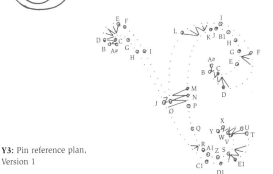

Y3: Pin reference plan, Version 1

Y2: Pricking

---

2 x (no 5)
R edge pr   2 x (no 5)
leaders   2 x (no 1)
(14 prs)

After pin L:
start patt – Cls thro 7 p prs, tw 1
leaders, Cls rem p prs.
Nr: tw 2 leaders, as before.
Nr: tw 3 leaders, as before.
Cont in patt, tw 3 leaders.
After pin M:
tw 2 leaders, as before.
Nr: tw 1 leaders, as before.

After pin N:
work locking st (tech 6, td 6) with 1st
p pr, secure all bobbins in order, and
leave to work Section 1a.

Section 1a

Start at pin A#:
using a two colour point start (tech 1, td
1), (Note L–R working direction), hang
1 pr (no 7) and 1 pr (no 5) to be edge
prs (diag y.2).
Add magic thread (tech 2, td 2a).
L edge pr is now (no 7).

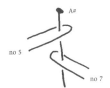

A#

no 5

no 7

Diagram y2:
Start, Section 1a

R edge pr is now (no 5).

On T P, add 1 pr (no 7) to be leaders.
(3 prs)

On T P, hang 2 prs in order L–R:
1 pr (no 6) and 1 pr (no 5).
Cls leaders thro 2 p prs and edge st at
pin B.
(5 prs)
Nr: add 1 pr (no 4) to be s ps 2 & 3
from R.
(6 prs)

After pin C:
change leaders (no 7) to (no 2), (tech 4,
td 4), cont row
adding 2 prs in order L–R:
1 x (no 3)
2 x (no 2)
1 x (no 3)
to be s ps 3, 4, 5 & 6 from R.

L–R order should be:
L edge pr   2 x (no 7)
                   2 x (no 6)
                   1 x (no 5)
                   1 x (no 4)
                   1 x (no 3)
                   2 x (no 2)
                   1 x (no 3)
                   1 x (no 4)
                   1 x (no 5)
R edge pr   2 x (no 5)
leaders   2 x (no 2)
(8 prs)

After pin D:
start patt: Cls thro 2 p prs, tw 1 leaders,
Cls rem p prs.
Nr: tw 2 leaders, as before.
Nr: tw 3 leaders, as before.
Cont in patt, tw 3 leaders.
After pin E:
tw 2 leaders, as before.
Nr: tw 1 leaders, as before.

After pin F:
cont in Cls.

After pin G:
change leaders (no 2) to (no 4), (tech 4,
td 4), cont row.
Nr: add 1 pr (no 6) to be s ps 10 & 11
from R.
Nr: T O & T B s ps 8 & 9 (no 2) from L.
Work 2 rows.
Nr: add 1 pr (no 6) to be s ps 10 & 11
from R.
(9 prs)

After pin H:
change leaders (no 4) to (no 7), (tech 4,
td 4), cont row T O & T B 2nd p pr (no
3) from R.
(8 prs)

At pin I:
change leaders (no 7) with R edge pr
(no 5), (tech 7, td 7).
After pin I:
change leaders (no 5) to (no 7), (tech 4,
td 4), cont row, adding 1 pr (no 6) to be
s ps 2 & 3 from L.
Work 1 row.
Nr: T O & T B 1 p pr (no 4).
Work 2 rows.
Nr: add 1 pr (no 7) to be 1st p pr from L.
Nr: T O & T B 1 p pr (no 5).
(8 prs)
After pin J:
Cls leaders thro all p prs, leave to return
to Section 1.

Return to Section 1

Undo locking st at pin M, Cls across all
p prs, leave.

87

Join sections

Cls & tw 2 R edge pr from Section 1a, (tech 22, td 22), and
L edge pr from Section 1, place pin O.
Cls leaders thro respective edge prs, work T S with leaders from both sections, replacing pin O as a support pin (tech 19, td 19), and T O & T B Section 1 leaders (no 1), cont with Section 1a leaders (no 7), working to R.
(21 prs)

After pin P:
T O & T B s ps 8 & 9 (no 1) from R.
Nr: cont, T O & T B 1 p pr per row, lightest colours first, till 10 p prs rem.
(13 prs)

At pin Q:
change leaders (no 7) with R edge pr (no 5), (tech 7, td 7).
After pin Q:
change leaders (no 5) to (no 7), (tech 4, td 4), cont row.
Nr: T O & T B 7th p pr (no 7) from L.
Work 1 row.
Nr: T O & T B s ps 12 & 13 (no 7) from L.
Work 1 row.
Nr: T O & T B 6th p pr (no 7) from L.
Work 1 row.
Nr: T O & T B 5th p pr (no 6) from L.
Work 1 row.
Nr: T O & T B 4th p pr (no 6) from L.
(8 prs)

After pin R:
add 1 pr (no 6) to be 6th p pr from R.
Work 1 row.
Nr: T O & T B 1st p pr (no 6) from R, and add 1 p pr (no 6) to be 1st p pr from L.
Work 1 row.
Nr: T O & T B 1st p pr (no 6) from R.
Work 1 row.
Nr: T O & T B 1st p pr (no 6) from R, and add 1 pr (no 5) to be 2nd p pr from L.
Work 1 row.
Nr: T O & T B 1st p pr (no 6) from R, and add 1 pr (no 5) to be s ps 4 & 5 from L.
Work 1 row.
Nr: add 1 pr (no 4) to be 4th p pr from R.
Nr: add 1 pr (no 3) to be s ps 6 & 7 from L.
(10 prs)

After completing blind pin S:
change leaders (no 7) to (no 5), (tech 4, td 4), cont row, start patt – tw 1 leaders between 3rd and 4th p prs from L.
Nr: tw 2 leaders, as before.
Nr: tw 3 leaders, as before.
Cont in patt, tw 3 leaders.
After pin T:
tw 2 leaders, as before.
Nr: tw 1 leaders, as before.
After pin U:
cont in Cls.

After completing blind pin V:
T O & T B s ps 8 & 9 (no 3) from R.
Nr: T O & T B 3rd p pr (no 4) from L.
(8 prs)
After pin W:
change leaders (no 5) to (no 7), (tech 4, td 4), cont row T O & T B s ps 4 & 5 (no 5) from L.
Nr: T O & T B 2nd p pr (no 5) from L.
Nr: T O & T B 2nd p pr (no 6) from R.
(5 prs)

After pin X:
Cls leaders thro 1st p pr, T O & T B both prs, T O & T B rem p pr, and secure to back of work with previously T B prs.

Finish at pin Y:
Cls & tw edge prs (no 7), place pin Y, Cls & T O.
These 2 prs to be used for rolled edge.

Notes for rolled edges
Roll from pin Y to pin A1 (tech 9, td 9):
rolling thread – 1 x (no 7)
rolled threads – 3 x (no 7)
Use both edge prs from pin Y for roll.
T B 1 thread from roll at pin S and pin Z (tech 14, td 14).
Finish at pin A1 (tech 10, td 10).

Roll from pin A#, Section 1 to pin J:
rolling thread – 1 x (no 7)
rolled threads – 3 x (no 7)
Using magic thread (tech 16, td 16a), add 2 prs (no 7) at pin A#.
T B 1 thread at pin H and pin B1 (tech 14, td 14).
Finish at pin J.

Roll from pin A#, Section 1a to pin E1:
rolling thread – 1 x (no 7)
rolled threads – 3 x (no 7)
Using magic thread, add 2 prs (no 7) at pin A#.
T B 1 thread at pin C1 and pin D1.
Finish at pin E1.

VERSION 2
Section 1
Start at pin A#:
follow instructions for Version 1, from pin A# to pin D.

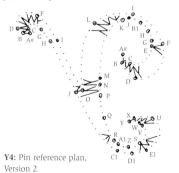

Y4: Pin reference plan, Version 2

(12 prs)
After pin D:
add 1 pr (no 2) to be 4th p pr from L.
(13 prs)
Nr: Cls thro 6 p prs, work T S with 7th p pr (no 2), work leaders (no 2) to their respective edges.
Nr: start Mittens (var) patt (diag y.3), Cls L leaders thro 2 p prs, tw 1 leaders,

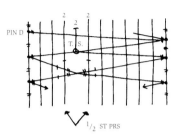

Diagram y3: Patt. 'Mittens' (var) after pin D, Section 1

tw 1 3rd p pr (no 2) from L, work ½ st with 3rd p pr from L, tw 1 leaders.
Cls R leaders thro 5 p prs, tw 1 leaders, tw 1 6th p pr (no 2) from R, work ½ st with 6th p pr from R, tw 1 leaders.
Cls & tw 2 each pr leaders, and work back to their respective edges.
Cont in patt, working ½ st with 1 patt pr only from each side.

After working 1st part of blind pin E:
working each side to match, Cls leaders to centre patt, work T S, cont in Cls working to L.
Nr: T O & T B 4th p pr (no 2) from L.
(12 prs)

After pin F:
follow instructions for Version 1 to pin L.
(14 prs)
Nr: add 1 pr (no 1) to be 8th p pr from L.
Nr: work T S with 5th p pr (no 1), work leaders (no 1) to their respective edges.
Nr: start Mittens (var) patt – Cls L leaders thro 6 p prs, tw 1 leaders, tw 1 7th
p pr (no 1) from L.
Cls R leaders thro 3 p prs, tw 1 leaders, tw 1 4th p pr (no 1) from R.
Cont in patt, working ½ st with 1 patt pr only from each side, as before.
After pin M:
Cls leaders to centre patt, work T S, cont in Cls working to L.
(15 prs)
After pin N:
work locking st (tech 6, td 6) with 1st p pr, secure all bobbins in order, and leave to work Section 1a.

Section 1a
Start at pin A#:
follow instructions for Version 1, from

pin A# to pin C.
(6 prs)
After pin C:
change leaders (no 7) to (no 2), (tech 4, td 4), cont row, adding 3 prs in order L–R:
1 x (no 3)
4 x (no 2)
1 x (no 3)
to be s ps 3, 4, 5, 6, 7 & 8 from R.
(9 prs)
After pin D:
work T S with 3rd p pr (no 2) from R, work leaders (no 2) to their respective edges.
Nr: start Mittens (var) patt – Cls L leaders thro 1 p pr, tw 1 leaders, tw 1 2nd p pr (no 3/no 2) from L.
Cls R leaders thro 2 p prs, tw 1 leaders, tw 1 3rd p pr (no 3/no 2) from R.

Cont in patt, working ½ st with 1 patt pr only from each side, as before.
Note There is no pin E in Version 2.

After pin F:
Cls leaders to centre patt, work T S, cont in Cls working to L.
Note Patt prs will not have returned to original colour positions.
Nr: T O & T B 4th p pr (no 2) from L.
(8 prs)

After pin G:
follow instructions for Version 1, from pin G, to pin J.
Note As patt prs will not have returned to their original colour positions after completion of patt, when following

Version 1 notes, decrease p prs in stated position.

After pin J:
Cls leaders thro all p prs, leave to return to Section 1.

Return to Section 1
Undo locking st at pin M, Cls across all p prs, leave.
Join sections
Cls & tw 2 R edge pr from Section 1a, (tech 22, td 22), and L edge pr from Section 1, place pin O.
Cls leaders thro respective edge prs, work T S with leaders from both sections, replacing pin O as a support pin (tech 19, td 19), and T O & T B Section 1 leaders (no 1), cont with Section 1a leaders (no 7), working to R.
(22 prs)
Nr: T O & T B 5th p pr (no 1) from R.
(21 prs)
After pin P:
follow instructions for Version 1 to pin R.
(8 prs)
After pin R:
add 1 pr (no 6) to be 6th p pr from R.
Work 1 row.
Nr: T O & T B 1st p pr (no 6) from R, and add 1 pr (no 6) to be 1st p pr from L.
Work 1 row.
Nr: T O & T B 1st p pr (no 6) from R.
Work 1 row.
(8 prs)
Nr: T O & T B 1st p pr (no 6) from R, and add 1 pr (no 5) to be 2nd p pr from L.
Nr: add 1 pr (no 5) to be s ps 4 & 5 from L.

Nr: T O & T B 1st p pr (no 6) from R, and add 1 pr (no 4) to be 3rd p pr from L.
Nr: add 1 pr (no 3) to be s ps 6 & 7 from L.
Nr: add 1 pr (no 3) to be 5th p pr from R.
(11 prs)

After completing blind pin S:
change leaders (no 7) to (no 3), (tech 4, td 4), cont row working T S with 4th p pr (no 3) from L, work leaders (no 3) to their respective edges.
Nr: start Mittens (var) patt – Cls L leaders thro 2 p prs, tw 1 leaders, tw 1 3rd p pr (no 5/no 4) from L.
Cls R leaders thro 3 p prs, tw 1 leaders, tw 1 4th p pr (no 5/no 4) from R.
Cont in patt,
working ½ st with 1 patt pr only from each side, as before.
Note There is no pin T in Version 2.

After working 1st part of blind pin V:
Cls leaders to centre patt, work T S, cont in Cls working to L.
After pin U:
T O & T B 4th p pr (no 3) from L.
(10 prs)
After completing blind pin V:
T O & T B s ps 8 & 9 (no 4) from R.
Nr: T O & T B 3rd p pr (no 3) from L.
(8 prs)
After pin W:
change leaders (no 3) to (no 7), (tech 4, td 4), and cont, following instructions for Version 1, to finish at pin Y.

Notes for rolled edges
As Version 1.

Z for ZIRCON

Colours
(no 1)	*White
(no 2)	Baby Blue
(no 3)	*Sky
(no 4)	*Pansy
(no 5)	Mid Purple
(no 6)	*Helio
(no 7)	*Mid Navy

VERSION 1
Section 1
Start at pin A#:
using a two colour point start (tech 1, td 1), (Note R–L working direction), hang 1 pr (no 6) and 1 pr (no 7) to be edge prs (diag z.1).
Add magic thread (tech 2, td 2).
L edge pr is now (no 6).
R edge pr is now (no 7).

Diagram z1:
Start, Section 1

On T P, hang 1 pr (no 6) to be leaders.
(3 prs)
On T P, hang 2 prs in order L–R:
1 pr (no 2) and 1 pr (no 5).
Cls leaders R–L thro 2 p prs and edge st at pin B (tech 3, td 3).
(5 prs)
After pin B:
add 1 pr (no 2) to be s ps 2 & 3 from L, and add 1 pr (no 4) to be 2nd p pr from R.
Nr: add 1 pr (no 1) to be 4th p pr from R.
Nr: add 1 pr (no 1) to be s ps 4 & 5 from L.
(9 prs)
After completing blind pin C:
add 1 pr (no 6) to be 1st p pr from R,

and T O & T B s ps 4 & 5 (no 1) from L.
Nr: T O & T B 2nd p pr (no 1) from L.
Nr: add 1 pr (no 7) to be 1st p pr from R, and T O & T B s ps 2 & 3 (no 2) from L.
Nr: T O & T B 1st p pr (no 2) from L, and add 1 pr (no 7) to be s ps 2 & 3 from R.
Nr: add 1 pr (no 6) to be 1st p pr from R.
(9 prs)
Nr: T O & T B 1st p pr (no 4) from L, and add 1 pr (no 6) to be s ps 2 & 3 from R.
Nr: add 1 pr (no 5) to be 2nd p pr from R.
Nr: T O & T B 1st p pr (no 5) from L, and add 1 pr (no 4) to be s ps 4 & 5 from R.
Nr: add 1 pr (no 3) to be 3rd p pr from R.
Nr: T O & T B 1st p pr (no 6) from L, and add 1 pr (no 2) to be s ps 6 & 7 from R.
(11 prs)
When completing blind pin D:
change leaders (no 6) with R edge pr (no 7), (tech 7, td 7).

After blind pin D:
add 1 pr (no 1) to be 4th p pr from R.
(12 prs)

At pin E:
change leaders (no 7) with L edge pr (no 6),
(tech 7, td 7).
After pin E:
add 1 pr (no 1) to be s ps 12 & 13 from L.
Nr: add 1 pr (no 1) to be 5th p pr from R.

After pin F:
start patt: Cls thro 6 p prs, tw 1 leaders,
work Cls & tw with 7th p pr (no 1), Cls rem
p prs.
Nr: cont in patt, Cls & tw 7th patt.pr, as
before.
Nr: cont in patt, Cls & tw 4th p pr (no 5/no
4), 7th patt.pr (no 1) and 10th p pr (no 4/no
5).
Cont in patt, Cls & tw 3 patt prs, as before.

After pin G
when patt prs have returned to their original
colour positions, work patt with 1 patt pr
(no 1) only.

After pin H:
cont in Cls.

After completing blind pin I:
T O & T B 6 p prs, 1 pr per row, lightest prs
first, till 5 p prs rem.
(8 prs)
After pin J:
add 1 pr (no 7) to be 2nd p pr from L, and
T O & T B 1 p pr (no 5).
Work 1 row.
Nr: add 1 pr (no 7) to be s ps 4 & 5 from L.
Nr' add 1 pr (no 7) to be 1st p pr from R,
and T O & T B s ps 10 & 11 (no 6) from L.
(9 prs)

At pin K:
change leaders (no 6) with L edge pr (no 7),
(tech 7, td 7).
At pin L:
change leaders (no 7) with R edge pr (no 6),
(tech 7, td 7).
After pin L:
T O & T B 2nd p pr (no 6) from R.
(8 prs)
After pin M:
add 1 pr (no 6) to centre.
After pin N:
add 1 pr (no 6) to centre.
(10 prs)

Finish at pin O and pin P:
T O all prs, set aside R edge pr (no 7) for
rolled edge, T B rem prs, and secure to back
of work with previously T B prs.

Notes for rolled edges
Roll from pin P to pin L (tech 9, td 9):
rolling thread – 1 x (no 7)
rolled threads – 3 x (no 7)

Use R edge pr (no 7) and add 3 prs (no 7) at pin P for rolled edge.
Use 4 of the 8 threads now at pin P for roll.
T B 1 thread from roll at pin Q and pin R (tech 14, td 14).
Finish at pin L (tech 10, td 10).

Roll from pin P to pin E:
rolling thread – 1 x (no 7)
rolled threads – 3 x (no 7)
Use rem 4 threads from pin P for roll.
T B 1 thread at pin S and pin T.
Finish at pin E.

Roll from pin A# to pin V:
rolling thread – 1 x (no 7)
rolled threads – 3 x (no 7)
Using magic thread (tech 16, td 16a), add 2 prs at pin A#.
T B 1 thread at pin C and pin U.
Finish at pin V.

Section 2

Start at pin A#:
using a one colour point start (tech 23, td 23), (Note L–R working direction), hang 2 prs (no 7) open, to be edge prs (diag z.2).
Add magic thread (tech 2, td 2b).
On T P, add 1 pr (no 6) to be leaders.
(3 prs)
On T P, add 2 prs (no 7) open, to be p prs.
Cls leaders L–R thro 2 p prs and edge st at pin B.
(5 prs)

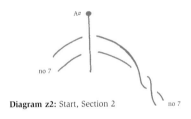

Diagram z2: Start, Section 2

After pin B:
add 1 pr (no 6) to centre.
Nr: add 1 pr (no 6) to centre.
Nr: add 1 pr (no 7) to be s ps 2 & 3 from R.
Work 1 row.
(8 prs)
Nr: add 1 pr (no 7) to be 2nd p pr from R.

Nr: add 1 pr (no 6) to be 3rd p pr from L, and add 1 pr (no 7) to be s ps 4 & 5 from R.
Nr: add 1 pr (no 6) to be 3rd p pr from R.
Nr: add 1 pr (no 6) to be s ps 6 & 7 from L, and 1 pr (no 7) to be s ps 8 & 9 from R.
(14 prs)
Nr: add 1 pr (no 6) to be s ps 6 & 7, and add 1 pr (no 7) to be s ps 11 &12, and add 1 pr (no 5) to be s ps 21 & 22 from R.
Nr: add 1 pr (no 5) to be s ps 8 & 9, and add 1 pr (no 6) to be s ps 24 & 25, and add 1 pr (no 6) to be s ps 28 & 29 from L.
(20 prs)
Nr: add 1 pr (no 5) to be 5th p pr from R, and 1 pr (no 4) to be 5th p pr from L.
Nr: add 1 pr (no 4) to be s ps 10 & 11 from L, and 1 pr (no 5) to be s ps 10 & 11 from R.
(24 prs)
After working 1st part of blind pin C:
add 1 pr (no 5) to be 6th p pr from R, and 1 pr (no 3) to be 6th p pr from L.
(26 prs)
After pin D:
add 1 pr (no 3) to be s ps 12 & 13 from L, and 1 pr (no 5) to be s ps 12 & 13 from R.
(28 prs)
After completing blind pin C:
work locking st (tech 6, td 6) and leave to split braid (tech 39, td 39).

Split braid

Work T S with 13th and 14th p prs (no 7) from R, to be centre edge prs (diag z.3), placing pin E as a support pin (tech 19, td 19), and adding magic thread (tech 2, td 2b), tw 2 both prs.

Return to pin C

Undo locking st, cont to pin F, adding 1 pr (no 6) to be 7th p pr from R.

At pin F:
edge st with R centre edge pr.
After pin F:
work locking st with 1st p pr (tech 6, td 6).

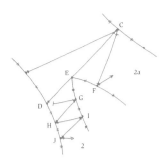

Diagram z3: Splitting braid

Cont with Section 2

After pin D:
add 1 pr (no 6) to be leaders (tech 31, td 31), and work to pin G.

At pin G:
edge st with L centre edge pr.
(14 prs)
After pin H:
add 1 pr (no 2) to be 7th p pr from L.
(15 prs)
After pin I:
T O & T B 2nd p pr (no 6) from R, and start patt – Cls thro 6 p prs, tw 1 leaders, work Cls & tw with 7th p pr (no 2) from L, Cls rem p prs.

After pin J:
T O & T B 2nd p pr (no 6) from L, and cont in patt, Cls & tw 2nd p pr (no 5), 5th patt.pr (no 2) and 8th p pr (no 5) from R.
Cont in patt, Cls & tw 3 patt prs, as before.
(13 prs)
After pin K:
add 1 pr (no 6) to be 2nd p pr from L, and add 1 pr (no 6) to be 2nd p pr from R, cont in patt with 1 patt pr (no 2) only.
(15 prs)
After pin L:
add 1 pr (no 6) to be 2nd p pr from L,

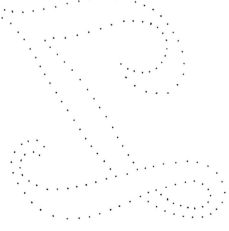

Z1: Order of work

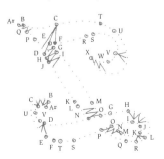

Z3: Pin reference plan, Version 1

Z2: Pricking

and add 1 pr (no 6) to be 2nd p pr from
R, cont in Cls.
(17 prs)

After pin M:
T O & T B 1 p pr (no 2).
Nr: T O & T B 1 p pr (no 3).
Nr: T O & T B 1 p pr (no 3), and add 1
pr (no 7) to be 1st p pr from R, and add
1 p pr (no 7) to be 2nd p pr from L.
Next 2 rows: T O & T B 1 p pr (no 4).
Nr: T O & T B s ps 12 & 13 (no 5) from L.
(13 prs)

Finish at pin N and pin O:
join to Section 1, using top sewings
(tech 12, td 12).
T O all prs, set aside 1st p pr (no 7)
from L, and L edge pr (no 7) to use for
rolled edge.
T B rem prs, and secure to back of work
with previously T B prs

Notes for rolled edge
Roll from pin N to pin A#:
rolling thread – 1 x (no 7)
rolled threads – 3 x (no 7)
Use 2 prs from pin N for roll.
T B 1 thread at pin P and pin Q.
Finish at pin A#.

Return to Section 2a

After pin F:
start patt – Cls thro 6 p prs, tw 1
leaders, work Cls & tw with 7th p pr
(no 6) from L.
Nr: cont in patt, Cls & tw 4th p pr (no
6), 7th patt.pr (no 6) and 10th p pr (no
6) from R.
(16 prs)
Cont in patt, Cls & tw 3 patt prs, as
before.

After pin R:
cont patt with 7th patt pr (no 6) only.

After pin S:
cont in Cls.

After pin T:
T O & T B 1 p pr per row from centre,
till 8 p prs rem.
(11 prs)

After pin U:
add 1 pr (no 6) to be 1st p pr from R,
and T O & T B 1 p pr (no 6) from centre.
Nr: T O & T B 1 p pr (no 6) from centre.
Nr: add 1 pr (no 6) to be s ps 2 & 3
from R, and T O & T B 1 p pr (no 6)
from centre.
Nr: T O & T B 1 p pr (no 6) from centre.
(9 prs)
Nr: add 1 pr (no 5) to be 2nd p pr from
R, and T O & T B s ps 4 & 5 (no 7) from L.
Nr: T O & T B 2nd p pr (no 7) from L,

and add 1 pr (no 5) to be s ps 4 & 5
from R.
Nr: add 1 pr (no 4) to be 3rd p pr from R.
Nr: add 1 pr (no 3) to be s ps 10 & 11
from L.
Nr: add 1 pr (no 2) to be 4th p pr from
R.
Nr: add 1 pr (no 1) to be s ps 12 & 13
from L.
Nr: add 1 pr (no 1) to be 5th p pr from R.
(14 prs)

After completing blind pin V:
start patt – Cls st thro 6 p prs, tw 1
leaders, work Cls & tw with 7th p pr
(no 1) from L.
Nr: cont in patt, Cls & tw 2nd p pr (no
5), 5th patt pr (no 1) and 8th p pr (no
5) from R.
Cont in patt, Cls & tw 3 patt prs, as before.

After pin W:
cont in patt with 1 patt pr (no 1) only.
Nr: cont in Cls.
Nr: T O & T B 7th p pr (no 1) from L.
Nr: T O & T B s ps 8 & 9 (no 1) from R.
Nr: T O & T B 6th p pr (no 2) from L.
Nr: T O & T B s ps 6 & 7 (no 3) from R.
Nr: T O & T B 5th p pr (no 4) from L.
Nr: T O & T B s ps 2 & 3 (no 6/no 5)
and s ps 6 & 7 (no 5/no 6) from R.
(7 prs)
Nr: Cls 2 centre p prs tog, and T O &
T B , Cls leaders thro 2 rem p prs (diag
z.4), T O & T B leaders and 2 rem p prs,
and secure all T B prs to back of work,
with previously T B prs.

Finish at pin X:
Cls & tw both edge prs (no 7), place pin
X, Cls & T O both prs.
These 2 prs to be used for rolled edge.

Notes for rolled edge
Roll from pin X to pin E:
rolling thread – 1 x (no 7)
rolled threads – 3 x (no 7)
Use both edge prs from pin X for roll.
Finish at pin E, using magic thread
(tech 16, td 16a).

VERSION 2
Section 1
Start at pin A#:
follow instructions for Version 1, from
pin A# to pin F.
(14 prs)

After pin F:
Cls thro 4 p prs, start Basketweave (var)
patt – (diag z.5), Cls tog next 4 p prs in
2 sets of 2 prs, Cls leaders thro 2 patt
sets, Cls rem p prs.

Nr: Cls thro 2 p prs, Cls tog next 4 p prs
in 2 sets of 2 prs, Cls leaders thro 2 patt

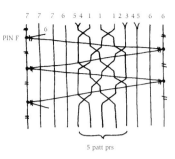

Diagram z5: 'Basketweave' (var). After pin F,
Section 1

sets, Cls rem p prs.
Cont in Basketweave (var), using 5
p prs, as before.
Note There is no pin G in Version 2.

After pin H:
cont in Cls, and follow instructions for
Version 1 to finish at pin P.
Note Patt prs will not have returned to
their original colour positions.

Notes for rolled edge
As Version 1.

Section 2
Start at pin A#:
follow instructions for Version 1, from
pin A# to pin I.
(15 prs)

After pin I:
T O & T B 2nd p pr (no 6) from R.
(14 prs)
After pin J:

T O & T B 2nd p pr (no 6) from R, and
Cls thro 3 p prs, start Basketweave (var)
patt, using next 5 p prs, as before, Cls
rem p prs.
(13 prs)
Nr: Cls thro 2 p prs, cont Basketweave
(var), using 5 p prs, as before.
Cont in Basketweave (var) patt, using 5
p prs, as before.
After pin K:
add 1 pr (no 6) to be 2nd p pr from L,
and add 1 p pr (no 6) to be 2nd p pr
from R, cont in patt.
(15 prs)
After pin L:
add 1 pr (no 6) to be 2nd p pr from L,
and add 1 p pr (no 6) to be 2nd p pr
from R.
(17 prs)

After pin M:
Cls 2 patt sets tog, to return threads to
original colour positions, T O & T B 1
p pr (no 2).
(16 prs)
Cont in Cls,
follow instructions for Version 1, to
finish at pin O.

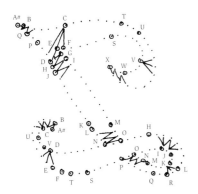

Diagram Z4: Pin reference plan, Version 2

Notes for rolled edge
As Version 1.

Return to Section 2a
After pin F:
Cls thro 4 p prs, start Basketweave (var) patt, using 5 p prs, as before.
Nr: Cls thro 4 p prs, cont Basketweave (var) patt, using 5 p prs, as before.
(16 prs)
Cont in Basketweave (var) patt, using 5 p prs, as before.
Note There is no pin R in Version 2.

After pin S:
cont in Cls.
Note Patt prs will not have returned to their original colour positions.

After pin T:
T O & T B 1 p pr per row, from near centre, lightest prs first, till 8 p prs rem.
(11 prs)
After pin U:
follow instructions for Version 1 to pin V.

After pin V:
Cls thro 4 p prs, start Basketweave (var) patt, using 5 p prs, as before.

Nr: Cls thro 2 p prs, cont Basketweave (var) patt, using 5 p prs, as before.
Cont in Basketweave (var) patt, using 5 p prs, as before.

After pin W:
Cls 2 patt sets tog,

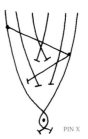

Diagram z4: Finish at pin X, Section 2a

Cont in Cls, T O & T B 9th p pr (no 1/no 2) from L.
Note Patt prs will not have returned to their original colour positions.
(13 prs)
Nr: T O & T B 5th p pr (no 1) from R.
Nr: T O & T B 6th p pr (no 2/no 1) from L.
Nr: T O & T B s ps 6 & 7 (no 3) from R.
Nr: T O & T B 5th p pr (no 4) from L.
Nr: T O & T B s ps 2 & 3 (no 6/no 5) and s ps 6 & 7 (no 5/no 6) from R.
(7 prs)
Nr: Cls 2 centre p prs tog, and T O & T B, Cls leaders thro 2 rem p prs (diag z.4), T O & T B leaders and 2 rem p prs, and secure all T B prs to back of work, with previously T B prs.

Finish at pin X:
follow instructions for Version 1 to finish.

Notes for rolled edge
As Version 1.

Hellebore (Extra)

One of the simplest methods of extending the design possibilities of a basic shape is illustrated by these two motifs. By referring to the original *H for Hellebore* pattern (page 29) it can be seen that Sections 1 and 1a have been duplicated, with one section reversed and placed on top of the other, to share the start pin A#. In order to unite the two pattern pieces, the sections to be worked have been carefully selected to suggest an intertwining plant form. The result of this selection is that the motif becomes more interesting, since the predictable symmetry is altered. Note that the central leaf shapes no longer form a mirror image.

In the motif using the basic colour arrangement (left), each section is worked in the same way as those of the original. However, in the version using the shaded colour arrangement (right), the colour tones are darker in the the areas that would be in shadow. This enhances the three-dimensional qualities of the plant form.

Note that although the original pattern shapes have been placed one on top of the other, when the piece is worked, the lower shape is finished and rejoined to the upper shape, while still keeping the pattern and colour sequence correct. If the lower shape were to be worked underneath the upper shape, the motif would be very bulky and threads from the lower shape would show through. Since the two pieces of lace would have no distance between them, there would be no sense of perspective and therefore the work's three-dimensional quality would be lost.

Hellebore (Extra)

(Basic colour arrangement)
Colours
As *H for Hellebore*.

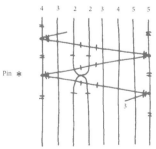

diagram h. extra 1: Pin*, Section 1

Hellebore Extra 1: Order of work

Hellebore Extra 3: Pin reference
plan, Sections 1 and 1a

Section 1

Start:
follow instructions for H for Hellebore,
Sections 1 and 1a, Version 2.

Note To ensure exact replication of
pattern it is useful to know the colour
order and pattern positions after pin C,
pin F and pin *.

L–R colour order after pin C:

L edge pr	2 x (no 7)
	2 x (no 7)
	2 x (no 6)
	2 x (no 5)
	4 x (no 4)
	2 x (no 5)
	2 x (no 6)
	2 x (no 7)
R edge pr	2 x (no 5)
leaders	2 x (no 5)
(11 prs)	

L–R colour order after pin F:

L edge pr	2 x (no 4)
	2 x (no 3)
	2 x (no 2)
	2 x (no 3)
	2 x (no 4)
	2 x (no 5)
	2 x (no 6)
	2 x (no 7)
R edge pr	2 x (no 5)
leaders	2 x (no 3)
(10 prs)	

L–R colour order after pin *, (see diag
h.e.1).
Cont changing p prs until 1 p pr (no 2)
has been added, and 9 prs rem, secure
all bobbins in order, and leave to work
Section 1a and Section 1b.

Section 1a

L–R colour order, after splitting braid,
before adding new leaders, at pin E:

L edge pr	2 x (no 7)
	2 x (no 7)
	2 x (no 6)
	2 x (no 5)
	2 x (no 4)
	2 x (no 3)
	2 x (no 2)
	2 x (no 3)
R edge pr	2 x (no 4)
(9 prs)	

Notes for rolled edges
As 'H', Version 2.
Note Replace magic thread (tech 16b, td
16b) pin A#, Section 1, for use at start
of rolled edge Section 1c, or, *add 2
extra prs (no 7) into loop for 1st rolled
edge, (tech 16a, td 16a) at pin A#,
Section 1a.
Roll from pin B1 to pin E1.
Roll from pin A# to pin G1.

Section 1b

Start:
as Section 1.
Note Reverse L–R instructions.
Notes for rolled edges
As 'H', Version 2.

Return to Section 1

Join to Section 1b using top sewings.

Notes for rolled edge
Roll from joining pin Section 1b to pin I:
rolling thread – 1 x (no 5)
rolled thread – 1 x (no 5)
Finish at pin I.

Section 1c

Start:

as Section 1a.

Note Reverse L–R instructions, and the blind pin before pin C.

Add R edge pr (no 7) and 1st p.pr (no 7), using magic thread at pin A# and top sewings at pin B, or, *2 extra prs (no 7) added previously, when working rolled edge, Section 1a.

After pin C:

change leaders (no 7) to (no 5), (tech 4, td 4).

After pin D:

change leaders (no 5) to (no 3), (tech 4, td 4).

After pin E:

change leaders (no 3) to (no 2), (tech 4, td 4).

Notes for rolled edges

As Section 1a.

Hellebore (Extra)

(Shaded colour arrangement)

Section 1

Start:

follow instructions for H for Hellebore, Sections 1 and 1a, Version 2.

Note R edge pr must be (no 6). Cont adding prs as for Basic colour arrangement.

After pin F:

T O & T B s ps 2 & 3 (no 7/no 6) from R. (10 prs)

After pin H:

work 2 rows, then T O & T B s ps 4 & 5 (no 5/no 4) from L. (9 prs)

After pin I:

gradually T O & T B p prs,` lightest first, and add (no 7) p prs to R edge till (no 7) and (no 6) p prs rem. (8 prs)

After pin J:

change leaders (no 3) to (no 7), (tech 4, td 4).

At R edge, before pin K:

change leaders (no 7) with R edge pr (no 6), (tech 7, td 7).

At next L edge:

change leaders (no 6) with L edge pr (no 4), (tech 7, td 7), then change leaders (no 4) to (no 7), (tech 4, td 4). Cont foll instructions for Basic colour arrangement.

Section 1a

Start:

foll instructions for Basic colour arrangement.

Notes for rolled edges

As Basic colour arrangement.

Section 1b

Start:

add prs to give L–R colour order after pin *, (see diag h.e.2).

After pin J:

change p prs, to ensure that L–R order is as foll, after completing blind pin M:

L edge pr	2 x (no 5)
	2 x (no 4)
	2 x (no 3)
	1 x (no 2)
	2 x (no 1)
	1 x (no 2)
	2 x (no 3)
	2 x (no 4)
	2 x (no 5)
	2 x (no 6)
R edge pr leaders	2 x (no 7)
	2 x (no 4)
(11 prs)	

To finish at pin Q:

Cls leaders (no 4) thro 2 rem p prs (no 5) & (no 6).

T O & T B leaders (no 4) and p.pr (no 5).

T O p.pr (no 6) and set aside, this pr to be used for rolled edge.

Cls & tw edge prs, place pin Q, Cls & to both prs.

T B L edge pr (no 5).

Set aside R edge pr to be used for rolled edge.

Secure rem threads in a bunch to back of work, using previously T B prs.

Notes for rolled edge

Roll from pin Q to pin I:

rolling thread – 1 x (no 7)

rolled threads – 1 x (no 7); 2 x (no 6)

Use threads set aside at pin Q for roll.

T B 1 thread from roll at pin M and pin L (tech 14, td 14).

Finish at pin I.

Return to Section 1

Join to Section 1b using top sewings.

Notes for rolled edge

As Basic colour arrangement, using L edge pr (no 6) for roll.

Hellebore Extra 2: Pricking

Hellebore Extra 4: Pin reference plan, Sections 1b and 1c

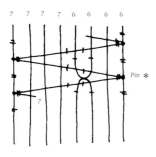

7 7 7 7 6 6 6 6

7

Pin *

Diagram h. extra 2: Pin*, Section 1b

Section 1c
Start:
as Basic colour arrangement, leaders (no 7), R edge pr (no 7) and 1st p.pr (no 7).
Add p prs to give L–R order at pin C:

	2 x (no 7)
	2 x (no 6)
	2 x (no 5)
	2 x (no 6)
	2 x (no 7)
R edge pr	2 x (no 7)
leaders	2 x (no 7)
(7 prs)	

Cont adding p prs to give order at pin E,

Section 1, T O & T B 1 p.pr (no 7) and 1 p.pr (no 6) from L as braid widens, also, after pin D, change leaders (no 7) to (no 5), (tech 4, td 4).

After pin E:
change leaders (no 5) to (no 2), (tech 4, td 4).
Cont as Basic colour arrangement to finish.

Notes for rolled edge
As Basic colour arrangement.

Chinese Seedling Collection

The *Chinese Seedling Motif* forms the basis for the *Chinese Seedling Collection* (illustrated on page 98). The motif has been developed from *I for Ice* (page 33). The patterns and colour choices were inspired by antique Chinese textiles and porcelain.

The *Chinese Seedling Motif* (centre), illustrated using colour set 1, is modified slightly when developed into the *Chinese Seedling Border* and *Chinese Seedlings* designs.

Chinese Seedling Border (left) is illustrated using two 7-colour sets: set 2 and set 3. The design is constructed of six motifs joined into a circle with each of the tonally similar colour sets alternating to give an undulating effect.

Chinese Seedlings (right) is illustrated using three 7-colour sets: set 4, set 5 and set 6. The design construction is similar to that of the *Chinese Seedling Border*, but three of the alternating motifs of the border are reversed, suggesting a triangular form, and three more motifs have been added in the centre. The swirling effect of this design is enhanced by a more clearly defined colour and tonal change, emphasised by these three extra motifs in the centre.

The techniques given for all the designs include the following: working a cloth stitch braid that changes to Tenstick, a supported Tenstick edge, decorative short rows while increasing and decreasing passive pairs, sewing into a supported Tenstick edge and rolled edges using the Withof technique, and also increasing and decreasing within the roll. Section 1 may be worked using Half-stitch or the Milanese braid Mittens. *Chinese Seedling Border* and *Chinese Seedlings* may use a combination of both.

Colours	Set 1	Set 2	Set 3		Set 4	Set 5	Set 6
(no 1)	*White	*White	*White	(no 1)	*White	*White	*White
(no 2)	Dark Ivory	Flesh	Flesh	(no 2)	Dark Ice	Ecru	Dark Ice
(no 3)	*Honey	Pastel Pink	Pastel Pink	(no 3)	*Ice	*Honey	*Baby Blue
(no 4)	*Champagne	*Pale Salmon	*Soft Beige	(no 4)	Eau de Nil	*Champagne	Powder Blue
(no 5)	*Mint	*Soft Beige	*Rose	(no 5)	Powder Blue	Eau de Nil	*Sky
(no 6)	Pale Sage	*Peach Pink	*Peach Pink	(no 6)	*Mint	*Mint	Pale Sage
(no 7)	Dark Sage	*Orchid	*Orchid	(no 7)	Pale Sage	Pale Sage	Dark Sage

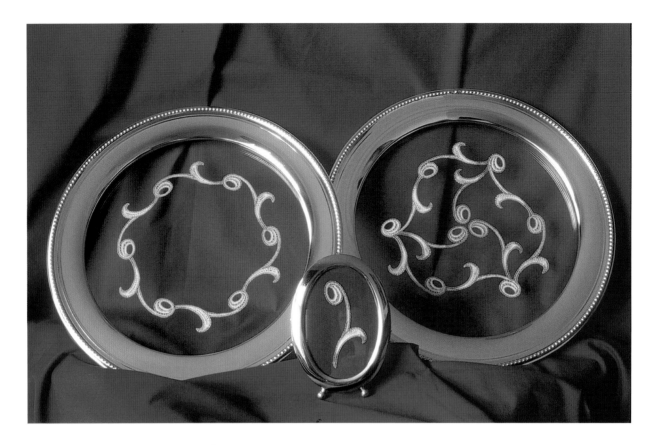

Chinese Seedling Motif

(Illustrated using colour set 1,
'Half-stitch')

Section 1
Start at pin A#:
Follow instructions for I for Ice, Version
1, Section 1,
from pin A# to pin H, reversing L–R
directions.
Note L–R working direction

After pin H:
T O & T B 1 pr (no 6).
Work 1 row.
Nr: T O & T B 1 pr (no 6)
(4 prs)
Nr: Cls thro rem p.pr (no 6), and T O &
T B rem p.pr and leaders.

Finish at pin I:
Cls & tw both edge prs, place pin I, Cls
prs tog & T O. T B R edge pr (no 6)

Notes for rolled edge
Roll from pin I to pin A#:
rolling thread – 1 x (no 7)
rolled threads – 3 x (no 7)
Use leaders and L edge pr for roll.
T B I thread from roll at pin F.
T B 1 thread at 2nd pin before finishing
at pin A#.

Section 2
Start at pin A#:
using a narrow angle start (tech 17, td
17):
add 1 pr (no 7) to be L edge pr, and into
its loop, add 1 pr (no 6) to be leaders,
and 1 pr (no 6) to be 1st p.pr from L,

tw 2 L edge pr (no 7).
(3 prs)
Nr: Cls leaders (no 6) thro 1st p. pr (no
6), tw 2 leaders to join at pin B1, tw 2
leaders.
Nr: work to pin B2: tw 2 leaders, place
pin B2, edge st at pin B2.
Nr: add from pin B1 – 1 pr (no 7) to be
2nd p.pr from L, Cls thro 2 p prs, join as
before, at pin B3.
(4 prs)
Work 1 row.
Nr: add from pin B3 – 1 pr (no 5) to be
3rd p.pr from L, add, on temp pins, in
L–R order,
1 pr (no 4) to be 4th p.pr,
1 pr (no 5) to be 5th p.pr, and
1 pr (no 6) to be 6th p.pr from L.
Cls thro 6 p prs, join as before, at pin B4.
(8 prs)

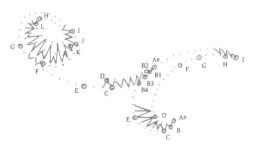

Chinese Seedling Motif 2:
Pin reference plan

Chinese Seedling Motif 1:
Pricking and order of work

Work 1 row.
Nr: add, from pin B4 – 1 pr (no 7) to be R edge pr, tw 2.
Cont in Cls.
(9 prs)
After pin C:
T O & T B 5th p.pr (no 7) from R.
(8 prs)
After pin D:
change L edge pr to be smooth edge pr, (tech 32, td 32) and work to R edge, edge st, work a locking st (tech 6, td 6) with leaders and 1st p.pr from R.
Untwist L edge pr, and Cls with 1st p.pr from L.
Undo locking st, and start Tenstick, i.e. Cls to L and work smooth edge st.
Cont in Tenstick.
(8 prs)
After pin E:
T O & T B 1 pr (no 4), and remove pin D and its preceding pin, to allow a smooth line to develop.
(7 prs)
At pin F:
cont Tenstick, placing pin F as a support pin (tech 19, td 19b).
Note When using support pins, leave pins in work for as little time as possible, aim to complete the section in one session.
Cont Tenstick, placing support pins, to pin H, on the smooth L edge.
Note Do not remove these support pins until after the side sewings have been made.

After pin G:
T O & T B 4th p.pr (no 7) from R.
L–R order should now be as foll:
smooth edge pr   2 x (no 6)
                   4 x (no 5)
                   2 x (no 6)
R edge pr   2 x (no 7)
leaders   2 x (no 6)
(6 prs)
After pin H:
when continuing to use support pins, only 2 or 3 pins need to left in the work at any time, as there will be no side sewings made into these pinholes.

After pin I:
add 1 pr (no 6) to be s ps 5 & 6 from R.
Nr: add 1 pr (no 4) to be s ps 8 & 9 from R.
Nr: add 1 pr (no 6) to be s ps 6 & 7 from R.
Nr: add 1 pr (no 6) to be s ps 7 & 8 from R.
(10 prs)
After pin J:
Cls R–L thro 3 p prs, work T S (tech 19, td 19) with 4th p.pr (no 6), place support pin K, work back to R edge, adding 1 pr (no 4) to be s ps 4 & 5 from R.

(11 prs)
Nr: work to L, adding 1 pr (no 3) to be s.p 15 & 16 from R.
Nr: work to R, adding 1 pr (no 1) to be s.ps 16 & 17, and add 1 pr (no 3) to be s ps 5 & 6 from R.
(14 prs)
Nr: work a T S with 6th p.pr (no 6) from R, place support pin, and work back to R, adding 1 pr (no 2) to be s ps 6 & 7 from R.
L–R order should be as foll:
smooth edge pr   2 x (no 6)
                   1 x (no 5)
                   1 x (no 4)
                   1 x (no 3)
                   2 x (no 1)
                   1 x (no 3)
                   1 x (no 4)
                   1 x (no 5)
                   6 x (no 6)
                   1 x (no 5)
                   1 x (no 4)
                   1 x (no 3)
                   2 x (no 2)
                   1 x (no 3)
                   1 x (no 4)
                   1 x (no 5)
                   2 x (no 6)
R edge pr   2 x (no 7)
leaders   2 x (no 6)
(15 prs)
Nr: *work to L edge.
Nr: work to R edge.
Nr: work to L edge, work T S with 7th p.pr from R,
place support pin, then work back to R edge*.
Cont rep * to *.
Note When using the support pins for decorative short rows, if they are allowed to remain in situ, and the threads tensioned accordingly, decorative holes will be created.

Join to existing braid at and after pin F with side sewings, tw 1 leaders.
Note Do not cut off edge pr, it will be required for rolled edge, also do not replace R side pins after sewings.
Decrease prs evenly, lightest prs first, as braid narrows.
At pin L:
work X T X instead of the normal T S, placing support pin after X T.

Finish at pin H:
sew smooth edge pr into pin H,
T O & T B rem prs in a bunch, and secure to back of work with previously T O & T B prs.

Notes for rolled edge
Roll from pin F to pin B4:
rolling thread – 1 x (no 7)
rolled thread – 1 x (no 7)
Using 1 pr (no 7) previously left at pin F.

Add 1 thread (no 6) at pin G (tech 13, td 13).
Finish at pin B4.

Chinese Seedling Border

(Illustrated using colour sets 2 & 3, Mittens)

Section 1 (colour set 2)
Note Sections 1, 3, 5, 7, 9 & 11, or an alternate combination, may also be worked in 'Half-stitch', follow instructions for Chinese Seedling Motif, Section 1.

Start at pin A#:
follow instructions for I for Ice, Version 2, Section 1 from pin A# to pin H, reversing L–R directions.
Note L–R working direction
After pin H:
T O & T B 1 pr from centre.
(5 prs)
Cont to pin M:
Tw 2 leaders,
Note Do not edge st.
Leave enough thread to join to Section 12, when completed, at pins M & N with top sewings.
Note Threads may be removed from bobbins, plaited loosely and placed away from work.

Notes for rolled edge
When Section 12 has been completed, and Section 1 has been joined using top sewings:
Note It may be advisable to hang in new threads for roll.
Roll from pin M to pin A#:
rolling thread   1 x (no 7)
rolled threads   3 x (no 7)
Use leaders and L edge pr for roll.
T B 1 thread from roll at pin F.
T B 1 thread at 2nd pin before finishing at pin A#.

Section 2 (colour set 2)
Follow instructions for Chinese Seedling Motif, Section 2.
Notes for rolled edge
As Chinese Seedling Motif, Section 2.

Section 3 (colour set 3)
Follow instructions for Chinese Seedling Border, Section 1, to pins M & N, using top sewings.
Join to Section 2 at pins M & N.
Notes for rolled edge
As Chinese Seedling Motif, Section 1.

Section 4 (colour set 3)
Follow instructions for Chinese Seedling Motif, Section 2.

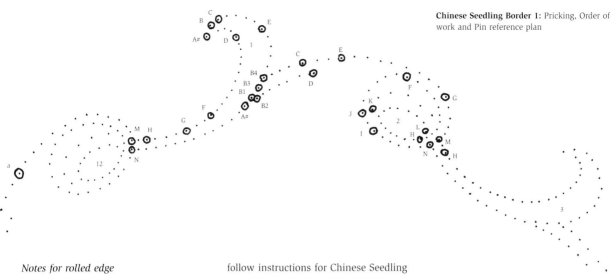

Notes for rolled edge
As Chinese Seedling Motif, Section 2.

Sections 5 and 9 (colour set 2)
Follow instructions for Chinese Seedling
Border, Section 3, joining to previously
worked section using top sewings.
Notes for rolled edge
As Chinese Seedling Motif, Section 1.

Sections 6 and 10 (colour set 2)
Follow instructions for Chinese Seedling
Motif, Section 2, joining to previously
worked section using top sewings.
Notes for rolled edge
As Chinese Seedling Motif, Section 2.

Sections 7 and 11 (colour set 3)
Follow instructions for Chinese Seedling
Border, Section 3, joining to previously
worked section using top sewings.
Notes for rolled edge
As Chinese Seedling Motif, Section 1.

Sections 8 and 12 (colour set 3)
Follow instructions for Chinese Seedling
Motif, Section 2, joining to previously
worked section with top sewings.
Notes for rolled edge
As Chinese Seedling Motif, Section 2.

*Note After Section 12 has been
completed, Section 1 may then be
completed and the edge rolled. See
Chinese Seedling Border, Section 1.*

Chinese Seedlings

(Illustrated using colour sets 4, 5, & 6,
'Half-stitch')

Section 1 (colour set 4)
Note Sections 1, 3, 5, 7, 9, 11, 13, 15 &
17, or any combination, may also be
worked in 'Mittens', follow instructions
for Chinese Seedling Border, Section 1.
Start at pin A#:

follow instructions for Chinese Seedling
Motif from pin A# to pin H.
Note L–R working direction
(5 prs)
Cont to pin I:
work edge st at pin I, Cls thro 2 passive
prs, and leave enough thread to join to
Section 12, when completed, at pins M
& N with top sewings.
Note Threads may be removed from
bobbins, plaited loosely and placed
away from work.
Notes for rolled edge
As Chinese Seedling Border, Section 1,
from pin M to pin A#.

Section 2 (colour set 4)
Follow instructions for Chinese Seedling
Motif, Section 2.
Notes for rolled edge
As Chinese Seedling Motif , Section 2,
finishing at pin B4.

Section 3 (colour set 5)
Follow instructions for Chinese Seedling
Motif, Section 1,
to pin H.
Note Reverse L–R instructions.

After pin H:
cont in Cls with 6 prs
to finish, using top
sewings, at pins M,
N & O.
Note There is no
pin I.

Notes for rolled edge
As Chinese Seedling Motif, Section 1,
from pin M to pin A#.

Section 4 (colour set 5)
Follow instructions for Chinese Seedling
Motif, Section 2.
Note Reverse L–R instructions.
Notes for rolled edge
As Chinese Seedling Motif, Section 2,
finishing at pin B4.

Sections 5 and 9 (colour set 4)
Follow instructions for Chinese Seedling
Motif, Section 1, to finish, using top
sewings, at pins M & N.
Notes for rolled edge
As Chinese Seedling Motif, Section 1,
from pin M to pin A#.

Sections 6 and 10 (colour set 4)
Follow instructions for Chinese Seedling
Motif, Section 2.

Notes for rolled edge
As Chinese Seedling Motif, Section 2,
finishing at pin B4.

Sections 7 and 11 (colour set 5)
Follow instructions for Chinese Seedling
Motif, Section 1, to pin H.
Note Reverse L–R instructions.
After pin H:
cont in Cls with 6 prs to finish, using
top sewings, at pins M, N & O.
Note There is no pin I.
Notes for rolled edge
As Chinese Seedling Motif, Section 1,
from pin M to pin A#.

Sections 8 and 12 (colour set 5)
Follow instructions for Chinese Seedling
Motif, Section 2.
Note Reverse L–R instructions.
Notes for rolled edge
As Chinese Seedling Motif, Section 2,
finishing at pin B4.
Note After Section 12 has been
completed, Section 1 may then be
completed and the edge rolled. See
Chinese Seedling Border, Section 1.

Sections 13, 15 and 17
(colour set 6)
Follow instructions for Chinese

Seedlings, Section 5,
to finish, using top sewings, at pins O &
P, Section 12.
Note There is no pin I.
Notes for rolled edge
As Chinese Seedling Motif, Section 1,
from pin P to pin A#.

Sections 14, 16 and 18
(colour set 6)
Follow instructions for Chinese Seedling
Motif, Section 2.
Notes for rolled edge
As Chinese Seedling Motif, Section 2,
finishing at pin B4.

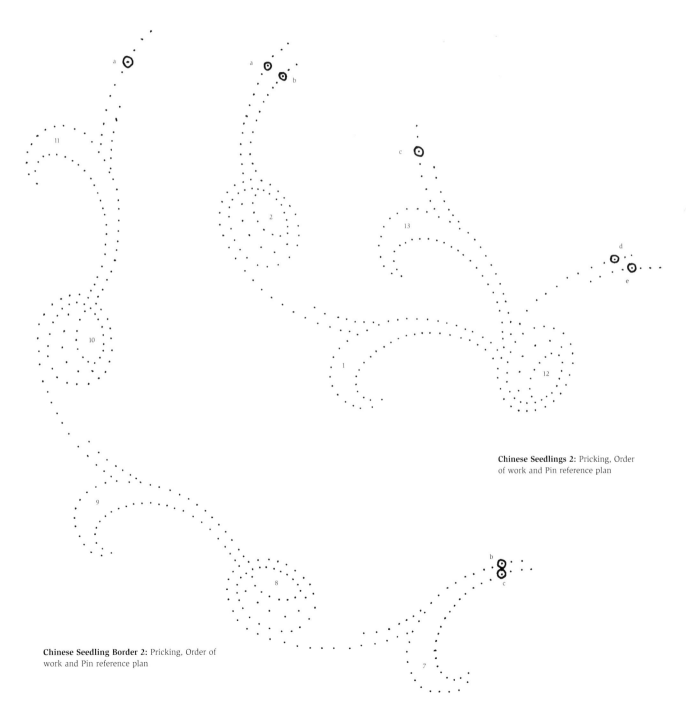

Chinese Seedlings 2: Pricking, Order
of work and Pin reference plan

Chinese Seedling Border 2: Pricking, Order of
work and Pin reference plan

Chinese Seedlings 1: Pricking, Order of work and Pin reference plan

J for Jay + Seedling (not illustrated) 1: Pricking

Plus Seedlings

This group of patterns offers examples of using the leaf curl shape from the Chinese Seedling Motif (page 98) to vary the patterns for the letters *I for Ice* (page 33), *J for Jay* (page 36), *Q for Quince* (page 61) and *T for Tilia* (page 69). Further visual interest may be created by the addition of Tenstick tendrils.

I for Ice, plus Seedling is worked using one colour set throughout, as is *Q for Quince, plus Seedling*, albeit a different set. *Q for Quince, plus Seedling* is also worked in the same colour set throughout. This colour set is shared with the seedling section in *T for Tilia, plus Seedling*, but the colour set used for the *T* is different from that of the *Q*, although it does contain some of the same colours. This serves to form an interesting visual link between the two patterns, without necessarily duplicating the exact colours.

Note: When making pattern additions, attention must be paid to the assumed light source in order to maintain the three-dimensional illusion.

I for Ice, plus Seedling

Colours:
(no 1)	*White
(no 2)	Sycamore
(no 3)	Pale Lettuce
(no 4)	*Jade
(no 5)	Kingfisher
(no 6)	Dark Kingfisher
(no 7)	Dark Tartan

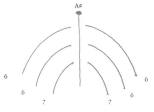

I plus 1: Start, Section 3

Section 1

Start at pin A#:
follow instructions for I for Ice, Version 2.
Notes for rolled edges
As I for Ice.

Section 2

Start at pin A#:
use a narrow angle start (tech 17, td 17) and side sewing into pin A#.
Hang 1 pr (no 7) to be R edge pr, and insert into its loop, 1 pr (no 7) to be L edge pr.
Tw 2 L edge pr.
Hang leaders 1 pr (no 6) on temp pin, and Cls leaders thro R edge pr.
Tw 2 both prs.
Hang 2 p prs (no 6) on temp pin, and Cls leaders R–L thro both p prs, tw 2 leaders, and edge st at pin B (tech 3, td 3).
(5 prs)
Work 1 row.
Nr: add 1 pr (no 5) to centre.
Work 1 row.
Nr: add 1 pr (no 5) to centre.
Work 1 row.
Nr: add 1 pr (no 4) to centre.
Work 1 row.
Nr: add 1 pr (no 3) to centre.
(9 prs)
After pin C:
T O & T B 1 pr (no 3).
(8 prs)
Cont foll instructions for Chinese Seedling Motif, after pin D to finish.
Notes for rolled edge
As Chinese Seedling Motif.

Section 3

Start at pin A#:
use a Tenstick colour point start (tech 41, td 41a).
Note Pinned edge is on the inner curve.
Hang 2 prs (no 6) and 1 pr (no 7) open around pin A#, (diag 'I' plus.1), L–R order should be as foll:
2 x (no 6)
2 x (no 7)

2 x (no 6)
(3 prs)
Cls centre pr (no 7) thro L pr (no 6), and tw 2 (no 7), which is now the pinned edge pr.
Note Both prs (no 6) will be leader prs in Tenstick.
Hang 1 pr (no 5) on a temp pin (td 41b), to be placed between both prs (no 6). Cls L pr (no 6) thro 1 pr (no 5), then work smooth Tenstick edge (tech 19, td 19) with both prs (no 6).
Work back thro 1 pr (no 5), tw 2 leader pr (no 6), place pin B, work edge st (tech 3, td 3), with pinned edge pr (no 7).
(4 prs)
Cont in Tenstick.

To finish: use top sewings to join to Section 1, T O & T B prs, securing them to back of work in a bunch

Q for Quince, plus Seedling

Colours
(no 1)	*Pale Salmon
(no 2)	*Rose
(no 3)	*Strawberry
(no 4)	*Hibiscus
(no 5)	Dark Cerise
(no 6)	Lime
(no 7)	*Mid Olive

Sections 1 and 2

Start at pin A#:
follow instructions for Q for Quince, Version 2.
Note Reverse L–R directions.

Notes for rolled edges
As Q for Quince.

Section 3

Start at pin #:
using top sewings, add 1 pr (no 7) to be

L edge pr, tw 2.
At pin B, Section 2:
add 1 pr (no 6) to be leaders.
On temp pin, add in L–R order, 1 pr (no 7) and 1 pr (no 6) to be p prs.
Cls leaders R–L thro 2 p prs, tw 2 leaders, and join to Section 1 at pin #, using a top sewing.
Nr: add 1 pr (no 6) to be 1st p.pr from L.
Cont joining to Section 2, using top sewings.
(5 prs)
After pin B1:
add 1 pr (no 5) to be 3rd p.pr from L.
After pin B2:
add 1 pr (no 5) to be s ps 6 & 7 from L.
At pin B3:
add 1 pr (no 7) to be R edge pr.
After pin B4:
add 1 pr (no 4) to be 4th p.pr from L.
(9 prs)
After pin C:
cont to pin D.
After pin D:
follow instructions for Chinese Seedling Motif to finish.
Note T O & T B L edge pr (no 7) after Cls with 1st p.pr (no 6) from L. This pr to be set aside for rolled edge.
(8 prs)

Notes for rolled edges
Roll from pin D to pin #:
rolling thread – 1 x (no 7)
rolled thread – 1 x (no 7)
Use pr set aside at pin D for roll, do not sew into pin D.
Add 1 thread (no 7) at next two alternate pins.
Finish at pin #.
Roll from pin F to pin B3:
As Chinese Seedling Motif.

Section 4

Start at pin #:
using a narrow angle start (tech 17, td 17), add 1 pr (no 7) to be L edge pr, and into its loop, 1 pr (no 6) to be leaders,

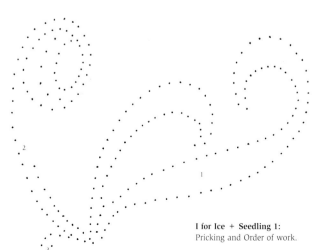

I for Ice + Seedling 1:
Pricking and Order of work.

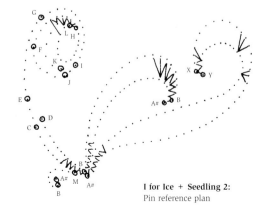

I for Ice + Seedling 2:
Pin reference plan

Q for Quince + Seedling 1:
Pricking and Order of work

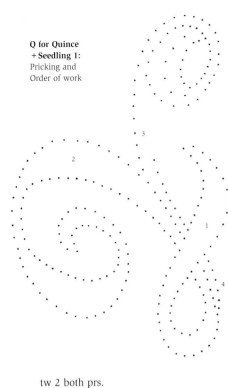

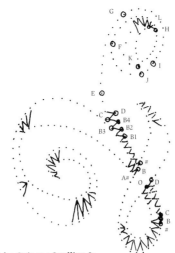

Q for Quince + Seedling 2:
Pin reference plan

tw 2 both prs.
Edge st at pin B (tech 3, td 3).
On temp pin, add 1 pr (no 7) to be 1st p.pr from L.
Cont, joining to Section 1 using top sewings.
(3 prs)
After pin C:
add 1 pr (no 6) to be 2nd p.pr from L.
(4 prs)
Finish at pin D:
using top sewings, set aside 2 prs (no 7) for rolled edge.
T O & T B rem prs in a bunch (tech 25, td 25).

Notes for rolled edge
Roll from pin D to next pin after #:

rolling thread – 1 x (no 7)
rolled threads – 3 x (no 7)
Use prs set aside at pin D for roll.
Work 3 pins, T B 1 thread from roll.
T B 1 thread from roll at pin C.
Finish at the next pin after start pin #, do not work pin #.

T for Tilia, plus Seedling

Colours
Sections 1 and 1a, as T for Tilia.
Section 2, as Q for Quince.

Sections 1 and 1a

Start at pin A#:
follow instructions for
T for Tilia, Version 2.
Note Reverse L–R
directions.

Notes for rolled edges
As T for Tilia.

Section 2

Start at pin A#:
using a narrow angle start (tech 17, td 17), and top sewings, add 1 pr (no 7) to be L edge pr, and add 1 pr (no 6) to be leaders, tw 2 both prs.
On temp pin, hang 2 prs (no 6) to be p prs.
Cls leaders R–L thro 2 p prs, edge st at pin B (tech 3, td. 3).
(4 prs)
Work 1 row.
Next row: add 1 pr (no 5) to centre of braid.
Next row: add 1 pr (no 5) to centre of braid.
Next row: add 1 pr (no 4) to centre of braid.
Next row: add 1 pr (no 3) to centre of braid.
Note Add 1 pr (no 7) to be R edge pr when Section 2 splits from Section 1a.
(9 prs)
After pin C:
T O & T B 1 pr (no 3).
(8 prs)
After pin D:
follow instructions for
Chinese Seedling Motif to finish.
Note Reverse L–R directions.

Notes for rolled edge
Roll from pin F to pin G, Section 1a:
rolling thread – 1 x (no 7)*BOT
rolled thread – 1 x (no 7)*BOT
Use 1 pr (no 7) set aside at pin F for roll.
Add 1 single thread (no 6) at pin G, Section 2.
Add 1 pr (no 5) at pin B, Section 2.
Add 1 pr (no 7) at pin after pin A#, Section 2.
Finish at pin G, Section 1a.

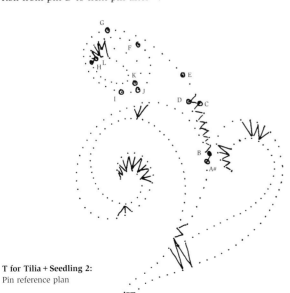

T for Tilia + Seedling 2:
Pin reference plan

T for Tilia + Seedling 1:
Pricking and Order of work

Above: Ribbon Grass Seedling

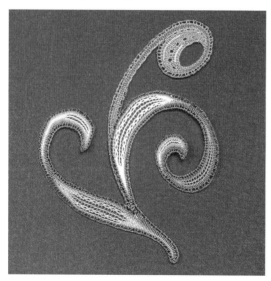

Above: T for Tilia, plus Seedling

Above: Q for Quince, plus Seedling

Ribbon Grass Seedling

Ribbon Grass Seedling continues with the idea of developing a design by simply adding another shape, but in this instance a substantial change has been made to the original design.

Sections 1 and 2 from *Ribbon Grass Seedling* are derived from *L for Leaves* (page 42). If the designs are compared, it will be seen that only part of Section 2 from *L for Leaves* is used. An amendment to the pattern is made to curtail the finish. Section 3, the *Seedling*, is added, though again pattern adjustments are required, this time to the start of Section 3.

Note The sense of the assumed direction of light is maintained.

Colours
(no 1)	*Sky
(no 2)	*Flax
(no 3)	*Pansy
(no 4)	Mid Purple
(no 5)	*Helio
(no 6)	*Dark Kingfisher
(no 7)	Dark Tartan

Ribbon Grass Seedling 1: Pricking and Order of work

Ribbon Grass Seedling 2: Pin reference plan

Section 1
Start at pin A#:
follow instructions for L for Leaves,
Version 2.

Notes for rolled edges
As L for Leaves, Section 1.

Section 2
Start at pin #:
follow instructions for L for Leaves,
Version 2, from pin # to after pin Z.
(9 prs)
Nr: T O & T B 1 p.pr (no 1).
Nr: add 1 pr (no 7) to be 1st p.pr from R.
Nr: T O & T B 1 p.pr (no 1).
Work 1 row.
Nr: T O & T B 1 p.pr (no 1).
Work 1 row.
Nr: T O & T B 1 p.pr (no 2).
Work 1 row.
Nr: T O & T B 1 p.pr (no 6),
(5 prs)
To finish: Cls thro rem 2 p prs, place pin
A1, edge st.
Cls thro 1st p.pr, T O & T B leaders.
T O & T B rem 2 p prs, do not cut them off.
Cls & tw edge prs and replace pin A1
between them, Cls & tw edge prs again
and T O.
Set aside 1 edge pr and 1 single thread
for rolled edge, T O & T B rem threads
and secure to back of work with
previously T B prs.

Notes for rolled edge
Roll from pin A1 to pin #:
rolling thread – 1 x (no 7)
rolled threads – 2 x (no 7)
Use 1 of the edge prs and 1 thread for roll.
Finish at pin #.

Section 3
Start at pin A#:
using a top sewing into pin A#, add 1 pr
(no 7) to be R edge pr, tw 2.

At pin B1:
add 1 pr (no 6) to be leaders, and add 1
p.pr (no 6).
Tw 2 leaders, Cls thro passive pr, tw 2
leaders, pin and edge st (tech 3, td 3).
(3 prs)
On temp pin, add 1 pr (no 7) to be 1st
p.pr from L, Cls thro 2 p prs.
(4 prs)
At pin B2:
using top sewing into top bar, add 1 pr
(no 5) to be 1st p.pr from L, work to R
edge.
(5 prs)
Nr: from lower bar, pin B2, add 1 pr (no
5) to be 4th p.pr from R, and add, on
temp pin, 1 pr (no 6) to be 1st p.pr from L.
(7 prs)
At pin B3:
using top sewing into top bar, add 1
p.pr (no 4) to be 3rd p.pr from L, and
work to R edge.

(8 prs)
Work 1 row.

Also at pin B3:
using top sewing into lower bar, add 1
pr (no 7) to be L edge pr.
(9 prs)
After pin C:
when changing to Tenstick, T O & T B
2nd pr (no 7) from R.
Note Set pr aside, to be used for rolled
edge.
(8 prs)
After pin D:
follow instructions for Chinese Seedling
Motif to finish.
Note Reverse L–R directions.

Notes for rolled edge
Roll from smooth edge start to pin A#:
rolling thread – 1 x (no 7)
rolled thread – 1 x (no 7)
Use 1 pr set aside at pin D for roll, do
not work pin D.
Work 2 pins, add 1 thread (no 7).
Finish at pin A#, using top sewings.

Roll from pin F to pin B3:
rolling thread – 1 x (no 7)
rolled thread – 1 x (no 7)
Use 1 pr (no 7) set aside at pin F.
Add 1 thread (no 6) at pin G.
Finish at pin B3, using top sewings.

Blackthorn Sprig

In *Blackthorn Sprig* the leaf curl shape becomes a sloe berry. It is worked in exactly
the same manner as the *Seedling*, but the support pins used when working the
decorative short rows are almost immediately removed. Careful tensioning of the
threads ensures that the *Seedling*'s decorative holes cannot develop, since they are
not required when suggesting the berry's solidity of form.

The drawing of a sprig from a blackthorn bush provided the original idea for this
motif. It was autumn, the leaves had turned an intense golden-yellow and the fruits,
the sloe berries, were still on the bush. The natural tonal contrast between the bright
leaves and the dark twigs was enhanced by the dampness of the twigs. When the
blues and purples of the sloe berry are added to the yellows and oranges of the
leaves, the full effect of using complementary colours (yellow and purple, blue and
orange) and tonal contrasts can be seen: the colours appear to glow.

This motif is an appropriate piece to celebrate a fiftieth birthday or anniversary, partly
due to the colour association with the golden leaves, but also to the composition of
the design. There are five leaves, and the figure 5 is additionally traced out using the
underside of the top leaf, down the straight stem, then following the curve of the
lower stem. The zero is formed by the sloe berry. Should the commemorative nature
of this piece not be required, the motif may simply be worked in reverse.

If the finished piece is mounted onto dark blue or purple fabric with a sheen (not
shine), then the effect will be to reflect the light and in so doing 'fill' the unworked
centre of the sloe berry with its characteristic 'bloom'. Alternatively, the berry centre
may be filled at the lacemaker's discretion (with a leadwork, for example).

Colours

(no 1)	*Honey
(no 2)	*Brass
(no 3)	*Marigold
(no 4)	*Dark Coral
(no 5)	Mid Purple
(no 6)	*Helio
(no 7)	Extra Dark Brown

Section 1

Start at pin A#:
use a one-colour point start (tech 23, td 23), (Note R–L working
direction), hang 2 prs (no 3) open, to be edge prs.
Add magic thread (tech 2, td 2).

On temp pin, hang 1 pr (no 2) to be leaders.
(3 prs)
On temp pin, add 2 prs (no 4) open to be p prs.
Cls leaders R–L thro 2 p prs, and edge st (tech 3, td 3).
(5 prs)
Cont in Cls, adding p prs to centre of braid, in order as foll:
Nr: 1 pr (no 3).
Nr: 1 pr (no 4) and 1 pr (no 3).
Nr: 1 pr (no 2) and 1 pr (no 3).
Nr: 1 pr (no 2).
Nr: 1 pr (no 2).
Nr: 1 pr (no 2).

After completing blind pin B:
L–R order should be

L edge pr	2 x (no 3)
	2 x (no 4)
	1 x (no 3)
	1 x (no 4)
	1 x (no 3)
	1 x (no 2)
	1 x (no 3)
	6 x (no 2)
	1 x (no 3)
	1 x (no 2)
	1 x (no 3)
	1 x (no 4)
	1 x (no 3)
	2 x (no 4)
R edge pr	2 x (no 3)
leaders	2 x (no 2)

(13 prs)

Work 2 rows.
Start Kisses patt (diag b.s.1).

After pin C:
*change 4th p.pr from L and 4th p.pr
from R (no 3/no 2) to (no 1), (tech 28,
td 28).

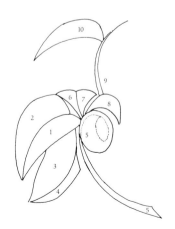

Blackthorn Sprig 1: Order of work

Cls 3rd and 4th p prs, from each side,
tog, as in patt*.
Cont in patt.
After pin D:
rep * to *.
After pin E:
cont in Cls.
Work 2 rows.
T O & T B p prs, lightest prs first, from
centre of braid.
Finish at pin F:
Cls 2 rem edge prs, pin and insert a
magic thread, Cls & T O both prs.
Note Include 1 pr (no 5) for the rolled
edge in the knot.

Notes for rolled edge
Roll from pin F to pin A#:
rolling thread – 1 x (no 5)
rolled threads – 1 x (no 5), 4 x (no 3)
T B 1 thread (no 5) at pin E,
T B 1 thread (no 3) at pin C,
T B 1 thread (no 3) at pin B,
cont roll to pin A#.
(1 x rolling thread and 2 x rolled threads
rem)

At pin A#:
add 1 pr (no 2) to be leaders, to start
Section 2, 2 rem threads (no 3) will
become R edge pr, to start Section 2, 1
rolling thread (no 5) will become 1st
thread at L edge.
(5 threads rem)

Blackthorn Sprig 2: Pricking

Section 2

Start at pin A#:
tw 2 R edge pr (no 3) from roll, (Note
L–R working direction).
Leaders (no 2) should be at L edge.
The rolling thread, (no 5) is 1st s.p
thread at L edge.

On temp pin, add I single thread (no 5)
to be 2nd s.p thread from L, and tie to
rolling thread (no 5).

On temp pin, add 2 prs (no 4), to hang
to R of 1st p.pr from L (no 5).
Cls L–R thro 3 p prs, pin, edge st.
Cont in Cls, adding prs to centre of
braid, (see after pin B, Section 1).

*Note: When joining Section 2 to Section 1,
use the twisted bar between pins for side
sewings, for an interesting vein effect,
instead of the usual method of sewing
into the pin holes. To start this effect,
insert hook to make sewing, just above 1st
pinhole, remove and do not replace pin.*

At pin G:
L–R order should be exactly the same as
after pin B, Section 1, except that
instead of a L edge pr (no 3), the 1st
p.pr from L is (no 5).
(13 prs)
After pin G:
start Kisses patt.
After pin H:

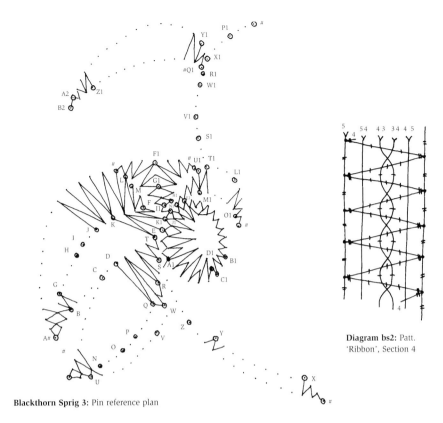

Blackthorn Sprig 3: Pin reference plan

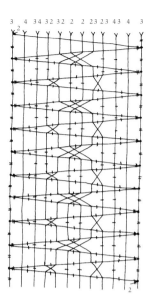

Diagram bs2: Patt. 'Ribbon', Section 4

Diagram bs1: Patt. 'Kisses', Section 1

T O & T B 1 pr (no 5).
(12 prs)
After pin I:
change 3rd p prs from L and R edges to
(no 1), (tech 28, td 28).
After pin J:
change 3rd p prs from L and R edges to
(no 1), (tech 28, td 28).
After pin K:
add 1 pr (no 5) to be 1st p.pr from L.
After pin L:
change to Cls, and T O & T B p prs from
centre of braid, lightest prs first.
After pin M:
add 1 pr (no 5) to be s ps 1 and 3 from R.
Finish at pin F:
Cls thro rem p prs, and T O & T B.
Join leaders and R edge pr into pin F,
T O & T B leaders.
Use R edge pr (no 3) for rolled edge.

Notes for rolled edge
Roll from pin F to pin A#:
rolling thread – 1 x (no 3)
rolled thread – 1 x (no 3)
Use R edge pr for roll.
Finish at pin A#.

Section 3
Start at pin #:
use a one colour point start (tech 23, td
23), (Note L–R working direction), hang
2 prs (no 4) open, to be edge prs.
Add magic thread.
On temp pin:
hang 1 pr (no 3) to be leaders.
(3 prs)
Cont in Cls, adding prs to centre of

braid, in order as foll:
Nr: 2 prs (no 4) and 1 pr (no 5).
Nr: 1 pr (no 5) and 2 prs (no 4).
Nr: 1 pr (no 4) and 1 pr (no 3).
Nr: 2 prs (no 3).
Nr: 2 prs (no 3).
Work 1 row.
At pin N:
L–R order should be
L edge pr   2 x (no 4)
                        5 x (no 4)
                        10 x (no 3)
                        3 x (no 4)
                        1 x (no 5)
                        1 x (no 4)
                        1 x (no 5)
                        1 x (no 4)
                        2 x (no 5)
R edge pr   2 x (no 4)
leaders   2 x (no 3)
(15 prs)
After pin N:
start Kisses patt.
After pin O:
change 3rd and 8th p prs (no 4) from L
to (no 2), (tech 28, td 28).
After pin P:
change 3rd and 8th p prs (no 3) from L
to (no 1), and change 4th and 7th p prs
(no 3/no 4) from L to (no 2) (tech 28,
td 28).
At pin C, Section 1:
join to Section 1 using top sewings, T O
& T B R edge pr (no 4).
Note Do not cut off R edge pr, it will be
required for the rolled edge.
Next R pin: T O & T B 1st p.pr from R.*
Rep * to *.

Note Do not cut off these 2 prs, they
will be required for the rolled edge.
(12 prs)
After pin Q:
change 4th and 7th p prs (no 1) from L
to (no 3), (tech 28, td 28).
After pin R:
change 4th and 7th p prs (no 2) from L
to (no 3), (tech 28, td 28).
After pin S:
change to Cls, T O & T B 4th and 7th
p prs (no 2).
Cont, T O & T B p prs from centre of
braid.
Finish at pin T:
T O & T B rem prs in a bunch.

Notes for rolled edge
Roll from pin C to pin #:
rolling thread – 1 x (no 5)
rolled threads – 2 x (no 5), 3 x (no 4)
Use R edge pr (no 4), 1 p.pr (no 5) and
1 p.pr (no 5/no 4) set aside at R edge
for roll.
T O & T B 1 thread from roll, in foll
order:
1 x (no 4)
1 x (no 5)
1 x (no 4)
1 x (no 5)
on alternate pins, leaving
rolling thread   1 x (no 5)
rolled thread   1 x (no 4)
to finish at pin #.

Section 4
Start at pin #:
using a narrow angle start (tech 17, td

17), (Note R–L working direction), add 1 pr (no 5) to be L edge pr, add 1 pr (no 4) to be leaders, add 1 pr (no 5) to be s ps 1 & 4, and add 1 pr (no 4) to be s ps 2 & 3 from L edge.
Cls leaders R–L thro 2 p prs, pin and edge st.
(4 prs)
Nr: add 1 pr (no 4) to be 2nd p.pr from L.

Note Join to Section 3, using the same method used for joining Section 2 to Section 1, this time insert the hook below 1st pinhole.

Nr: add 1 pr (no 3) to be s ps 4 & 5 from L.
At pin U:
L–R order should be
L edge pr	2 x (no 5)
	1 x (no 5)
	2 x (no 4)
	2 x (no 3)
	2 x (no 4)
	1 x (no 5)
leaders	2 x (no 4)
(6 prs)
After pin U:
Cls thro 1st p.pr, tw 1 leaders, and start Ribbon patt with 2nd and 3rd p prs (diag b.s.2), tw 1 leaders, Cls thro rem pr.
Cont in patt.
After pin V:
change 2nd p.pr from L (no 4/no 3) to (no 2), (tech 28, td 28).
After pin W:
change to Cls, and T O & T B p prs from centre, lightest prs first.
Finish at pin R:
sew leaders and L edge pr into pin R, set aside to use for rolled edge.
T O & T B rem prs and secure to back of work with previously T B prs.

Notes for rolled edge
Roll from pin R to pin #:
rolling thread – 1 x (no 5)
rolled threads – 1 x (no 5), 2 x (no 4)
Use leaders (no 4) and L edge pr (no 5) for roll.
T O & T B 1 thread from roll, on alternate pins, leaving:
rolling thread – 1 x (no 5)
rolled thread – 1 x (no 5)
to finish at pin #.

Section 5
Start at pin #:
use a one colour point start, (Note R–L working direction), hang 2 prs (no 7) open, to be edge prs.
Add magic thread.
On temp pin, hang 1 pr leaders (no 6).
On temp pin, add 2 prs (no 6) open, to be p prs.
Cls leaders thro 2 p prs, tw 2 leaders, pin and edge st.

(5 prs)
Nr: add 1 pr (no 5) to be s ps 3 & 5 from L, and add 1 pr (no 7) to be s ps 4 & 6 from L.
Nr: add 1 pr (no 4) to be 3rd p.pr from R, and add 1 pr (no 7) to be 5th p.pr from R.
Nr: add 1 pr (no 5) to be 3rd p.pr from L.
Nr: add 1 pr (no 3) to be s ps 6 & 7 from R.
Work 3 rows.
Note It will be necessary to tie ½ knot with leaders after Cls 1st p.pr at pin X, to keep p.pr in position close to pin.
(11 prs)
Nr: T O & T B 1 p.pr (no 3).
Work 4 rows.
Nr: T O & T B 1 p.pr (no 5/no 4).
Work 6 rows.
Nr: T O & T B 1 p.pr (no 7/no 4).
(8 prs)
After pin Y,
change L edge pr to be smooth edge pr, (tech 32, td 32), work to R edge, edge st, work a locking st (tech 6, td 6) with leaders and 1st p.pr from R.
Untwist L edge pr, and Cls with 1st p.pr from L.
Undo locking st, and start Tenstick, i.e. Cls to L and work smooth edge st. Cont in Tenstick.
(8 prs)
After pin Z:
T O & T B 4th pr (no 7), and remove pin Y and its preceding pin, to allow a smooth line to develop.
L–R order is:
smooth edge pr	2 x (no 6)
	2 x (no 7)
	3 x (no 5)
	1 x (no 7)
	2 x (no 6)
R edge pr	2 x (no 7)
leaders	2 x (no 6)
(7 prs)
At pin A1,
cont in Tenstick, placing pin A1 as a support pin (tech 19, td 19b).
Note When using support pins, leave in pins in work for as little time as possible, aim to complete the section in one session.
Cont in Tenstick, placing support pins at smooth L edge.
Join to Section 1 with top sewings, T O & T B R edge pr (no 7),
Note Do not cut off, it will be required for the rolled edge.
(6 prs)
After 2nd sewing into Section 1, T O & T B 4th p.pr (no 7) from R, and add, with top sewing, a new R edge pr (no 6).
L–R order should be:
smooth edge pr	2 x (no 6)
	3 x (no 5)
	1 x (no 7)
	2 x (no 6)

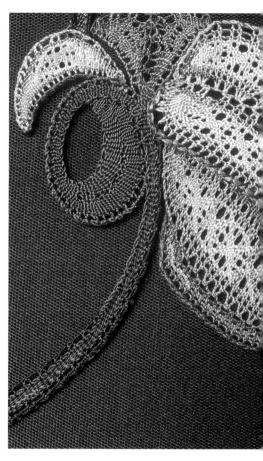

Blackthorn Sprig, detail

| R edge pr | 2 x (no 6) |
| leaders | 2 x (no 6) |
(6 prs)
After pin B1:
add 1 pr (no 6) to be s ps 5 & 6 from R.
Nr: add 1 pr (no 6) to be s ps 8 & 9 from R.
Nr: add 1 pr (no 6) to be s ps 6 & 7 from R.
Nr: add 1 pr (no 6) to be s ps 7 & 8 from R.
(10 prs)
After pin C1:
Cls R–L thro 3 p prs, work T S with 4th pr (no 6), place support pin D1:
work back to R edge, adding 1 pr (no 6) to be s ps 5 & 6 from R.
Note: The support pins used when working the decorative short row must be removed almost immediately, the threads must be carefully tensioned to ensure that the decorative holes are not allowed to develop in this pattern.
(11 prs)
Nr: work to L, adding 1 pr (no 6) to be s ps 13 & 14 from R.
(12 prs)
Nr: work to R, adding 2 prs (no 6) to be s ps 14 & 15, and 6 & 7 from R.
(14 prs)
Nr: work T S with 6th p.pr (no 6) from R, place support pin, and work back to R, adding 1 pr (no 6) to be s ps 7 & 8 from R.

(15 prs)
Nr: *work to L.
Nr: work to R.
Nr: work to L, work T S with 7th p.pr from R, place support pin, then work back to R.*
Cont rep * to *.
Join to existing braid at and after pin A1 with side sewings, tw 1 leaders.
Note Do not cut off edge pr, it will be required for rolled edge. Decrease prs evenly as braid narrows.
To finish, T O & T B rem prs in a bunch, and secure to back of work with previously T O & T B prs.

Notes for rolled edge
Roll from pin E, Section 1, to pin X:
rolling thread – 1 x (no 7)
rolled thread – 1 x (no 7)
Work 4 pins, then start adding threads to roll, at alternate pins, in order:
1 x (no 7)
1 x (no 6)
1 x (no 6)
1 x (no 5)
placing lighter threads to outside of roll:
rolling thread – 1 x (no 7)
rolled threads – 2 x (no 7), 2 x (no 6), 1 x (no 5)
After pin #, T B 1 thread from roll at each pin, lightest threads first.
Finish at pin X.
Roll from pin A1 to pin E1:
rolling thread – 1 x (no 6)
rolled thread – 1 x (no 6)
At next pin, start adding threads to roll:
1 x (no 6)
1 x (no 5)
one at each pin, lighter thread to outside of roll:
rolling thread – 1 x (no 6)
rolled threads – 2 x (no 6), 1 x (no 5)
T B 1 thread from roll, lightest threads first, at each of the 3 pins before finishing at pin E1.

Section 6
Start at pin #:
using a narrow angle start (tech 17, td 17), (Note L-R working direction), and top sewings, add
1 pr (no 5) to be R edge pr,
1 pr (no 4) to be L edge pr, and
1 pr (no 4) to be leaders.
Tw 2 both edge prs and leaders.
(3 prs)
***On temp pin, hang 2 p prs (no 4)*COR, and 1 p.pr (no 5), to give L-R order as foll:

L edge pr	2 x (no 4)
	3 x (no 4)
	1 x (no 5)
	1 x (no 4)
	1 x (no 5)
R edge pr	2 x (no 5)
leaders	2 x (no 4)

(6 prs)
Cls leaders L-R thro 3 p prs, tw 2 leaders, pin and edge st.
Nr: add 1 pr (no 4) to be s ps 2 & 3 from L.
Nr: add 1 pr (no 3) to be s ps 3 & 5 from L.
Work 1 row.
(8 prs)
Nr: *Cls L-R thro 2 prs, tw 1 leaders, start Ribbon patt with next 2 p prs, tw 1 leaders, Cls rem pr.
Nr: Cls thro 1 pr, tw 1 leaders, patt next 2 prs, tw 1 leaders, Cls rem 2 prs.*
Cont in patt, rep * to *

After pin F1:
tie ½ knot with leaders after Cls 1st p.pr.

After pin G1:
cont in Cls, prs will have returned to original colour positions.
Nr: *T O & T B 1 p.pr (no 3/no 4).
Nr: rep * to *.
***

(4 prs)
Work a locking st (tech 6, td 6) with leaders and 1st p.pr.
Secure bobbins, and leave to work Section 7.

Section 7
Start at pin #:
use a two colour point start (tech 1, td 1), (Note R-L working direction), hang 1 pr (no 5) and 1 pr (no 4).
L edge pr is now (no 5).
R edge pr is now (no 4).
On temp pin, hang 1 pr (no 4) to be leaders.
(3 prs)
Follow instructions for Section 6, from *** to ***.
Note Reverse L-R directions.

At pin F1:
join to Section 6, with a side sewing into pin F1, also T O & T B L edge pr (no 5).
Note Thereafter, join to Section 6, using the same method previously used when joining Section 2 to Section 1.

After *** pin H1:
Cls thro p prs, leave.
Join rem prs from Section with rem prs from Section 7, thus:
undo locking st at left side of Section 6, and Cls thro p prs, T O & T B R edge pr (no 5) from Section 6.
At pin I1 (tech 22, td 22):
work T S with leaders from both sections, place pin I.
Cls to left.
Nr: T O & T B 3 p prs (no 4).
At pins J1 and K1:
finish by joining to Section 5, T O & T B rem prs in a bunch.

Section 8
Start at pin #:
use a two colour point start (tech 1, td 1), (Note R-L working direction), hang 1 pr (no 3) and 1 pr (no 5) to be edge prs.
Add magic thread (tech 2, td 2).
L edge pr is now (no 3).
R edge pr is now (no 5).
On temp pin, hang 1 pr (no 2) to be leaders.
(3 prs)
On temp pin, hang 2 p prs (no 4) open.
Cls leaders R-L thro 2 p prs, pin and edge st.
(5 prs)
Nr: add 2 p prs (no 3) and 1 p.pr (no 2).
Nr: add 1 p.pr (no 2).
L-R order should be as foll:

L edge pr	2 x (no 3)
	2 x (no 4)
	1 x (no 3)
	1 x (no 2)
	1 x (no 3)
	2 x (no 2)
	1 x (no 3)
	1 x (no 2)
	1 x (no 3)
	2 x (no 4)
R edge pr	2 x (no 5)
leaders	2 x (no 2)

(9 prs)
Work 4 rows, and complete blind pin.
Nr: *add 1 pr (no1) to centre.*
Nr: rep * to *.
(11 prs)
After pin L1:
start Kisses patt.
After pin M1:
cont in Cls.
Nr: *T O & T B 1 pr (no 1).*
Nr: rep * to *.
Nr: T O & T B 2 p prs, not central prs, (no 2/no 3).
Nr: T O & T B 1 p.pr (no 2/no 3).
Work 1 row.
(6 prs)
At pin E1:
join to Section 5.
Nr: T O & T B 1 p.pr (no 2/no 3).
(5 prs)
Finish at pin N1:
T O & T B rem prs in a bunch (tech 25, td 25).

Notes for rolled edge
Roll from pin E1 to pin #.
rolling thread – 1 x (no 5)
rolled thread – 1 x (no 5)
Use R edge pr (no 5) for roll.
Add 1 thread (no 6) to roll, at next pin.
T B 1 thread (no 6) at pin O1.
Finish at pin #.

Section 9
Start at pin #:
use a Tenstick colour point start (tech 41, td 41a), hang 3 prs (no 7) open.

On temp pin, add 1 pr (no 5) to be p.pr (td 41b).
(4 prs)
Cont in Tenstick.

After pin P1:
add 1 pr (no 6) to be 2nd p.pr from L.
L–R order should now be as foll:

L edge pr	2 x (no 7)
	2 x (no 5)
	2 x (no 6)
smooth edge pr	2 x (no 7)
leaders	2 x (no 7)

(5 prs)
After placing pin Q1:
the pinned edge is changed from the L side to the R side, (tech 42, td 42).
Untwist pinned edge pr, Cls leaders thro 2 p prs, tw 2 leaders and R edge pr.
Place pin R1 under leaders,
edge st (tech 3, td 3) with R edge pr.
Cont in Tenstick.

Nr: add 1 pr (no 6) to be s ps 2 and 3 from R, work Tenstick smooth edge st at L edge.

After pin S1:
add 1 pr (no 4) to be s ps 5 & 7 from R.
(7 prs)
Finish at pins T1 and U1:
ensure that R edge pr (no 7) and 1st p.pr from R (no 6) are sewn into pin T1. These 2 prs will be used for the rolled edge.
T O & T B rem prs in a bunch.

Notes for rolled edge
Roll from pin T1 to pin R1:

rolling thread – 1 x (no 6)
rolled threads – 2 x (no 7), 1 x (no 6)
Use 2 prs set aside at pin T1 for roll.
After pin V1:
T B 1 thread (no 7) at pin V1 and pin W1.
Finish at pin R1:
T O 2 threads (no 6), sew into pin Q1#, and tw 2, to become R edge pr, at start of Section 10.

Section 10
Start at pin Q1#:
add, using a top sewing, 1 pr (no 2) to be leaders, to existing pr (no 6) from roll of Section 9

At pin X1:
add 1 pr (no 3) to be L edge pr.
Tw 2 leaders and both edge prs.

On temp pins, hang 7 p prs, to give L–R order as foll:

L edge pr	2 x (no 3)
	2 x (no 5)
	1 x (no 4)
	1 x (no 3)
	1 x (no 4)
	4 x (no 3)
	1 x (no 4)
	1 x (no 3)
	1 x (no 4)
	2 x (no 5)
R edge pr	2 x (no 6)
leaders	2 x (no 2)

(10 prs)
Nr: add 3 prs (no 2) to be s ps 7 & 9, 10 & 11, and 12 & 14 from R.
Nr: add 2 prs (no 1) to be s ps 11 & 12, and 13 & 14 from R.

(15 prs)
At pin Y1:
T O & T B 1st p.pr from L (no 5).
Start Kisses patt, also Cls 1st p.pr (no 5) from R, throughout.
(14 prs)
After pin Z1:
cont in Cls, also T O & T B 1 p.pr (no 1) and 2 p prs (no 2).
Nr: T O & T B 1 p.pr (no 1).
Nr: T O & T B 1 p.pr (no 2).
Nr: *T O & T B 1 p.pr (no 3).*
Nr: rep * to *.
Nr: T O & T B s ps 4 & 5 (no 3/no 4) from R.
Nr: T O & T B 1 p.pr (no 3/no 4).
(5 prs)
After pin A2:
T O & T B 1 p.pr (no 4).
(4 prs)
Finish at pin B2:
Cls leaders thro rem p.pr (no 5), T O & T B both prs.
Note Do not cut off rem pr (no 5); this pr will be used for rolled edge.
Cls tog L and R edge prs.
Place pin B2, Cls & T O both prs.
T B L edge pr (no 3).
Set aside R edge pr (no 6) for roll.
Secure rem prs to back of work with previously T B prs.

Notes for rolled edge
Roll from pin B2 to pin Q1#:
rolling thread –1 x (no 6)
rolled threads – 1 x (no 6), 2 x (no 5)
Use R edge pr (no 6) and p.pr (no 5) set aside at pin B2 for roll.
Finish at pin Q1#.

Sprouting Seedlings

Colours:

(no 1)	*Champagne
(no 2)	*Brass
(no 3)	*Sky
(no 4)	*Flax
(no 5)	*Pansy
(no 6)	Mid Purple
(no 7)	*Helio

By using very simple methods a further pattern worked in an entirely different way has been developed from *I for Ice* (page 33).

Part of a section from the original design has been repeated and reversed. Although it is possible to work the design in many different ways, full instructions are provided for two suggested versions. Many of the elements involved in their execution are interchangeable and so allow plenty of scope for further customisation.

The construction of the motif, in both versions, involves the joining together of two braids while maintaining the working of the patterned section and logical continuation of the descriptive colour elements.

The design has been planned to enable both those relatively new to the field of lacemaking and the highly experienced to experiment with colour in a painterly way.

The techniques chosen illustrate a few of the ways to make the necessary colour changes to indicate the effect of light and shade falling across leaves, while using a limited range of colours. One effect where the considered use of colour manifests itself can be seen where the yellow leaders used in the patterned sections of Version 1 are replaced with blue leaders in Version 2. The passive pairs in both versions are yellow, so the visual perception is that the patterned sections in Version 2 appears slightly green.

VERSION 1
('Half-stitch')

Section 1
Start at pin A#:
use a two colour point start (tech 1, td 1), (Note L–R working direction), hang 1 pr (no 7) and 1 pr (no 6) to be edge prs (diag s.s.1).
Add magic thread (tech 2, td 2).
L edge pr is now (no 7).
R edge pr is now (no 6).

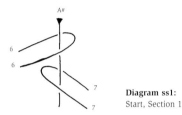

Diagram ss1:
Start, Section 1

On temp pin, hang 1 pr (no 6) to be leaders.
(3 prs)
On temp pin, hang 2 prs in L–R order:
1 pr (no 7) and 1 pr (no 6) to be p prs.
Cls leaders L–R thro 2 p prs, edge st at pin B (tech 3, td 3).
(5 prs)
Nr: add 1 pr (no 7) to be s ps 4 & 5 from R.
Nr: add 1 pr (no 6) to be s ps 6 & 7 from L.
(7 prs)
After pin C:
cont in Cls, and
add 1 pr (no 6),
add 1 pr (no 5),
add 1 pr (no 4),
add 1 pr (no 3), 1 pr per row in order to centre.
(11 prs)
Nr: T O & T B 2nd p.pr (no 7) from L.

Nr: Add 2 prs (no 2), 1 pr per row, to near centre of braid.
(See L–R thread order, after Pin D.)
Nr: T O & T B 2nd p.pr (no 6), from R, and add 1 pr (no 1) to centre.
Nr: add 1 pr (no 1) to centre.
(13 prs)

After completing blind pin D:
change leaders (no 6) to (no 1), (tech 4, td 4) cont row, adding 1 pr (no 1) to centre.
L–R order should be as foll:
L edge pr	2 x (no 7)
	2 x (no 7)
	1 x (no 6)
	1 x (no 5)
	1 x (no 4)
	1 x (no 3)
	2 x (no 2)
	6 x (no 1)
	2 x (no 2)
	1 x (no 3)
	1 x (no 4)
	1 x (no 5)
	3 x (no 6)
R edge pr	2 x (no 6)
leaders	2 x (no 1)

(14 prs)
After pin E:
start patt: Cls thro 4 prs, tw 1 leaders, ½ st 3 p prs (no 1), Cls rem prs.
Nr: Cls thro 3 p prs, tw 1 leaders, ½ st 5 prs (no 1) and (no 2), Cls rem prs.
Cont in patt, ½ st 5 prs.
After pin F:
make locking st with leaders (tech 6, td 6).

Leave to work Section 1a.

Section 1a
Start at pin A#:
follow instructions for Section 1, from pin A# to pin F (diag s.s.2).
Note Reverse L–R instructions.

After pin F:
cont in Cls, Cls thro all p prs.
Note Do not tw leaders or include L edge pr. Leave.

Return to Section 1
Undo locking st, cont in patt thro all p prs.
Note: Do not tw leaders or include R edge pr.

Join Sections
Cls & tw 2 edge prs from Sections 1 and 1a (tech 22, td 22), placing pin G between them.
(28 prs)
Work T S with leaders, using pin G as support pin, cont working to R, T O & T B 6th p.pr (no 1) from R.
(27 prs)
Note Section 1 p prs, cont in patt.
Section 1a p prs, cont in Cls.

Nr: T O & T B s ps 10 & 11 (no 1), and s ps 23 & 24 (no 1) from R (old leaders).
(25 prs)
Nr: T O & T B s ps 22 & 23 (no 6), s ps 26 & 27 (no 6) and s ps 35 & 36 (no 1) from L.
Nr: T O & T B s ps 8 & 9 (no 2) and s ps 16 & 17 (no 6) from R.
(20 prs)
Nr: T O & T B 11th p.pr (no 6) and 14th p.pr (no 2) from L.
Nr: T O & T B s ps 6 & 7 (no 3) and s ps 10 & 11 (no 6) from R.
(16 prs)
After pin H:
when p prs from Section 1 have returned to their original colour positions, cont in Cls, T O & T B 5th p.pr (no 1), 7th p.pr (no 1) and 11th p.pr (no 4) from L.
(13 prs)
Nr: T O & T B s ps 4 & 5 (no 5) and s ps 11 & 12 (no 1) from R.
Nr: T O & T B s ps 8 & 9 (no 2) from L.

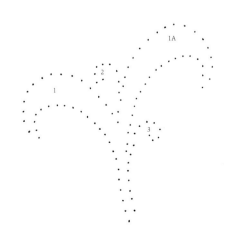

Sprouting Seedlings 1: Pricking and Order of work

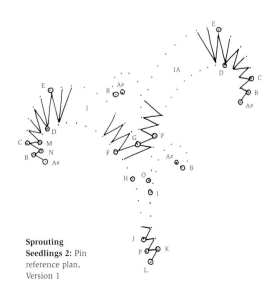

Sprouting Seedlings 2: Pin reference plan, Version 1

(10 prs)

After pin I:
change leaders (no 1) to (no 6), (tech 4, td 4), cont row T O & T B 4th p.pr (no 2) from L.
(9 prs)
Nr: T O & T B 1 p.pr (no 3).
Nr: T O & T B 1 p.pr (no 4).
Cont in Cls.
(7 prs)
After pin J:
T O & T B 1 p.pr (no 5).
Work 1 row.
Nr: T O & T B 1 p.pr (no 6).
(5 prs)
After pin K:
Cls thro 2 rem p prs, T O & T B leaders and all p prs in a bunch, and secure to back of work with previously T B prs.
(2 prs)
Finish at pin L:
Cls & tw both edge prs tog, insert magic thread (tech 2a, td 2a), Cls & T O.
Use both edge prs (no 7) for rolled edge.

Diagram ss2:
Start, Section 1a

Rolled edge notes

Roll from pin L to pin A# (Section 1):
rolling thread – 1 x (no 7)
rolled threads – 3 x (no 7)
Use both edge prs from pin L for roll.
T B 1 thread at pin M and pin N.
Finish at pin A#.

Roll from pin A# to pin O (Section 1a):
rolling thread – 1 x (no 7)
rolled thread – 1 x (no 7)
Using magic thread, add 1 pr (no 7) at pin A#.
Finish at pin O.

Section 2

Start at pin A#.
follow instructions for "I for Ice, plus Seedling", Section 3.
Use a Tenstick colour point start (tech 41, td 41).
Note Pinned edge is on the inner curve.

To finish:
join to Section 1a, using top sewings.
T O & T B 2 prs (no 6) and 1 pr (no 5).

Cont with pinned edge pr (no 7) to form rolled edge, finishing at pin G.

Section 3

Follow instructions given for Section 2.
Note Reverse L–R directions.

To finish:
join to Section 1, using top sewings.
T O & T B 2 prs (no 6) and 1 pr (no 5).

Cont with pinned edge pr (no 7) to form rolled edge, finishing at pin P, using magic thread at pin L.

VERSION 2
(Illustrated using Ribbon variation)

Section 1

Start at pin A#:
follow instructions for Version 1, Section

1, from pin A# to pin D.
(13 prs)
After completing blind pin D:
change leaders (no 6) to (no 4), (tech 4, td 4) cont row,
start Ribbon (var) patt using 2 central p prs (no 1).
Work 1 patt rep. (diag s.s.3)
Note There is no pin E in Version 2, Section 1.
Nr: cont in patt with 2 p prs (no 1).
Nr: cont in patt with 2 p prs (no 1), also working Cls & tw with 1 p.pr (no 2) either side of patt prs, (diag s.s.3).
Cont in patt with 4 p prs (no 1 & no 2).
(13 prs)

After pin F1:
make locking st with leaders (tech 6, td 6), secure bobbins in order.

Leave to work Section 1a.

Section 1a

Start at pin A#:
follow instructions for Version 1, Section 1, from pin A# to pin D (diag s.s.2).
Note Reverse L–R instructions.

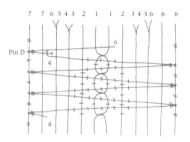

Diagram ss3: After pin D, Section 1

After pin D:
follow instructions for Version 2, Section 1, from pin D, Section 1, to pin F1, Section 1A.
(See pin reference plan.)
Note Start patt after pin E, reversing patt diag.

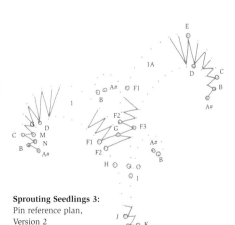

Sprouting Seedlings 3:
Pin reference plan,
Version 2

After pin F1:
work patt with 2 p prs (no 1) only.

Next row: rep * to *.

After pin F2:
Cls 2 p prs (no 1) tog to complete patt, and cont in Cls.
After pin F3:
Cls thro all p prs.
Note Do not tw 2 leaders or include L edge pr.

Leave.

Return to Section 1

Follow instructions for Version 1 to join sections.

After replacing pin G for T S:
cont working to R edge, and T O & T B s ps 10 & 11 (no 1) from R.
(25 prs)
Note Cont in patt for Section 1 p prs, Cls Section 1a p prs

Nr: T O & T B s ps 9 & 10 (no 1), and s ps 21 & 22 (no 4) from R (old leaders).
(23 prs)
After pin F2 (Section 1):
Cls 2 p prs (no 1) tog to complete patt, cont in Cls, T O & T B s ps 20 & 21 (no 6) and s ps 24 & 25 (no 6) from L.
(21 prs)
Nr: T O & T B s ps 8 & 9 (no 2) and s ps 16 & 17 (no 6) from R.
Nr: T O & T B 10th p.pr (no 6) and 13th p.pr (no 2) from L.

Nr: T O & T B s ps 6 & 7 (no 3) and s ps 10 & 11 (no 6) from R.
(15 prs)
After pin H:
T O & T B s ps 10 & 11 (no 1) and s ps 19 & 20 (no 4) from L
(13 prs)
Cont following instructions for Version 1, to finish at pin L.

Rolled edge notes
As Version 1, Sections 1 and 1a.

Sections 2 and 3
Follow instructions for Version 1, Sections 2 and 3.

The Silverfish Collection

Colours: As *S for Silverfish* (page 67).

The 'Chinese Whispers' nature of design development, discussed in the introduction to this book, is perfectly illustrated by the *Silverfish Collection*. With *Bud*, the original shape of *S for Silverfish* is repeated, reversed and the design developed. The same reversed shapes are rearranged and the earlier design development is further altered and developed to produce *Bloom*.

By the time we reach *Quadrille* and *Trefoil* (not illustrated), the original *S* shape has been discarded: *Quadrille* repeats and reverses *Trefoil*, the developed flower shape from *Bloom*. *Interval* then joins and alters both a positive and negative diagonal shape from *Quadrille*.

Bud, *Bloom*, *Trefoil* and *Interval* are designed to be complete patterns in their own right, but equally they may be used to enhance and develop other patterns. They may also be rotated and positioned or joined to provide a border or an embellishment for one of the alphabet's letters.

Interval is designed to create decorative 'intervals' when two or more letters from the alphabet are to be placed together. *Trefoil* may be repeated and reversed for the same effect, while *Quadrille*, in contrast, is intended to be used as a single motif.

The ways in which these shapes may continue to be developed are many and varied, especially since all sections of the designs may be worked using basic stitches, Version 1, or Milanese techniques, Version 2.

Bud 1: Pricking
and Order of work

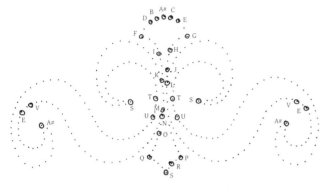

Bud 2: Pin
reference plan

Bud (Half-stitch)

Sections 1 and 2

Start at pin A#:
follow instructions for S for Silverfish,
Version 1.
Note Add magic thread at pin S. Reverse
L–R working direction for Section 2.

Notes for rolled edges
Roll from pin S to pin S, via pin A#
(tech 9, td 9):
rolling thread – 1 x (no 6)
rolled threads – 3 x (no 6)
Use edge prs from pin S for roll.
T B I thread from roll at pin T and pin U
(tech 14, td 14).
At pin A# add 2 threads (no 6) to roll.
T B 1 thread from roll at pin E and pin V.
Finish at pin S.

Section 3

Start at pin A#:
using a one-colour flat start (tech 21, td
21), (Note R–L working direction), hang
on 2 prs (no 6) to be edge prs.
Add magic thread.
On temp pin, add 1 pr (no 1) to be
leaders.
(3 prs)
On temp pin, add 2 prs (no 7) open, to
be p prs.
Cls R–L thro 2 p prs, edge st at pin B.
(5 prs)

After pin B:
add 4 prs (no 3) to centre.
(9 prs)
After pin C:
add 4 prs (no 2) to centre.
(13 prs)
After pin D:
add 3 prs (no 1) to centre.
L–R order should be as foll:

L edge pr	2 x (no 6)
	2 x (no 7)
	4 x (no 3)
	4 x (no 2)
	6 x (no 1)
	4 x (no 2)
	4 x (no 3)
	2 x (no 7)
R edge pr	2 x (no 6)
leaders	2 x (no 1)
(16 prs)	

After pin E:
start patt: work ½ st with 3 central
p prs, Cls rem p prs.
After pin F and pin G:
Cls thro 1 p.pr, tie ½ knot with leaders.
Note This will hold 1st p prs in place
near pins.
After pin H:
cont in Cls.
After pin I:
T O & T B 4th, 6th, 8th and 10th p prs,
2 p prs (no 2) and 2 p prs (no1), from L.
(12 prs)

Nr: T O & T B 3rd, 5th and 7th p prs,
2 p prs (no 3) and 1 p.pr (no 1), from R.
(9 prs)
Nr: T O & T B 1 p.pr (no 2) from centre.
Nr: T O & T B 1 p.pr (no 2).
Nr: T O & T B 1 p.pr (no 3).
(6 prs)
After pin J:
change leaders (no 1) to (no 6), (tech 4,
td 4) cont row, T O & T B 1 p.pr (no 3).
(5 prs)
At pin K and pin L:
join edge prs to Sections 1 and 2, using
top sewings.
T O & T B R edge pr at pin L.
Note Do not cut off L edge pr, set aside
for rolled edge. Rem 3 p prs will cont in
Cls for Section 3a.

Notes for rolled edges
Roll from pin K to pin L:
rolling thread   1 x (no 6)
rolled thread   1 x (no 6)
Use L edge pr from pin K for roll.
Sew twice into pin G and pin F, to turn
corners.
Finish at pin L.

Section 3a

Cont in Cls with prs from Section 3:
p prs   2 x (no 7)
leaders   1 x (no 6)
(3 prs)
After pin M:
add 1 pr (no 6) to centre.
(4 prs)
After pin N:
add 1 pr (no 5) to centre and, using top
sewings into Sections 1 and 2, add 2 prs
(no 6) to be edge prs, tw 2.
(7 prs)
Nr: add 1 pr (no 6) and 1 pr (no 5) to
centre, in L–R order:
1 x (no 6
2 x (no 5)
1 x (no 6)
(9 prs)
Nr: add 2 prs (no 4) and 1 pr (no 6) to
centre, in L–R order:

1 x (no 4)
1 x (no 6)
2 x (no 4)
1 x (no 6)
1 x (no 4)
(12 prs)
Nr: add 2 prs (no 4) to centre,
L–R order should be as foll:

L edge pr	2 x (no 6)
	2 x (no 7)
	1 x (no 6)
	1 x (no 5)
	1 x (no 6)
	1 x (no 5)
	1 x (no 4)
	1 x (no 6)
	6 x (no 4)
	1 x (no 6)
	1 x (no 4)
	1 x (no 5)
	1 x (no 6)
	1 x (no 5)
	1 x (no 6)
	2 x (no 7)
R edge pr	2 x (no 6)
leaders	2 x (no 6)
(14 prs)	

After pin O:
change leaders (no 6) to (no 4), (tech 4, td 4),
start patt: work ½ st with 3 central
p prs (no 4),
Cls rem p prs.
After pin P and pin Q:
Cls thro 1 p.pr, tie ½ knot with leaders.

After pin R:
cont in Cls.
Nr: T O & T B 3rd, 5th, 7th and 9th
p prs, 2 p prs (no 6/no 5) and 2 p prs
(no 4), from R.
(10 prs)
Nr: T O & T B s ps 4 & 5 (no 5/no 4),
4th p.pr (no 4) and s ps 10 & 11 (no
4/no 5) from L.
(7 prs)
Nr: T O & T B 2 central p prs (no 6).
Cls tog rem 2 p prs (no 7), Cls leaders
thro rem 2 p prs, T O & T B leaders and
2 rem p prs.
Secure all T B prs to back of work,
using previously T B prs.
(2 prs)
Finish at pin S:
Cls & tw edge prs (no 6), place pin S,
Cls & T O.
Set aside to use for rolled edges.

Notes for rolled edges
Roll from pin S to join Section 1 or
Section 2.
rolling thread   1 x (no 6)
rolled thread   1 x (no 6)
Use 1 edge pr, for each side, from pin S.
Finish by joining with top sewings at
Section 1 or Section 2.

Bloom (Maltese Spot)

Sections 1 and 2
Start at pin A#:
follow instructions for S for Silverfish,
Version 2.
Note Add magic thread at pin S. Reverse
L–R working direction for Section 2.

Notes for rolled edges
Roll from pin S to pin S, via pin A#
(tech 9, td 9):
rolling thread – 1 x (no 6)
rolled threads – 3 x (no 6)
Use edge prs from pin S for roll.
T B I thread from roll at pin T and pin U
(tech 14, td 14).
At pin A# add 2 threads (no 6) to roll.
T B 1 thread from roll at pin E and pin V.
Finish at pin S.

Section 3
Start at pin A#:
follow instructions for 'Bud' to pin E.

(16 prs)

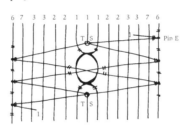

Diagram sb1: Patt. 'Maltese Spot', Bloom
after pin E

After pin E:
start patt: work supported T S (tech 19,
td 19), with central p.pr (no 1), work a
Maltese Spot (diag s.b.1).
After pin F and pin G:
Cls thro 1 p.pr, tie ½ knot with leaders.
Note This will hold 1st p prs in place
near pins.
Work supported T S to finish Maltese
Spot, cont in Cls, working to L.
Note Adjust p prs carefully, remove
support pins. There is no pin H.
After pin I:
follow instructions for 'Bud'.
Note Work blind pin.

Notes for rolled edge
As 'Bud', Section 3.

Section 3a
After pin M:
add 1 pr (no 6) to centre.

After pin N:
using top sewings, add 2 edge prs (no
6), and on the same row, begin to add 8
prs.
1 pr per row to centre in order:

1 pr	(no 5)
1 pr	(no 6)
1 pr	(no 5)
4 prs	(no 4)
1 pr	(no 6)

to give L–R order:

L edge pr	2 x (no 6)
	2 x (no 7)
	1 x (no 6)
	1 x (no 5)
	1 x (no 6)

Bloom 1: Pricking and Order of work

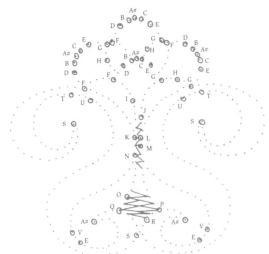

Bloom 2: Pin reference plan

1 x (no 5)
4 x (no 4)
2 x (no 6)
4 x (no 4)
1 x (no 5)
1 x (no 6)
1 x (no 5)
1 x (no 6)
2 x (no 7)
R edge pr   2 x (no 6)
leaders   2 x (no 6)
(14 prs)
After pin O:
start patt – work supported T S with
central p.pr (no 6), work a Maltese Spot.

At pin P and pin Q:
join edge prs to Sections 1 and 2, using
top sewings.
Note Set aside edge prs for rolled edges.

After pin P and pin Q:
Cls thro 1 p.pr, tie ½ knot with leaders,
work supported T S cont in Cls, working
to R.

Cont, follow instructions from pin R,
Bud to finish at pin S, Bloom, using top
sewings to join Section 1 and Section 2.
Note When decreasing, colours will not

be identical, therefore, T O & T B by
thread positions.

Notes for rolled edges
Roll from pin Q to join Section 1, and
pin P to join Section 2:
rolling thread – 1 x (no 6)
rolled thread – 1 x (no 6)
Use 1 edge pr, from either pin Q or pin
P, for each side.
Finish by joining with top sewings at
Section 1 or Section 2.

Sections 4, 5 and 6
Start at pin A#:
follow instructions for Section 3.
(16 prs)
After working Maltese Spot, cont in Cls.

After pin H:
T O & T B 5th, 7th and 9th p prs from R.
(13 prs)
Nr: T O & T B s ps 6 & 7, s ps 10 & 11
and s ps 14 & 15 from L.
(10 prs)
Nr: T O & T B 2nd, 4th and 6th p prs
from R.
(7 prs)
Finish by joining previously worked
section using top sewings.

T O & T B rem prs in a bunch (tech 25,
td 25).
Set aside one of the edge prs, it will be
used for rolled edge.

Notes for rolled edges
As 'Bud', Section 3.

Trefoil (Maltese Spot)

(not illustrated)

Sections 1, 1a, 2, 3 and 4
Start at pin A#:
follow instructions for Bloom, Sections
3, 3a, 4, 5 and 6 to finish.
Notes: Add magic thread when finishing
at pin S, Section 1a, and all pins A# in
all sections. Set aside both edge prs for
rolled edges at pin S, do not set aside at
pin P and pin Q.
May also be worked in half-stitch (see
Bud).

Notes for rolled edges
Roll from pin R, to pin R.
rolling thread – 1 x (no 6)
rolled thread – 3 x (no 6)
Use both edge prs at pin R to work
rolled edge around all exterior edges.
Use magic thread to finish at pin R.
Note When following instructions for
Bloom, ignore all other notes for rolled
edges.

Quadrille
(Maltese Spot)

Sections 1, 1a, 2, 3 and 4:
Start at pin A#:
follow instructions for Trefoil.

Notes for rolled edges
As Trefoil.
Note Edges are rolled after all sections
have been completed.

Section 5
Start at pin A#:

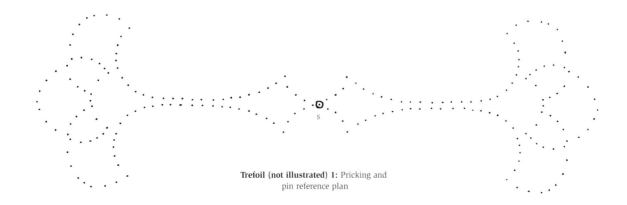

Trefoil (not illustrated) 1: Pricking and
pin reference plan

Quadrille (Maltese Spot)

using a one colour flat start (tech 21, td 21), (Note L–R working direction), hang 2 prs (no 6) open to be edge prs.
Add magic thread (tech 2, td 2).
On temp pin, hang 1 pr (no 6) to be leaders.
(3 prs)
On temp pin, hang 2 prs (no 7) open, to be p prs.
Cls leaders L–R thro 2 p prs, edge st at pin B (tech 3, td 3).
(5 prs)
Note Cont adding prs to centre as shown after pin B, to give thread order as after pin N, Section 3a, Bloom.
After pin B:

add

| 1 pr | (no 6) |
| 1 pr | (no 5). |

(7 prs)
After pin C:
add

1 pr	(no 6)
1 pr	(no 5)
1 pr	(no 4)

(10 prs)
After pin D:

| 3 prs | (no 4) |
| 1 pr | (no 6) |

(14 prs)
After pin E:
cont in Cls.

After pin F:
start patt – work supported T S (tech 19, td 19), with central p.pr (no 6), work a Maltese Spot.
After pin G and pin H:
Cls thro 1 p.pr, tie ½ knot with leaders.
Note This will hold 1st p prs in place near pins.
Work supported T S to finish Maltese Spot, cont in Cls, working to R.

After pin I:
T O & T B 1 pr per row from centre till 3 p prs rem.
(6 prs)
After pin J:

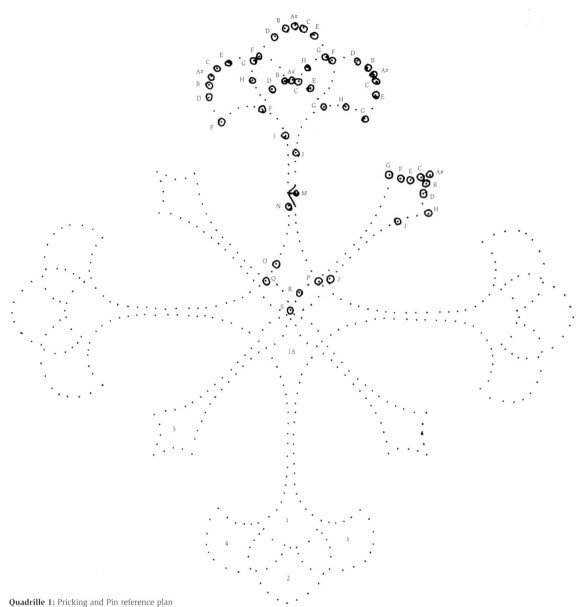

Quadrille 1: Pricking and Pin reference plan

T O & T B 1 p.pr (no 6) from centre.
(5 prs)
To finish at pin P and pin Q:
join to previously worked sections using
top sewings.

Notes for rolled edges
Roll around all edges of spaces at centre:
rolling thread – 1 x (no 6)
rolled threads – 1 x (no 6)
After 4th Section 5 has been completed,
use L edge pr to roll around all edges of
spaces, the lower edges of Sections 1a.
Note It is not necessary to join 4 points
of Sections 1a at centre.

Roll around all outside edges from pin Q
to pin Q.
rolling thread – 1 x (no 6)

rolled threads – 3 x (no 6)
Use leaders and R edge pr for rolled
edges.

Interval

VERSION 1
('Half-stitch')

Section 1
Start at pin A#:
follow instructions for 'Quadrille',
Section 5, from pin A# to after pin D.

After pin D:
add 1 pr (no 6) and 3 prs (no 4).
L–R order should be as foll:
L edge pr   2 x (no 6)

	2 x (no 7)
	1 x (no 6)
	1 x (no 5)
	1 x (no 6)
	1 x (no 5)
	1 x (no 4)
	1 x (no 6)
	6 x (no 4)
	1 x (no 6)
	1 x (no 4)
	1 x (no 5)
	1 x (no 6)
	1 x (no 5)
	1 x (no 6)
	2 x (no 7)
R edge pr	2 x (no 6)
leaders	2 x (no 6)
(14 prs)	
After pin E:	

120

start patt – work ½ st with 3 centre
p prs (no 4).

Note There is no pin F.

After pin G and pin H:
Cls thro 1 p.pr, tie ½ knot with leaders.
Note This will hold 1st prs in place near
pins.
After 7 rows,
when leaders return to original colour
position, cont in Cls.
After pin I:

follow instructions for 'Quadrille',
Section 5.
Note When T O & T B, thread colour
order will not be exactly the same.

After pin J:
add 1 pr (no 5) to centre.
Nr: add 1 pr (no 4) and 1 pr (no 3) to
centre.
Nr: add 2 prs (no 2) to centre.
Nr: add 2 prs (no 1) to centre.
L–R order should be as foll:

L edge pr	2 x (no 6)
	2 x (no 7)
	1 x (no 6)
	1 x (no 5)
	1 x (no 4)
	1 x (no 3)
	2 x (no 2)
	4 x (no 1)
	2 x (no 2)
	1 x (no 3)
	1 x (no 4)
	1 x (no 5)
	1 x (no 6)

	2 x (no 7)
R edge pr	2 x (no 6)
leaders	2 x (no 6)
(13 prs)	

Work 4 rows.
Nr: T O & T B 2 p prs (no 1).
Nr: T O & T B 2 p prs (no 2)
Nr: T O & T B 1 p.pr (no 3) and 1 p.pr
(no 4).
Nr: T O & T B 1 p.pr (no 5).

After pin K:
add 1 p.pr per row to centre, to give
order as after pin D.
(14 prs)

After pin L:
start patt: work ½ st with 3 centre p prs.

After pin M and pin N:
Cls thro 1 p.pr, tie ½ knot with leaders.
*Note This will hold 1st prs in place
near pins.*

After pin O:
work 1 row, then cont in Cls.
Cont to finish at pin P:
follow instructions after pin R, Section
3a, Bud.
Note Add magic thread when placing
pin P.

Notes for rolled edge
Roll from pin P, via pin A#, to pin P:
rolling thread – 1 x (no 6)
rolled threads – 3 x (no 6)
Use edge prs at pin P for roll.
Work twice into pinholes to turn corners.
Finish at pin P.

VERSION 2
(Maltese Spot)

Section 1
Start at pin A#:
follow instructions for Quadrille, Section
5, from pin A# to pin J.
(5 prs)

After pin J:
follow instructions for Version 1, to pin K.

After pin K:
add p prs, 1 pr per row to centre, to give
order as after pin N, Section 3a, Bloom.

After pin L:
start patt: work supported T S with cen
tre p.pr, work Maltese Spot.
At pin M and pin N:
Cls thro 1 p.pr, tie ½ knot with leaders.
*Note This will hold 1st prs in place near
pins.*

Work supported T S to finish Maltese
Spot, cont in Cls, working to R.

After pin O:
work 1 row, then cont in Cls.

Cont to finish at pin P:
follow instructions after pin R, Section
3a, Bud.
Note Add magic thread when placing
pin P.

Notes for rolled edge
As Version 1.

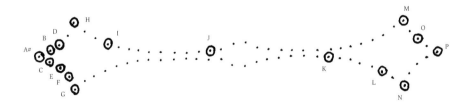

Interval 1: Pricking and pin reference plan

Antique Blossoms

The *Antique Blossoms*, both round and oval, are worked in a set of colours that suggest the softly faded silk blooms found in Victorian glass-domed flower displays.

The motifs illustrate how colours may be chosen to indicate a particular mood or period of time and to create a certain atmosphere, while also describing shape and form. It is due to the successful blending of the disparate colours that the finished motif maintains its subtle visual interest. If a bright and vibrant set of colours were chosen, instead of the soft colours, the form of the flowers would be described in the same manner, but the overall result would be entirely different – lively rather than gentle. When making the colour decisions for a piece of work, the emotive response of the viewer to the finished piece is an important consideration, since the overall choice of colours affects the character of the piece in its entirety.

Colours:

(no 1)	*White
(no 2)	Flesh
(no 3)	Pastel Pink
(no 4)	*Honey
(no 5)	Light Slate
(no 6)	*Mauve
(no 7)	*Crocus

Antique Blossoms (round)

The blossoms have detached sepals, which are joined to the petal with one sewing at the tip of the sepal. The sepals are worked in Tenstick for a daintier appearance than can be achieved using the more conventional two-pinned edge

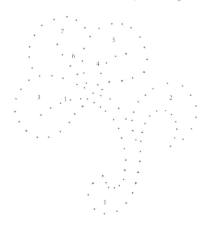

Antique Blossoms round 1: Pricking and Order of work

method. The Tenstick changes into the two-pinned edge style of working where the sepals join the stem. An unusual method of achieving 'holes' within Cloth Stitch is a feature of this piece. The outer edges of the petals and parts of the stem and leaf are rolled.

Section 1
(Cloth stitch with Holes/Ribbon, var)

Start at pin A#:
Use a Tenstick colour point start (tech 41, td 41), (Note Pinned edge is on the inner curve), hang 2 prs (no 6) to be leader prs, and 1 pr (no 7) to be pinned edge pr on pin A# (td 41a).
L–R order is as foll:
2 x (no 6)
2 x (no 7)
2 x (no 6)
(3 prs)
Add magic thread (tech 2, td 2b)
Cls centre pr (no 7) thro L pr (no 6), and tw 2 (no 7), which is now the pinned edge pr.
At next pin:
tw 2 leaders (no 6), place pin, and work smooth Tenstick edge (tech 19, td 19).
Nr: add 1 pr (no 6) to be 1st p.pr from L. (4 prs)
Cont in Tenstick, adding 1 pr (no 6) after next two pins, to centre of p.pr/prs at each addition. (6 prs)
At the base of the sepal, pin B:
change from smooth edge to pinned edge (tech 33, td 33), tw 2 leaders, place pin B, and edge st at pin B.
Note Take care to identify to correct Pin

B, Section 1.

After pin C:
add 1 pr (no 7) to be 1st p.pr from L. (7 prs)

After pin D:
add 1 pr (no 7) to be s ps 2 & 3 from L. (8 prs)
Nr: T O & T B 2nd p.pr (no 6) from R, and add 1 p.pr (no 7) to be 2nd p.pr from L.
Nr: add 1 pr (no 7) to be s ps 4 & 5 from L.
Work 1 row.
Nr: add 1 pr (no 7) to be 3rd p.pr from L.
Nr: T O & T B 2nd p.pr (no 6) from R. (9 prs)

After pin E:
add 1 pr (no 6) to be s ps 2 & 3 from R. (10 prs)
Nr: T O & T B 3rd p.pr (no 7) from L.
Nr: add 1 pr (no 5) to be 2nd p.pr from R.
Nr: T O & T B s ps 4 & 5 (no 7) from L.
Nr: add 1 pr (no 4) to be s ps 4 & 5 from R.
Nr: T O & T B 2nd p.pr (no 7) from L, and add 1 pr (no 4) to be 3rd p.pr from R.
Nr: add 1 pr (no 4) to be s ps 6 & 7 from R.
Nr: add 1 pr (no 3) to be 6th p.pr from L.
Nr: add 1 pr (no 3) to be s ps 8 & 9 from R.
(13 prs)

After working 1st part of blind pin F:
T O & T B 2nd p.pr (no 7) from L, start Holes/Ribbon (var) patt (diag a.b.r.1)

thus – *Cls tog 5th and 6th p prs (no 3) from L, Cls leaders thro 5 p prs, tw 2 leaders, Cls rem 4 p prs.
Nr: tw 2, 4th and 5th p prs (no 3) from R, Cls leaders thro 4 p prs, tw 2 leaders, Cls rem 5 p prs.*
(12 prs)
Cont in patt, rep * to *.
(12 prs)
After completing blind pin G:
when 3 sets of holes have been worked, Cls tog 5th and 6th p prs (no 3), cont in Cls.

Nr: T O & T B s ps 8 & 9 (no 3) from R.
Nr: T O & T B 3rd p.pr (no 5/no 6), 5th p.pr (no 3), and 7th p.pr (no 4/no 5) from L.

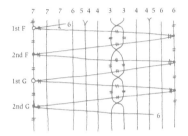

Diagram abr 1: After pin F and pin G, Section 1

(8 prs)
After pin H:
use a wide-angle finish (diag a.b.r.2) as foll – Cls tog 2nd and 3rd p prs (no 4) from R, and T O & T B.
Cls tog 1st and 2nd p prs (no 6), then Cls leaders thro all 3 rem p prs.
T O & T B L p.pr (no 6) and leaders (no 6).
T O 1st p.pr (no 7) from L, and T O 1st p.pr (no 6) from R.
Note: Do not cut off these 2 prs, they will be included in T O of edge prs, and used for the rolled edges.
Cls tog & tw 2 L & R edge prs (no 7) and (no 6), place pin I. Cls tog edge prs.

T O L edge pr (no 7).
Note Include p.pr (no 7) in knot when T O, these 2 prs will be used for rolled

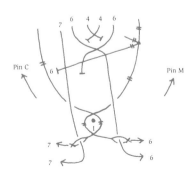

Diagram abr 2: Wide angle finish, Section 1

edge from pin I to pin C.

T O R edge pr (no 6).
Note Include p.pr (no 6) in knot when T O, these 2 prs will be used for rolled edge from pin I to pin N.

Secure T O & T B prs to back of work with previously T B prs.

Notes for rolled edges
Roll from pin I to pin C:
rolling thread – 1 x (no 7)
rolled threads – 3 x (no 7)
Use L edge pr and 1st p.pr from L for rolled edge.
T B 1 thread at pin J and pin D.
Finish at pin C.

Roll from pin I to pin M:
rolling thread – 1 x (no 6)
rolled threads – 3 x (no 6)
Use R edge pr and 1st p.pr from R for rolled edge.
T B 1 thread from roll at pin K and pin L.
Finish at pin M.

Section 2
Start at pin A#:
use a two colour point start (tech 1, td 1), (Note R–L working direction), hang 1 pr (no 6) and 1 pr (no 7) to be edge prs.
Add magic thread (tech 2, td 2).
L edge pr is now (no 6).
R edge pr is now (no 7).

On temp pin, hang 1 pr (no 6) to be leaders.
(3 prs)
On temp pin, hang 2 p prs in order L–R: 1 pr (no 6) and 1 pr (no 7).
Cls leaders R–L thro these 2 p prs and edge st at pin B.
(5 prs)
After pin B:
add 1 pr (no 6) and 1 pr (no 5) open on a temp pin.
L–R order is as foll:
1 x (no 6)
2 x (no 5)
1 x (no 6)
hanging in positions to become s ps 2, 3, 4 & 5 from L.
(7 prs)
Nr: add 1 pr (no 5) to be s ps 6 & 7 from R.
Nr: add 1 pr (no 4) to be 3rd p.pr from L.
Nr: add 1 pr (no 4) to be s ps 8 & 9 from R.
Nr: add 1 pr (no 3) to be 4th p.pr from L.
Nr: add 1 pr (no 2) to be s ps 10 & 11 from R.
Nr: add 1 pr (no 2) to be 5th p.pr from L.
Nr: add 1 pr (no 1) to be s ps 12 & 13 from R.
(14 prs)
After pin C:

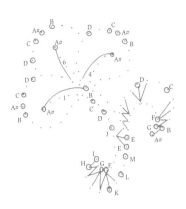

Antique Blossoms round 2: Pin reference plan

start patt, 'Holes/Ribbon', var (diag a.b.r.3), use 5th p.pr (no 2/no 1) and 6th p.pr (no 1/no 2) from L.
Cont in patt.
(14 prs)
After pin D:
when 3 holes have been worked, Cls 5th and 6th p prs tog to complete patt, cont in Cls.
(14 prs)
Nr: T O & T B s ps 12 & 13 (no 1) from R.
Nr: add 1 pr (no 7) to be 1st p.pr from L, and
T O & T B 5th p.pr (no 3) and 7th p.pr (no 3) from R.
Work 1 row.
Nr: add 1 pr (no 7) to be s ps 2 & 3 from L, and
T O & T B 5th p.pr (no 2) from R.
Work 1 row.
Nr: T O & T B s ps 10 & 11 (no 4) from L.
Nr: add 1 pr (no 7) to be s ps 2 & 3 from R.
Nr: T O & T B 5th p.pr (no 4) from L.
(11 prs)
Cont in Cls,
T O & T B from centre, 1 p.pr per row, lightest prs first, joining to Section 1 using top sewings.

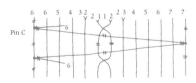

Diagram abr 3: Pin C, Section 2

Finish at pin E.
Note Do not cut off R edge pr (no 7) or rem 1st p.pr (no 7) from R, they will be used for rolled edge.
T O & T B rem prs.

Rolled edge notes
Roll from pin E to pin A#:
rolling thread – 1 x (no 7)

rolled threads – 3 x (no 7)
Use R edge pr and 1st p.pr from R for
rolled edge.
T B 1 thread at pin F and pin G.
Finish at pin A#.

Section 3
Note Blossom petal (Section 3) is
worked over top of Blossom sepal
(Section 1), all other petal sections are
also worked in a similar manner.

Start at pin A#:
Using a one colour flat start (tech 21, td
21) (Note R–L working direction), hang
2 prs (no 1) to be edge prs.
Add magic thread (tech 2, td 2a)

On temp pin: hang 1 pr (no 3) to be
leaders.
(3 prs)
On temp pin, hang 4 prs (no 1) open.
Cls leaders R–L thro 4 p prs and edge st
at pin B.
(7 prs)
After pin B:
on a temp pin, add 6 prs (no 2) open, to
be centre p prs.
(13 prs)
After pin C:
add 3 prs (no 3) to centre.
Work 3 rows.
(16 prs)

After pin D:
start Holes/Ribbon (var) patt thus (diag
a.b.r.4) – Cls leaders R–L thro 2 p prs,
tw 2 leaders, Cls leaders thro 4 p prs,
join central p.pr (no 3) to Section 1,
sewing into pin A#, Cls leaders thro 4
p prs, tw 2 leaders, Cls leaders thro 2 p prs.
Nr: tw 2, 2nd , 3rd, 11th and 12th p prs
from L, Cls leaders thro 2 p prs,
tw 2 leaders, Cls leaders thro 9 p prs, tw
2 leaders, Cls leaders thro 2 p prs.
Nr: Cls tog 2nd & 3rd and 11th & 12th
p prs from R, Cls leaders thro all p prs.
Nr: Cls thro all p prs.
Nr: Cls tog 2nd & 3rd and 11th & 12th
p prs from R, Cls leaders thro 2 p prs,
tw 2 leaders, Cls leaders thro 9 p prs, tw
2 leaders, Cls leaders thro 2 p prs.

Nr: tw 2, 2nd & 3rd and 11th & 12th
p prs from L, Cls leaders thro 2 p prs,
tw 2 leaders, Cls leaders thro 9 p prs, tw
2 leaders, Cls leaders thro 2 p prs.
Cont in Cls,
T O & T B p prs as section narrows.

Finish at base of petal.
Note Do not cut off R edge pr, or 1
thread from 1st p.pr from R, they will be
used for rolled edge.

Notes for rolled edge
Roll from pin B, Section 1, to L edge at

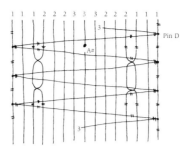

Diagram abr 4: Pin D, Section 3

base of petal.
rolling thread – 1 x (no 1)
rolled threads – 2 x (no 1)
Use R edge pr and 1 thread from 1st
p.pr from R.
Roll around edge of petal.
Finish at L edge at base of petal.

Section 4
Start at pin A#:
follow instructions for Section 1, from
pin A# till 4 prs.
Note Pinned edge is on the inner curve.
Reverse L–R directions.
(4 prs)
Finish by joining to previously worked
sections using top sewings.

Section 5
Note Blossom petal (Section 5) is
worked over top of Blossom sepal
(Section 4), all other petal sections are
also worked in a similar manner.

Start at pin A#:
Note L–R working direction
follow instructions for Section 3, from
pin A# to finish.
Note Reverse L–R directions.

Notes for rolled edge
As Section 3.
Note Reverse L–R directions.

Section 6
Start at pin A#:
follow instructions for Section 1, from
pin A# till 4 prs.
Note Pinned edge is on the inner curve.
Reverse L–R directions.
(4 prs)
Finish by joining to previously worked
sections using top sewings.

Section 7
Note Blossom petal (Section 7) is
worked over top of Blossom sepal
(Section 6), all other petal sections are
also worked in a similar manner.

Start at pin A#:
follow instructions for Section 3, from
pin A# to finish.

Note L–R working direction (i.e. reverse
R–L directions given for Section 3). Join
to previously worked sections using top
sewings. T O & T B edge prs and 1st
p prs from each side where petals meet,
do not cut off prs from L, they will be
used for rolled edge.

T O & T B p prs where section narrows.
Finish at base of petal.
Note Due to decreasing of p prs, where
section narrows, only 1st pair of holes
will be worked.

Notes for rolled edge
Roll from L edge where petals meet, to
R edge where petals meet:
rolling thread – 1 x (no 1)
rolled threads – 2 x (no 1)
Use L edge pr and 1 thread from 1st
p.pr from L to roll around edge of petal.
Finish at R edge where petals meet.

Antique Blossoms
(oval)

As with Antique Blossoms (round),
these blossoms have detached sepals,
which are joined to the petal with one
sewing at the tip of the sepal. The
sepals are worked in Tenstick for a
daintier, lighter appearance than can be
achieved using the more conventional
two-pinned edge method. The petals are
worked in Half-stitch. The Milanese
braid Basketweave is used to work
sections of the stem and the leaf. The
unusual use of a shaped section of
Tenstick for one side of the leaf is a
feature of this piece. The outer edges of
the petals and parts of the stem and leaf
are rolled.

*Note: It is advised that a marked
pricking is made (tech 43, td 43) to
indicate the Tenstick smooth edge guide
line, Section 1a.*

Section 1
(Basketweave, Tenstick and Half-stitch)
Start at pin A#:
using a one colour point start (tech 23,
td 23), (Note L–R working direction),
hang 2 prs (no 7) open, to be edge prs.
Add magic thread (tech 2 ,td 2).

On temp pin, hang 1 pr (no 7) to be
leaders.
(3 prs)
On temp pin, hang 2 prs (no 7) open, to
be p prs.
Cls leaders L–R thro 2 p prs and edge st
at pin B (tech 3, td 3).
(5 prs)
After pin B:

add 1 p.pr per row to centre, in foll
order:

1 p.pr	(no 6)
1 p.pr	(no 6)
1 p.pr	(no 5)
1 p.pr	(no 5)
1 p.pr	(no 4)
1 p.pr	(no 4)
1 p.pr	(no 3)
1 p.pr	(no 3)

(13 prs)
Nr: T O & T B s ps 4 & 5 (no 6/no 5)
from R.
(12 prs)

After pin C:
T O & T B s ps 4 & 5 (no 6/no 5) from
L, Cls thro 2 p prs, start Basketweave
patt with 4 p prs (no 4 and no 3), (diag
ABO.1), Cls rem 2 p prs.
(11 prs)
Nr: Cls 2 p prs, patt 4 p prs, Cls rem 2
p prs.
Cont in patt.

After pin D:
when p prs have returned to original
colour positions, cont in Cls, cont row
T O & T B 1 p.pr (no 3) from centre.
Work 1 row.
(10 prs)
Nr: T O & T B 1 p.pr (no 3).
Nr: add 1 pr (no 7) to be s ps 2 & 3
from R.
Nr: T O & T B 1 p.pr (no 4).
Nr: add 1 pr (no 7) to be 2nd p.pr from R.
Nr: T O & T B 1 p.pr (no 4).
Nr: add 1 p.pr (no 7) to be s ps 4 & 5
from R.
Nr: T O & T B 1 p.pr (no 5).
Nr: add 1 p.pr (no 7) to be 3rd p.pr
from R.
Nr: T O & T B 1 p.pr (no 6).
(9 prs)
When working 1st part blind pin E:
tw 2 leaders, place pin, do not work
edge st.
Cont to pin F.

After pin F:
Cls thro 2 p prs, take pr just worked
thro as new leaders, Cls back thro 1 p.pr
to pin G.

After pin G:
T O & T B 2nd p.pr from L, and T O &
T B 2nd p.pr from R.
(7 prs)
At blind pin E:
complete blind pin, working edge st.

Finish at pin H and pin I:
join to previously worked braid using
top sewings, set aside R edge pr (no 7)
and 1st p.pr from R (no 7) for rolled
edge.
T O & T B rem prs in a bunch.

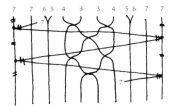

Diagram abo 1: After Pin C, Section 1

Notes for rolled edges
Roll from pin H to pin E:
rolling thread – 1 x (no 7)
rolled threads – 3 x (no 7)
Use set aside prs at pin H for roll.
T B 1 thread from roll at pin J and pin K.
Finish at pin E.

Roll from pin F to pin A#:
rolling thread – 1 x (no 7)
rolled threads – 3 x (no 7)
Add 1 pr (no 7) at pin F.
Add 1 thread to roll at pin L and pin M.
T B 1 thread at pin N and pin O.
Finish at pin A#, adding 1 pr (no 7) into
loop, created by rolling thread at pin A#.
Note Do not T O & T B these 2 prs (no
7), they will be used as the leaders and
smooth edge pr for Tenstick, Section 1a.

Section 1a
Start at pin A#:
using 2 prs (no 7) from rolled edge, to
be leaders and smooth edge pr, (Note
See notes for rolled edge, Section 1),
start Tenstick thus – work smooth edge
st with both prs, tw 2 R pr, leaders, join
to Section 1, using top sewing, tw 2
leaders.
Nr:*add 1 pr (no 7) to be 1st p.pr from
R, positioned between leaders and
smooth edge pr, Cls leaders thro p.pr
and work smooth edge st.
Nr: Cls to R edge, adding 1 pr (no 6)
to be 1st p.pr from R, tw 2 leaders, join

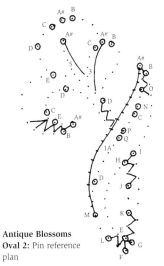

Antique Blossoms
Oval 2: Pin reference
plan

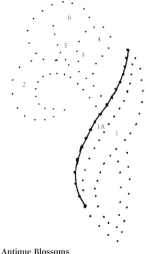

Antique Blossoms
Oval 1: Pricking and
Order of work

to Section 1 using top sewing, tw 2
leaders.*
(4 prs)
Cont rep * to * till 9 prs.
(9 prs)
Cont in Tenstick.
Note Care must be taken to ensure the
Tenstick section follows the shape of the
smooth edge guide line, shown on the
marked pricking (tech 43, td 43) and pin
reference diag.

After pin D:
T O & T B 1st p.pr from R, 1 pr per row.

Finish at pin M.

Section 2
Start at pin A#:
use a two-colour point start (tech 1, td
1), (Note L–R working direction), hang
1 pr (no 7) and 1 pr (no 6) to be edge
prs.
Add magic thread (tech 2, td 2).
L edge pr is now (no 7).
R edge pr is now (no 6).

On temp pin, hang 1 pr (no 7) to be
leaders.
(3 prs)
On temp pin, hang 2 prs (no 7) open, to
be p prs.
Cls leaders L–R thro 2 p prs, and edge st
at pin B.
(5 prs)
After pin B:
add 1 pr per row to centre of braid, in
foll order:

1 p.pr	(no 6)
1 p.pr	(no 6)
1 p.pr	(no 5)
1 p.pr	(no 5)
1 p.pr	(no 4)
1 p.pr	(no 4)

Section 4

Note Blossom petal (Section 4) is worked over top of Blossom sepal (Section 3), other petal section is also worked in a similar manner.

Start at pin A#:
using magic thread at pin A# (tech 16, td 16a), (Note L–R working direction) – add 1 pr (no 3) to be leaders, and into its loop, hang 1 pr (no 1) to be R edge pr. Tw 2 R edge pr.

On temp pin, hang 2 prs (no 1) open, to be p prs.
Cls L–R thro 2 p prs and edge st at pin B. (4 prs)
On temp pin, add 3 prs (no 2) open, placing them between Section 3 and 2 p prs (no 1), Cls thro all 5 p prs. (7 prs)
Join to Section 3 using top sewings.

After pin C:
start patt: work ½ st with 3 p prs (no 2), Cls rem 2 p prs (no 1).
Nr: Cls 2 p prs (no 1), patt ½ st 3 p prs (no 2).
Cont in patt.

Join to Sections 2 and 3 using top sewings.

Finish at pin C, Section 3, and pin D, T O & T B prs to decrease.
Set aside R edge pr and 1 thread from 1st p.pr from R, for rolled edge.

Notes for rolled edge
Roll from pin D to pin A#:
rolling thread – 1 x (no 1)
rolled threads – 2 x (no 1)
Use set aside threads for roll.
T B 1 thread from roll at pin B.
Finish at pin A#.

Section 5
Start at pin A#:
Follow instructions for Section 1, 'Antique Blossoms (round)', from pin A# till 4 prs.
(4 prs)

Cont in Tenstick.
Join to previously worked sections using top sewings.
T O & T B prs in a bunch.

Section 6
Start at pin A#:
Follow instructions for Section 3, Antique Blossoms (round) from pin A# to pin C.
Note Reverse L–R directions.
(13 prs)
After pin C:

1 p.pr   (no 3)
1 p.pr   (no 3)
1 p.pr   (no 3)
(14 prs)

After pin C:
T O & T B s ps 4 & 5 (no 6/no 5) from L, work Basketweave patt with 5 p prs (no 4 and no 3), Cls rem prs.
(13 prs)
Nr: T O & T B s ps 4 & 5 from R, cont patt with 5 p prs (no 3 and no 4).
(12 prs)
Cont in patt.

After pin D:
when prs have returned to original colour positions, cont in Cls and T O & T B 5th p.pr (no 3) from L.
(11 prs)
Nr: T O & T B s ps 6 & 7 (no 4 / no 3), and s ps 10 & 11 (no 3 / no 4) from R.
Nr: T O & T B s ps 6 & 7 (no 3) from L.
Nr: T O & T B 3rd p.pr (no 4) from R.
Nr: add 1 pr (no 7) to be s ps 2 & 3 from L.
Nr: T O & T B s ps 4 & 5 (no 5) from R.
Nr: add 1 pr (no 7) to be 2nd pr from L.

Nr: T O & T B 2nd p.pr (no 6) from R.
(7 prs)
Cont in Cls to finish at pin P and pin Q, Section 1, working over top of Tenstick section.
T O & T B all prs except L edge pr and leaders, to be set aside for rolled edge.

Notes for rolled edge
Roll from pin Q, Section 1, to pin A#, Section 2:
rolling thread – 1 x (no 7)
rolled threads – 3 x (no 7)
Use prs set aside at pin Q for rolled edge.
T B 1 thread from roll at pin C and pin E.
Finish at pin A#.

Section 3
Start at pin A#:
follow instructions for Section 1, Antique Blossoms (round), from pin A# till 4 prs.
(4 prs)
Cont in Tenstick.

Join to Section 2 using top sewings.
T O & T B prs in a bunch.

start patt:*Cls thro 2 p prs, tw 1 leaders, work ½ st with 6 p prs (no 2), Cls rem 2 p prs.*
Cont in patt, rep * to *.

After pin D:
Cls thro 2 p prs, ½ st 2 p prs, join to Section 5, by making a sewing with leaders, using magic thread at pin A#, ½ st 4 p prs, Cls rem 2 p prs.
Cont with in patt.

Note No further sewings into Section 5 required.

To finish, join to Sections 2, 4 and 5 using top sewings, decreasing prs as section narrows.
Set aside R edge pr and 1 thread from 1st p.pr from R, for rolled edge.
Note Optional: after joining Section 2, Cls may be resumed.

Notes for rolled edge
Roll from pin A#, Section 3, to pin E, Section 6:
rolling thread – 1 x (no 1)
rolled threads – 2 x (no 1)
Use set aside threads for roll.
Finish at pin E.

X Blossoms

(Half-stitch and Tenstick)

The blossoms from *Antique Blossoms (round)* (page 123) and *(oval)* (page 125) have both been used to create *X Blossoms*: the blossoms from the round version have been reversed and merge into the pattern for *X for Xenon* (page 83), whereas the blossoms from the oval version are simply repeated.

If preferred, the blossoms may be worked with the Holes/Ribbon variation, in which case refer to *Antique Blossoms (round)*. The *X* sections may also be worked as *X for Xenon*, Version 2.

Colours: As *X for Xenon.*

Section 1
Start at pin A#:
follow instructions for Antique Blossoms (round), from pin A# to pin B.
Note Reverse L–R directions
(6 prs)
After pin B:
change from smooth edge to pinned edge (tech 33, td 33), place pin B and edge st (tech 3, td 3).
After pin C:
follow instructions for X for Xenon, Version 1, Section 1, to finish at pin R.

Notes for rolled edges
Roll from pin R to pin K:
as X for Xenon, Version 1, Section 1.

Roll from pin C to pin I:
rolling thread – 1 x (no 7)
rolled threads – 3 x (no 7)
Add 1 pr at pin C, using top sewings.
Add 1 thread at pin U and pin D.
T B 1 thread at pin G and V.
Finish at pin I.

Section 2
Follow instructions for X for Xenon, Version 1, Section 2.

Notes for rolled edge
As X for Xenon, Version 1, Section 2.

Section 3
Follow instructions for X for Xenon, Version 1, Section 3.

Notes for rolled edge
As X for Xenon, Version 1, Section 3.

Section 4
Follow instructions for X for Xenon, Version 1, Section 2, from pin A# to pin F.

After pin F:
change leaders (no 3) to (no 7), (tech 4, td 4) cont row.
(12 prs)
Work 1 row.
Nr: T O & T B 6th p.pr (no 3) from L.
Nr: T O & T B s ps 6 & 7 (no 4) from R.

Nr: T O & T B 5th p.pr (no 4) from L.
Nr: T O & T B s ps 4 & 5 (no 5) from R.
Nr: T O & T B 4th p.pr (no 5) from L.
(7 prs)

Join to Section 1:
using top sewings, decreasing prs from R.
Finish by joining 1 p.pr from L at pin G, and L edge pr at pin H.

Notes for rolled edge
Roll from pin H to pin A#:
rolling thread – 1 x (no 7)
rolled threads – 3 x (no 7)
Use L edge pr and 1st p.pr from L for rolled edge.
T B 1 thread at pin D and pin I.
Finish at pin A#.

Sections 5, 7 and 9
Note Blossom petal (Section 5) is worked over top of Blossom sepal (Section 1), all other petal sections are also worked in a similar manner.
Start at pin A#:

Follow instructions for Antique Blossom
(round), Sections 3, 5 and 7, from pin
A# to C.
Note Reverse L–R directions.
(13 prs)

After pin C:
start patt – Cls thro 2 p prs, work ½ st
with 6 centre p prs (no 2), Cls rem p prs.
Cont in patt.

After pin D:
Cls thro 2 p prs, ½ st 4 p prs, join
section to tip of sepal, ½ st 2 p prs, Cls
rem p prs.
Cont in patt, ½ st 6 p prs.
Note No further sewings into sepal are
required.

After pin E:
when patt prs have returned to their
original colour positions, cont in Cls.
Note Follow instructions for Antique
Blossoms (round), to join and finish
Sections 7 and 9, reversing L–R
directions where necessary.
Nr: T O & T B 2nd, 4th, s ps 10 & 11,
7th and 9th p prs from L.
(8 prs)
At pin F:

join leaders and R edge pr to Section 1.
T O & T B R edge pr, and T O & T B 3
p prs.
(4 prs)

Finish at pin B, Section 1:
join leaders and L edge pr to Section 1,
T O L edge pr and set aside for rolled
edge.
T O leaders and rem prs, set aside 1
thread from 1st p.pr from L for roll.
T B rem prs in a bunch.

Notes for rolled edges
As Antique Blossom (round).

Sections 6 and 8
Start at pin A#:
Follow instructions for Antique
Blossoms (round).
Note Reverse L–R directions.

Sections 10, 11, 12 and 13
Start at pin A#:
follow instructions for Antique Blossoms
(oval), Sections 3, 4, 5 and 6, from pin
A# to finish.

Notes for rolled edges
As Antique Blossoms (oval).

Y Blossoms
(Mittens var and Holes/Ribbon var)

The blossoms from *Antique Blossoms
(oval)* have been used to create *Y
Blossoms*: the blossoms from the oval
version have been reversed; the top part
of Section 1 has been repeated as an
extra leaf and is worked normally,
though the rest of the *Y* sections are
reversed.
If preferred, the blossoms may be
worked in Half-stitch, in which case
refer to *Antique Blossoms (oval)*. The *Y*
sections may also be worked as Version
1, *Y for the Reason Because...*

Colours
As *Y for the Reason Because...*

Sections 1 and 1a
Start at pin A#:
follow instructions for Y for the Reason
Because..., Version 2, Sections 1 and 1a,
from pin A# to finish.
Note Reverse L–R directions.
Notes for rolled edges
As Y for the Reason Because..., Version
2, Sections 1 and 1a.

X Blossoms 1:
Pricking and
Order of work

X Blossoms 2: Pin reference plan

Section 2

Start at pin A#:
Follow instructions for Y for the Reason Because..., Version 2, Section 1, from pin A# to pin I.
(7 prs)

At pin I: change leaders (no 7) with R edge pr (no 5), (tech 7, td 7).

After pin I:
change leaders (no 5) to (no 7), (tech 4, td 4), cont in Cls.
(7 prs)

After pin J:
add 1 pr (no 6) to be 1st p.pr from R.
Nr: T O & T B 1st p.pr (no 6) from L and add 1 pr (no 7) to be s ps 8 & 9 from R.
Nr: add 1 pr (no 7) to be 5th p.pr from R.
(9 prs)

After pin K:
use top sewings to join to Section 1a. Cont T O & T B prs from L as section narrows.

Finish at pin L:
set aside leaders (no 7) and R edge pr (no 7) for rolled edge.
T O & T B rem prs, and secure to back of work with previously T B prs.

Notes for rolled edge
Roll from pin L to pin A#:
rolling thread – 1 x (no 7)
rolled threads – 3 x (no 7)
Use prs set aside at pin L for roll.
T B 1 thread from roll at pin M and pin C.
Finish at pin A#.

Sections 3 and 5

Start at pin A#:
follow instructions for Antique Blossoms (oval), Sections 3 and 5 from pin A# to finish.
Note Reverse L–R directions.

Section 4

Start at pin A#:
follow instructions for Antique Blossoms (oval), Section 4, from pin A# to pin C.
Note Reverse L–R directions.
(7 prs)
After pin C:
add 2 p prs (no 3) to be 1st and 2nd p prs from R.
Work 1 row.
(9 prs)
Nr: start Holes patt (diag y.b.1) – Cls leaders R–L thro 4 p prs, tw 2 leaders, Cls leaders thro 2 p prs.
Nr: tw 2, 2nd and 3rd p prs (no 1 and no 2), Cls leaders thro 2 p prs, tw 2 leaders, Cls leaders thro 4 p prs.
Cont in Cls.

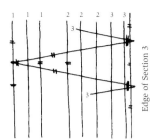

Diagram yb 1: Patt. 'Holes', Section 4

Join to Section 1a using top sewings, T O & T B p prs as braid narrows.

Finish at pin D:
set aside L edge pr (no 1) and 1 thread (no 1) from 1st p.pr from L for roll.
T O & T B rem threads in a bunch.

Notes for rolled edge
As Antique Blossoms (oval).

Section 6

Start at pin A#:
follow instructions for Section 3, Antique Blossoms (round) from pin A to finish.

Notes for rolled edge
As Antique Blossoms (oval).
Note Reverse L–R directions.

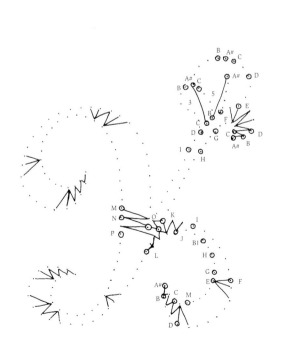

Y Blossoms 2: Pin reference plan

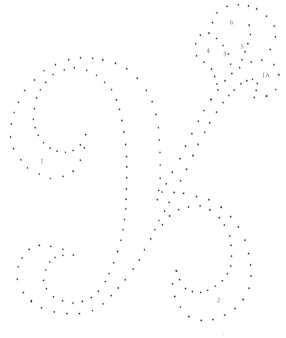

Y Blossoms 1: Pricking and Order of work

Z Blossoms

(Basketweave var and Half-stitch)

The blossoms from *Antique Blossoms (oval)* (page 125) have been used to create *Z Blossoms*. The blossoms are worked in exactly the same manner as those from the oval version. The Z sections are also worked normally, though the motif is rotated.

If preferred, the blossoms may be worked in Holes/Ribbon var, in which case refer to *Y Blossoms*, reversing the L–R directions. The Z sections may also be worked as Version 1, *Z for Zircon*.

Colours
As *Z for Zircon* (page 89).

Sections 1, 2 and 2a
Start at pin A#:
Follow instructions for Z for Zircon, from pin A# to finish.

Notes for rolled edges
As Z for Zircon, Version 2, Sections 1, 2 and 2a.

Section 3
Start at pin A#:
using a two-colour point start (tech 1, td 1), (Note L–R working direction), hang 1 pr (no 7) and 1 pr (no 6) to be edge prs.
Add magic thread (tech 2, td 2).
L edge pr is now (no 7).
R edge pr is now (no 6).
On temp pin, hang 1 pr (no 6) to be leaders.
(3 prs)
On temp pin, hang 2 prs in order L–R: 1 pr (no 7) and 1 pr (no 6) to be p prs, Cls leaders L–R thro 2 p prs and edge st

at pin B.
(5 prs)
Nr: add 1 pr (no 6) to be s ps 2 & 3 from R.
Nr: add 1 pr (no 5) to be 3rd p.pr from L.
Nr: add 1 pr (no 5) to be s ps 4 & 5 from R.
Nr: add 1 pr (no 4) to be 4th p.pr from L.
Nr: add 1 pr (no 3) to be s ps 6 & 7 from R.
Nr: add 1 pr (no 2) to be 5th p.pr from L.
Nr: add 1 pr (no 2) to be s ps 8 & 9 from R.
Nr: add 1 pr (no 1) to be 6th p.pr from L.
(13 prs)
After pin C:
start Basketweave patt – Cls thro 3 p prs, Basketweave patt with 5 p prs, Cls rem 2 p prs.
Nr: Cls thro 2 p prs, patt 5 p prs,

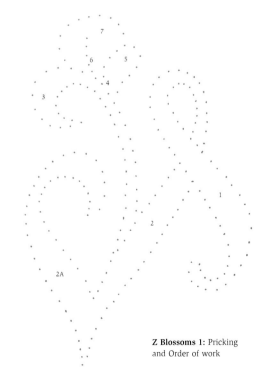

Z Blossoms 1: Pricking and Order of work

Cls rem 3 p prs.
After pin D:
Cls patt tog to complete patt, to return
patt prs to original colour positions, cont
row, T O & T B 1 pr (no 1).
(12 prs)
After pin E:
T O & T B 1 p.pr per row, from near
centre, lightest prs first, till 4 p prs rem.
Work 1 row.
(7 prs)
Nr: add 1 pr (no 7) to be s ps 2 & 3
from L.
Nr: T O & T B 2nd p.pr (no 5) from R.
Nr: add 1 pr (no 7) to be 2nd p.pr from L.
Nr: T O & T B s ps 2 & 3 (no 6) from R.

Cont in Cls to finish at pin F and pin G:
joining to Section 2 using top sewings,

and decreasing prs from R.
Set aside L edge pr (no 7) and 1st p.pr
from L (no 7) for rolled edge.

Notes for rolled edge
Roll from pin G to pin A#:
rolling thread – 1 x (no 7)
rolled threads – 3 x (no 7)
Use prs set aside at pin G for roll.
T B 1 thread from roll at pin C and pin
H.
Finish at pin A#.

Sections 4, 5, 6 and 7
As Antique Blossoms (oval), Sections 3,
4, 5 and 6.

Notes for rolled edges
As Antique Blossoms (oval).

Z Blossoms 2: Pin reference plan

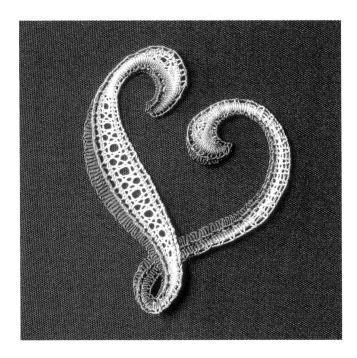

Colours
(no 1)   *White
(no 2)   Pastel Pink
(no 3)   *Pale Salmon
(no 4)   *Peach Pink
(no 5)   Apple Green
(no 6)   Lime Green
(no 7)   *Mid Olive
(no 8)   *Helio

Piper's Silks 80/3 0r *90/3
or
Gutermann Silk S303 (100/3) Colour nos: 800, 658,
659, 43, 582, 585, 841, 309.

Shadow Valentine

As the name of this motif implies, the effects of light falling over a three-dimensional shape and the
shaded areas it creates are explored in the design of this piece, where coloured threads are used in a
painterly way. The design is a development from the motif *F for Fairy Moss*, but in order to enrich
the additional shadow sections, an eighth colour is required. This choice has not only the tonal
value expected to depict a shadow but also the colour.

Shadow Valentine is illustrated using the Milanese techniques of Version 2, from *F for Fairy Moss* to
work Sections 1 and 4. If preferred, the working techniques of Version 1 may be substituted.

This motif, as the name suggests, may be used as a Valentine or perhaps, worked in different
colours or in white, it could be used as a wedding motif.

*Note It is advised that a marked pricking is made (tech 43, td 43) to indicate the Tenstick smooth
edge guide lines for Sections 2, 3, 5, 6 and 7.*

Section 1

Start at pin A#:
Follow instructions for F for Fairy Moss, Version 2, from pin A# to pin O.

After pin O:
work locking st (tech 6, td 6).
Note Leave to work rolled edges and Section 2 and Section 3.

Notes for rolled edges
Roll from pin U to pin Y:
rolling thread – 1 x (no 6)
rolled threads – 3 x (no 6)
Hang on 1 pr (no 6) at pin U.
Add 1 thread to roll at pin V and pin K.
T B 1 thread from roll at pin W and pin X.
Finish roll at pin Y.
Roll from pin A# to pin T:
Note Replace magic thread at pin A# (tech 16b, td 16b)
rolling thread – 1 x (no 7)
rolled threads – 3 x (no 7)
Hang 2 prs (no 7) at pin A#.
T B 1 thread from roll at pin S and pin F.
Finish roll at pin T.

Roll from pin J to pin B1:
rolling thread – 1 x (no 4)
rolled threads – 3 x (no 4)
Hang on 1 pr (no 4) at pin J, add 1 thread (no 4) at next following 2 pins.
T B 1 thread from roll at pin Z and pin A1.
Finish at pin B1.

Section 2

Start at pin A# to work Tenstick section (shadow):
using magic thread (tech 16, td 16),
hang on 1 pr (no 8) to be leaders, tw 2.
Replace pin A#.
On a temp pin, to L of pin A#:
hang 4 prs, side by side and staggered,

(tech 35, td 35), in L–R order as foll:
smooth edge pr	2 x (no 8)
	2 x (no 8)
	1 x (no 7)
	1 x (no 8)
	1 x (no 7)
	1 x (no 8)
leaders	2 x (no 8)
(5 prs)	

Cls leaders R–L thro 3 prs, work T S with rem pr (no 8), placing pin B after X T of X T X T X.
Work back to pin C:
tw 2 leaders, using top sewings join to Section 1, cont working Tenstick.
After a few pins have been worked, remove pin B.
Using the marked pricking as a guide, decrease Tenstick, T O & T B prs from R edge, when joining to Section 1.
Finish at pin H, Section 1.

Section 3

Start at pin A# to work Tenstick section (shadow):
using top sewing, hang on 1 pr (no 8) at pin A#, adding 1 pr (no 8) thro loop of 1st pr.
Work T S with both prs at B, tw 2 leaders (L pr), join to Section 1 with top sewing at pin C, tw 2 leaders.
Cont working Tenstick, joining to Section 1, and add 1 pr (no 8) to be 1st p.pr at L edge.
Work 1 row.
(3 prs)
Nr: add 1 pr (no 8) to be 1st p.pr at L edge.
(4 prs)
Using marked pricking as a guide, and support pins if necessary, cont Tenstick, adding prs to left edge, 1 per row, staggered when required, to give L–R order after pin D, as foll:

	3 x (no 8)
	1 x (no 7)
	1 x (no 8)
	1 x (no 7)
	1 x (no 8)
	1 x (no 7)
	1 x (no 8)
	1 x (no 7)
	1 x (no 8)
	1 x (no 7)
	1 x (no 8)
	1 x (no 7)
	4 x (no 8)
smooth edge pr	2 x (no 8)
leaders	2 x (no 8)
(11 prs)	

After pin E:
start decreasing prs from L edge, T O & T B 1 pr after each pin till 6 prs rem.
Thereafter, T O & T B after each alternate pin till 4 prs rem.
Cont T O & T B prs after each pin, to finish at pin F (pin M, Section 1).

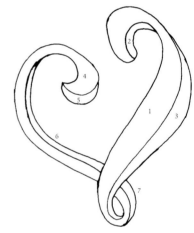

Shadow Valentine 1: Order of work

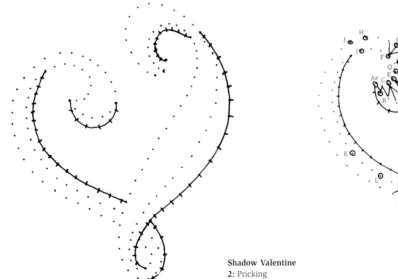

Shadow Valentine
2: Pricking

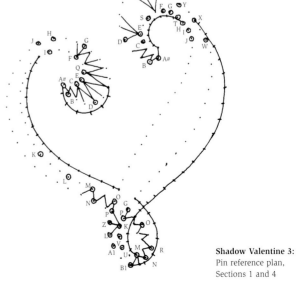

Shadow Valentine 3:
Pin reference plan,
Sections 1 and 4

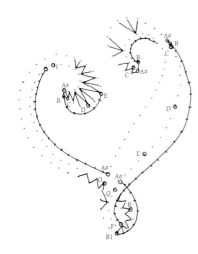

Shadow Valentine 4: Pin reference plan, Sections 2, 3, 5, 6 and 7

Return to Section 1
Undo locking st, and tension all prs.
Cont in Cls, working over Tenstick, Section 3.
Finish at pin P and pin Q, Section 1, using top sewings over the rolled edge.
Note Use R bar at pin Q only.
Use L edge pr and 1st p.pr from L for roll.
T O & T B rem prs in a bunch.

Notes for rolled edge
Roll from pin Q to pin N, Section 1:
rolling thread – 1 x (no 7)
rolled threads – 3 x (no 7)
Use prs set aside at pin Q for roll.
T B 1 thread at pin O and pin R.
Finish at pin N, Section 1.

Section 4
Start at pin A#:
follow instructions for F for Fairy Moss, Version 2, Section 2, from pin A# to finish.

Notes for rolled edge
Roll from pin O to pin A#:
rolling thread – 1 x (no 7)
rolled threads – 3 x (no 7)
T B 1 thread from roll at pin Q and pin C.
Finish at pin A#.

Section 5
Start at pin A#, to work Tenstick section (shadow):
using a magic thread, hang on 2 prs (no 8), follow instructions for Section 3, until there are 3 prs.
Note Reverse L–R instructions.
(3 prs)
Using marked pricking as a guide, cont Tenstick, adding prs, 1 pr per row, to R edge, to give L–R order at pin D, as foll:

smooth edge pr	2 x (no 8)
	4 x (no 8)
	1 x (no 7)
	1 x (no 8)
	1 x (no 7)
	1 x (no 8)
leaders	2 x (no 8)

(6 prs)
Work 1 row.

After pin D:
T O & T B 1 pr each row, from R edge, to finish at pin E.

T O & T B rem prs, secure to work with previously T B prs.

Section 6
Start at pin O, Section 4, and pin A#, to work Tenstick section (shadow).

At pin O, Section 4:
using magic thread, hang 1 pr (no 8) to be leaders, and thro its loop, 1 pr (no 8) to be 1st p.pr from R edge.
(2 prs)
At pin A#:

using top sewings, hang 1 pr (no 8) to be smooth edge pr, and 1 pr (no 8) to be 1st p.pr from smooth edge pr.
(4 prs)
On temp pins, between 2 prs from pin A#, and 2 prs from pin O, Section 1, add 4 prs, staggered, to give L–R order as foll:

smooth edge pr	2 x (no 8)
	3 x (no 8)
	1 x (no 7)
	1 x (no 7)
	1 x (no 8)
	1 x (no 7)
	1 x (no 8)
	1 x (no 7)
	2 x (no 8)
leaders	2 x (no 8)

(8 prs)
Cls leaders R–L thro p prs, work smooth edge st with L pr.
Cont in Tenstick, T O & T B prs from R edge, using marked pricking as a guide.
Finish at the pin before pin I.

Section 7
Start at pin Q, Section 1, and pin A#, to work Tenstick section (shadow).

Using top sewings at pin Q, Section 1, and pin A#:
hang on 8 prs as Section 6.
Note Reverse L–R directions and thread order.
Cont in Tenstick.
After pin B:
using marked pricking as a guide, start decreasing prs, T O & T B prs from L edge.

Finish at pin B1, Section 1.

FRILLY FLOWERS

The Frilly Flower patterns have their origins in the letters *B* (page 11) and *K* (page 39). The defined shapes of these letters could be considered difficult to develop into patterns that lose their original identity but, as with other designs, it is just a question of selecting the particular shape that can be changed, perhaps repeated and sometimes worked in a different style.

Frilly Flower B

Colours
(no 1)	*White
(no 2)	Sycamore
(no 3)	Eau de Nil
(no 4)	*Ice
(no 5)	Baby Blue
(no 6)	Spring Green
(no 7)	*Jade

Sections 1 and 1a

Follow instructions for B for Bauhinia, Sections 2 and 2a, Version 1, from pin A♯ to after pin S.
(8 prs)
After pin T:
T O & T B centre pr (no 6).

After pin U:
add 1 pr (no 5) to centre.
(8 prs)
At pin V:
work locking st (tech 6, td 6) and leave to work rolled edge, Section 1a.

Notes for rolled edges

Roll from pin A♯, Section 1 to pin W (via pin U):
rolling thread – 1 x (no 5)
rolled threads – 3 x (no 5)
Add 2 prs at pin A♯, cont to pin U.
Leave to cont Section 1.
When Section 1 has been completed*, cont to pin W.

*To complete Section 1

After pin V:
add 1 pr (no 5).
(9 prs)
Finish at pin W:
T O & T B all prs.

*Cont roll from pin U, to finish at pin W.

Notes for rolled edge

Roll from pin A♯, Section 1 to pin X:
rolling thread – 1 x (no 5)
rolled threads – 3 x (no 5)
Add 2 prs at pin A♯.
T B 1 thread at pin C and pin D.
Finish at pin X.

Section 2

Start at pin A♯:
using a one-colour point start (tech 23, td 23), (Note R–L working direction), add 2 prs (no 5) open, to be edge prs.
Add magic thread (tech 2, td 2).

On a temp pin, hang 1 pr (no 6) to be leaders.
(3 prs)
On temp pin, add 2 prs (no 7) open, to be p prs.
Cls leaders R–L thro 2 p prs and edge st (tech 3, td 3) at pin B.
(5 prs)
After pin B:
add 2 prs (no 6) to centre.
Nr: add 2 prs (no 5) to centre.
Nr: add 2 prs (no 4) to centre.
(11 prs)
After pin C:
change leaders (no 6) to (no 3), (tech 4, td 4) cont row, adding 1 pr (no 3) to centre.
(12 prs)
After pin D:
start patt: work ½ st with 3 centre p prs (no 4).
After pin E:
tie ½ knot after 1st p pr, to keep p pr in position near pin, cont in patt.

After pin F:
when p prs have returned to original colour positions, change leaders (no 3) to (no 6), (tech 4, td 4) cont row, T O & T B 5th p.pr (no 3) from R, cont in Cls.
(11 prs)
Nr: T O & T B s ps 10 & 11 (no 4) from R, join to Section 1 using top sewings.
Nr: T O & T B 4th p.pr (no 4) from L.
(9 prs)
Finish at pin F:
set aside L edge pr (no 5) for rolled edge, T O & T B rem prs in a bunch (tech 25, td 25).

Notes for rolled edge

Roll from finish to pin A♯.
rolling thread – 1 x (no 5)
rolled threads – 3 x (no 5)
Use L edge pr from pin F and add 1 pr (no 5) for roll.
T B 1 thread from roll at pin E and pin B.
Finish at pin A♯.

Section 3

Start at pin A♯:
using a one colour flat start (tech 21, td 21), (Note L–R working direction), hang 2 prs (no 1) to be edge prs.
Add magic thread.

On temp pin, hang 1 pr (no 1) to be leaders.
(3 prs)
On temp pin, hang 2 prs (no 3) and 2 prs (no 2),
in L–R order: 2 x (no 3)
                 4 x (no 2)
                 2 x (no 3)
and edge st at pin B (tech 3, td 3).
After pin B:
add 2 prs (no 2) and 2 prs (no 1),
in L–R order: 2 x (no 2)
                 4 x (no 1)
                 2 x (no 2) to centre.
(11 prs)
After pin C:
Cls thro 2 p prs,
start patt: work ½ st with 4 centre p prs (no 1) and (no 2), Cls rem p prs.
Cont in patt.
Join to previously worked sections using top sewings, set aside both edge prs at

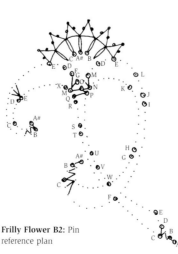

Frilly Flower B2: Pin reference plan

Frilly Flower B1: Pricking and Order of work

pin D, to use for rolled edge, and Plait and Picot border.
Tie ½ knot after 1st p.pr at each edge to hold p prs in position.
Cls final row to finish at pin O, Sections 1 and 1a.
T O prs in a bunch (tech 25, td 25).

Notes for rolled edge
Roll from pin D to pin D, via pin A#:

rolling thread – 1 x (no 1)
rolled threads – 3 x (no 1)
Use 1 edge pr set aside at pin D to roll across top edge of Section 3 to pin D, via pin A#.
Note Replace magic thread (tech 16b,td 16b) at pin A#.

Plait and Picot border
Use both prs (no 1) at pin D to form

one plait for border, add 2 more prs (no 1) to form second plait at pin E.
Work plait to pin E, cont working Ninepin edge (Bedfordshire lace), (see pin reference plan) tw 5 to make picots.
Use Windmill Crossings (tech 45, td 45).
Finish at pin D and pin E.

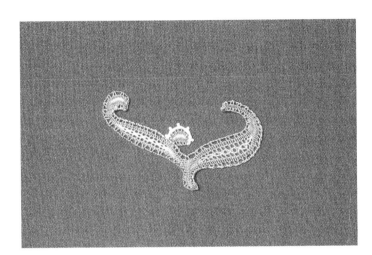

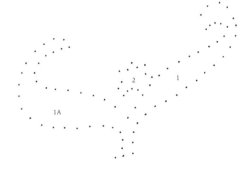

Frilly Flower K

Colours

(no 1)	*White
(no 2)	*Citrus
(no 3)	Pale Lettuce
(no 4)	Apple
(no 5)	Lime
(no 6)	*Mid Olive
(no 7)	*Pewter

Frilly Flower K2: Pin reference plan

Frilly Flower K1: Pricking and Order of work

Sections 1 and 1a

Follow instructions for K for Kingfisher, Sections 2 and 2a, Version 2, from pin A# to finish at pin K.

Note After working 1st part of blind pin before pin J, T O & T B 2nd p.pr (no 6) from L.
After pin J:
T O & T B 2nd p.pr (no 6) from R.
Nr: T O & T B 3rd p.pr from L.
(5 prs)

To finish at pin K:
Cls leaders thro 2 rem prs, T O & T B leaders and 2 rem p prs.
Cls & tw edge prs, place pin K, Cls & T O, set aside to use for rolled edge.

Notes for rolled edges
Roll from pin K to pin A#, Section 1a:
rolling thread – 1 x (no 7)
rolled threads – 1 x (no 7), 2 x (no 6)

Use set aside prs at pin K for rolled edge.
T B 1 thread (no 6) at pin L and pin B. Finish at pin A#.

Roll from Pin A# to pin H, Section 1.
As K for Kingfisher, Section 2, Version 1.

Section 2

Start at pin A#:
using a two-colour start (tech 1, td 1), (Note L–R working direction), hang 1 pr (no 7) and 1 pr (no 2) to be edge prs.
Add magic thread.
L edge pr is now (no 7).
R edge pr is now (no 2).

On temp pin, add 1 pr (no 4) to be leaders.
(3 prs)
Cont, foll instructions for Section 1.
Join to Section 1, using top sewings.

After sewing into L pin F:
T O & T B 3 p prs, work to next R pin and join.
When sewing in R edge pr, add 1 pr (no 1) to its loop.
These 2 prs will be used for rolled edge with picots.
T O & T B rem p prs in a bunch (tech 25, td 25).

Rolled edge with picots
Roll from base of R edge, pin D, Section 2 to pin A#:
rolling thread – 1 x (no 2)
rolled threads – 1 x (no 2)
picots – 2 x (no 1)
Cls prs tog to ensure (no 1) pr is the L pr, tw 5, make picot.

Cls, make sewing with (no 2) into next pinhole, enclosing all 3 threads for roll.
Cont making picots and roll to finish at Pin A#.

SECTION THREE
Techniques

The general techniques listed are arranged in an order which relates to their appearance in the book. (Specific techniques are included in the instructions for the individual patterns.)

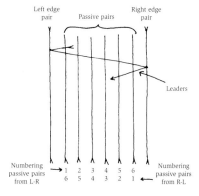

Working diagram 1: Numbering passive pairs

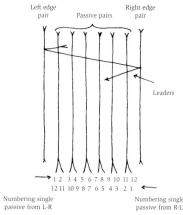

Working diagram 2: Numbering single passives

1 Two-colour start (L–R working direction)

Using a two-colour start (td 1), hang 1 pr, to become L edge pr, and to the L of it, 1 pr to become R edge pr.
Cls edge prs tog, inserting magic thread (tech 2a) after X T of X T X (td 2).
Tw 2 R edge pr.
On T P, hang 1 pr to be leaders, Cls leaders L–R thro L edge pr, tw 2 both leaders and L edge pr.
(3 prs)
On T P, hanging between leaders and R edge pr, hang p prs as specified in instructions.
Cls leaders thro p prs, tw 2 leaders and place edge pin, under leaders.
Work a No (Colour) Change Edge stitch at edge pin (tech 3, td 3).
Note: If the working direction is to be R–L, simply reverse the instructions.

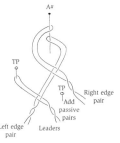

TD 1: Two colour start, L–R working direction

2 Magic thread

A magic thread (td 2a & td 2b) is used to enable a future sewing to be made, in a situation where the pinhole is likely to close immediately the pin is removed.

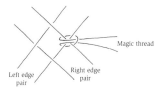

TD 2A: Inserting magic thread, two colour start

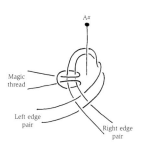

TD 2B: Inserting magic thread, one colour start

3 No (colour) change edge stitch

The no (colour) change edge stitch is essential to the concept of working with coloured threads in a painterly way. Its use enables the existing colours of the leaders and edge prs to be maintained and is worked thus; X T T X T T (td 3). Note: This edge stitch is worked throughout all patterns, unless specified otherwise.

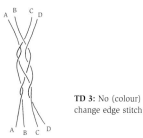

TD 3: No (colour) change edge stitch

4 Changing leaders

This is worked after the pin has been placed and the edge st completed (td 4).
Cls leaders thro 1st p pr, hang new leaders on T P, to hang between old leaders and 2nd p pr, Cls old leaders thro new leaders, T O & T B old leaders, cont with new leaders.

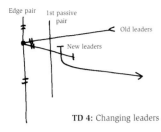

TD 4: Changing leaders

TD 6: Locking stitch XTXTX

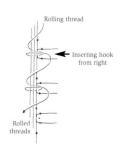

TD 9: Working a Withof roll

5 Splitting a braid (R–L working direction, continuing with R braid)

After pin a; Cls thro 1st p pr from R edge, work locking st (tech 6, td 6) with 1st p pr and leaders, leave (td 5).
At pin b; between specified p prs, hang two prs to become centre edge prs.
Cls these 2 prs tog and tw 2 both prs.
Return to prs left after pin a; undo locking st, cont to work across all p prs for R side braid to pin c.
At pin c; work edge st with right centre edge pr and cont with R side braid.
Secure in order all bobbins from L side braid.
When returning to L side braid at pin z; add specified leaders thus: hang leaders on T P, between L edge pr and 1st p pr from L, Cls leaders L–R across all p prs, edge st with L centre edge pr, release T P and tension leaders carefully (tech 36, td 36), cont with L side braid.
Note: If the working direction is to be R–L, simply reverse the instructions. See also tech 38, td 38, diag t.2, tech 39, td 39 and diag w.3, the choice of technique is dependent upon the shape of the braid and the angles of the split sections.

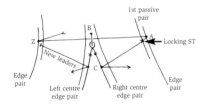

TD 5: Splitting a braid, R–L working direction, continuing with right braid

6 Locking stitch (also used as turning stitch)

Used to hold the tension on designated threads, usually leaders and another pair, while another section of work is completed. Worked thus; X T X T X (td 6).
Note: It is important to undo this stitch before resuming work with the threads concerned.

7 Changing leaders with an edge pr

This may be worked thus; X T X T T at either side of braid as required (td 7).

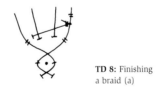

TD 7: Changing leaders and edge pair

8 Finishing a braid (a)

Cls leaders thro rem p prs (usually 2prs), T O & T B leaders and rem p prs. Tie them in a bunch, and secure them to back of work with previously T B prs. The 2 rem edge prs will be used for the rolled edge; Cls & tw edge prs, place final pin, Cls prs tog & T O (td 8).

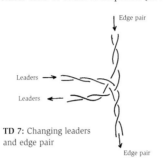

TD 8: Finishing a braid (a)

9 Working a (Withof) roll (and finishing at a point)

A minimum of two threads are required to work a (Withof) roll, a rolling thread and a rolled thread, although there may be as many rolled threads as the lacemaker chooses (td 9).

Consideration must be given to the position of the rolled edge, the number of rolled threads at the start and finish of the roll and their relationship to the maximum number of threads included in the roll. This is dependent upon the effect the lacemaker wishes to achieve, since the roll will create its own shadow when viewed from the correct side. This consideration is as important as the choice of colours within the roll and that of the rolling thread.

The rolling thread binds and encloses the rolled thread/s to the edge of the lace. The working direction of the roll is towards the lacemaker.

To start, place the chosen threads to be included in the roll alongside the edge of the lace, the rolling thread placed to the outside.
Remove the pin from the first pinhole to be worked.
Insert a fine 0.4mm crochet hook from across the lace towards the outer edge under the edge, to make a side sewing (td 11), ensuring that the roll threads to be enclosed are over the top of the hook.
Pull the rolling thread thro, under the roll threads to make a loop.
Pass the end of the rolling thread bobbin thro the loop that has been created, enclosing the roll threads and edge pr.
Pull up the rolling thread gently across the work to tighten around the enclosed threads. Correct tension is achieved by pulling the rolling thread to the left and right across the work, always finishing across the work.
Also, pull the rolled threads straight to ensure that the rolling thread has not been adjusted to tightly.
Replace pin and continue to the next pinhole.
Finish the rolled edge, usually at a point, by making a sewing into the last pinhole, then into the same pinhole, make a top sewing into the next bar.

10 Finishing a (Withof) roll on a straight edge

Make a side sewing (td 11) into the last pinhole to be worked.
Turn the pillow thro 90 degrees (td 10).
Make a top sewing (td 12) into the next

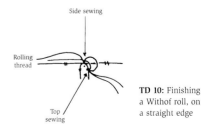

TD 10: Finishing a Withof roll, on a straight edge

137

available bar of the same pinhole, then T O & T B both prs.

11 Side sewings

A side sewing is made by inserting a fine 0.4mm crochet hook across the work at a 90 degree angle, into the pinhole and under the edge pr (td.11).

If two pieces of work have been joined using this method, when viewed from the correct side they will appear to sit side by side.
The side edges will be flat.

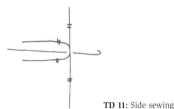

TD 11: Side sewing

12 Top sewings

A top sewing is made by inserting a fine 0.4mm crochet hook across the work at a 45 degree angle, into the pin-hole under the side bar and over the edge pr (td 12).

If two pieces of work have been joined using this method, when viewed from the correct side the first piece to have been worked will appear to sit on top of the second piece.
The side edge from the first piece of work will form a ridge.

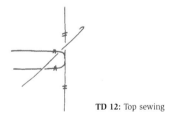

TD 12: Top sewing

13 Adding a thread to a (Withof) roll

At the marked pin where a thread is to be added to the roll;

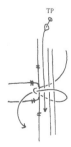

TD 13: Adding a thread to a Withof roll

before making the side sewing, hang the thread on a T P above the work and include it in the roll with the other threads, preferably placed in a position close to the inner edge of the roll (td13). Do not cut off any threads until the roll is completed.

14 Decreasing threads from a (Withof) roll

At the marked pin where a thread is to be decreased from the roll, after making the side sewing enclosing the thread, place the thread to the back of the work. Where possible, ensure the thread to be removed is in a position close to the inner edge of the roll (td14). Do not cut off any threads until the roll is completed.

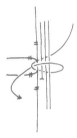

TD 14: Decreasing (throwing back) a thread from a Withof roll

15 Finishing a braid (b)

To use a passive pr for a rolled edge instead of an edge pr, Cls thro rem pr/prs (td 15), T O & T B leaders and any other non-required p prs, T O required p pr for rolled edge and set aside, Cls & tw edge prs, place pin, Cls, T O & T B non-required edge pr, T O required edge pr for rolled edge enclos-ing set aside p pr in knot.
Secure all T B prs to back of work with previously T B prs.

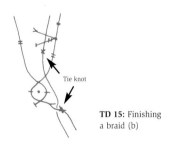

TD 15: Finishing a braid (b)

16 Using a magic thread (adding prs, replacing a magic thread)

Adding prs (td 16a): insert the pr to be added thro the loop of the magic thread, pull both ends of the magic thread until the thread from the new pair is thro the pinhole, forming a loop, pass one end of the new pair thro its own loop, and remove the magic thread.

Note: More threads may be added by threading them thro the loop of the newly added pr.

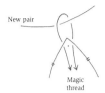

TD 16A: Using a magic thread, adding pairs

Replacing a magic thread (td 16b): In a situation where the pinhole will need to be used again, the magic thread may be replaced at the same time as it is being used for the first occasion When threading the first bobbin thro the loop of the original magic thread, at the same time hang in another magic thread doubled.

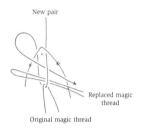

TD 16B: Using a magic thread, adding pairs

When the original magic thread is pulled thro, along with the looped thread from the bobbin, so will the loop from the replacement magic thread. Place loose ends thro the replacement magic thread, to secure it. Cont to complete the sewing.

17 Narrow angle start

Adding 2 prs (td 17), use a top sewing (tech 12, td 12) into the bar of the pin-hole to add I pr, and pass one end of the added pr thro its own loop, then pass one end of the other pr into the loop.

Note: More prs may be added into the loop.

TD 17: Narrow angle start

18 Blind pins

Using a pin twice, to gain on a pin, around a curve: the first time the blind pin is worked, tw 2 leaders, place a T P in the marked hole under leaders, do not work an edge st (td 18).

The second time of working (when the blind pin is completed), tw 2 leaders, remove T P and replace it under leaders (the loop from the first working is not included), edge st, and continue.

Adjust the tension of the leaders carefully, holding the 1st p pr from the blind pin's edge in position. This will ensure that the passive prs are not pulled out of line, but will allow the leaders' excess thread (from the first working) to be taken up.

Note: This working method relates to the patterns in this book, there are other methods of working a blind pin.

Blind pin as shown on reference plan

TD 18A: Blind pins

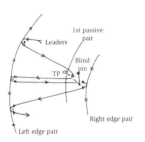

TD 18B: Blind pins

19 Turning stitch (also used as a locking stitch and tenstick smooth edge stitch)

Used to create a second pr of leaders in a Milanese braid.

The original leaders are worked usually to the centre of the braid, where they work the T S with the designated pr thus: X T X T X (td 19a). This results in one thread from the original leader pr and one thread from the p pr forming two sets of leader prs, see also (tech 6, td 6).

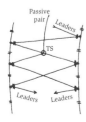

Passive pair
Leaders
TS
Leaders   Leaders

TD 19A: Turning stitch, using a support pin

Note: It is sometimes useful to use a support pin after the X T of X T X T X (td 19b).

TD 19B: Turning stitch, using a support pin

20 Changing leaders, by exchanging with a p pr

Exchanging the leaders with a p pr is a convenient way of making a colour change without the need to add a new pr and T O & T B the old pr. It is most successful when the exchange is made in a closely worked section with one of the central prs (td 20).

After the edge st, Cls thro 1 p pr, exchange leaders with the second p pr (or chosen p pr), work X T T X, and cont with new leaders.

The original leaders have now become the second passive pr.

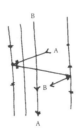

TD 20A: Changing leaders by exchanging with a passive pair

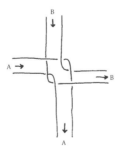

TD 20B: Changing leaders by exchanging with a passive pair

21 One-colour flat start

This one-colour start method (td 21) is exactly the same as for the two colour start (tech 1, td 1). It is used when starting at a corner or on a round shape.

Note: This technique may also be used when starting at a point, when the start pin will have a rolled edge added.

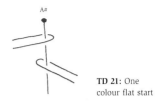

TD 21: One colour flat start

22 Joining sections

This is the principle by which most sections are joined together; there may be individual variations (td 22). Cls & tw 2 R edge pr from L section and L edge pr from R section, place pin (td 22a).

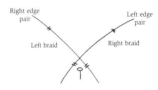

Right edge pair
Left edge pair
Left braid
Right braid

TD 22A: Joining two sections of braid

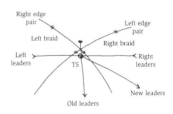

Right edge pair
Left edge pair
Left braid
Right braid
Left leaders
TS
Right leaders
Old leaders
New leaders

TD 22B: Joining two sections of braid

Cls L leaders thro L edge pr, Cls R leaders thro R edge pr, work T.S. with leaders from both sections (td 22b), replacing pin as a support pin (tech 19, td 19), work to next pin and cont.

23 One-colour point start (R–L working direction)

Using a one-colour point start (td 23), hang 2 prs to be edge prs (diag c.1) tw 2.

Note This is the same as a False Picot start when prs are tw 5.

Add magic thread (tech 2, td 2) before Cls prs tog.

Tw 2 L edge pr.

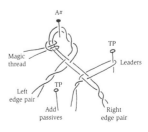

Magic thread
Left edge pair
Add passives
TP
TP
Leaders
Right edge pair

TD 23: One colour point start, R–L working direction

On T P, hang 1 pr to be leaders, Cls leaders R–L thro R edge pr, tw 2 both leaders and R edge pr.
(3 prs)
On T P, hanging between leaders and L edge pr, hang p prs as specified in instructions.
Cls leaders thro p prs, tw 2 leaders and place edge pin under leaders.
Work a No (Colour) Change Edge st at edge pin (tech 3, td 3).
Note: If the working direction is to be L–R, simply reverse the instructions.

24 Adding a single thread to beginning of Withof roll

When a single thread is required at the start of a rolled edge; add the single thread thro the loop created when the pr is added, then tie a knot with the thread from the pr to be included in the roll (td 24).

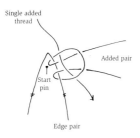

TD 24: Adding a single thread when beginning a roll

25 Finishing by tying off prs in a bunch

When all prs have been T O, take the outer thread from either side, cross it underneath the other threads and T O (td 25).

Note: This method may also be used before T B the bundle over work, and T O over the bundle with previously T B prs.

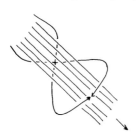

TD 25: Finishing, tying back pairs in a bunch

26 Changing leaders with a (1st) p pr, T O & T B old leaders

This is a convenient method of changing the colour of the leaders and decreasing 1 p pr at the same time,

usually worked with the 1st p pr. After working the edge st, Cls thro 1st p pr, T O & T B old leaders (td 26), and cont with new leaders (previously the 1st p pr from the edge).
Note: Similar to (tech 20, td 20).

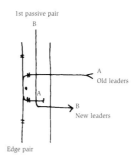

TD 26: Changing leaders with a 1st passive pair, tying off and throwing back old leaders

27 Working a part row, to fill a space (when leaders and p prs are different colours)

When there is a space to be filled, usually due to an acute angle, if the leaders and p prs differ in colour the leaders may be worked from the outside edge, across the required number of p prs, tw 1, and returned to the outside edge (td 27). Adjust tension carefully.

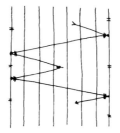

TD 27: Working a part row (decorative short row) to fill a space

28 Changing patt p prs:

The general principle is to hang the new pr alongside the old pr in a position that will ensure the ends of the old pr will be hidden in the pattern when the threads are cut.
The new patt pr is hung on a T P, Cls

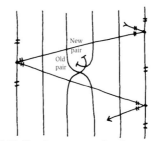

TD 28: Changing pattern passives (pattern may not be as illustrated)

thro old patt pr, T O & T B old patt pr (td 28). Cont working patt with new patt pr.

29 Finishing at a point, filling a gap

When finishing at a point, where there is a possibility of a gap appearing before the final pin, the p prs may be Cls tog before the leaders are worked thro them. All prs may then be T O & T B, leaving the edge prs to work the rolled edge (td 29).

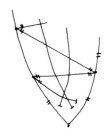

TD 29: Finishing at a point and filling a gap

30 Working into and out of a sharp point

To allow a sharp point to be negotiated (td 30), the inside edge pr and p pr or p prs are left out of the work at each of the pinholes, to be collected and included again after the point has been worked.

Notes: When the edge pr is to be included again; if the edge st was previously worked, in order to make the join, a sewing is made into its pinhole, tw 2 leaders and cont, or if no edge st was previously worked, make the edge st, paying particular attention to its tension and position and cont.
The discarded pr/prs may be twisted or plaited for extra decoration.
In other patterns, where there are no additional pinholes into the point, the lacemaker may add them at her own discretion.

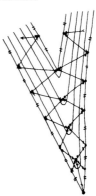

TD 30: Working into a point

31 Changing leaders, adding new leaders at edge

This method of changing leaders is useful when there are few p prs in the braid, or when the colour change would be less noticeable.

After working edge st; Cls leaders thro 1st p pr and T O & T B leaders (td 31). Add new leaders on T P, between worked edge pr and 1st p pr, Cls new leaders across all p prs and cont.

Notes: Care must be taken when tensioning leaders for a few rows. The original leaders may be Cls thro more than 1 p pr if the colour change would be less noticeable.

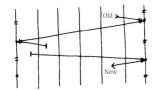

TD 31: Changing leaders, adding new leaders at edge

32 Tenstick: changing from pinned edge to smooth edge

When changing from a pinned edge to a smooth edge, the edge pr to be the smooth edge must first be untwisted after pin a (td 32a). If the braid consists of few p prs, it may be desirable to Cls the edge pr with the 1st p pr to fill a potential gap (td 32b).

Note: This would depend upon the colour arrangement being desirable, and may also be used to change a colour to suit.

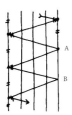

TD 32A: Tenstick, changing from a pinned edge to a smooth edge

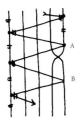

TD 32B: Tenstick, changing from a pinned edge to a smooth edge

The leaders then work a Turning Stitch; X T X T X at pin b, this T.S. is used throughout as the smooth edge st (see also, tech 6, td 6 and tech 19, td 19).

Note: After a few rows have been worked, remove pin a, to allow a smoother line to develop tension p prs carefully.

33 Tenstick: changing from smooth edge to pinned edge

When changing from a smooth edge st, tw 2 the smooth edge pr after the last smooth edge st at pin position a (td 33). Cont working pinned edge normally at pin b.

Note: After a few rows have been worked, remove pin a to allow a smoother line to develop. Tension p prs carefully.

TD 33: Tenstick, changing from a smooth edge to a pinned edge

34 Changing an edge pr (exchanging with a new pr)

An edge pr may be changed to the required colour by adding a new pr (td 34); hang the new pr (a) on a T P, untwist the old edge pr (b), Cls old pr (b) thro new pr (a), tw 2 new pr (a), place pin, T O & T B old pr (b).

TD 34: Changing an edge pair with a new pair added

35 Staggered hanging of p prs

When more than two prs, of the same colour, are to be added at the same time, a staggered arrangement of threads is advisable (td 35).

A similar arrangement may be used when there are prs of more than one colour, but the threads may have to be rearranged (e.g. by twisting) to achieve the required thread order.

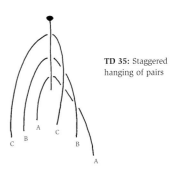

TD 35: Staggered hanging of pairs

36 Adding new leaders, when splitting a braid

When a braid has been split, the original leaders will continue with one side of the braid, therefore a new pr of leaders will need to be added (td 36).

Note: Tension new leaders carefully. This method may be used for either side of a braid.

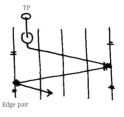

TD 36: Adding new leaders, when splitting braid

37 Changing leaders, continuing with a p pr

When the braid is closely worked, e.g. during the working of a blind pin (tech 18, td 18) the leaders may be changed as follows: Cls thro 1st p pr, T O & T B leaders, cont with 1st p pr (td 37). This method may employed using the 2nd or 3rd p prs on an inner curve, but is less noticeable with the 1st p pr and when changing to new leaders of a similar tonal value or colour (see also tech 20, td 20.)

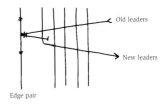

TD 37: Changing leaders with 1st passive pair

38 Splitting a braid (L–R working direction, continuing with R braid)

After pin x, Cls thro 1st p pr from L edge, work locking st (tech 6, td 6), with 1st p pr and leaders, leave (td 38).

At pin y; between specified p prs, hang 2 prs to become centre edge prs.
Return to pin X; undo locking st, Cls across all prs, including centre edge prs, to pin z.
Cont with R side of braid.
When returning to L side of braid at pin x; add specified leaders thus: hang leaders on T P, between L edge pr and 1st p pr from L, Cls leaders L–R across all p prs, edge st with L centre edge pr, release T P and tension leaders carefully, cont with L side of braid.
Note: If the working direction is to be R–L, simply reverse the instructions. See also (tech 5, td 5, diag t.2, tech 39, td 39, and diag w.3), the choice of technique is dependent upon the shape of the braid and the angles of the split sections.

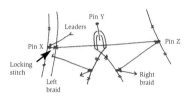

TD 38: Splitting a braid, L–R working direction, adding two centre edge pairs, continuing with right braid

39 Splitting a braid using p prs to become centre edge prs (L–R working direction, continuing with R braid)

After pin X; Cls across all p prs, adding extra p prs as required (td 39).
At pin Y; Cls & tw 2 specified prs to be centre edge prs.
Return to pin Z;cont with R side of braid.
Note: If the working direction is to be R–L, simply reverse the instructions. See also (tech 5, td 5, tech 38, td 38, diag t.2 and diag w.3), the choice of technique is dependent upon the shape of the braid and the angles of the split sections.

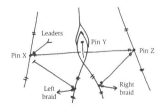

TD 39: Splitting a braid, L–R working direction, adding one pair and using one passive pair to be centre edge pairs, continuing with right braid

40 Straight edge start (R–L working direction)

Note: This method may be used for a one or two colour start, add edge prs as instructed in pattern on start pin A#.
Tw 2 L edge pr.
On T P, hang 1 pr to be leaders (td 40).
Cls leaders R–L thro R edge pr, tw 2 both prs.
(3 prs)
On T P, hang designated number of p prs, side by side, to hang between leaders and L edge pr.
Cls leaders thro p prs, tw 2 leaders, edge st (tech 3, td 3) at pin B, and cont.

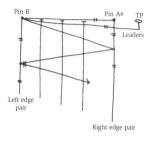

TD 40: Straight edge start, R–L working direction

41 Tenstick colour point start (pinned edge pr at L edge)

This method is used when the pinned edge pr is required to be of a different colour from that of the two leader prs (smooth edge prs).

Note: It may also be used when all prs are the same colour.

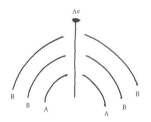

TD 41A: Tenstick colour point start, pinned edge pair at left edge

Hang 2 prs (b) to be leader prs, and 1 pr (a) to be pinned edge pr, open, on pin A# (td 41a).
Cls centre pr (a) thro L pr (b), and tw 2 (a), which is now the pinned edge pr.
Note: Both prs (b) will be leader prs in Tenstick.
Hang 1 p pr (c) on a T P (td 41b), to be placed between both prs (b).
Cls L pr (b) thro 1 p pr (c), then work smooth Tenstick edge (tech 19, td 19), with both prs (b).
Work back thro 1 p pr (c), tw 2 leader

pr (b), place pin B, work edge st (tech 3, td 3), with pinned edge pr (a).
(4 prs)
Cont in Tenstick.
Note: As many p prs as required may be gradually added.
Reverse directions if pinned edge pr is to be at R edge.

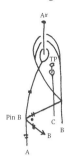

TD 41B: Tenstick colour point start, pinned edge pair at left edge

42 Changing Tenstick pinned edge pr from L–R

After placing pin Y, the pinned edge is changed from the L side to the R side (td 42).
Untwist pinned edge pr, Cls leaders thro p prs, tw 2 leaders and R edge pr (smooth edge pr).
Place pin Z under leaders, edge st with R edge pr (tech 3, td 3).
Cont in Tenstick, R edge pr is now pinned edge pr.
Note: To change pinned edge pr from R - L, reverse L–R directions.

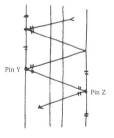

TD 42: Changing tenstick pinned edge pr from L–R

43 Making and using a marked pricking

When a wide shaped section is to be worked in Tenstick, e.g. one side of a leaf, or a shadow, it is advisable to make a marked pricking. The marked pricking acts as a guide, not only enabling the width of the section to be judged, but also the working angle of the leaders. The section of the pricking to be marked is shown by a line punctuated by dots (td 43).

Note: This indicates the Tenstick smooth edge, not the pinned edge.

The dots are pricked just enough to allow a small mark to be visible on the pricking card, the holes are not made all the way through. This distinguishes the marked pinholes from the normally pricked pinholes on the pricked pattern. It is not necessary to draw the guide line on the pricking card, since unless the line is accurate, it will only serve to confuse.

Note: If a supported Tenstick section is required (td 19b), the holes may be pricked in the normal way.

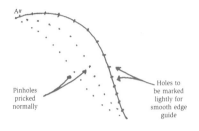

TD 43: Marked pricking, guiding marks for working a curved tenstick smooth edge

44 Withof rolled edge with picots

A rolled edge with picots worked at the same time will need at a minimum of four threads. The roll is worked in the normal way into the edge pinhole; two of the rolled threads form the picot (tw 5), place pin into the picot pinhole, Cls the picot threads together and include as rolled threads at the next edge pinhole.

Notes: The position of the pinholes for the picots are to the outside and in between those of the edge pins (td 44). If the picot threads are to be a different colour from those of the roll, it will be necessary to adjust their positions within the roll to suit.

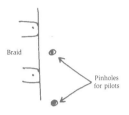

TD 44: Pricked edge, for withof roll with pilots

45 Windmill crossing (Bedfordshire)

A windmill crossing uses four pairs to make a Cls using each of the pairs as one thread (td 45).

TD 45: Windmill crossing

FURTHER READING

Woods, Sandi. *Special Effects in Bobbin Lace*. B T Batsford, 1998

Read, Patricia & Kincaid, Lucy. *Milanese Lace*. B T Batsford, 1988

Read, Patricia & Kincaid, Lucy. *New Braids and Designs in Milanese Lace*. B T Batsford, 1994

Heijden-Biemans, Trude v.d., Scheele Kerkhof, Yvonne, & Smelter-Hoekstra, Puck. *Withof Lace*. B T Batsford 1991

Underwood, Barbara M. *Traditional Bedfordshire Lace*. Ruth Bean, 1988

Springett, Christine & David. *The Torchon Lace Book*. Christine and David Springett, 1993

Interval plus S: pattern on pages 67 and 120

INDEX